FERGUSON

CAREER RESOURCE GUIDE FOR

WOMEN

AND

MINORITIES

VOLUME 2

Ferguson

An imprint of Infobase Publishing

Ferguson Career Resource Guide for Women and Minorities

Copyright © 2006 by Infobase Publishing

Ferguson
An imprint of Infobase Publishing
132 West 31st Street
New York NY 10001

Library of Congress Cataloging-in-Publication Data
Ferguson career resource guide for women and minorities.
    v. cm
    Includes indexes.
    Contents: v. 1. Resources for women — v. 2. Resources for minorities.
    ISBN 0-8160-6130-0 (set) (hc : alk. paper)
    ISBN 0-8160-6131-9 (vol. 1)— ISBN 0-8160-6132-7 (vol. 2)
    1. Vocational guidance for women—United States—Directories. 2. Women—Unemployment—United States. 3. Vocational guidance for minorities—United States—Directories. 2. Minority women—Unemployment—United States. I. Title: Career resource guide for women and minorities.
HF5382.65F46 2006
331.702082'0973   2005035411

Text design by David Strelecky
Cover design by Salvatore Luongo

Printed in the United States of America

VB FOF 10 9 8 7 6 5 4 3 2 1

This book is printed on acid-free paper.

CONTENTS

PART I
INTRODUCTION AND OVERVIEW

FOREWORD: A NOTE TO CAREER COUNSELORS AND MINORITY STUDENTS

by Paul Phifer
Director of Career Development Services
Grand Rapids Community College, Grand Rapids, Michigan

One of the most important proficiencies individuals can acquire in the 21st century is the ability to accurately understand and manage their career. A significant amount of this understanding is knowing what information is credible, what should be disregarded, and what requires further exploration (a skill in itself). These tasks can be overwhelming for anyone who is starting a serious postsecondary pursuit.

At no time in the history of the United States has the need for information, in what seems to be an unending list of key areas, been so important to an individual's career success. One can only imagine how prospective and current college students, as well as those who plan to attend graduate school, must feel when faced with sorting through and determining where to start their research. Indeed, of significant value are the combination of key precollege and postgraduate preparatory resources that consider the special interests of minorities and offer options that can help them to overcome obstacles.

As an Afro-American career counselor who has worked with hundreds of minority students over the years, I have become keenly aware of the following: Information about and access to appropriate and accurate career information has been traditionally accessible and available to most in the majority population. On the other hand, resources that serve as special guides for minority students, while increasing in recent years, are too often not known about or made available. The lack of reliable information about careers and how to effectively enter them can result in a serious disadvantage for any aspiring student, but especially so if one is a minority.

While many institutions of higher education have experienced increasing enrollment of minorities, too often they have also witnessed an unacceptable number who do not complete, graduate, or continue on after attending for a semester or two. Although multiple factors usually contribute to the lack of completion or success, some minority students are able to overcome obstacles with appropriate resources provided at the right time and delivered in an effective way.

For example, many minority students may not respond to or be motivated by traditional mailing, make-an-announcement/appointment, or "it's in the career library" approaches. Therefore, it is important to combine such methods with efforts that reflect genuine personal care and commitment. It could mean verbalizing the benefits and availability of helpful resources to minority students in informal settings, visiting minority student organizations, or making individual contacts. Upward Bound, Special Services, and similar programs implemented in high schools and on college campuses have shown that specialized outreach efforts combined with the right resources can and have resulted in many minority students being able to overcome barriers.

Ferguson Publishing Company seems to have a knack for finding niche markets, particularly within diverse populations, and then producing resources that respond to their unique challenges. I have and continue to share with both prospective and current students, as well as make available in our college's career center, some of these materials. *Ferguson Career Resource Guide for Women and Minorities* should prove to be another helpful tool to add to a growing list of successful publications.

If you are a career service provider, I strongly recommend that you familiarize yourself with this publication as one of your career informational options. This choice could be one of a number of approaches that will most likely be required in order to reduce the number of minorities who either do not begin or, after enrollment, fail to complete or continue their academic studies. If you are a prospective or current student and find this publication beneficial, I encourage you to share this resource with others, particularly your career center, library, and counseling office personnel.

Paul Phifer is the author of several career books from Ferguson Publishing, including Great Careers in Two Years: The Associate Degree Option, Quick Prep Careers: Good Jobs in One Year or Less, *and* College Majors and Careers: A Resource Guide for Effective Life Planning.

PART II
ESSAYS

MENTORS IN SCHOOL AND THE WORKPLACE

Whether you're in high school, college, or in your first years of work, you can benefit from a mentor—somebody on the "inside" who has found success within his or her profession and industry, and who is willing to give advice and share experiences. Mentors can help you make informed decisions about your future. For minority students, mentors also serve as role models, showing students that, regardless of their background, color, or race, great success is achievable for anyone who works hard and acquires the right skills.

And a need for guidance doesn't end once you begin a job. Starting a new job can be exciting, but also can be stressful—you have to learn a whole new set of rules, meet many new people, and figure out all the unique aspects of the workplace. It can take you months to learn all the details of the job, big and small—from which coworkers to trust and which tasks are top priority, to whether it's okay to take breaks outside the building. Minorities often have additional questions—such as whether discrimination exists in the workplace, and if the company regularly promotes minority workers.

MENTORS IN SCHOOLS AND COMMUNITIES

Many corporations, professional associations, colleges, and minority organizations are working together to provide role models to young people through mentoring programs and internships. Mentorships in the community, in which professionals are assigned to grade school and high school students, are often part of a company's diversity initiatives. For example, a technology company might initiate a program for students at an area inner-city school. Company employees would serve as mentors to the students and involve the students with regular computer use. These mentors, many of whom are information technology professionals, would teach students how to use the Internet as a research tool for school projects, and keep in close contact with their students through e-mail. Such a program would help students learn about the business world while developing important computer skills. Another successful mentorship program began in the early 1970s at Northrop Corporation (now called Northrop Grumman), an aviation contractor. Not only has the company's High School Involvement Partnership program linked students, including minorities, with workers in a number of departments, it also has involved minority students in internships and has hired many of these students after graduation.

Various nonprofit organizations have aided corporations in their outreach efforts. INROADS (http://www.inroads.org), with its 52 affiliates throughout the United States and the world, is dedicated to placing minority high school and college students into careers in business, engineering, computer and information sciences, sales, marketing, allied health care, healthcare management, and retail management. College students with a GPA of 2.8 or better, as well as high school seniors with a GPA of 3.0 or better, can apply to this program, which offers access to training workshops, summer employment, and mentors. Nearly 90 percent of INROADS students take on full-time jobs with their sponsoring companies (one of which is Northrop Grumman). More than 8,000 graduates of the INROADS programs have gone on to pursue professional and managerial careers.

A Better Chance is another organization that pairs mentors and minority students. Its Business Professional Partnership Program gives selected high school juniors and seniors access to the organization's corporate partners through internships, seminars, and employment opportunities. Its College Preparatory Schools Program links A Better Chance students to mentors who assist with college preparation and the admissions process. Nearly all of the graduating high school seniors (more than 99 percent) with A Better Chance enroll in college.

Some colleges and universities have formed their own outreach programs that bring students to campus for special seminars and introduce them to faculty and college students. Mentorship opportunities often become available to students once they have started college as well, through minority assistance programs. Some universities have set up electronic mentoring programs for minority students. Using e-mail and the Internet, students can communicate with mentors from participating institutions across the state. Electronic mentoring allows students to develop computer skills while making connections with the students and faculty of various departments.

COLLEGES AND UNIVERSITIES
No matter what college or university you attend, there likely will be a thriving minority organization to assist you with your educational path and career development. You also may choose to attend a college that has traditionally served an African-American, Hispanic, or Native American student population. Historically Black Colleges and Universities (HBCUs), Hispanic Serving Institutions (HSIs), and Tribal Colleges and Universities (TCUs) are those institutions devoted particularly to minority students. The U.S. Department of Education maintains a list of accredited postsecondary minority institutions; in 2004, more than 800 such institutions were listed. As more corporations and professional organizations recognize the importance of a diverse workplace, more mentoring programs have developed for the students of HBCUs, HSIs, and TCUs.

Many organizations are dedicated to promoting minority institutions and to helping them expand. The National Association for Equal Opportunity in Higher Education (http://www.nafeo.org) represents our nation's HBCUs, which include public four-year, public two-year, private four-year, and private two-year institutions. The Association sponsors conferences, internships, and scholarships. Also in support of HBCUs, *Black Enterprise Magazine* (http://www.blackenterprise.com) ranks the 50 top colleges and universities where African Americans are most likely to succeed.

The Hispanic Association of Colleges and Universities (http://www.hacu.net) represents more than 400 Hispanic Serving Institutions, and aids students through internship programs, scholarships, and college preparation. The association also maintains a detailed Web site, and publishes the monthly newsletter *The Voice of Hispanic Higher Education*. HispanicOnline.com provides rankings of the top colleges and universities for Hispanic Americans.

In the last 35 years, tribal colleges have developed to meet the needs of the Native American population. The American Indian Higher Education Consortium (http://www.aihec.org) represents 34 tribal colleges that serve more than 30,000 students from 250 tribes across the United States and Canada.

MENTORS IN THE WORKPLACE
Traditionally, a mentor is someone with experience who plays an almost parental role in guiding a new employee's career, forming both a personal and professional bond with the protégé (the person learning the ropes). A mentor-protégé relationship sometimes forms naturally, when two people take an interest in each other. In the workplace today, these relationships have become more institutionalized, and often are established before mentor and protégé ever meet. Many companies have incorporated mentorships into their diversity plans, giving every new employee access to someone with a great deal of experience and success within the company. These special mentoring programs have proven valuable to minority and nonminority workers alike, allowing new employees to learn about their workplaces from the inside out.

Though the mentor-protégé relationship is not new, its development as part of company policy has evolved rapidly over the last decade. By the mid-1990s, large corporations such as General Motors, AT&T, and DuPont had established formal mentoring programs, along with about one-third of the nation's largest corporations. By 1998, a special task force of the Equal Employment Opportunity Commission listed mentoring as an important management practice, and today mentoring programs are commonplace. The U.S. military, recognizing the success of mentoring programs in the business sector, has also initiated such programs. Several books published in the last several years—*Mentoring: How to Develop Successful Mentor Behaviors* (Menlo Park, Calif.: Crisp Learning, 2001), *Managers as Mentors: Building Partnerships for Learning* (San Francisco: Berrett-Koehler Publishers, 2002), and *Mentor Manager/Mentor Parent: How to Develop Responsible People and Build Successful Relationships at Work and at Home* (Austin, Tex.: Turnkey Press, 2002) among them—aim to teach mentoring skills.

Even if your workplace has no formal mentoring program, you may be able to find a mentor on your own. Once you meet people in the workplace, you can begin to look for someone with a great deal of experience, with whom you also have much in common: maybe you come from similar backgrounds, went to the same college, or participate in some of the same activities outside the workplace. Once you have made a connection with this person, you may be able to rely on him or her for future guidance.

"Networking" also can be an important aspect of establishing productive workplace relationships. This system of meeting people and making connections with others in your profession can lead you to more job opportunities and a better understanding of your profession and the industry in which you work. Professional associations are often the best sources for networking opportunities. For most individual professions, there are associations that allow people to meet and exchange ideas and concerns, as well as direct people toward accredited educational programs, certification, and job opportunities. Many of these associations include minority chapters or councils; some professional associations, such as the National Association of Hispanic Journalists and the National Society of Black Engineers, are devoted entirely to minority members. Many associations sponsor national networking conferences, allowing professionals to meet each other, attend seminars, and speak to corporate recruiters. (For more information on professional associations, see Part II, Section B, "Organizations.") Online communities also are developing among professionals, allowing you to exchange e-mail addresses, post questions on Web site forums, and reserve Web pages for your resume.

Whether you're just starting out, or on your way to becoming well established in your profession, mentoring and networking may be your most essential tools in finding success. And as more companies and industries stress workplace diversity, opportunities to form strong bonds among other minority professionals will increase.

FOR MORE INFORMATION
A Better Chance
240 West 35th Street, 9th Floor
New York, NY 10001
646-346-1310
http://www.abetterchance.org
Contact A Better Chance for information on its Business Professional Partnership and College Preparatory Schools Programs.

American Indian Higher Education Consortium
121 Oronoco Street
Alexandria, VA 22314
703-838-0400
aihec@aihec.org
http://www.aihec.org
Contact the consortium for information on Native American postsecondary institutions. Visit its Web site to read *Tribal College Journal*, *Tribal Colleges: An Introduction*, and *What Makes Tribal Colleges Unique?*

Hispanic Association of Colleges and Universities
8415 Datapoint Drive, Suite 400
San Antonio, TX 78229
210-692-3805
hacu@hacu.net
http://www.hacu.net
Contact this association for information on Hispanic-serving postsecondary institutions, scholarships, loans, internships, and The *Voice of Hispanic Higher Education*.

INROADS
10 South Broadway, Suite 300
St. Louis, MO 63102
314-241-7488
info@inroads.org
http://www.inroads.org
Contact INROADS for information on its internship and training and development programs.

National Association for Equal Opportunity in Higher Education
8701 Georgia Avenue, Suite 200
Silver Spring, MD 20910
301-650-2440
http://www.nafeo.org
Contact this association for information on educational opportunities at Historically Black Colleges and Universities, as well as scholarships, internships, and fellowships.

MINORITIES IN MEDIA

Careers in the media—such as jobs in television and film, journalism, publishing, recording, and the ever-expanding electronic-based media (such as the Internet)—are some of the most sought after in the nation. Of course, not all jobs in the entertainment industry and the media are lucrative and glamorous, but many do offer the potential for great success. Unfortunately, minorities may not have the same opportunities in the media as nonminorities, according to some professional and minority organizations. Groups such as the National Association for the Advancement of Colored People (NAACP), the National Association of Hispanic Journalists (NAHJ), and UNITY (an alliance of minority journalism organizations) are closely examining the media and are offering solutions for how to expand the number of minorities in newsrooms, broadcast stations and networks, and other media workplaces.

THE MEDIA "WHITEWASH"

When the major television networks announced their new schedules for 1999–2000, red was the only color many minorities saw. The casts of the new shows featured too few people of color, prompting Kweisi Mfume, head of the NAACP, and other leaders of minority organizations to call for meetings with network executives, boycotts, and legal action. Ultimately, Mfume purchased 100 shares of the four major networks (ABC, CBS, Fox, and NBC) to allow him to attend shareholders meetings and the opportunity to voice his opinions directly to the network decision-makers. He also brought the issue to the attention of the nation, as major newspapers, magazines, and network news programs featured reports of this "whitewash" of television programming for the many weeks leading up to the new fall season. As a result, the networks quickly made efforts to introduce minority actors to the casts of their new and returning series.

Today, there is only slightly less of a "whitewash" at major television networks, and great strides are still necessary for minority groups to attain appropriate representation on television. African Americans have seen the largest improvements in major roles on network television, but Hispanics and other minorities are still greatly underrepresented. Much had been written in the media lately about the increasing influence of Latin culture on America—how Hispanics were showing clout in elections, on the consumer market, and as entertainers—but television executives still largely fail to recognize this when developing new programming.

This exclusion of minority actors and characters is all particularly puzzling when you consider that advertisers encourage the inclusion of programming featuring minority actors so that they can reach a viable market. A study released by Nielsen Media Research in 2001 shows that African-American households watch 75 hours of television per week—an amount well above any other ethnic group. So the problem is not a lack of viewers. The problem, according to Mfume and professionals within the entertainment industry, is too few minority executives, resulting in too few minority directors, producers, and performers hired to create original programming.

THE IMPACT

The failure of an industry to hire minorities for powerful positions can have far-reaching consequences—not only can it result in poor minority representation in television and the movies, but also poor representation in the front pages of the newspaper. Without minority reporters and editors making the important decisions in the nation's newsrooms, the issues important to minorities may be ignored, and serious issues in minority communities may go unrecognized.

The American Society of Newspaper Editors (ASNE) responded to the dearth of minority editors by setting a goal for the nation's newspapers—by 2025 news staffs would mirror the general population's make-up of minorities. In a study released in 2005, the ASNE reported that the number of minority journalists inched up nearly a half of a percentage point from the previous year to 13.42

percent in 2004. In 2005, minorities made up 31.7 percent of the U.S. population. Original projections were for news staffs to mirror the general population by the year 2000 (at that time 29 percent minority), but when this failed to become reality, the target date was changed drastically, causing a fair amount of controversy regarding the actual commitment to diversity in newsrooms. While editors are increasing their hiring and retention of minority journalists at a time when diversity in the United States grows at historic rates, newsrooms are still not changing quickly enough for the industry to achieve its goal of parity of newsrooms with their communities by 2025.

The Radio-Television News Directors Association (RTNDA) releases an annual survey that details minority participation in local broadcast journalism. In 2004, the percentage of minorities working in local television news was largely unchanged from that of the previous year. The percentage of minorities working in local radio actually dropped. Minorities comprised 21.2 percent of local television news staffs in 2004, compared with 21.8 percent in 2003. In local radio, the minority workforce fell to 7.9 percent in 2004 from 11.8 percent in 2003, though this could be due—at least in part—to the ongoing consolidation of radio newsrooms and significant shifts from year to year as to which radio stations respond to the survey, making year-to-year comparisons difficult. The percentage of minority TV news directors in 2004 was 12 percent, compared with 12.5 percent in the 2003 survey. In radio, the percentage of minority news directors rose from 8 percent to 11 percent. "The survey suggests that we may have hit a plateau at a time when having a diverse newsroom, especially in decision making positions, is so important," said Janice Gin, RTNDA diversity chairman and associate news director at KTVU-TV in Oakland, California, at the RTNDA Web site. "Successful newsrooms have learned that having a diverse staff generates better stories, better storytelling, and better serves our viewers. As an industry, we can do more to improve the recruiting, hiring and retention of minorities."

Despite some improvements over the past decade, many minority journalists are frustrated with the pace of diversity implementation in newsrooms. A 1999 report by the International Women's Media Foundation (IWMF) focused on opportunities for minority women in the nation's newsrooms. Only 15 percent of the women surveyed were satisfied with the frequency of promotions, and 28 percent were satisfied with their opportunities of career advancement in general. Fifty-one percent believed they were discriminated against in promotions because of their color and ethnic heritage.

The IWMF report also found that only 25 percent of the minority women journalists interviewed believe the news they cover is representative of the markets they serve. As a result, the IWMF developed leadership workshops to help provide minority women journalists with the skills they need to make their voices heard in newsrooms. Women journalists from print, broadcast and Internet media participated in workshops from 1999–2002. However, with percentages of both women and minorities in newsrooms remaining relatively unchanged from 2003 to 2004, and the number of both women and minority news directors down from 2003, according to the Radio-Television News Directors Association and Foundation, the issue remains at the forefront—women and minorities are not advancing in the industry at the rate they should be.

This disparity in news coverage has long been a concern, even as far back as 1968 when the Kerner Commission Report criticized the news media for failing to accurately analyze racial problems. Media studies in recent years have found that the desire to end affirmative action, aid to cities, and other benefits to minorities correlate with distorted perspectives of the population: a *Washington Post* study found that those supporting such cuts believed that the average African American had the same advantages (good education, job, health care) as the average white person. However, the U.S. Census and many other studies and statistics dispute such beliefs.

Media scholars and organizations continue to blame the press for these distorted views, and for promoting racism through insensitive, unbalanced reporting. Research has shown that minorities are typically portrayed in news stories as contributing to social problems and conflicts. For example, The Freedom Forum, an organization that sponsors studies of the media, found in 1998 that 92 percent of sound-bites from "experts" were from nonminorities. The NAHJ sponsored a study of the 1997 network news stories and found a 25 percent drop from the previous year in the number of Hispanic-focused stories (which accounted for only 112 of 12,000 total stories). Today, The Freedom Forum's publication, *Top 10 Tips on News Research,* suggests (among other things) that identifying authoritative and diverse experts to contact is highly important. One such way to ensure diversity in sources, it suggests, is to use the Society of Professional Journalists' *Rainbow Sourcebook.* This sourcebook allows journalists to search for qualified experts across a spectrum of industries from demographic groups traditionally underrepresented in the news. The sourcebook is an outgrowth of the Society's mission because it helps make diversity in coverage easier.

Employment opportunities for minorities in broadcasting are also threatened by minorities losing ground as owners of radio and television stations. A 2000 survey by the National Telecommunications and Information Administration showed that only 3.8 percent of commercial broadcast stations were owned by minorities in 2000, although minorities made up an estimated 29 percent of the U.S. population. Despite recent gains, minority ownership still lags behind the general growth of the industry. Minority owners cite the difficulty of attracting advertisers and industry consolidation as two of the problems facing their stations.

SOLUTIONS

Some efforts are underway to remedy the problems in today's newsrooms and broadcast stations. In February 1999, President Clinton encouraged the advertising industry to develop guidelines that would take minority-owned outlets and agencies into consideration, and would result in more fair distribution of dollars spent. The American Advertising Federation (AAF) picked up the gauntlet in May 1999, forming a committee to study the multicultural market and advertising practices. The AAF Mosaic Center on Multiculturalism, formed to expand AAF's well-established leadership capabilities on multicultural marketing/advertising and diversity issues, not only implements all AAF multicultural and diversity initiatives, but is also the only national ad industry resource of its kind.

To encourage more balanced coverage of the news affecting society as a whole, a group called UNITY developed as an alliance of minority journalists. UNITY hosted a conference in 2004, attended by more than 8,000 people, including members of the Asian American Journalists Association, the NABJ, the NAHJ, and the Native American Journalists Association.

Many other media organizations also serve minority media professionals, including the Black Publishers Association (http://www.blackpublishers.org) and the National Association of Minority Media Executives (http://www.namme.org).

In 2003, the National Association of Hispanic Journalists launched The Parity Project, a five-year strategic program to increase the number of Hispanic journalists in our nation's newspaper and television newsrooms. You can learn more about this project by visiting http://www.nahj.org/parityproject/parityproject.shtml.

The Newspaper Association of America offers internships and minority fellowships, as well as diversity training and recruiting kits, for the nation's newsrooms. Its Broadcasting Training Program introduces minority students to broadcasting, and a number of job banks direct minorities to jobs in the media: The National Diversity Newspaper Job Bank (http://www.newsjobs.com), Workplace Diversity (http://www.workplacediversity.com), the Journalism and Women Symposium Job Bank (http://www.jaws.org), among them.

Though many of the statistics compiled by the organizations detailing the underrepresentation of minorities in the media are discouraging, and show that much work must be done in the coming years, the fact that such reports are beginning to receive serious attention from the media shows some progress. As media companies and executives give consideration to these facts and figures, talented minority journalists, directors, producers, writers, and actors of the 21st century should find the paths to success better paved.

FOR MORE INFORMATION

Asian American Journalists Association
1182 Market Street, Suite 320
San Francisco, CA 94102
415-346-2051
National@aaja.org
http://www.aaja.org
This association seeks to increase employment of Asian American print and broadcast journalists. It provides support to Asian American students via scholarships and fellowships, offers a newsletter and other publications, and provides job services to professionals.

Media Action Network for Asian Americans
PO Box 11105
Burbank, CA 91510
888-906-2622
manaaletters@yahoo.com
http://www.manaa.org
The network strives to ensure that Asians are depicted accurately and respectfully by the media. It regularly meets with representatives from the four major television networks to encourage diversity in the television industry.

National Association of Black Journalists
8701-A Adelphi Road
Adelphi, MD 20783-1716
301-445-7100

nabj@nabj.org
http://www.nabj.org
The National Association of Black Journalists is the largest media organization for people of color in the world. It awards scholarships and internships to students throughout the country, as well as fellowships for seasoned professionals. Visit its Web site to learn more about the association's programs and services.

National Association of Hispanic Journalists

1000 National Press Building
529 14th Street, NW
Washington, DC 20045-2001
202-662-7145
nahj@nahj.org
http://www.nahj.org
The NAHJ is dedicated to the recognition and professional advancement of Hispanics in the news industry. It offers regional workshops and seminars, a national convention and career expo, mid-career and professional development programs, an online job bank, journalism awards, internship and fellowship listings, student journalism workshops, a newsletter, scholarships, and The Parity Project, a program to increase the number of Hispanic journalists at newspapers and television stations.

National Hispanic Media Coalition (NHMC)

1201 West Fifth Street, Suite T-205
Los Angeles, CA 90017-2019
213-534-3026
info@nhmc.org
http://www.nhmc.org

The NHMC is a nonprofit coalition of Hispanic American organizations that strives to "improve the image of Hispanic Americans as portrayed by the media and . . . increase the number of Hispanic Americans employed in all facets of the media industry." It releases an annual report card that grades the major networks' efforts at including minorities in its programming.

Native American Journalists Association

Al Neuharth Media Center
555 Dakota Street
Vermillion, SD 57069
605-677-5282
info@naja.com
http://naja.com
This organization promotes Native American journalism. It monitors and analyzes tribal and national news, maintains educational services, and awards scholarships. Visit its Web site for job listings and additional information about its programs and services.

UNITY: Journalists of Color Inc.

7950 Jones Branch Drive
McLean, VA 22107
703-854-3585
info@unityjournalists.org
http://www.unityjournalists.org
UNITY represents more than 10,000 minority journalists. It consists of four national associations: the Asian American Journalists Association, the National Association of Black Journalists, the National Association of Hispanic Journalists, and the Native American Journalists Association

LEGAL RIGHTS AND RECOURSE

Although affirmative action as we know it may be in trouble (see the essay "Leveling the Playing Field: Affirmative Action"), programs to end workplace discrimination have been particularly effective in the last 40 years. These programs have succeeded in part because minorities have legal recourse and access to mediation when they feel they've been mistreated. Any kind of discrimination based on race, color, or national origin is prohibited by law. Minorities are protected from being excluded in job advertisements and training and recruitment programs, from being passed over for promotions and raises, and from being denied retirement plans. Not only is intentional discrimination illegal, but so are special workplace practices that result in discrimination, such as employers prohibiting the speaking of any language other than English in the office.

Thanks to the efforts of the Equal Employment Opportunity Commission (EEOC), employers and their employees often can reach agreement without the case going to court. The EEOC was formed as a result of the Civil Rights Act passed in 1964. This act prohibits employment discrimination on the basis of race, color, or national origin, as well as on the basis of religion, age, sex, and disability. Private employers, state and local governments, and educational institutions that employ 15 or more individuals are held accountable when discrimination occurs.

Some who oppose affirmative action make the claim that discrimination no longer exists. However, the EEOC continues to investigate thousands of cases every year. In 2004, there were nearly 27,700 individual filings with the EEOC charging discrimination on the basis of race and national origin. And many of these individual filings claim multiple types of discrimination. These numbers reveal that a great deal of disharmony among the races remains in the workplace, despite more than 40 years of affirmative action. But the EEOC is resolving cases faster than they are being filed. And these resolutions, through settlement and conciliation, have helped those who have been discriminated against (including minorities, women, the disabled, those over 40 years of age, and other victims of discrimination) receive millions in monetary benefits. Though monetary awards don't make up for acts of discrimination, they do help to compensate individuals for unfair promotion practices, unfair raise and benefits distribution, and other discrepancies. And they require individual businesses to address issues of discrimination, and help to end unfair practices in the workplace.

WHAT CAN I DO IF I'VE BEEN A VICTIM OF DISCRIMINATION?

Though we often read in the newspaper of court cases involving workplace discrimination and large monetary settlements, litigation is usually a last resort for those who feel they have been the victim of discrimination. Court cases can be expensive, time-consuming, and incredibly disruptive to the lives of all involved. (And after you've sued your employer, you will most likely have to look for work elsewhere.) Many companies have established their own affirmative action policies and programs in efforts to eliminate discrimination and to avoid lawsuits. Human resources departments may employ professionals to deal with disputes in-house, and a company may employ diversity counselors to whom employees can voice complaints. Some companies also provide areas within their intranets (electronic networks used only within the company) for the posting of complaints. Mentors and special minority peer groups can also help guide individuals through a process of complaint.

According to a survey conducted by Korn/Ferry International, an executive placement firm, 40 percent of the minority executives surveyed believed they had been passed over for deserved promotions as a result of race discrimination. These executives believed that positive approaches were the most effective in dealing with unfairness in the workplace. Such positive approaches included direct feedback and careful analysis, which allowed them to handle the situations and to learn from them without damaging their careers.

In case you're unable to persuade the company to deal fairly with your complaint of discrimination, you may need additional assistance. In some states, outside mediation, or alternative dispute resolution (ADR), is required by the courts. Mediators are trained professionals, unbiased in the case, who listen to both sides of an argument and help employer and employee reach a satisfactory settlement. Both parties must agree before settlement can be reached. ADR seeks a quick resolution of the dispute and helps to reduce backlogs in the courts. Your employer may even have it written into your contract that you must first seek mediation through a third party before filing a lawsuit. ADR has been encouraged by the Supreme Court, the Civil Rights Act of 1991, and the Americans with Disabilities Act. The Association for Conflict Resolution (http://www. acrnet.org) states that mediated agreements are adhered to more often than judgments of the court.

If you choose to speak to your employer about your charges of discrimination, you may decide together to pursue mediation. Mediate.com maintains a database of trained mediators and can provide you with more information about mediation. You can also learn more about mediation from the National Association for Community Mediation (http://www.nafcm.org), the American Arbitration Association (http://www.adr.org), and the Association for Conflict Resolution.

If you'd rather not pursue a discrimination case by yourself, you can seek help from the EEOC. If your workplace employs more than 15 individuals, your options in the event of discrimination must be posted somewhere in the workplace for all employees to read. A phone number may be all you need to contact the EEOC. The EEOC has 50 field offices across the country with employees who can help you file a charge. If there are state laws prohibiting the kind of discrimination you've experienced, you may file with your state's own equal opportunity office. These state offices are often called Fair Employment Practices Agencies (FEPAs). When a case of discrimination violates both state and federal laws, a FEPA will work together with the EEOC to resolve a problem. Tens of thousands of discrimination charges are processed annually by the EEOC contracting with more than 100 FEPAs across the country.

You only have 180 days from the date that an incident occurs to file a charge with the EEOC. If you feel that filing a charge may greatly jeopardize your professional standing in the workplace, you may ask someone else to file a charge for you. Any individual or organization can file on your behalf. You should keep in mind that, even if filing through someone else in order to remain anonymous, there is a level of risk involved. Should the case

be investigated closely, your identity will likely become apparent to your employers. But, to rectify a case of discrimination, risks might be necessary.

If you are unable to find a posting about discrimination at your workplace, look in the federal government section of your telephone book for your local EEOC office, or you can visit the EEOC's Web site, http://www.eeoc.gov. (If you're a federal employee, you'll have to contact the EEO counselor within your department.) You also can learn more about the EEOC by calling 800-669-4000 (voice) or 800-669-6820 (TTY). When filing a charge, you'll be asked to provide your name, address, and phone number, as well as that of whomever you're charging with discrimination. You'll also need to describe the act of discrimination, and the date it occurred. You also should know the approximate number of people employed by the company or organization charged.

After interviewing you about the situation, and asking you questions about how you believe you were discriminated against, the EEOC will then decide whether to proceed. The EEOC may dismiss your charge, determining that there is no case of discrimination. In this case, you'll be issued a notice, and you'll have 90 days to file your own lawsuit against the charged party if you choose. If your charge has merit, the EEOC will investigate by gathering information and documents and interviewing the various parties involved.

HOW ARE CASES OF DISCRIMINATION SETTLED?

As mentioned above, mediation has become a popular and effective form of settling employment disputes, even with charges handled by the EEOC. According to an independent survey, 96 percent of all respondents and 91 percent of all charging parties would participate in the EEOC mediation program again, if necessary.

The EEOC's mediation program is offered as an alternative to investigation. When both employer and employee agree to use EEOC mediation, a third party will meet with them, listen to the complaint, and help them settle the issue within one to five hours of discussion. Once an agreement is reached, the charging party is not allowed to take the case to court (unless the agreement ultimately goes unrecognized by the employer). A settlement may allow you promotion, back pay, or other remedies of discrimination. If no settlement is reached, an investigation will continue without the involvement of the mediator. The mediation is entirely confidential, and no written record or tape recordings are made, so nothing discussed in the mediation session is used in the investigation. If no settlement can be reached, the EEOC may choose to sue, or to close the case, allowing the charging party to pursue litigation.

As the EEOC statistics demonstrate, the nation's workplaces have a long way to go before they will be free of discrimination. In the meantime, minority workers can rely on mentors, diversity departments, mediators, and the EEOC in getting the promotions, raises, and respect entitled to them.

FOR MORE INFORMATION
Alliance for Justice
11 Dupont Circle, NW, 2nd Floor
Washington, DC 20036
202-822-6070
alliance@afj.org
http://www.afj.org
The Alliance for Justice is a national association of environmental, civil rights, mental health, women's, children's, and consumer advocacy organizations. Its Web site links to the web pages of its members, which provide a wealth of legal resources.

American Arbitration Association
335 Madison Avenue, Floor 10
New York, NY 10017-4605
800-778-7879
http://www.adr.org
This organization provides comprehensive resources on mediation, arbitration, and other forms of alternative dispute resolution.

Association for Conflict Resolution
1015 18th Street, NW, Suite 1150
Washington, DC 20036
202-464-9700
acr@ACRnet.org
http://www.acrnet.org

This organization provides information on conflict resolution. It offers publications such as *ACResolution Magazine* and *Conflict Resolution Quarterly*.

U.S. Equal Employment Opportunity Commission
PO Box 7033
Lawrence, KS 66044
800-669-4000, 800-669-6820 (TTY)
info@ask.eeoc.gov
http://www.eeoc.gov
The U.S. Equal Employment Opportunity Commission handles employment discrimination complaints based on race and other criteria. Visit its Web site for more information and to access online publications such as *Federal Laws Prohibiting Job Discrimination: Questions and Answers; Fact Sheet: Race/Color Discrimination; Fact Sheet: National Origin Discrimination;* and *Fact Sheet: Questions and Answers about the Workplace Rights of Muslims, Arabs, South Asians, and Sikhs under the Equal Employment Opportunity Laws*.

Mediate.com
PO Box 51090
Eugene, OR 97405
541-345-1629
admin@mediate.com
http://www.mediate.com
This Web site offers a database of trained mediators, a section on diversity, and useful publications.

National Association for Community Mediation
1527 New Hampshire Avenue, NW
Washington, DC 20036-1206
202-667-9700
http://www.nafcm.org
This organization supports the development and growth of community-based mediation programs and processes.

ADVICE FOR MINORITY ENTREPRENEURS AND BUSINESS OWNERS

You are your own boss: you set your own hours, hire your own staff, work in an office in your home, and make a comfortable living. Does this describe your job? Or just your dream? For many, success in small business is a reality. More and more people are setting out to be entrepreneurs. According to the U.S. government's Small Business Administration (SBA), the 22.9 million small businesses in America employ more than 50 percent of the private workforce and generate nearly 50 percent of the nation's gross domestic product. And in the past 10 years, this boom has been helped along by minority-owned businesses. The number of businesses in the United States increased by 10 percent between 1997 and 2002, according to the U.S. Census Bureau. But minority-owned businesses enjoyed even stronger growth during this time span. Despite this growth, a study released by the Milken Institute in 1999 found that minorities are still underrepresented in business ownership, compared to nonminority males. Just as obstacles exist for minorities seeking employment, so do obstacles exist in the pursuit of self-employment.

However, obstacles aren't necessarily stumbling blocks: the SBA's Office of Advocacy reported that the more than 3 million minority-owned businesses in the United States generated more than $591 billion in revenues in 1997. In 1999, Miami-based MasTec became the first Hispanic company to have revenues exceeding $1 billion. And many organizations and lending institutions are becoming more involved in helping minorities develop businesses. The SBA has been working to increase the number of guaranteed loans to minorities. Banks such as Wells Fargo (http://www.wellsfargo.com/biz/intentions/women_minority_services.jhtml) have begun special lending programs that provide support to minorities interested in starting or expanding a business. The Federal Reserve Board has been closely studying disparities in access to loans between minorities and nonminorities, and Chairman Alan Greenspan has cited these disparities as an impediment to national wealth. "It is important for lenders to understand," Greenspan said in a 1999 speech, "that failure to recognize the profitable opportunities represented by minority enterprises not only harms these firms, it harms the lending institutions and, ultimately, robs the broader economy of growth potential."

FUNDING AND INFORMATION

Money and know-how: the two go hand in hand in establishing a business. To get your small business off the ground, and to keep it growing and developing, you'll need financial support and as much information as you can find. You may know everything there is to know about the goods and services you'll be offering, but you also must know about all the different aspects of small business: financing, marketing, long-term planning, labor requirements, and area competition.

Without proper funding, it can be difficult to start a business. Though some small businesses have few start-up costs, others require thousands of dollars—potential entrepreneurs typically look to loans, grants, personal savings, and investments from friends and relatives. But for some minorities, such options are limited: they may come from poor families and neighborhoods; they may have unverifiable credit and no collateral; they may live in the inner-city, where few banks are located; and they may face discrimination by lenders who, new to making small loans, believe that investment in minority-owned business is too big of a risk. Though commercial banks are the leading source of credit for small businesses, 40 percent of minority-owned businesses with gross sales of $1 million or more have never received bank loans, according to the U.S. Department of Commerce. A 1997 study by Wells Fargo found that 50 percent of the Hispanic business owners surveyed had been turned down for credit, compared to only 38 percent of non-Hispanics. Fifty-three percent of the Hispanic business owners had not even approached a bank for a loan.

In the last few years, some banks have begun to recognize the benefits of helping small business owners grow and succeed. Many minorities have been aided by the SBA. The SBA's Office of Minority Enterprise Development (http://www.sba.gov/gcbd/whoweare.htm) is seriously dedicated to helping minority businesses by providing specialized training, professional consulting, and other assistance. The SBA works with banks, guaranteeing the loans offered to selected minority businesses. It also actively recruits banks and other funding companies to invest in small, unproven businesses, and to allow these businesses time to become established.

The Minority Business Development Agency (http://www.mbda.gov), which is part of the U.S. Department of Commerce, also has dedicated itself to the creation and expansion of minority-owned businesses. Through their development and resource centers across the nation, the agency offers assistance in management, financial planning, marketing, and information about sources of funding.

The National Minority Supplier Development Council (http://www.nmsdcus.org) oversees the Business Consortium Fund. This fund provides minority businesses with contract financing through a network of local banks. The regional councils of the council certify minority-owned businesses and match them with member corporations needing to purchase goods and services, helping the businesses to expand clientele.

Of course, these and other organizations, along with the banks that offer special programs for minority-owned businesses, are faced with many more applicants than they can fund. This is where preparation and wealth of information may pay off. With a detailed business plan that shows you've done your research and clearly understand such things as the marketplace, future trends, the demands of the business, and the competition, you can show investors that you're a good risk. (See the For More Information section for useful Web sites about creating a business plan.) You also must be prepared for complicated and detailed loan applications.

To help you prepare for all the ins and outs of starting and running a business, and to direct you to the information you'll need for success, community colleges and universities across the nation offer courses in small business administration and management. Some schools of business administration, such as at the University of Wisconsin-Milwaukee (http://cfprod01.imt.uwm.edu/sce/program_area.cfm?id=2142), have specific programs geared toward minority entrepreneurship. There are also a number of organizations that offer

training. The Minority Business Development Agency has regional centers located all across the country, and offer one-on-one assistance in writing business plans, as well as help with financial planning and management. The National Minority Supplier Development Council offers educational seminars and training, business opportunity fairs, and publications to help you learn about small business. The National Center for American Indian Enterprise Development (http://www.ncaied.org) also provides assistance with business plans, along with advice on loan packaging, taxes, and Web page design. Asian American Economic Development Enterprises (http://www.aaede.org) sponsors workshops, events, and seminars to train Asian Americans in entrepreneurship, as well as arranges for financial support for new businesses. Other organizations focused on the success of minority businesses include the National Minority Business Council (http://www.nmbc.org) and the National Association of Black Women Entrepreneurs (http://www.nabwe.org). Also, most states have minority councils and development centers for small business owners. Your local chamber of commerce and the offices of the mayor and governor can also direct you to relevant information.

A number of publications focus on minority-owned business, including the magazines *Minority Business Entrepreneur* (http://www.mbemag.com), *Hispanic Business* (http://www.hispanicbusiness.com), *The Network Journal: Black Professional and Small Business Magazine* (http://www.tnj.com), and *Black Enterprise* (http://www.blackenterprise.com), which also publishes a series of books that includes *The Black Enterprise Guide to Starting Your Own Business* by Wendy Beech. *Hispanic Magazine* (http://www.hispaniconline.com) publishes an annual list of the fastest growing Hispanic-owned businesses in the United States.

Technology and Internet resources also are becoming increasingly important to minority entrepreneurs. A survey conducted by the software company Intuit found that minority business owners use technology for managing finances, finding information on the Internet, tracking customers, and forecasting budgets. Databases, articles, editorials, and information about training are available through the Web sites of many of the organizations and magazines listed in this directory. Web sites such as http://www.ideacafe.com direct minority entrepreneurs to information about funding, as does http://www.creativeinvest.com, the Web site for Creative Investment Research. The site also includes lists of minority-owned banks. Additionally, the Federal Reserve Board lists minority-owned banks at its Web site, http://www.federalreserve.gov. And a small business can greatly benefit from its own Web site; business owners use their own sites to promote their businesses, answer questions, and provide customer service through e-mail and other methods.

All of the efforts mentioned above are paying off for minority business owners, as entrepreneurs post high revenues and set records for success. The SBA reports that business expansion rates for three minority business groups (Hispanic American, 34.0 percent; Asian American 32.1 percent; and Native American, 27.8 percent) exceeded that of nonminority owned business (27.4 percent) from 1997 to 2001.

FOR MORE INFORMATION

Asian American Economic Development Enterprises
216 West Garvey Avenue, Suite E
Monterey Park, CA 91754
626-572-7021
info@aaede.org
http://www.aaede.org
This nonprofit organization provides entrepreneurial
training, technical assistance, and financial consulting
to Asian American businesses.

Bplans.com
144 East 14th Avenue
Eugene, OR 97401
541-683-6162
http://www.bplans.com/sp/businessplans.cfm
Bplans.com offers 60 free business plans in a variety
of industries, as well as useful articles.

Minority Business Development Agency
U.S. Department of Commerce
1401 Constitution Avenue, NW
Washington, DC 20230
888-324-1551
http://www.mbda.gov
The agency does not provide funding, but helps
minorities locate financial resources, including loans.

Money Hunt
http://www.moneyhunter.com
The Money Hunt Web site is the online companion to the
Money Hunt TV program. It offers a free download of
an award-winning business plan template.

National Center for American Indian Enterprise Development
953 East Juanita Avenue
Mesa, AZ 85204
480-545-1298
http://www.ncaied.org
This nonprofit organization works to establish business
relationships between Indian enterprises and private
industry.

National Minority Business Council
25 West 45th Street, Suite 301
New York, NY 10036
212-997-4753
nmbc@msn.com
http://www.nmbc.org
The council assists minority and women small business
owners develop and expand their businesses. It
provides loans, seminars, workshops, consulting,
and newsletters and other publications.

National Minority Supplier Development Council
1040 Avenue of the Americas, 2nd Floor
New York, NY 10018
212-944-2430
http://www.nmsdcus.org
The Council offers loan and financial assistance programs,
educational seminars and training, business
opportunity fairs, and publications.

Small Business Television
20 Allen Avenue, Suite 344
St. Louis, MO 63119
314-533-7288
http://www.sbtv.com/default.asp?cid=10
Small Business Television calls itself "the first television
network on the Web devoted 100 percent to the small
business market." Its Web site has an excellent section
that features videos and other content that will be
useful to minority business owners.

Small Office Home Office America
http://www.soho.org
Small Office Home Office (SOHO) America is an
online community where you can exchange
ideas and interact with small-office/home-office
professionals. SOHO Online has information and
resources for starting and succeeding at home-
based business.

U.S. Small Business Administration

http://www.sba.gov

The U.S. Small Business Administration provides a wealth of resources on starting, financing, and managing a business at its Web site. It also offers workshops on topics such as starting a business, writing a business plan, and locating funding in cities and towns throughout the United States. It also has an Office of Native American Affairs (http://www.sba.gov/naa) and an Office of Minority Enterprise Development (http://www.sba.gov/gcbd/whoweare.htm).

Wells Fargo

Women/Minority Services
420 Montgomery Street
San Francisco, CA 94104
800-869-3557
http://www.wellsfargo.com/biz/intentions/women_minority_services.jhtml

This financial services company provides a variety of loans and other financial resources to minority business owners.

MINORITIES IN THE ARTS: OPPORTUNITIES FOR PERFORMERS, VISUAL ARTISTS, AND WRITERS

Do you play in a band? Write poetry or create original illustrations for your own magazine? Maybe you've grown up studying the skills and artistry of a parent or grandparent gifted in a particular art form. Or maybe you have little artistic background, but possess an original perspective on your life and the world around you. In any case, the art world, whatever the discipline, offers opportunities to help minorities develop as artists and to introduce their work to the public. Pursuing a career in the arts can be difficult—receiving recognition for your work can take years of dedication and involve much rejection, disappointment, and serious competition from the thousands of other talented people seeking the same awards and opportunities for exposure. Because of these challenges, organizations have evolved to help minority artists with scholarships, reaching an audience, and mentoring with established artists.

A number of organizations, such as the Association of Hispanic Arts (http://www.latinoarts.org), the Asian American Arts Alliance (http://www.aaartsalliance.org), and the International Agency for Minority Artist Affairs (http://www.aboutharlemarts.org), assist individual artists and groups, as well as promote the significance of the work of minority artists. Not only have these organizations created opportunities for artists, but also for those interested in careers supporting artists—including careers as arts administrators, gallery and museum curators, teachers, and agents. Colleges and universities across the country offer minority scholarships for their master's of fine arts programs (studio-based graduate programs for writers, dancers, painters, actors, filmmakers, and other artists). There are many state art councils and leagues that offer special opportunities for artists. Minority artists should contact their own city and state arts organizations about such programs. (To find out the phone number and address of your arts organizations, contact the offices of your mayor and governor.)

With the exception of some art disciplines and opportunities, the arts do not typically offer a great deal of financial reward. Many artists must supplement their arts careers with jobs that may be outside their fields of interest, or do freelance work to afford them the freedom and time to commit to their art. According to the 2004–05 *Occupational Outlook Handbook* (*OOH*) of the U.S. Bureau of Labor Statistics, more than 50 percent of visual artists are self-employed—a percentage that is significantly higher than the proportion in all professional occupations. The *OOH* also reports that photographers and musicians pursue self-employment in much higher numbers than average. More than 33 percent of musicians employed in 2002 worked part time. Many of the organizations and groups mentioned in this essay must struggle to survive and to secure funds for the artists they support. But, for artists with drive and ambition, the rewards of having work recognized and appreciated far outweighs financial reward.

THE PERFORMING ARTS— MUSIC, DANCE, THEATER, FILM

As the percentage of Hispanic Americans in the U.S. population has increased over the past two decades, Latin music has crossed cultural boundaries and, in many instances, become mainstream. The spotlight on Jennifer Lopez, Marc Anthony, and musical groups such as the Buena Vista Social Club also cast some glow on many other Latin American musicians perhaps not as famous, but certainly benefiting from the growing success of Latin music in America. Clubs such as Sounds of Brazil in Manhattan and HotHouse in Chicago are cropping up in major cities, giving more Hispanic musicians opportunities to perform and build an audience, and powerful people in the industry are paying close attention. David Byrne, former leader of the 1980s band Talking Heads, promotes world music with his record company Luaka Bop, and the Internet company Descarga.com has found great success selling only Latin dance music. African-American-influenced music—rap, hip-hop, jazz, blues, and other genres—continues to enjoy immense popularity in the United States. Even Asian American and Pacific Islander musicians (such as Yo-Yo Ma, Henry Kapono, Rachael Yamagata) and Native American musicians (such as R. Carlos Nakai, Robbie Robertson, and Joanne Shenandoah) are gaining more recognition as the American public seeks out diversity in the arts, including music.

Though ballet does not typically have the same impact on American culture as pop music, the Ballet Hispanico (http://www.ballethispanico.org) is allowing many talented dancers the opportunity to perform in front of thousands of people across the nation. And with its school of dance, the Ballet Hispanico trains children in classical ballet and traditional Spanish dance (Jennifer Lopez is an alumnus of the school); with its arts education program, the Ballet Hispanico visits schools across the nation to work with kids of all ages.

For performers interested in theatrical opera, Opera Ebony (http://www.operaebony.org) provides opportunities for African American and other minority artists. The opera stages such standards as *Carmen* and *Porgy & Bess,* while also showcasing the work of new minority composers. In addition to these performers and composers, Opera Ebony supports directors, choreographers, and technicians.

While many performing arts groups are based in New York City (including Ballet Hispanico and Opera Ebony), other major cities offer special opportunities for minority performers. The African-American Shakespeare Company (http://www.african-americanshakes.org) tours throughout the Bay area of California, and also performs a regular production season on its main stage in San Francisco. Along with the tours and performances, the African-American Shakespeare Company invites high school students to take part in its Summer Youth Troupe. The program involves students in production, direction, and management of a touring show.

The East West Players (http://www.eastwestplayers. org) of Los Angeles is the nation's foremost Asian American theater, with main stage productions of new and classic plays and musicals, as well as a great deal of actor training. Workshops involve training in acting, voice, auditions, choreography, and other skills needed for stage and film work. Its Alliance of Creative Talent Services program allows for actors to network and meet with industry professionals.

Arguably the most competitive art form, filmmaking has provided great, albeit limited, opportunities for minorities. Hispanic American film professionals are receiving critical acclaim and professional support at film festivals throughout the world. One of the most popular festivals is the Los Angeles Latino International Film Festival, which is sponsored by the popular Latino actor Edward James Olmos. In addition to film screenings, attendees can participate in a writing workshop and a screenwriting lab. Other popular festivals include the Toronto Latino Film and Video Festival (http://www.alucinefestival.com), the San Diego Latino Film Festival (http://www.sdlatinofilm. com), and the Chicago Latino Film Festival (http://www. latinoculturalcenter.org/Filmfest/index.htm).

To introduce more African-American filmmakers to the world, the Urbanworld Film Festival (http://www. uwff.com) is going beyond showcasing the works of African-American directors, producers, and actors to New York audiences; it also sponsors a college tour, which is designed to encourage young African-American college students around the country. Having reached more than 200,000 students at Historically Black Colleges and colleges with film programs, the festival has helped African-American students learn about the film industry and see films being made by African-American filmmakers.

Many new Asian American filmmakers have had their work showcased as part of the San Francisco International Asian American Film Festival (http://www.naatanet.org/ festival/2005/html). Some of the films shown at the festival are funded in part by the National Asian American Telecommunications Association (NAATA), which has set out to develop new Asian Pacific American programs for public television.

The Sundance Institute, long committed to new filmmakers, has established the Native American Initiative (http://www.sundance.org), a program that offers professional support to Native American filmmakers. Its efforts include screenwriters and directors labs, and the showcasing of Native American films at the annual Sundance Film Festival. It also sponsors Native American producers who attend its Independent Producers Conference. In addition to working with Native American screenwriters and directors, the institute has begun reaching out to Native American playwrights, music composers, and nonfiction arts writers, as well as working with indigenous artists from all of North America and the South Pacific.

THE VISUAL AND FINE ARTS— PAINTING, PHOTOGRAPHY, SCULPTURE

Toward the end of the 20th century, multiculturalism in the nation's universities and museums began to allow for a more inclusive display of the artwork created by minorities. Some of the traditional artistry of minority groups—such as the prayer books, jewelry, and altarpieces much a part of Hispanic culture—has been appreciated in the past by the mainstream art world, but mostly as folk art or handicraft, something less than fine art. These attitudes are changing with the efforts of such organizations as the National Hispanic Cultural Center of New Mexico (http://www.nhccnm.org), and the galleries and museums across the country that exhibit the works of Hispanic artists who break traditional molds and experiment with the art forms of their culture. Also, the popularity of Latin American artists Frida Kahlo, Fernando Boteros, and others has heightened interest in the collection of Hispanic art. Galleries such as the Galeria de La Raza (http://www.galeriadelaraza.org) in San Francisco regularly feature the work of new Hispanic artists. The Museum of Latin American Art (http://www.molaa.com) in Long Beach, California, is dedicated entirely to promoting the work of Hispanic artists; not only does the museum exhibit the work, it also organizes art courses and lectures.

Many contemporary African-American, Native American, and Asian American artists also are working within the traditions of their cultures, and exhibiting their work in galleries and museums nationwide. The Studio Museum in Harlem (New York) exhibits the work of African-American artists and offers an artists in residence program to African-American artists. Visit http://www.studiomuseum.org for more information. The Asia Society and the Asia/American Center of Queens College (http://www.qc.cuny.edu/index.php) support the work of Asian American artists through national exhibits and publications. The Asia/American Center also hosts an artist intern. The Institute of American Indian Arts (http://www.iaiancad.org) in Santa Fe, New Mexico, helps Native American artists to develop and exhibit their work, and is also home to The National Collection of Contemporary Indian Art. The Smithsonian's National Museum of the American Indian (http://www.nmai.si.edu) provides support and creative avenues to contemporary Native American artists.

LITERATURE—POETRY, FICTION WRITING, PLAYWRITING

Isabel Allende, Sandra Cisneros, Toni Morrison, Ernest Gaines, Amy Tan, Ha Jin, Louise Erdrich, and Sherman Alexie are just a few of the minority writers whose work has gained wide readership around the world; and Oprah's Book Club has helped the novels of several minority writers reach the bestseller lists. While most writers of contemporary fiction, poetry, and theater write for relatively small audiences, the desire to publish, or to see a play produced, remains strong. Many publishing houses, literary magazines, and Web pages are devoted to the publication of work by minority writers.

The Open Book Committee (http://www.pen.org/page.php?prmID/151) of the PEN American Center provides opportunities for African-American, Native American, Hispanic American, Caribbean, and Asian American writers. It features an online network, online job bank, and other programs to help writers gain access to publishers. It also offers PEN/Beyond Margins Awards for writers of color.

African-American writers can receive support from the Center for Black Literature (http://www.mec.cuny.edu/academic_affairs/black_lit.asp) at Medgar Evers College in New York. The center sponsors workshops and seminars, scholarships, and opportunities for new writers to meet established writers and publishing professionals.

The Asian American Writers' Workshop (http://www.aaww.org) provides Asian American writers with opportunities to develop and publish their work. Based in New York City, the workshop promotes the work of new writers nationwide, and sponsors numerous events and programs.

Native American writers have the opportunity to publish with the prestigious University of Nebraska Press—the North American Indian Prose Award (http://blackelkspeaks.unl.edu/writer.html) was initiated by the press (and is cosponsored by the University of California-Berkeley) to promote works of literary merit and originality in dealing with North American Indian life. Though the contest does not invite submissions of novels, plays, or poetry, it does invite biography, autobiography, history, literary criticism, essays, nonfiction works for children, and political commentary.

For Asian American playwrights, East West Players sponsors the David Henry Hwang Writers Institute. Those writers accepted into the program have the opportunity to study with professionals, and are expected to complete a number of one-act and full-length plays. African-American playwrights can benefit from the Lorraine Hansberry Playwriting Award (http://www.kennedy-center.org/education/actf/actflha.html) sponsored by the Kennedy Center American College Theater Festival. The first-place winner receives a cash award of $2,500, as well as a fellowship to attend a writing retreat. The winning play is published and leased for production. You can read some of the winning plays in *The Lorraine Hansberry Playwriting Award: An Anthology of Prize-Winning Plays* (Topeka, Kans.: Clark Publishing, 1996). Additionally, the Playwrights' Center (http://www.pwcenter.org) offers the Many Voices Residency to help artists of color pursue the opportunity to develop new work in the field of playwriting.

FOR MORE INFORMATION

Opportunities for African-American Artists
African-American Shakespeare Company
762 Fulton Street, Suite 306
San Francisco, CA 94102
http://www.african-americanshakes.org
This organization offers main stage productions, tours, and student programs.

Center for Black Literature
1650 Bedford Avenue
Brooklyn, NY 11225
718-270-6976
bgreene@mec.cuny.edu
http://www.mec.cuny.edu/academic_affairs/black_lit.asp
This organization is dedicated to the development of African-American writers and the promotion of their work. It is associated with Medger Evers College in Brooklyn and reaches writers nationally through its Web site.

International Agency for Minority Artist Affairs
The Harlem Art Council
163 West 125th Street, Suite 909
New York, NY 10027
212-749-5298
iamaa@pipeline.com
http://www.aboutharlemarts.org
This agency sponsors a variety of programs and services for artists, including training, newsletter, information about jobs.

The Lorraine Hansberry Playwright Award
American College Theater Festival
The John F. Kennedy Center for the Performing Arts
2700 F Street, NW
Washington, DC 20566
800-444-1324
http://www.kennedy-center.org/education/actf/actflha.html
This organization offers a first-place award of $2,500 and publication for new playwrights in annual competition.

Opera Ebony
2109 Broadway, Suite 1418
New York, NY 10023
212-877-2110
info@operaebony.org
http://www.operaebony.org
This organization introduces performers, conductors, stage directors, choreographers and others to theatrical opera.

Urbanworld Film Festival
c/o Montage Entertainment
104-106 East 126th Street, 4th Floor
New York, NY 10035
212-941-3845
inquiries@urbanworld.org
http://www.uwff.com
This organization offers an annual film festival; sponsors a college tour, bringing films to students across the country.

Opportunities for Asian American Artists
Asian American Arts Alliance
74 Varick Street, Suite 302
New York, NY 10013
212-941-9208
A4@aaartsalliance.org
http://www.aaartsalliance.org
This organization provides assistance to Asian American artists and art groups through publications, grants, networking opportunities, and advocacy.

Asian American Writers' Workshop
16 West 32nd Street, Suite 10A
New York, NY 10001
212-494-0061
desk@aaww.org
http://www.aaww.org
This organization supports the work of Asian American writers via readings, book parties, panel discussions, and creative writing workshops.

Asia Society
725 Park Avenue at 70th Street
New York, NY 10021
212-288-6400
info@asiasoc.org
http://www.asiasociety.org
This organization sponsors exhibits of Asian American art

and supports Asian American arts through a variety of programs. Its Web site features many links to other arts organizations around the world.

East West Players
120 North Judge John Aiso Street
Los Angeles, CA 90012
213-625-7000
info@eastwestplayers.org
http://www.eastwestplayers.org
This organization sponsors actors workshops and main stage productions and is home of the David Henry Hwang Writers Institute.

National Asian American Telecommunications Association
145 Ninth Street, Suite 350
San Francisco, CA 94103
415-863-0814
http://www.naatanet.org
This organization funds public television projects developed by Asian Americans.

Opportunities for Hispanic American Artists
Association of Hispanic Arts Inc.
161 East 106th Street
New York, NY 10029
212-876-1242
ahanews@latinoarts.org
http://www.latinoarts.org
This is a clearinghouse of information about Hispanic arts organizations; it publishes a quarterly magazine and a directory of organizations, and also maintains a database of information about fellowships and grants.

Ballet Hispanico
167 West 89th Street
New York, NY 10024
212-362-6710
http://www.ballethispanico.org
This organization offers main stage performances, a school of dance, and an arts-in-education program.

Museum of Latin American Art
628 Alamitos Avenue
Long Beach, CA 90802
562-437-1689
info@molaa.org

http://www.molaa.org
This museum offers exhibitions of Hispanic artists, lectures and seminars on a variety of arts-related subjects, a summer art camp:

South Coast Repertory
655 Town Center Drive, PO Box 2197
Costa Mesa, CA 92628-2197
714-708-5500
http://www.scr.org
This organization sponsors of the Hispanic Playwrights Project.

Opportunities for Native American Artists
Institute of American Indian Arts
83 Avan Nu Po Road
Santa Fe, NM 87508-1300
505-424-2302
http://www.iaiancad.org
This school for Native American artists offers instruction in a variety of disciplines; it is also home of the National Collection of Contemporary Indian Art.

Sundance Institute
Native American Initiative
8530 Wilshire Boulevard, 3rd Floor
Beverly Hills, CA 90211-3114
310-360-1981
native@sundance.org
http://www.sundance.org
This organization sponsors workshops for Native American screenwriters and offers professional support for filmmakers.

North American Indian Prose Award
University of Nebraska Press
233 North Eighth Street
Lincoln, NE 68588-0255
gdunham1@unl.edu
http://blackelkspeaks.unl.edu/writer.html
This competition invites the work (autobiography, biography, history, literary criticism, and essays) of Native American writers. Winners are published by the press.

Other Arts Programs for Minorities
Open Book Committee
PEN American Center
588 Broadway, Suite 303

New York, NY 10012
212-334-1660, ext. 109
stacyleigh@pen.org
http://www.pen.org/page.php/prmID/151
This organization assists minority writers with publication and offers the PEN/Beyond Margins Awards for writers of color.

Playwrights' Center
2301 Franklin Avenue East
Minneapolis, MN 55406-1099
612-332-7481
info@pwcenter.org
http://www.pwcenter.org/fellowships_MV.asp
This organization provides the Many Voices Residency.

LEVELING THE PLAYING FIELD: AFFIRMATIVE ACTION

We hear the phrase "affirmative action" tossed about in debates, political campaigns, and the media. We're asked to vote on the issue in state elections. But, for many of us, the phrase is unclear. The issue of affirmative action, along with all its controversies, is very complicated. In this essay, you'll read about some of these controversies, as well as the origins of affirmative action programs, the effect of these programs on the colleges and workplaces of the United States, and what experts predict for affirmative action in the future.

The Affirmative Action Review, a White House report written in 1995 in response to President Clinton's questions about the effectiveness of affirmative action, well-defined the issue: "Affirmative action," it reads, "is used first and foremost to remedy specific past and current discrimination or the lingering effects of past discrimination—used sometimes by court order or settlement, but more often used voluntarily by private parties or by governments." This is the basic premise behind the affirmative action programs enforced by the state and federal governments. In addition:

Affirmative action programs cannot require "quotas" (policies requiring the hiring of specific numbers or percentages of minority group members). Though courts may order specific institutions that have shown long histories of discrimination to hire a certain number of minorities, these court-ordered "consent decrees" can not be part of affirmative action programs. Consent decrees are mandated only in extreme situations, and on an individual basis. Consent decrees will continue to be issued by judges even if affirmative action is ended.

Affirmative action programs cannot promote reverse discrimination. According to opinion polls, some members of the majority feel threatened by the existence of affirmative action programs, fearing that they will be passed up for jobs, promotions, and college entry because institutions are eager to promote minorities. Reverse discrimination, however, is illegal, and victims of such discrimination have won their cases in lower and higher courts.

Affirmative action programs cannot promote the hiring of unqualified minorities over qualified white applicants. Affirmative action programs attempt to promote those qualified minorities who might otherwise fail to get job interviews because of discrimination or because they have been unable to make the proper connections and contacts.

AFFIRMATIVE ACTION TIMELINE

The following timeline lists key events in the history of the development and revision of affirmative action:

1961—President Kennedy encourages contractors working for the federal government to "take affirmative action" in employment practices, and to assure that all workers "are treated . . . without regard to their race, color, religion, sex, or national origin."

1964—The Civil Rights Act is enacted, making it illegal to discriminate in employment. This Act also results in the creation of the Equal Employment Opportunity Commission (EEOC).

1969—The Philadelphia Plan is developed by President Nixon. This plan furthers President Kennedy's call for contractors working for the federal government to actively seek out minorities for employment.

1972—The Equal Opportunity Act expands affirmative action policies to include colleges and universities.

1978—The Supreme Court case *The University of California vs. Bakke* concerns admission policies of the medical school of the University of California at Davis. The school uses a rigid quota system, accepting a predetermined number of minority students each year. The Court declares this practice unconstitutional, though it does uphold the rights of schools to take such issues as race and ethnicity into consideration when evaluating applicants.

1979—The Supreme Court case *The United Steelworkers vs. Weber* concerns special training programs geared toward minorities. Such temporary programs, even if they give preference to minorities, are deemed constitutional when they are devised to make up for past discrimination within an institution or business.

1991—The 1980s saw more conservatives appointed to the bench of the Supreme Court, and therefore a number of conservative rulings. The Civil Rights Act of 1991 overturns some of these rulings, strengthening anti-discrimination laws.

1995—The Supreme Court case *Adarand Constructors, Inc. vs. Pena* concerns programs using racial/ethnic classifications. The Court declares that affirmative action programs should be carefully scrutinized and "narrowly tailored." As a result, President Clinton calls for the federal government to make changes in its programs. "We should have a simple slogan," Clinton says. "Mend it, but don't end it."

1996—Proposition 209, an act to end affirmative action in the state, is passed by the voters of California, despite the fact that a majority of these voters believe that some forms of affirmative action are necessary. (Note: Proposition 209, due to legal challenges, was not enacted until November 1997.)

1998—Initiative 200, a proposition similar to 209, is passed in the state of Washington, and other states consider putting such propositions on their own ballots in the near future.

1999—A number of changes in affirmative action policies occur on campuses across the nation: a federal judge finds unconstitutional a University of Georgia admission policy giving preferential treatment to black applicants; the University of Texas at Austin discontinues a special minority professor recruitment program; the University of Washington considers eliminating minority scholarships; the University of Washington Law School experiences a 41 percent drop in black applicants from the previous year when affirmative action policies were still in effect; and the University of California, in an effort to increase enrollment of minority students, decides to admit all high school students in the state graduating in the top 4 percent of their classes.

2000—In February, Florida's legislature bans race as a factor in college admissions, a move geared at discontinuing affirmative action in the state. Later that year, in December, a federal judge ruled that the University of Michigan's use of race as a factor in undergraduate admissions was constitutional (*Gratz vs. Bollinger*).

2001—In March, a judge ruled that the University of Michigan Law School's policy of using race as a factor in admissions was unconstitutional (*Grutter vs. Bollinger*). (This was reversed in 2002.)

2003—The Supreme Court issues a landmark ruling on affirmative action, upholding the use of race as a factor in admissions at the University of Michigan Law School (*Grutter vs. Bollinger*). However, the Supreme Court rules against the use of race as a factor in the University of Michigan's undergraduate admissions program (*Gratz vs. Bollinger*).

WHAT'S SO CONTROVERSIAL ABOUT AFFIRMATIVE ACTION?

Those in support of affirmative action are of one basic view: that affirmative action is necessary to create a level playing field—to allow minorities the same opportunities for jobs, contracts, promotions, and college acceptances as those allowed the majority. However, those against affirmative action may be of a variety of views: Some believe that affirmative action is unnecessary because discrimination in the workplace no longer exists, and that minority workers have no more challenges than do white workers; some believe that affirmative action results in reverse discrimination and the promotion of unqualified minority workers; some believe that current affirmative action policies are ineffective and need to be re-examined and replaced. Still others object to affirmative action simply because it causes such controversy and dispute, and gives some the impression that minorities are not deserving of their successes.

While some analysts believe that affirmative action has worked in many ways for the benefit of minorities and of the nation as a whole, other critics conceive of affirmative action as a failure, an unfair and outdated practice. Regardless of whatever facts exist, this negative public conception will likely determine the fate of affirmative action. And just what facts do exist?:

■ There are thousands of charges of racial discrimination each year, and few of reverse discrimination. In fiscal year 2004 alone, there were 27,696 charge filings of racial discrimination filed with the EEOC, and another 8,361 filings of discrimination based on national origin. However, the few cases of reverse discrimination, even when dismissed by courts, often draw the most attention from the media.

■ The Alliance for Board Diversity, created by Catalyst, The Executive Leadership Council, and the Hispanic Association on Corporate Responsibility to examine barriers in the workplace for women and minorities, reported in 2005 that minorities made up only 14.9 percent of Fortune 100 corporate boards. Minority women made up only 3 percent of board members at Fortune 100 companies.

■ "Before the Civil Rights Act of 1964," states *The Affirmative Action Review,* "the median black male worker earned only about 60 percent as much as the median white male worker." Though the median income of black males has greatly improved since then, in 2003 it was still approximately $8,970 less than the average income for white men, according to the U.S. Census Bureau. Hispanic men fared even worse. They earned $15,128 less than white males in 2004.

These facts don't make strong arguments for either side of the affirmative action debate—they show that discrimination and unfair hiring and promotion practices still greatly hurt minorities, requiring special programs and policies. Yet, our current policies of affirmative action, after more than 40 years in practice, have failed to create equal opportunity for everyone.

Despite attempts to eliminate affirmative action across the nation, most Americans believe that special minority programs are important. Sixty-three percent of Americans surveyed by The Pew Research Center in 2003 favored "affirmative action programs designed to help blacks, women, and other minorities get better jobs and education." But the idea of giving "preferences" creates different responses depending on the race of those surveyed. A 2003 survey by The Pew Research Center found that 49 percent of white Americans opposed affirmative action programs giving preferences to minorities, while 82 percent of minorities favored preferences.

WHAT'S TO BECOME OF AFFIRMATIVE ACTION?

Just as many disagree on the effectiveness of affirmative action, so do many disagree on its future. Some believe that the defeat of affirmative action in California, Washington, and select public postsecondary programs means that the nation is ready to overturn affirmative action policies. Politicians like John Carlson (who headed the campaign for Washington's Initiative 200) and Ward Connerly (the California businessman behind Proposition 209) have taken their efforts to other states, most notably in Florida and Michigan. But these efforts to place anti-affirmative action initiatives onto the ballots in other states, particularly in states with high minority popula-

tions, have often failed. And exit polls showed that the anti-affirmative action initiative in Washington state may have passed because of its vague language.

Even when these anti-affirmative action initiatives pass, it doesn't necessarily mean the end of opportunities for minorities. After the passing of Proposition 209 in California, the private sector began stepping in to improve issues, and the San Francisco Board of Supervisors expanded a program that gave preferences to minorities in city contracting. The University of California System (consisting of 10 campuses) introduced new policies to assist in the recruitment of minority students (see the Affirmative Action Timeline). Similar policies were introduced in Texas: following the federal court-ordered elimination of affirmative action policies at Texas colleges and universities, minority enrollment dropped by half. The state responded by introducing a "10 percent plan," which automatically admitted to public universities any student in the state who graduated in the top 10 percent of his or her high school class. The state of Florida also initiated a similar plan for its public colleges and universities.

Affirmative action policies are being most hotly contested in colleges and universities—most recently at the University of Michigan (see the Affirmative Action Timeline). For decades, minorities were not allowed to attend the same colleges and universities as white students. Today, any minority wanting to go to college will likely have many choices. Since the Civil Rights Movement, university and college boards have attempted to make up for past discrimination by enacting policies that increase enrollment of minorities. Special minority scholarships (of which many are listed in the resource section of this book), recruitment programs, and preferences given minority applications have helped minorities gain access to higher education. These efforts are not only in the name of fair practice; colleges also recognize the educational value of a racially diverse environment and social interaction between students of differing backgrounds and cultures. In the book *The Shape of the River: Long-Term Consequences of Considering Race in College and University Admissions* (Princeton, N.J.: Princeton University Press, 1998), William Bowen and Derek Bok provide evidence that racial preferences greatly benefit minorities, and therefore society, and argue that eliminating preferences would have very little positive effect on the majority.

Despite these findings, universities in Georgia, Texas, Massachusetts, California, Washington, and other states have eliminated certain minority application procedures, and other schools are following suit. As a result, the University of Michigan in 1999, faced by lawsuits (which have since been heard by the Supreme Court, see the Affirmative Action Timeline) by white students accusing the institution of reverse discrimination in its application policies, put together a defense that shows, through extensive research by social scientists, that such racial preferences are of great value to the success of the university and its students. Meanwhile, a group of minority students and organizations filed suit against the University of California at Berkeley, charging that the school's emphasis on standardized test scores violates anti-bias laws.

Standardized test scores, such as the SAT, have long been criticized as inadequate measures of student success. In 1997, an advisory group of professors and community activists in Texas stated that classroom performance in high school is a more effective gauge of a graduate's potential. The "percent" plans initiated in Texas, California, and Florida, which effectively increase minority enrollment without using racial consideration, bypass SAT scores in the application process. Though standardized testing will likely continue to be used in evaluating college applicants, more universities may adopt new policies for evaluation in order to increase minority enrollment while avoiding reverse-discrimination lawsuits.

While it's uncertain what role affirmative action will play in the nation's future, the issue at hand—establishing equality among the races—will likely continue to inspire great controversy. As affirmative action is eliminated in some states, there remains hope for something more effective and less divisive to take its place.

FOR MORE INFORMATION
Affirmative Action and Diversity Project
http://aad.english.ucsb.edu
This website examines both sides of the affirmative action debate.

American Association for Affirmative Action
888 16th Street, NW, Suite 800
Washington, DC 20006
800-252-8952
http://www.affirmativeaction.org
This organization is dedicated to the advancement of affirmative action.

American Civil Rights Institute
PO Box 188350
Sacramento, CA 95818
916-444-2278
http://www.acri.org
This organization works to repeal affirmative action programs. Its motto is "race has no place in American life or law."

Civilrights.org: Affirmative Action
http://www.civilrights.org
This Web site provides resources regarding affirmative action.

Coalition to Defend Affirmative Action, Integration and Immigrant Rights and Fight for Equality by Any Means Necessary
PO Box 24834
Detroit, MI 48224
313-438-3748
http://www.bamn.com
This organization defends affirmative action, integration, and immigrant rights.

WORKPLACE DIVERSITY: PROVIDING A COMPETITIVE EDGE IN THE BUSINESS WORLD

Just as state and federal affirmative action policies are threatened across the country (see the essay "Leveling the Playing Field: Affirmative Action"), the private sector is more dedicated than ever to diversity initiatives. Many large companies have long recognized a commitment to diversity as a moral responsibility. These companies recruit and train minority workers, and provide them with clear paths of promotion and a sense of inclusion, helping minorities achieve fair representation in their workforce. Company executives also are beginning to recognize a commitment to diversity as good business sense. Diversely staffed companies have seen greater productivity—by hiring more minority workers and managers, they have increased sales, built better relationships with other companies, and improved public relations. But, critics say that a number of factors can contribute to a company's success, and these factors are difficult to measure. Some critics argue that those companies devoted to diversity initiatives are devoted to their workers in general, providing all employees with more perks and benefits, and thereby creating a happier, more productive staff. Others believe that diversity can introduce serious problems into the workplace, resulting in reverse discrimination and a divided workforce. Despite the controversies, one thing is given: "diversity" will remain a business-world buzzword for years to come.

Considering the number of complaints of workplace discrimination filed annually with the Equal Employment Opportunity Commission (see the essay "Legal Rights and Recourse"), and the continued underrepresentation of minorities in many industries and in college enrollment, U.S. companies are still a long way from true diversity. Altruistic intentions and more than 40 years of affirmative action haven't been enough to solve the problems facing minorities in the workplace. But economic growth in certain sectors of the American economy has forced company executives to carefully consider the benefits of diversity initiatives. Companies are competing against each other for talented employees and becoming more concerned about retaining experienced workers. Some industries, particularly high-tech industries such as engineering and information technology (for more information, see the essay, "Information = Success: Minorities and Technology"), are faced with severe employment shortages, and must immediately address issues of recruitment and training. But even those industries with more workers than jobs are setting out to improve percentages of minority employment. For example, the American Society of Newspaper Editors (http://www.asne.org) has set long-term diversity goals, hoping for the percentage of minorities in the nation's newsrooms to be the same as the percentage in the general population by 2025. Also, the American Association of University Professors (http://www.aaup.org) has instituted mentoring programs and other initiatives to introduce more minority professors to universities across the country. And those are only a few of the many professional associations that have surveyed, studied, and analyzed the minority numbers in their workforces.

The business world's recent commitment to diversity is reflected in the annual "Best Companies for African Americans, Asian Americans, Hispanic Americans, and Native Americans" lists created by *Fortune* magazine and other publications. These lists typically feature highly successful companies. *Fortune* has emphasized the correlation between the success of a company and its commitment to diversity—noting that stock prices and earnings often rose right along with minority employment percentages. Studies by the Alliance for Board Diversity, also seem to support these findings—2004 numbers showed that America's largest companies (by annual revenue) had more minority board directors than the average. Companies on this list included DuPont, Pepsico, Walt Disney, and General Electric, among others. Though there's no way to directly attribute company growth to diversity, it makes sense to most executives that a cohesive workforce can move a company forward. In addition to better production internally, companies with minority executives and a history of diversity can make better connections with other diversely staffed companies. They also become better reflections of the increasing diversity of the American population—almost all minority groups have experienced significant population growth. And with business being conducted on an international level, a company represented by workers from different cultural backgrounds will make stronger impressions globally.

Despite the correlation between diversity and strong financial performance, minorities and women are still severely underrepresented on corporate boards of Fortune 100 companies. According to the report, *Women and Minorities on Fortune 100 Boards,* which was created by the Alliance for Board Diversity, minorities held nearly 15 percent of the seats on Fortune 100 boards in 2004 despite the fact that minorities make up more than 30 percent of the population in the United States. African Americans held 10 percent of the seats; Hispanic Americans, 3.9 percent; and Asian Americans, 1 percent. In short, American corporations still have a lot of work ahead in creating diverse boards that are representative of America's increasingly diverse population.

WHAT ARE DIVERSITY INITIATIVES?

Companies achieve diversity in a variety of ways—these efforts often are referred to as initiatives. To accomplish their initiative, human resource departments often employ trained professionals experienced in promoting diversity, or companies form whole diversity "councils" or equal opportunity departments—groups of professionals dedicated to the many facets of creating a comfortable workplace for all employees regardless of their race, nationality, gender, age, religion, disability, or sexual orientation. Many freelance consultants specialize in diversity and help guide companies in creating initiatives and setting diversity goals.

In their efforts to increase minority employment, companies actively recruit new workers by visiting minority job fairs and placing ads in minority magazines and on Web sites. They also work with job placement firms and programs, such as the Hispanic Alliance for Career Enhancement (http://www.hace-usa.org). Some companies recruit college students early on in their education by offering scholarships to those going into the industry. They may form initiatives with minority colleges, forming a link between the company/industry and the school.

But diversity initiatives can't stop with recruitment— a company must also assure that minorities are allowed to advance, and encouraged to stay. Some companies offer their executives special bonuses for successfully initiating new diversity programs. Such programs would likely include a system of regular feedback and evaluation for

workers. One of the most effective methods of introducing minorities to the workplace is mentoring (see the essay, "Mentors in School and the Workplace"). Many companies have begun formal mentoring programs, in which new employees are linked with experienced employees, typically in upper management, who can offer guidance in setting career goals. A minority employee also may be invited to join a group composed of other members of the same minority, in order to network within the company, and to share concerns and ideas.

Some diversity councils also organize multicultural events, such as celebrations of the holidays of other nations, to increase understanding and awareness of the various cultures represented in the workplace. Also, English as a second language (ESL) courses may be instituted to help facilitate communication.

It's important to note that, as with the term "affirmative action," the word "diversity" sparks controversy and confusion. Some believe that a company with diversity initiatives is more committed to hiring minorities than to hiring nonminorities. Though a company with a history of discrimination may be ordered by the court to quickly increase its number of minority workers, quotas and racial preferences are against the law. And even with court orders, a company will hire only qualified minority workers. Diversity initiatives, like all affirmative action programs, are instituted for the sake of equality—to give minorities the same opportunities as nonminorities. However, it's possible for a diversity program, as with any corporate program, to fall short of its ideals, creating the problems it is intended to prevent. If diversity training is not handled sensitively, it can lead to divisiveness within a workplace, heightening hostilities and misunderstandings—nonminority workers may come to believe minorities receive special preferences in hiring, raises, and promotions, and minorities may feel that the company's diversity policies give the impression that the workers are not deserving of their success.

HOW DO YOU KNOW IF A COMPANY IS DEDICATED TO DIVERSITY?

Once you've received your degree and have gained some experience through internships, you'll likely have many job options. When considering a company's job offer, you should carefully examine its relationship with diversity and minority employment. If you have the opportunity to meet with a company's recruiters, ask them about the company's history with minority workers. Is the company only committed to recruiting minorities, or does it also assure that new minority hires feel an important part of the workforce and have clear paths of advancement? You may also be able to learn about a company through a professional organization. Most industries have at least one such organization, and some have organizations devoted entirely to minority professionals in the field. These organizations also can guide you in your career pursuit—they can help you choose a college, network with minority professionals already in the field, and pursue scholarships. For more information on such organizations, see "Organizations."

You should read trade and professional magazines and general business magazines—these publications offer insight into the industry, and may feature articles about companies particularly committed to minority employment. If you've chosen a specific city or state where you'd like to work, subscribe to the area's newspapers and read the business pages. Some companies also publish information about minority employment in their annual reports and other publications for stockholders. On the Internet, you can visit a company's Web site, which may feature a career page and e-mail addresses of professionals within the company. Additionally, the Hispanic Association on Corporate Responsibility (http://www.hacr.org) serves as a watchdog group of corporations, recognizing those companies committed to the Hispanic community. *Fortune* magazine, as mentioned earlier, publishes annual lists of the best companies for minorities. *Hispanic Magazine* (http://www.hispaniconline.com) publishes an annual list of the companies offering the strongest opportunities for Hispanics. And *Asian Enterprise* (http://www.asianenterprise.com) magazine publishes an annual list of the best companies for Asian Americans.

You may learn a lot about a company's commitment to diversity by contacting its human resources department. A company's human resources professional may be able to direct you to his or her company's diversity department. If a company doesn't have a special diversity department or council, it doesn't mean it's without diversity initiatives. A company's human resources department may handle the particulars of minority hiring and promotion, and may be able to give you the percentage of minorities in the workforce and in management positions, as well as information about special diversity initiatives.

You should be careful when examining a company's previous problems with discrimination and racial conflict, and not dismiss the company as uncommitted to diversity; often highly publicized lawsuits and charges of discrimination lead a company to introduce effective new diversity policies and programs. For example, the corporation that owns Denny's restaurants had to deal with charges of discrimination in recent years, yet made *Fortune* magazine's 2004 list of best companies for minorities. Nearly 50 percent of its franchisees, 33 percent of its restaurant managers, and 20 percent of its executives are minorities.

FOR MORE INFORMATION

Asian Enterprise
23824 Twin Pines Lane
Diamond Bar, CA 91765
909-860-3316
http://www.asianenterprise.com
Asian Enterprise publishes an annual list of the best
    companies for Asian Americans.

Diversity Pipeline Alliance
1600 Tysons Boulevard, Suite 1400
McLean, VA 22102
703-893-2063
info@diversitypipeline.org
http://www.diversitypipeline.org
This alliance of 10 nonprofit organizations seeks to
    increase the number of African Americans, Hispanic
    Americans, and Native Americans in business careers.

Executive Leadership Council
1010 Wisconsin Avenue, NW, Suite 520
Washington, DC 20007
202-298-8226
http://www.elcinfo.com
The council works to increase the diversity in the business
    world and the number of African Americans on
    corporate boards.

Fortune
http://www.fortune.com/fortune
This magazine publishes comprehensive rankings of
    the best companies for African Americans, Asian
    Americans, Hispanic Americans, and Native Americans.

Hispanic Alliance for Career Enhancement
25 East Washington, Suite 1500
Chicago, IL 60602
312-435-0498
abetomas@hace-usa.org
http://www.hace-usa.org
This nonprofit organization assists Hispanics with career
    development from college through their professional
    years.

Hispanic Association on Corporate Responsibility
1444 I Street, NW, Suite 850
Washington, DC 20005
202-835-9672
hacr@hacr.org
http://www.hacr.org
This organization ranks Fortune 100 companies on their inclusion practices by using the following criteria: corporate executive leadership, corporate governance, workforce representation, Hispanic community reciprocity, and minority supplier outreach and development.

Hispanic Magazine
http://www.hispaniconline.com
Hispanic Magazine provides resources for Hispanics in business. It also publishes an annual list of the best companies for Hispanic Americans.

GENERAL MINORITY WORK ISSUES

The U.S. Census Bureau predicts that minorities will account for nearly 50 percent of the population by 2050. (In 2004, the number of minorities in the United States was approximately 30 percent.) The population of Hispanics is expected to increase nearly 100 percent by 2050, with a projected population of 102.6 million. To meet the needs of a much more diverse society, the nation's industries and professions are in the process of great change. Efforts by private businesses, government agencies, and universities are underway to better assist minorities in the workforce. No matter what changes may occur in the political arena, no matter how affirmative action may be altered, career and educational opportunities will greatly increase for the minority population. Private industry in particular has recognized the need for multicultural staffing, looking ahead to a more diverse clientele; in order for a company or a profession to progress, it will need to reflect the diversity of the society it serves.

In the essays that follow, you may find some of the information contradictory. In "Information = Success: Minorities and Technology" about the need for minorities in the technology industry, and in "Workplace Diversity: Providing a Competitive Edge in the Business World" about private companies committing to multiculturalism, you'll read of industries and companies anxious to develop ways to employ and sustain minority professionals and employees. But in "Leveling the Playing Field: Affirmative Action," you will read how government affirmative action policies are threatened across the nation, limiting special opportunities in education and employment. As a result of lawsuits and government propositions, some of the scholarship opportunities and other programs listed in this directory have been changed from minority opportunities to scholarships benefiting only the economically disadvantaged or individuals from urban and rural areas. Colleges and universities are changing their entrance policies, careful to avoid giving special preference to minorities.

However, many of these changes are political in nature, and not practical, and not necessarily reflective of the pub-

lic interest. Polls have shown that even those who voted against affirmative action in California, Washington, and Florida actually were in support of programs assisting minorities. And colleges are fighting in the courts for their right to encourage and support a diverse campus, recognizing the educational importance of a multicultural student body. Most colleges and universities have active departments dedicated to the needs of minority students, helping these students to find scholarships and offering career guidance. And scholarship committees are eager to reward talented minority students. Terminology and policies may change, but society will find a way to fill the ranks of its workforce with qualified, educated minorities.

The success of many industries absolutely depends on the training and hiring of minorities. In order to effectively serve diverse communities, the health care industry needs more minority administrators and medical professionals; to effectively cover the news that impacts a multicultural readership, the newspaper industry must have more minority reporters and editors; to meet the increasing demands of technological development, more minority engineers must enter the rapidly growing field of information technology. Practically every professional association in the country is studying the numbers of minorities in its workforce, and devising ways to provide minority students with more educational opportunities, and professionals with more networking opportunities.

Whether you are just starting out, or looking to further yourself in your established career, or hoping to change professions, you have every reason to be optimistic about the job market. A *Newsweek* poll conducted in 1999 found that 71 percent of African Americans anticipated that their family incomes would increase in the next 10 years. (Only 59 percent of whites were as optimistic about their own incomes.) The future is bright, but obstacles, other than political, still exist. Cases of workplace discrimination still fill the courtrooms, and still impede workplace productivity. Although the employment and home ownership of African Americans is increasing, for example, too many middle class African-American students lag behind their white peers. An article in the *New York Times* focused on this issue, interviewing students and educators. Professionals find a number of reasons for the gap—too few minority teachers and role models, and too low expectations for the success of African-American students. Peer pressure and low self-esteem also play a part, according to the article.

But for every troubling statistic about minority career and education, there are many more encouraging ones. Despite obstacles, minorities in the United States are finding more opportunities for success than ever before. To recruit minority students, industries are linking established professionals with high school and college students. The American Psychological Association (http://www.apa.org), for example, has established many projects to interest minorities in psychology doctoral programs. The engineering profession is also active in sending professionals to lecture at Historically Black Colleges and Universities, and developing mentorships between professionals and students. The American Society of Newspaper Editors (http://www.asne.org) has comprehensive programs in place to encourage minorities to pursue careers in journalism.

Today's students and job seekers have the added benefit of the Internet. It is difficult for some minorities to get access to the Internet (see the essay, "Information = Success"), but government and private programs are working to change this. Hopefully, if you are reading this book in a library, you are only a few feet away from a computer. If Internet access is not available through your library, check with area social service agencies, cultural centers, and schools about reserving time to use the Internet. With the World Wide Web, you can research professions, colleges and universities, scholarship opportunities, and the cities where you would like to live. The Web also offers many employment-related Web sites for minorities, allowing you to search for jobs and read useful articles about work issues that are of special interest to minorities. Some of these Web sites include http://www.imdiversity.com, http://www.minoritycareer.com, and http://www.diversepro.com. Companies seeking to hire minorities also post job listings at these sites. Most of these Web sites enable you to view listings for free, and to even post your resume for employers. Free e-mail accounts are available from a variety of services, allowing you to communicate directly with college admissions departments, professional organizations, and potential employers. There is also a wealth of career guidance information on the Web, to assist you with writing a resume and searching for jobs. Some people even interview for jobs over the Internet.

A number of publications are also dedicated to professional guidance for minorities. *The Black Collegian* is a free magazine available through the career services department of your college or university, or you can read it online at http://www.black-collegian.com. *Black Enterprise* (http://www.blackenterprise.com), *Hispanic Business* (http://www.hispanicbusiness.com), and *Asian Enterprise* (http://www.asianenterprise.com) provide resources and advice to minority business professionals. You should also contact the association(s) dedicated to the profession you are pursuing; most professional associations publish journals and newsletters for their members. See Section B: Organizations for more information.

To read more about minority work and education issues, check out these books:

Beckham, Barry, ed. *Beckham's Guide to Scholarships: For Black and Minority Students,* Silver Spring, Md.: Beckham Publications Group, 2005.

Bell, Ella L. J. Edmondson, and Stella M. Nkomo. *Our Separate Ways: Black and White Women and the Struggle for Professional Identity,* Cambridge, Mass.: Harvard Business School Press, 2001.

Black, Isaac. *Black Excel African American Student's College Guide: Your One-Stop Resource for Choosing the Right College, Getting In, and Paying the Bill,* Hoboken, N.J.: Wiley, 2000.

Gabarro, John J., and David A. Thomas. *Breaking Through: The Making of Minority Executives in Corporate America,* Cambridge, Mass.: Harvard Business School Press, 1999.

Gutierrez, Gina T., ed. *Sources of Financial Aid Available to American Indian Students,* Las Cruces, N.M.: Indian Resource Development, 2004.

Hyun, Jane. *Breaking the Bamboo Ceiling: Career Strategies for Asians.* New York: HarperBusiness, 2005.

Johnson, Michelle T. *Working While Black: The Black Person's Guide to Success in the White Workplace,* Chicago: Lawrence Hill Books, 2004.

Larimore, Colleen, and Andrew Garrod, eds. *First Person, First Peoples: Native American College Graduates Tell Their Life Stories,* Ithaca, N.Y.: Cornell University Press, 1997.

May, Robin M. *The HBCU Guide: 100+ Things to Know (and a Few Other Things You Need to Do)!,* Lincoln, Neb.: iUniverse, Inc., 2005.

Peterson's. *Scholarships for African-American Students,* Lawrenceville, N.J.: Peterson's Guides, 2003.

Peterson's. *Scholarships for Asian-American Students,* Lawrenceville, N.J.: Peterson's Guides, 2003.

Schlachter, Gail Ann. *Financial Aid for Hispanic Americans,* El Dorado Hills, Calif.: Reference Service Press, 2005.

Stith, Anthony. *How to Build a Career in the New Economy: Guide for Minorities and Women,* Los Angeles: Warwick Publishing, 1999.

Turnock, Judith L., and Price M. Cobbs. *Cracking the Corporate Code: The Revealing Success Stories of 32 African-American Executives,* New York: American Management Association, 2003.

Watkins, Dr. Boyce. *Everything You Ever Wanted To Know About College: A Guide For Minority Students,* Camillus, N.Y.: Blue Boy Publishing, 2004.

INFORMATION EQUALS SUCCESS: MINORITIES AND TECHNOLOGY

It's obvious to some people that knowledge of computers and technology leads to better jobs and better pay in the workplace. To other people, particularly those without computer and Internet access, it's not so obvious. Despite many successful minorities reaping great rewards in the area of information technology (IT), many more minorities could be taking advantage of the surplus of jobs within this industry of computer-based careers. But if you don't have a computer, and have never used the Internet, then you probably aren't aware of the significance of computers in the majority of jobs today. Not only are computer skills necessary in technology-based careers such as computer database management and consulting, Web site development, and electrical and electronic engineering, but also in library science, administration, business, sales, social services, and hundreds of other careers.

Five of the top 20 fastest growing careers in the United States from 2002 through 2012 will be in computer science and IT, according to the U.S. Department of Labor. And countless other jobs require workers to have at least a basic knowledge of computers, the Internet, and related technology. To fill these jobs, the nation will have to work hard to bridge the gap between the "information rich"— those with computers and Internet access—and the "information poor"—a group that too many minorities, particularly African Americans, Hispanic Americans, and Native Americans, fall into. (Note: Asian Americans made up 11.8 percent of the IT workforce in 2002, a percentage that exceeds their representation in the U.S. workforce.)

MINORITIES UNDERREPRESENTED IN THE IT INDUSTRY

African Americans made up 12.7 percent of the U.S. workforce, but only 8.2 percent of the IT workforce in 2002, according to the International Technology Association of America (ITAA). Hispanics made up 12.2 percent of the U.S. workforce, but only 6.3 percent of the IT workforce. Native Americans made up .9 percent of the

U.S. workforce, but only .6 percent of the IT workforce. And recent statistics show that the outlook is not much better at the college level. African Americans, Hispanic Americans, and Native Americans constitute more than 30 percent of college students in the United States today, but earn only 6 percent of the doctorates annually in computer science and computer engineering. According to a 1999 study by the Computing Research Association (CRA): "If these groups [Hispanic Americans, African Americans, and Native Americans] were represented in the IT workforce in proportion to their representation in the U.S. population, this country would have more than an adequate supply of workers to fill even the most dire estimates of a shortage."

The remainder of this essay examines factors responsible for minority underrepresentation in information technology, as well as provide solutions to increase the number of underrepresented minorities in the IT workforce.

WHY ARE AFRICAN AMERICANS, HISPANIC AMERICANS, AND NATIVE AMERICANS UNDERREPRESENTED IN INFORMATION TECHNOLOGY?

The Digital Divide

Experts have many theories about why minorities are underrepresented in technology, but the most alarming statistics concern those minorities attending poor schools and living in low-income communities—many of which lack computers and access to the Internet. The U.S. Department of Commerce has released six reports since 1994 that examine the use of the Internet, computers, and other information technology tools by people in the United States. According to its 2004 report, A Nation Online: Entering the Broadband Age, nearly 59 percent of American households had Internet access—whether it be in a home, school, or other location. But the percentage of black and Hispanic households that had Internet access lagged far behind the national average. In October 2003, only 41.1 percent of blacks and 33.4 percent of Hispanic households had Internet access.

Educational Challenges

In 1999, Harris Interactive surveyed students regarding their favorite subject. Although the majority of students chose mathematics, the survey found that 74 percent of minority girls and 65 percent of minority boys wanted to take advanced math classes, but only 46 percent of girls and 45 percent of boys reported that their schools offered such classes. This dearth of advanced mathematics classes may be why many young, intelligent minorities are not pursuing careers in technology, and are not taking advantage of the fact that there are more job openings in the IT workplace than there are skilled workers to fill them.

The quality of education that minorities receive may also play a role in minority IT shortages. Grade school and high school teachers may be poorly trained in computer skills themselves, and therefore unable to give students anything more than a basic overview of computer use. Even college programs can fall behind in preparing students for the rapidly changing technology of today's workplace.

Minorities also may have different learning styles than their white peers, and may not, as mentioned earlier, gain access to some of the upper-level math and science courses that are key to preparing tomorrow's IT professionals. Otherwise high-achieving minority students may not score well on the standardized tests that are considered heavily for entrance to such courses and to highly selective college computer science and engineering programs.

A Lack of Role Models

Role models and mentors play an important role in helping students and early career professionals find success in the world of work. Fewer minorities in IT means fewer minority mentors for minority students who are interested in learning more about career options. As a result, according to The ITAA Blue Ribbon Panel on IT Diversity, a "vicious cycle" ensues in which minorities are unable to receive appropriate mentoring and support during critical stages of career exploration and planning, and, therefore, fewer minorities enter the IT field.

The Geek Factor

There's also reason to believe that some minorities, along with people from other ethnic groups, perceive information technology careers as "nerdy," dull, and overly technical. They may also feel that IT is a solitary profession despite the fact that many careers in IT are highly collaborative and team-based in nature. Additionally, minorities who don't have access to computers and the Internet, for whom digital technology has little significance, may have doubts about its significance in the workplace and the world-at-large. Information technology careers also may be unappealing to those minorities pursuing work in a socially conscious field; those wanting careers that address the problems in their communities may perceive computer skills to be unnecessary.

Stereotypes

Underrepresented minorities may have to fight stereotypes regarding their aptitude for math and science—stereotypes that begin as early as grade school and continue into the hiring process and beyond. Teachers laboring under these stereotypes may steer minority students away from advanced math and science courses, and recruiters and human resources personnel may also, perhaps even subtlety, take these stereotypes into consideration when choosing between equally qualified minority and nonminority candidates. This unfortunate stereotype may be especially harmful to female minority candidates due to outdated societal attitudes about women of all races in math- and science-based professions.

SOLUTIONS: ENCOURAGING SUCCESS FOR MINORITIES IN IT CAREERS

Government programs, private institutions, and IT companies have recognized the need to bring more minorities into the digital age. Over the past decade, federal and state governments have created programs to ensure that more technology is available to students. But new computers and new services don't necessarily bring students closer to technological proficiency. Many schools, particularly schools in urban areas, need many improvements before computers can be introduced: more desks and classrooms to house the computer units; more outlets and better wiring; and teachers better trained in computer use. And rewiring an old school is often very expensive, because asbestos in the walls makes such tasks difficult. To address these infrastructure issues, corporations, government programs, and nonprofit organizations are offering free equipment and technology, as well as hands-on assistance.

Computer and Internet availability is not just a problem in the schools. The Department of Commerce's 2002 report, *A Nation Online: How Americans Are Expanding their Use of the Internet,* found that African Americans and

Hispanics Americans were more likely than whites to use the Internet outside of their homes. For example, Internet use at public libraries varies by race and income: only 8.6 percent of whites who use the Internet use the public library as an access point, while the comparable figures for African Americans and Hispanics are 18.7 percent and 13.8 percent, respectively. Community-based initiatives to bring more computers to more neighborhoods are under way. The U.S. Department of Housing and Urban Development (HUD) has started Neighborhood Networks (http://www.hud.gov/offices/hsg/mfh/nnw/nnw aboutnn.cfm), which introduces computer workstations to its HUD-assisted housing. The National Association for the Advancement of Colored People's Technology Capacity Building Initiative (http://www.naacp.org) receives funding from corporate giants such as Microsoft, SBC, and AT&T to create community technology centers. Other corporations, such as Lucent Technologies, Cisco Systems, and 3Com Corporation, are also dedicated to building technology centers, donating equipment, and providing training across the country.

Organizations such as the Computing Research Association (http://www.cra.org), the Coalition to Diversify Computing (http://www.cdc-computing.org), and the International Technology Association of America (http://www.itaa.org) are working to expand opportunities for minority workers in computing fields. A study of the workplace by the International Technology Association of America (ITAA) in 1998 found a shortage of 346,000 programmers, systems analysts, and computer scientists. The ITAA's latest study, based on data from the U.S. Bureau of Labor Statistics Current Population Surveys, found that racial minorities and women made few inroads into high tech employment between 1996 and 2002. In response, some companies, therefore, have incorporated new training and recruitment programs and have partnered with colleges and universities to attract more workers. These companies send their representatives to minority student career fairs, to minority colleges, and they advertise in minority publications. Some also offer scholarships and education assistance programs.

But many Silicon Valley companies—leaders of IT industry—have failed to attract minorities, despite the fact that about half of the region's population is composed of minorities. None of the companies based in Silicon Valley made *Fortune* magazine's 2004 list of "50 Best Companies For Minorities." Asian Americans, well-represented in the industry, do hold 31 percent of the jobs and own nearly a quarter of the start-ups. The industry may need to incorporate better diversity initiatives (see the essay,

"Workplace Diversity: Providing a Competitive Edge in the Business World") in order to reach out to minority engineers and IT professionals.

Many organizations are promoting and rewarding success in IT fields in various ways. In an effort to dramatically increase the representation of African Americans, Native Americans, and Hispanic Americans in the critical field of engineering, the National Action Council for Minorities in Engineering (NACME) has selected 32 universities to participate in the NACME Scholars (Block Grant) Program (http://www.nacme.org/university/others.html). This program will not only support the success of individual students, but also build the participating institutions' capacity to improve their minority enrollment and degree-completion rates. The Technology Transfer Project, sponsored by the Executive Leadership Council (http://www.elcinfo.com), prepares African-American graduates at 12 Historically Black Colleges and Universities to compete for management and leadership positions in a corporate environment that is more and more affected by and dependent on technology. The National Association for the Advancement of Colored People sponsors a Diversity and High Tech Job Fair. The Black Engineer of the Year Awards Conference (http://blackengineeroftheyear.org/v3) hosts workshops and seminars that allow African-American students, scientists, engineers, and professionals to meet and network. Professional organizations such as the Society of Hispanic Professional Engineers (http://www.shpe.org), the Society of Mexican American Engineers and Scientists (http://www.maes-natl.org), and the National Society of Black Engineers (http://www.nsbe.org) have formed to serve minorities in the IT workforce.

There are also publications geared specifically toward minorities in IT. Equal Opportunity Publications (http://www.eop.com) offers many titles focusing on the issues of a diverse workplace, including *Minority Engineer* magazine. *Minority Engineer* is distributed free to minority IT students and professionals. The magazine features career articles, job listings, and information about career fairs and recruitment. *Workforce Diversity for Engineering and IT Professionals* is another publication from Equal Opportunity Publications for those in the technology workforce. *Diversity/Careers in Engineering and Information Technology* is a free publication distributed by DIVERSITY/CAREERS to IT professionals and students. It features articles, profiles of minority professionals, and updates on technical careers. Twice a year, a special "Minority College Issue" of *Diversity/Careers* provides information about diversity on campus, an overview of the job market, and profiles of recent graduates. The magazine's Web site (http://www.diversitycareers.com) posts articles from the current issue, features an online forum, and links to companies.

Though still underrepresented in the information technology industry, minorities can take encouragement from the number of opportunities available in the IT industry. For those minorities well-trained in technology, the workplace should prove welcoming. And as companies and corporate leaders slowly but surely recognize the need for minorities to fill their many job openings, better training programs and job placement will bring more minority workers into the fold.

FOR MORE INFORMATION

American Indian Science and Engineering Society (AISES)
PO Box 9828
Albuquerque, NM 87119-9828
505-765-1052
info@aises.org
http://www.aises.org
The AISES provides many programs and opportunities for students and professionals in the fields of science and engineering, including a national conference, professional and college chapters, a student science fair, college scholarships, and internships. It also publishes a magazine, *Winds of Change*.

Black Engineer of the Year Awards Conference
410-244-7101
http://blackengineeroftheyear.org/v3
This organization helps African-American students, scientists, engineers, and professionals meet and network.

Center for the Advancement of Hispanics in Science and Engineering Education
8100 Corporate Drive, Suite 401
Landover, MD 20785
301-918-1014
http://www.cahsee.org
The center seeks to overcome the underrepresentation of Hispanics in the engineering and scientific community.

Coalition to Diversify Computing
http://www.cdc-computing.org
The coalition seeks to increase the number of underrepresented minorities who pursue careers in computing. It is co-sponsored by the Computing Research Association, the Association for Computing Machinery, and the IEEE-Computer Society.

Equal Opportunity Publications
445 Broad Hollow Road, Suite 425
Melville, NY 11747
631-421-9421
info@eop.com
http://www.eop.com
This company publishes several periodicals for minority engineering students.

International Technology Association of America
1401 Wilson Boulevard, Suite 1100
Arlington, VA 22209
703-522-5055
http://www.itaa.org
This organization encourages diversity in the information technology industry.

National Action Council for Minorities in Engineering
440 Hamilton Avenue, Suite 302
White Plains, NY 10601-1813
914-539-4010
http://www.nacme.org and http://www.guidemenacme.org/guideme
This organization seeks to increase the number of African Americans, Native Americans, and Hispanic Americans in engineering, technology, math-, and science-based careers. It offers scholarships to students.

National Society of Black Engineers (NSBE)
1454 Duke Street
Alexandria, VA 22314
703-549-2207
info@nsbe.org
http://www.nsbe.org
The society provides support to African-American engineers and students. It has more than 270 chapters on college and university campuses, 75 Alumni Extension chapters nationwide, and 75 PreCollege chapters. Services provided include tutorial programs, group study sessions, high school/junior high outreach programs, technical seminars and workshops, two national magazines (*NSBE Magazine* and *NSBE Bridge*), a professional newsletter (Career Engineer), career fairs, scholarships, internships, research opportunities, and an annual national convention.

National Technical Association

26100 Bush Avenue, Suite 315
Cleveland, OH 44132
216-289-4682
http://www.ntaonline.org
The National Technical Association is an organization
for minority scientists and engineers. It encourages
minority youth and women to choose careers in
science and technology via science fairs, an annual
conference, mentoring, scholarships, and a career fair.

Society of Hispanic Professional Engineers

5400 East Olympic Boulevard, Suite 210
Los Angeles, CA 90022
323-725-3970
http://www.shpe.org
This professional society for Hispanic engineers provides
support to Hispanic American engineering students
via student chapters, scholarships, and the Advancing
Careers in Engineering program.

Society of Mexican American Engineers and Scientists

711 West Bay Area Boulevard, Suite 206
Webster, TX 77598-4051
281-557-3677
questions@maes-natl.org
http://www.maes-natl.org
The society works to increase the number of Mexican
Americans and other Hispanics in technical and
scientific fields. It offers a variety of resources for
students, including undergraduate and graduate
scholarships, student chapters, and high school clubs.

PART III

DIRECTORY

FINANCIAL AID

For the purposes of this directory, there are five types of financial aid: awards, fellowships, grants, loans, and scholarships. Readers should always check with the organization regarding eligibility requirements before applying for financial aid.

AWARDS

Awards are generally given in recognition of achievement, either to a promising young person moving up in his or her career field or to an experienced professional for a lifetime of achievement. Many awards include a monetary stipend; others don't grant any money at all but are valuable recognition by one's peers and excellent resume-builders.

American Academy of Child and Adolescent Psychiatry

Attn: Camille Jackson
3615 Wisconsin Avenue, NW, Suite 2
Washington, DC 20016
202-966-7300, ext. 117
cjackson@aacap.org
http://www.aacap.org/awards/index.htm
Award Name: Jeanne Spurlock Lecture and Award on Diversity and Culture. *Academic Area: Medicine (psychiatry). *Age Group: Open. *Eligibility: Nominees must be individuals who have made outstanding contributions to the advancement of the understanding of diversity and culture in the United States and the world as it pertains to children's mental health and who will support the recruitment of child and adolescent psychiatrists from all cultures. Nominees need not be psychiatrists. *Application Process: Nominations must come from academy members. Visit the academy's Web site to download an application. *Amount: $2,500. *Deadline: May 2.

American Association of Law Libraries (AALL)

53 West Jackson, Suite 940
Chicago, IL 60604
312-939-4764
http://www.aallnet.org/about/award_mlda.asp
Award Name: Minority Leadership Development Award. *Academic Area: Library sciences. *Age Group: Recent graduates of a graduate program. *Eligibility: Applicant must be a member of a minority group as defined by current U.S. government guidelines; have a strong academic record and have earned a master's degree in library/information science; have no more than five years of professional (post-MLS or post-JD) library or information service work experience; be a current member of the AALL at the time application is submitted; have been a member of the AALL for at least two years or have two years of full time, professional law library work experience; and demonstrate leadership potential. *Application Process: Applicants should submit a completed application along with an official transcript from all relevant graduate programs attended; three letters of reference; a personal statement discussing their professional interests, goals, and leadership potential; and a stamped self-addressed envelope. A copy of the applicants resume is optional. Visit the association's Web site to download an application. *Amount: Travel, lodging, and registration expenses for the recipient to attend the annual meeting of the AALL; an experienced AALL leader to serve as the recipient's mentor for at least one year; and an opportunity to serve on an AALL committee during the year following the monetary award. *Deadline: April 1.

American Psychiatric Association

Attn: Barbara Matos
1000 Wilson Boulevard, Suite 1825
Arlington, VA 22209-3901
703-907-8512
http://www.psychfoundation.org/awardsandfellowships/index.cfm
Award Name: Award for Advancing Minority Mental Health. *Academic Area: Medicine (general), Medicine (psychiatry). *Age Group: Open. *Eligibility: Applicants must show a commitment to increasing access to quality mental health services for underserved minorities and/or improving the quality of care for underserved minorities, particularly those in the public health system or those with severe mental illness. *Application Process: Applicants should submit a completed application along with a four-page narrative, two or more recommendations, and any additional supporting materials such as news clips or publications. Applicants should submit one original packet and three complete copies. Visit the association's Web site to download an application. *Amount: $5,000. *Deadline: November 1.

Asian American Journalists Association

1182 Market Street, Suite 320
San Francisco, CA 94102
415-346-2051
national@aaja.org
http://www.aaja.org/programs/awards/diversity
Award Name: Asian American Journalists Association Leadership in Diversity Award. *Academic Area:

Journalism. *Age Group: Open. *Eligibility: Nominees can be either individuals or corporations that have made strides in promoting and demonstrating diversity in the news media industry. *Application Process: Contact the association for information on the nomination procedure. Application forms are available online in January of each year. *Amount: Awards vary. *Deadline: March 15.

Asian American Psychological Association (AAPA)

Attn: Dr. Jean Lau Chin
AAPA Awards Committee Chair
614 Dedham Street
Newton, MA 02459
617-965-8964
http://www.aapaonline.org/resources/resources.htm

Award Name: The Asian American Psychological Association provides several awards to recognize the achievement of its members. *Academic Area: Psychology. *Age Group: Open. *Eligibility: Nominees should demonstrate a strong commitment of advocating for the Asian American and Pacific Islander communities through scholarship, practice, and leadership. *Application Process: Candidates may be nominated by sending a formal letter of nomination in their behalf. This letter should state the areas of contribution and the qualifications of the person relative to such areas. Nominations should also include letters of recommendation and the nominee's curriculum vita. Visit the association's Web site to view descriptions and qualifications necessary for individual awards. *Amount: Awards vary. *Deadline: Deadlines vary.

Asian American Writers' Workshop

16 West 32nd Street, Suite 10A
New York, NY 10001
212-494-0061
desk@aaww.org
http://www.aaww.org/aaww_awards.html

Award Name: Asian American Literary Award. *Academic Area: English/literature, writing. *Age Group: Open. *Eligibility: Applicants must demonstrate expertise in a literary genre and/or experience in academic environments relevant to Asian American literature. Applicants must be of Asian descent living in the United States. The work must have been published originally in English during the calendar year preceding the award year. *Application Process: Applicants should submit a completed application along with four copies of the work and a $100 entry fee. Visit the workshop's Web site to download an application. *Amount: Awards vary. *Deadline: April 22.

Asian Cultural Council

437 Madison Avenue, 37th Floor
New York, NY 10022-7001
212-812-4300
acc@accny.org
http://www.asianculturalcouncil.org/programs.html

Award Name: John D. Rockefeller 3rd Award of the Asian Cultural Council. *Academic Area: Performing arts (general), visual arts (general). *Age Group: Open. *Eligibility: Candidates, from Asia or the United States, must have made significant contributions to the international understanding, practice, or study of the visual or performing arts of Asia. *Application Process: Candidates must be nominated by artists, scholars, and others professionally involved in Asian art and culture. Contact the council for further information about nominating a candidate. *Amount: $30,000. *Deadline: Contact the council for deadline information.

Association of Black Cardiologists

6849 B2 Peachtree Dunwoody Road, NE
Atlanta, GA 30328
678-302-4222, 800-753-9222
abcardio@abcardio.org
http://www.abcardio.org/awards.htm

Award Name: The Association of Black Cardiologists offers several awards to cardiologists who have made strong contributions to their profession and the African-American community. *Academic Area: Medicine (physicians). *Age Group: Open. *Eligibility: Applicants should have made significant contributions to the field of cardiology while improving the health status and risks for minority populations. *Application Process: Applicants should contact the organization for further information about the nomination or application procedures for individual awards. *Amount: Awards vary. *Deadline: Contact the association for deadline information.

Association of Black Women Historians

Attn: Wanda A. Hendricks, Ph.D.
Attn: University of South Carolina
204 Flinn Hall
Columbia, SC 29208
803-777-4007

nationaldirector@abwh.org

http://www.abwh.org

Award Name: The Lillie M. Newton Hornsby Memorial Award is given for exemplary historical research. *Academic Area: History. *Age Group: Undergraduate students. *Eligibility: African-American females with accomplishments in historical research may be nominated. Applicants must be either at the end of their junior year or beginning their senior year. *Application Process: Candidates must be nominated for the award. Contact the association for more information. *Amount: $250. *Deadline: September 1.

Black Caucus of the American Library Association

Attn: Andrew P. Jackson, President

Queens Borough Public Library

100-01 Northern Boulevard

Corona, NY 11368

718-651-1100

andrew.p.jackson@queenslibrary.org

http://www.bcala.org/awards/literary.htm

Award Name: Black Caucus of the American Library Association Trailblazer's Award. *Academic Area: Library sciences. *Age Group: Professionals. *Eligibility: Applicants must have made significant, unique, and pioneering contributions to the field of library science. This prestigious award is given once every five years. *Application Process: Contact the caucus for information about the nominating procedure. *Amount: Awards vary. *Deadline: Contact the caucus for deadline information.

Black Caucus of the American Library Association

Attn: Andrew P. Jackson, President

Queens Borough Public Library

100-01 Northern Boulevard

Corona, NY 11368

718-651-1100

andrew.p.jackson@queenslibrary.org

http://www.bcala.org/awards/literary.htm

Award Name: DEMCO/American Library Association Black Caucus Award for Excellence in Librarianship. *Academic Area: Library sciences. *Age Group: Professionals. *Eligibility: Applicants must have made significant contributions to promoting the status of African Americans in the library profession. Specific contributions may include, but are not limited to, research and scholarship, recruitment, professional development, planning or implementation of programs, or advocacy (public relations). *Application

Process: Submit nominations for the award to the BCALA president via e-mail. *Amount: $500. *Deadline: Contact the association for deadline information.

Black Caucus of the American Library Association

Attn: John S. Page, Chair

BCALA Literary Award Committee

Washington, DC 20008

202-274-6030

jpage@wrlc.org

http://www.bcala.org/awards/literary.htm

Award Name: Black Caucus of the American Library Association Fiction Award. *Academic Area: English/literature, writing. *Age Group: Professionals. *Eligibility: Applicants must be African American, and their work must portray some aspect of the African-American experience past, present, or future and be published in the United States in the year preceding presentation. This award recognizes depictions of sensitive and authentic personal experience either within the framework of contemporary literary standards and themes or which explore innovative literary formats. *Application Process: Applicants should contact the committee chair for information on the application process. *Amount: $500. *Deadline: Contact the caucus for deadline information.

Black Caucus of the American Library Association

Attn: John S. Page, Chair

BCALA Literary Award Committee

Washington, DC 20008

202-274-6030

jpage@wrk.org

http://www.bcala.org/awards/literary.htm

Award Name: Black Caucus of the American Library Association Nonfiction Award. *Academic Area: English/literature, writing. *Age Group: Professionals. *Eligibility: Applicants must be African American, and their work must portray some aspect of the African-American experience past, present, or future and be published in the United States in the year preceding presentation. This award honors cultural, historical, political, or social criticism or academic and/or professional research which significantly advances the body of knowledge currently associated with the people and the legacy of the Black Diaspora. *Application Process: Applicants should contact the committee chair for information on the application process. *Amount: $500. *Deadline: Contact the caucus for deadline information.

California Chicano News Media Association

University of Southern California Annenberg School of Journalism

300 South Grand Avenue, Suite 3950

Los Angeles, CA 90071-8110

213-437-4408

ccnmainfo@ccnma.org

http://www.ccnma.org

Award Name: Ruben Salazar Journalism Awards are given to California journalists in four categories: print, television, radio, and photography. These awards recognize excellence in journalism and fair and accurate portrayals of Latinos in the media in the state of California. *Academic Area: Broadcasting, journalism. *Age Group: Professionals. *Eligibility: Journalism professionals in California may apply. *Application Process: Applicants should submit a cover letter that summarizes their submission. Entries may be in English or Spanish. Contact the association for specific application requirements about radio, print, and television submissions. There is a $25 application fee for association members, and a $40 application fee for nonmembers. *Amount: A cash prize is awarded; the amount varies. *Deadline: Typically in September.

Columbia College

Attn: Chuck Smith

Theatre Department

72 East 11th Street

Chicago, IL 60605

312-344-6136

theatre@colum.edu

http://www.colum.edu/undergraduate/theater/calendar.php?action=full&id=66

Award Name: Theodore Ward Prize for African American Playwriting. *Academic Area: English/literature, performing arts (general), writing. *Age Group: Open. *Eligibility: Applicants should be African Americans who are addressing the African-American experience in their work, and who wish to have the opportunity to gain exposure to Chicago's professional theater community through staged readings and/or fully mounted productions. *Application Process: Interested candidates should contact the college for submission instructions. *Amount: Awards vary. *Deadline: Contact the college for deadline information.

Committee on Institutional Cooperation

Attn: Chris Cosat

1819 South Neil Street, Suite D

Champaign, IL 61820

217-265-8005

cosat@uiuc.edu

http://www.cic.uiuc.edu/programs/FreeApp/archive/RequestForm/GraduateRecruitment.shtml

Award Name: Committee on Institutional Cooperation FreeApp Award. *Academic Area: Open. *Age Group: Graduate students. *Eligibility: Applicants must be underrepresented minority students seeking admission to graduate school. A bachelor's degree must be completed by the August preceding enrollment in the graduate program. Applicants must be applying for admission to a Ph.D. program or master of fine arts program, be a U.S. citizen or permanent resident, have a minimum GPA of 3.0, and intend to pursue an academic and/or research career. *Application Process: Applicants should visit the committee's Web site to download an application. *Amount: Awards vary. *Deadline: Deadlines vary.

Conference of Minority Public Administrators (COMPA)

Attn: Chris Snead, Chair

COMPA Awards Committee

22 Lincoln Street

Hampton, VA 23669

757-727-6377

csnead@hampton.gov

http://www.natcompa.org/awards.htm

Award Name: Conference of Minority Public Administrators Public Service Award *Academic Area: Government. *Age Group: Professionals. *Eligibility: Applicants should be minority public administrators who have demonstrated outstanding achievement in the field of public service. Eligible candidates include non-elected administrators in local, state, and federal government agencies; nonprofit and community based organization; or public academic institutions that have at least 15 years of public service experience. *Application Process: Candidates may be elected by a colleague or by oneself by submitting a nomination package that includes a narrative explaining the basis for the nomination; a biographical sketch of the nominee, which includes professional achievements, volunteer work, honors, awards and other information relevant to the nomination; and three letters of nomination, at least one of which must be from a COMPA member. The nomination package should include one original and five copies of all enclosed materials. *Amount: Awards vary. *Deadline: December 16.

Conference of Minority Public Administrators (COMPA)
Attn: Chris Snead, Chair
COMPA Awards Committee
22 Lincoln Street
Hampton, VA 23669
757-727-6377
csnead@hampton.gov
http://www.natcompa.org/awards.htm
Award Name: Sylvester Murray Distinguished
Mentor Award. *Academic Area: Government.
*Age Group: Professionals. *Eligibility: Applicants
should be minority public administrators who have
demonstrated outstanding mentorship capabilities
in the field of public service. Eligible candidates
include non-elected administrators in local, state,
and federal government agencies; nonprofit and
community based organization; or public academic
institutions that have at least 15 years of public
service experience. *Application Process: Candidates
may be elected by a colleague or by oneself by
submitting a nomination package that includes a
narrative explaining the basis for the nomination; a
biographical sketch of the nominee, which includes
professional achievements, volunteer work, honors,
awards and other information relevant to the
nomination; and three letters of nomination, at least
one of which must be from a COMPA member. The
nomination package should include one original and
five copies of all enclosed materials. *Amount: Awards
vary. *Deadline: December 16.

Hispanic Heritage Foundation
2600 Virginia Avenue, NW, Suite 406
Washington, DC 20037
202-861-9797
contact@hispanicheritageawards.org
http://www.hispanicheritageawards.org
Award Name: Hispanic Heritage Youth Award. *Academic
Area: Open. *Age Group: High school students.
*Eligibility: Applicants must demonstrate leadership
in their communities as well as academic achievement
in the classroom. The award's purpose is to identify
and promote the next generation of Hispanic role
models. *Application Process: Interested candidates
should visit the foundation's Web site for further
information. Contact the foundation with questions
about the application procedure. *Amount: $3,000 to
$5,000 (plus travel expenses and prizes for national
award winners). *Deadline: Contact the foundation for
deadline information.

Hispanic Theological Initiative
12 Library Place
Princeton, NJ 08540
609-252-1721
hti@ptsem.edu
http://www.htiprogram.org/awards/book-prize.htm
Award Name: Hispanic Theological Initiative Book Prize
and Lectureship. *Academic Area: Religion. *Age
Group: Professionals. *Eligibility: Applicants must
be Hispanic junior faculty members of an academic
institution in the United States who have written
a book that engages the intellectual traditions of
Christianity, Judaism, or Islam. *Application Process:
Applicants should submit a completed application,
a brief biography of author, and five copies of their
book or bound page proofs. Visit the initiative's Web
site to download an application. *Amount: Awards
vary. *Deadline: January 20.

Japanese American Citizens League
1765 Sutter Street
San Francisco, CA 94115
415-921-5225
jacl@jacl.org
http://www.jacl.org/scholarships.html
Award Name: Ruby Yoshino Schaar Biennium Playwright
Award. *Academic Area: Writing. *Age Group: Open.
*Eligibility: Applicants must be interested in telling the
story of the Japanese American or Japanese Canadian
experience in North America. *Application Process:
Applicants should contact the Japanese American
Citizens League for application procedures. *Amount:
Awards vary. *Deadline: Contact the organization for
deadline information.

Kennedy Center American College Theater Festival
2700 F Street, NW
Washington, DC 20566
202-416-8000
http://www.kennedy-center.org/education/actf
Award Name: Paula Vogel Award in Playwriting.
*Academic Area: English/literature, performing
arts (general), writing. *Age Group: Undergraduate
students, graduate students. *Eligibility: Applicants
must be full-time degree seeking students who
have written a play that celebrates diversity and
encourages tolerance while exploring issues of
disempowered voices not traditionally considered
mainstream. *Application Process: All scripts should
be typed following the standard play manuscript

format (e.g., Samuel French style sheet). Clear photocopies or letter-quality computer printouts are acceptable. All manuscripts must be firmly bound in a cover. Visit the organization's Web site for a more detailed description of submission guidelines. *Amount: $2,500, and the playwright will be awarded a fellowship to attend at New Play Development Laboratory; $1,000, and a grant of $250 to the producing department of the play for its support of the work. *Deadline: Contact the organization for deadline information.

Lee and Low Books
Attn: New Voices Award, #1205
95 Madison Avenue
New York, NY 10016
212-779-4400
general@leeandlow.com
http://www.leeandlow.com/editorial/voices.html
Award Name: Lee and Low Books, a publisher of multicultural children's literature, offers the Lee and Low New Voices Award for a picture book story by a writer of color. *Academic Area: English/literature, writing. *Age Group: Professionals. *Eligibility: Writers of color who are U.S. residents and who have not published a children's picture book may apply. *Application Process: Applicants should include a cover letter (which features their contact information, a short biographical note, and relevant cultural and ethnic information) and a self-addressed, stamped envelope for return of the manuscript. Agented submissions will not be accepted. Manuscripts may be fiction or nonfiction, but must focus on the interests of children of color ages two to 10. They must also be no longer than 1,500 words. *Amount: New Voices Award: $1,000, plus a standard publication contract with the publishing company; Honor Award: $500. *Deadline: October 31.

National Association of Black Accountants (NABA)
7249-A Hanover Parkway
Greenbelt, MD 20770
301-474-6222
http://www.nabainc.org/NationalAwards/
   Professional2004NA.jsp
Award Name: The National Association of Black Accountants offers several National Awards to its members who demonstrate excellence in accounting or community service. *Academic Area: Accounting. *Age Group: Professionals. *Eligibility: Members of

the NABA may apply. *Application Process: Contact the NABA for application requirements for specific awards. *Amount: These are not monetary awards, but provide an excellent opportunity for African-American accountants to gain professional recognition. *Deadline: February 1.

National Association of Black Accountants (NABA)
7249-A Hanover Parkway
Greenbelt, MD 20770
301-474-6222
http://www.nabainc.org/pages/Student_
   CaseCompetition.jsp
Award Name: The National Association of Black Accountants offers the Student Case Competition for student members of the association. *Academic Area: Accounting. *Age Group: College students. *Eligibility: Student members of the NABA may apply. *Application Process: Teams of four to six students are asked to solve an accounting-related issue at the association's annual convention. A panel of judges from public accounting firms, corporate accounting firms, and academia choose the winners. *Amount: A monetary award is provided to winning teams. *Deadline: Contact the NABA for details.

National Association of Black Journalists (NABJ)
University of Maryland
8701-A Adelphi Road
Adelphi, MD 20783-1716
301-445-7100
nabj@nabj.org
http://www.nabj.org/awards/honors/index.html
Award Name: National Association of Black Journalists Special Honors Award. *Academic Area: Journalism. *Age Group: Open. *Eligibility: Candidates should demonstrate excellence in journalism, according to one of the many awards outlined. *Application Process: Self-nominations are not accepted. Candidates should be nominated by an association member. Visit the association's Web site to review the list of available awards. Each award has its own nomination criteria. *Amount: Awards vary. *Deadline: February 25.

National Association of Health Services Executives
8630 Fenton Street, Suite 126
Silver Spring, MD 20910
202-628-3953
nahsehq@nahse.org

http://www.nahse.org/eweb/DynamicPage.aspx?Sit
e=NAHSE&WebKey=15d71c6b-6843-43d5-b539-
c95d2c1a37f6

Award Name: Everett V. Fox Student Case Competition.
*Academic Area: Medicine (general). *Age Group:
Graduate students. *Eligibility: Applicants must be
minority graduate students in health administration
programs or a related field who are interested in
applying their creativity, knowledge, and experience
to analyze the real and diverse issues facing a health
care organization. *Application Process: Applicants
must apply as teams of one to three students. Three
weeks prior to the competition each team receives
the case study to analyze and form recommendations.
During the competition, each team has 20 minutes to
present their analysis and recommendations, which is
followed by a 10-minute question and answer period.
Presentations are made before a panel of judges
representing leaders in the health care field, corporate
sponsors, and academia. Visit the association's
Web site to download a registration form. A $150
registration fee, per team, is required. *Amount:
$1,000 to $3,000. *Deadline: September 2.

**National Association of Health Services Executives
    (NAHSE)**
Attn: Eric L. Conley
8630 Fenton Street, Suite 126
Silver Spring, MD 20910
202-628-3953
nahsehq@nahse.org
http://www.nahse.org/eweb/DynamicPage.aspx?Sit
e=NAHSE&WebKey=759872fa-1389-417c-be62-
c76598947baf

Award Name: Hall of Fame Award. *Academic Area:
Medicine (general). *Age Group: Professionals.
*Eligibility: Nominees should have a minimum of
25 years of experience in related fields of the health
care industry, demonstrated leadership and vision
in the health care field, exemplary service in the
promotion and advancement of African-American
participation in the health care industry, and
evidence of dedication and commitment to fostering
excellence and professionalism in the health care
industry. Nominees also exhibit the positive impact
of networking by serving as a mentor to influence
the advancement of young aspiring professionals
in the health care industry. A commitment to
community involvement and outstanding community
service is also necessary as well as commitment

and involvement to attainment of the goals of the
National Association of Health Services Executives.
*Application Process: Candidates must be nominated
by other NAHSE members. Visit the organization's
Web site to download a nomination form. *Amount:
Awards vary. *Deadline: July 29.

**National Association of Health Services Executives
    (NAHSE)**
Attn: Eric L. Conley
8630 Fenton Street, Suite 126
Silver Spring, MD 20910
202-628-3953
nahsehq@nahse.org
http://www.nahse.org/eweb/DynamicPage.aspx?Sit
e=NAHSE&WebKey=759872fa-1389-417c-be62-
c76598947baf

Award Name: Senior Healthcare Executive Award.
*Academic Area: Medicine (general). *Age Group:
Professionals. *Eligibility: Nominees must be NAHSE
members (minimum of 10 years) who are actively
involved either at the local or national level. Nominees
must also have a minimum of 15 years in the health
care industry with demonstrated leadership and a
commitment to the advancement and development
of African-American health care professionals and
to the advancement and/or inclusion of African
Americans in health care. Additionally, nominees
should be active participants in community
organizations. *Application Process: Candidates must
be nominated by other NAHSE members. Visit the
organization's Web site to download a nomination
form. *Amount: Awards vary. *Deadline: July 29.

**National Association of Health Services Executives
    (NAHSE)**
Attn: Eric L. Conley
8630 Fenton Street, Suite 126
Silver Spring, MD 20910
202-628-3953
nahsehq@nahse.org
http://www.nahse.org/eweb/DynamicPage.aspx?Sit
e=NAHSE&WebKey=759872fa-1389-417c-be62-
c76598947baf

Award Name: Young Healthcare Executive Award.
*Academic Area: Medicine (general). *Age Group:
Professionals. *Eligibility: Nominees must be NAHSE
members (minimum of five years) under age 40 who
are actively involved either at the local or national
level. Nominees must also have a minimum of seven

years of progressive management experience in a health care organization and a demonstrated commitment to the development of young health care professionals. Additionally, nominees should be active in community organizations. *Application Process: Candidates must be nominated by other NAHSE members. Visit the organization's Web site to download a nomination form. *Amount: Awards vary. *Deadline: July 29.

National Association of Hispanic Nurses

Attn: Maria Castro
1501 16th Street, NW
Washington, DC 20036
202-387-2477
info@thehispanicnurses.org
http://www.thehispanicnurses.org

Award Name: The National Association of Hispanic Nurses provides several awards to Hispanic nurses who demonstrate professional excellence and service to the community. *Academic Area: Nursing (general). *Age Group: Open. *Eligibility: Nominees must be Hispanic nurses with accomplishments in the field of nursing and must be an active participant as a member of the National Association of Hispanic Nurses. *Application Process: Nurses are encouraged to nominate fellow nurses. Visit the association's Web site for specific criteria required for individual awards. *Amount: Awards vary. *Deadline: April 15.

National Hispana Leadership Institute (NHLI)

1901 North Moore Street, Suite 206
Arlington, VA 22209
703-527-6007
NHLI@aol.com
http://www.nhli.org/mujer.htm

Award Name: Mujer Award. *Academic Area: Open. *Age Group: Adults. *Eligibility: Hispanic woman who have served their communities and acted with justice, love, and pride in culture are eligible to apply. *Application Process: Visit the institute's Web site to download an application. *Amount: There is no monetary award; the NHLI honors the Mujer Award recipient at an annual gala event. *Deadline: Typically in the spring.

National Medical Fellowships

Five Hanover Square, 15th Floor
New York, NY 10004
212-483-8880
info@nmfonline.org
http://www.nmf-online.org/Programs/MeritAwards/meritawards.htm

Award Name: Aura E. Severinghaus Award. *Academic Area: Medicine (physicians). *Age Group: Medical students. *Eligibility: Applicants must belong to one of the following underrepresented, minority groups: African Americans, mainland Puerto Ricans, Mexican Americans, Native Hawaiians, Alaska Natives, or American Indians. Applicants must also be seniors attending the College of Physicians and Surgeons of Columbia University who demonstrate outstanding academic achievement, leadership, and service to the community. *Application Process: There is no application for this award. A committee of faculty and administrators at the College of Physicians and Surgeons of Columbia University selects the student most deserving of this award and presents the candidate's dossier to NMF for final approval. *Amount: $2,000. *Deadline: Deadlines vary.

National Medical Fellowships

Five Hanover Square, 15th Floor
New York, NY 10004
212-483-8880
info@nmfonline.org
http://www.nmf-online.org/Programs/MeritAwards/meritawards.htm

Award Name: Franklin C. McLean Award. *Academic Area: Medicine (physicians). *Age Group: Medical students. *Eligibility: Applicants must be students in their senior year of medical school who have exhibited outstanding academic achievement, leadership, and service to their communities. Applicants also must be African Americans, mainland Puerto Ricans, Mexican Americans, Native Hawaiians, Alaska Natives, or American Indians who are U.S. citizens attending medical degree-granting institutions accredited by the Liaison Committee on Medical Education of the Association of American Medical Colleges, or in D.O. degree-granting colleges of osteopathic medicine accredited by the Bureau of Professional Education of the American Osteopathic Association. *Application Process: Candidates must be nominated by their medical school deans. Schools are required to submit letters of recommendation and official academic transcripts for each candidate. *Amount: $3,000. *Deadline: July 21.

National Medical Fellowships
Five Hanover Square, 15th Floor
New York, NY 10004
212-483-8880
info@nmfonline.org
http://www.nmf-online.org/Programs/MeritAwards/
meritawards.htm
Award Name: Henry G. Halladay Award. *Academic Area: Medicine (physicians). *Age Group: Medical students. *Eligibility: Applicants must be African-American men enrolled in the first year of medical school who have overcome significant obstacles to obtain a medical education. Applicants must be U.S. citizens by the application deadline. Applicants born outside of the United States, or whose parents were born outside the United States, must submit proof of citizenship. *Application Process: There is no special application for these awards. NMF staff members review first-year, need-based scholarship applications and select five students who, on the basis of recommendations, personal statements, and financial need, are most deserving of these awards. For more information on need-based scholarships visit the association's Web site. *Amount: $760. *Deadline: Deadlines vary.

National Medical Fellowships
Five Hanover Square, 15th Floor
New York, NY 10004
212-483-8880
info@nmfonline.org
http://www.nmf-online.org/Programs/MeritAwards/
meritawards.htm
Award Name: Metropolitan Life Foundation Award for Academic Excellence in Medicine. *Academic Area: Medicine (physicians). *Age Group: Medical students. *Eligibility: Applicants must be second-through fourth-year underrepresented medical students who demonstrate outstanding academic achievement and leadership. Applicants must also demonstrate financial need and must also attend medical school or have legal residence in a select group of cities. Visit the association's Web site to view a list of eligible cities. *Application Process: Applicants should submit a completed application along with a letter of recommendation, transcripts, a 500-word essay, documented proof of financial need, proof of residency, and a curriculum vitae. Contact the association for an official application. *Amount: $4,000. *Deadline: February 25.

National Medical Fellowships (NMF)
Five Hanover Square, 15th Floor
New York, NY 10004
212-483-8880
info@nmfonline.org
http://www.nmf-online.org/Programs/MeritAwards/
meritawards.htm
Award Name: National Medical Association Special Award Program. *Academic Area: Medicine (physicians). *Age Group: Medical students. *Eligibility: Applicants must be African-American medical students who demonstrate extraordinary accomplishments, academic excellence, leadership and potential for outstanding contributions to medicine. Applicants should also be active participants in their communities. *Application Process: Applicants should submit an application along with a letter of recommendation, a 500-word essay, and academic transcripts. There are several awards offered in this category. Visit the association's Web site to view additional requirements for specific awards. Visit the association's Web site to download an application. *Amount: $2,250 to $5,000. *Deadline: May 7.

National Medical Fellowships
Five Hanover Square, 15th Floor
New York, NY 10004
212-483-8880
info@nmfonline.org
http://www.nmf-online.org/Programs/MeritAwards/
meritawards.htm
Award Name: Ralph W. Ellison Memorial Prize. *Academic Area: Medicine (physicians). *Age Group: Medical students. *Eligibility: Applicants must in their senior year of medical school and must be African Americans, mainland Puerto Ricans, Mexican Americans, Native Hawaiians, Alaska Natives, or American Indians who are U.S. citizens attending medical doctor degree-granting institutions accredited by the Liaison Committee on Medical Education of the Association of American Medical Colleges, or in D.O. degree-granting colleges of osteopathic medicine accredited by the Bureau of Professional Education of the American Osteopathic Association. *Application Process: Applicants must submit a letter of recommendation from their dean, a statement of 500 words or more that details their interest in medicine and career plans, a curriculum vitae, an academic transcript, and a completed

application (available at the organization's Web site). *Amount: $500. *Deadline: March 18.

National Medical Fellowships
Five Hanover Square, 15th Floor
New York, NY 10004
212-483-8880
info@nmfonline.org
http://www.nmf-online.org/Programs/MeritAwards/
meritawards.htm

Award Name: William and Charlotte Cadbury Award. *Academic Area: Medicine (physicians). *Age Group: Medical students. *Eligibility: Applicants must in their senior year of medical school and must be African Americans, mainland Puerto Ricans, Mexican Americans, Native Hawaiians, Alaska Natives, or American Indians who are U.S. citizens attending medical doctor degree-granting institutions accredited by the Liaison Committee on Medical Education of the Association of American Medical Colleges, or in D.O. degree-granting colleges of osteopathic medicine accredited by the Bureau of Professional Education of the American Osteopathic Association. *Application Process: There is no open application for this program. Candidates must be nominated by their medical school deans. Schools are required to submit letters of recommendation and official academic transcripts for each candidate. Those wishing to be nominated for the award should contact their medical school dean. *Amount: $2,000. *Deadline: July 21.

National Women's Studies Association Women of Color Caucus Student Essay Awards
Attn: Dr. Pat Washington
4537 Alamo Drive
San Diego, CA 92115
619-582-5383
Themorgangirl@aol.com
http://www.nwsa.org/wocscol.html

Award Name: ABAFAZI-Women of Color Caucus Student Essay Award. *Academic Area: Women's studies, writing. *Age Group: Undergraduate students, graduate students. *Eligibility: Applicants must submit scholarly essays that provide critical theoretical discussions and/or analyses of issues/experiences of women and girls of African descent in the United States and/or throughout the Diaspora. Applicants must be women of African descent. *Application Process: Applicants should submit three copies of a 15- to 25-page, original and unpublished essay via

mail. For further information, visit the association's Web site. *Amount: $400. *Deadline: February 15.

National Women's Studies Association Women of Color Caucus Student Essay Awards
Attn: Dr. Pat Washington
4537 Alamo Drive
San Diego, CA 92115
619-582-5383
Themorgangirl@aol.com
http://www.nwsa.org/wocscol.html

Award Name: Women of Color Caucus Student Essay Writing Award. *Academic Area: Women's studies, writing. *Age Group: Undergraduate students, graduate students. *Eligibility: Applicants must submit scholarly essays that provide critical theoretical discussions and/or analyses of issues/experiences of Latina, Asian/Asian American/Pacific Islander, or Native American/American Indian/Alaskan Native women and girls. The focus of the essay may be national or international, and the writer submitting the essay must be a woman of Latina/o, Asian/Asian American/Pacific Islander, or Native American/ American Indian/Alaskan Native descent. *Application Process: Applicants should submit three copies of a 15- to 25-page, original and unpublished essay via mail. For further information, visit the association's Web site. *Amount: $400. *Deadline: February 15.

Native American Journalists Association
555 North Dakota Street
Al Neuharth Media Center
Vermillion, SD 57069
605-677-5282
info@naja.com
http://www.naja.com/programs/awards

Award Name: The association provides several Native Media Awards to members and associate members. *Academic Area: Journalism. *Age Group: Open. *Eligibility: Applicants must be voting members of the association, except in categories specifically aimed at non-native individual journalists. In those cases, non-native entrants must be associate members of the association. The contest is open to journalists throughout the United States, Canada, and Latin America. *Application Process: Applicants should visit the association's Web site for information on various categories and how to submit applications. *Amount: Awards vary. *Deadline: Contact the association for deadline information.

Organization of American Historians
112 North Bryan Avenue, PO Box 5457
Bloomington, IN 47408-5457
812-855-7311
http://www.oah.org/activities/awards/hugginsquarles/
index.html
Award Name: Organization of American Historians
Huggins-Quarles Award. *Academic Area: History.
*Age Group: Graduate students. *Eligibility:
Applicants must be graduate students of color at the
dissertation research stage of their Ph.D. program.
*Application Process: Applicants should submit
a five-page dissertation proposal (which should
include a definition of the project, an explanation
of the project's significance and contribution to
the field, and a description of its most important
primary sources), along with a one-page itemized
budget explaining travel and research plans. The
application should be accompanied by a letter from
the dissertation advisor. A complete copy of the
application should be mailed to each committee
member. Visit the OAH's Web site for a complete
listing of committee members and their addresses.
*Amount: $1,000 to $2,000. *Deadline: December 1.

PEN American Center
Attn: Stacy Leigh
588 Broadway, Suite 303
New York, NY 10012
212-334-1660, ext. 109
stacyleigh@pen.org
http://www.pen.org/page.php/prmID/151
Award Name: The PEN American Center offers the
PEN/Beyond Margins Award for book-length works by
authors of color. *Academic Area: English/literature,
writing. *Age Group: Professionals. *Eligibility: African,
Arab, Asian, Caribbean, Latino, and Native American
writers who have published a book in the United States
during the current calendar year may apply. Preference
is given to works of fiction, literary nonfiction,
biography/memoir, and other works of literary
character. *Application Process: Book submissions
(including an official letter of recommendation) must
be made by publishers and agents only. Books that
have been self published are not eligible. *Amount:
$1,000. *Deadline: December 30.

Radio and Television News Directors Foundation
RTNDA/UNITY Awards
1600 K Street, NW, Suite 700

Washington, DC 20006-2838
awards@rtnda.org
http://www.rtnda.org/asfi/awards/unity.shtml
Award Name: Radio and Television News Directors
Association/UNITY Award. *Academic Area:
Broadcasting, journalism. *Age Group: Open.
*Eligibility: Entries may be submitted by stations,
networks, syndication services, or program services.
The award is presented to news organizations that
show an ongoing commitment to covering the
diversity of the communities they serve. *Application
Process: News organizations must submit an entry that
demonstrates excellence in covering issues of race and
ethnicity. Materials to be submitted include an edited
tape/CD, not to exceed 60 minutes and a written
presentation that includes a list of material on the
tape/CD and an explanation of the news organization's
philosophy related to the coverage of diversity issues.
Visit the foundation's Web site for additional award
criteria. *Amount: Awards vary. *Deadline: January 31.

REFORMA
Attn: ALSC
50 East Huron
Chicago, IL 60611-2795
barbara_scotto@brookline.mec.edu
http://www.reforma.org/belpreawardGeneric.html
Award Name: Pura Belpré Award. *Academic Area:
Visual arts (general), writing. *Age Group: Open.
*Eligibility: Applicants must be Latino/Latina writers
and illustrators whose work best portrays, affirms,
and celebrates the Latino cultural experience in an
outstanding work of literature for children and youth.
Books for children 0-14 are considered. The books
must be published in the United States or Puerto Rico,
and the author(s) or illustrator(s) must be residents
or citizens of the United States or Puerto Rico.
*Application Process: Applicants should contact the
association by e-mail for further information about
how to apply. *Amount: Awards vary. *Deadline:
December 31.

REFORMA
Attn: Loida Garcia-Febo, Librarian of the Year Award Chair
Queens Library-New Americans Program
89-11 Merrick Boulevard
Jamaica, NY 11432
http://www.reforma.org/loty.htm
Award Name: Trejo Librarian of the Year Award.
*Academic Area: Library sciences. *Age Group: Open.

*Eligibility: Nominees must have distinguished themselves in the field, advanced services to the Spanish-speaking and Latina/o community, and filled an unmet need within the community. Nominees should also have made significant contributions to REFORMA. *Application Process: Applicants must be nominated by a REFORMA member and endorsed by the local chapter. Visit the association's Web site for a nomination form. *Amount: Awards vary. *Deadline: Contact the association for deadline information.

Society for Advancement of Chicanos and Native Americans in Science (SACNAS)

Attn: Awards Committee
PO Box 8526
Santa Cruz, CA 95061-8526
831-459-0170, 877-722-6271
info@sacnas.org
http://www.sacnas.org/Distinsci05.html

Award Name: Society for Advancement of Chicanos and Native Americans in Science Distinguished Award. *Academic Area: Science. *Age Group: Open. *Eligibility: Nominees must be individuals who have dedicated themselves to science, education, and mentoring. Nominees are those who have reached the top of their field and continue to serve as role models for the next generation of minority scientists. *Application Process: Individuals are encouraged to nominate colleagues or themselves for the SACNAS Distinguished Awards by submitting an application packet that includes a cover letter, curriculum vita for nominated individual, biographical sketch, three letters of recommendation, and supporting materials such as a list of research interests or articles written about the individual. *Amount: Expenses paid for attendance at the SACNAS convention and award ceremony. *Deadline: June 17.

FELLOWSHIPS

Fellowships are generally offered at the graduate, postgraduate, or doctoral level, often for research projects or dissertation assistance.

American Academy of Child and Adolescent Psychiatry

Attn: Earl Magee
3615 Wisconsin Avenue, NW
Washington, DC 20016-3007
202-966-7300, ext. 115
emagee@aacap.org
http://www.aacap.org/awards/index.htm
Fellowship Name: Jeanne Spurlock Minority Medical Student Clinical Fellowship in Child and Adolescent Psychiatry. *Academic Area: Medicine (psychiatry). *Age Group: Medical students. *Eligibility: Applicants must be in good academic standing at an accredited U.S. medical school and be of African American, Asian American, Native American, Alaskan Native, Mexican American, Hispanic, or Pacific Islander descent. *Application Process: Applicants should submit a completed application along with a two-page personal statement, resume, letter verifying good standing in medical school, and a letter of support from the student's mentor. Visit the academy's Web site to download an application. *Amount: $3,000. *Deadline: March 15.

American Academy of Child and Adolescent Psychiatry

Attn: Earl Magee
3615 Wisconsin Avenue, NW
Washington, DC 20016-3007
202-966-7300, ext. 115
emagee@aacap.org
http://www.aacap.org/awards/index.htm
Fellowship Name: Jeanne Spurlock Research Fellowship in Drug Abuse and Addiction. *Academic Area: Medicine (psychiatry). *Age Group: Medical students. *Eligibility: Applicants must be in good academic standing at an accredited medical school in the United States and be of African American, Asian American, Native American, Alaskan Native, Mexican American, Hispanic, or Pacific Islander descent. *Application Process: Applicants should submit a completed application along with a two-page personal statement, a resume, a letter verifying good standing in medical school, and a letter of support from their mentor. Visit the academy's Web site to download an application. *Amount: $3,000. *Deadline: March 15.

American Indian Graduate Center

4520 Montgomery Boulevard, NE, Suite 1B
Albuquerque, NM 87109
505-881-4584, ext. 108
marveline@aigc.com
http://www.aigc.com
Fellowship Name: Graduate Fellowship. *Academic Area: Open. *Age Group: Graduate students. Eligibility: Applicants must be pursuing a post-baccalaureate graduate or professional degree as a full-time student at an accredited institution in the United States, able to demonstrate financial need, and an enrolled member of a federally recognized American Indian tribe or Alaska Native group, or provide documentation of descendency (possess one-fourth degree federally recognized Indian blood). *Application Process: Applicants should submit a completed application along with a financial need form, a tribal eligibility certificate form, and three self-addressed, stamped postcards. Visit the organization's Web site to request an application. *Amount: Awards vary. *Deadline: Contact the organization for deadlines.

American Institute of Certified Public Accountants

1211 Avenue of the Americas
New York, NY 10036-8775
212-596-6223
http://www.aicpa.org/nolimits/become/ships/AICPA.htm
Fellowship Name: Minority Doctoral Fellowship. *Academic Area: Accounting. *Age Group: Graduate students. Eligibility: Applicants must have applied to and/or been accepted into an accredited doctoral program with a concentration in accounting; have earned a master's degree and/or completed a minimum of three years full-time experience in the practice of accounting; attend or plan to attend school on a full-time basis and; and agree not to work full time in a paid position or accept responsibility for teaching more than one course per semester as a teaching assistant or, dedicate more than one quarter of their time as a research assistant. Applicants must be African American, Native American/Alaskan Native, or Pacific Island races, or of Hispanic ethnic origin. *Application Process: Applicants should submit a completed application along with official

transcripts, and two letters of recommendation. Visit the institute's Web site to download an application. *Amount: Up to $12,000. *Deadline: April 1.

American Nurses Association
Substance Abuse and Mental Health Services
    Administration Minority Fellowship Program
Attn: Janet Jackson, Program Coordinator
8515 Georgia Avenue, Suite 400
Silver Spring, MD 20910-3492
301-628-5247
http://nursingworld.org/emfp
Fellowship Name: Clinical Research Pre-Doctoral Fellowship. *Academic Area: Nursing (substance abuse and mental health). *Age Group: Graduate students. *Eligibility: Applicants must be master's-prepared nurses who are members of a minority group and committed to pursuing doctoral study on minority psychiatric-mental health and substance abuse issues. They must also be U.S. citizens and members of the association. *Application Process: Applicants must complete and electronically submit an application form, a scientifically based essay, and a curriculum vitae. Additionally, four letters of recommendation, transcripts, a copy the applicant's active RN license, published articles or scholarly writing, and proof of admittance to a Ph.D. program must all be sent via mail. Visit the association's Web site for more information and to submit an application.*Amount: Fellowship awards vary. *Deadline: March 1.

American Physiological Society
9650 Rockville Pike
Bethesda, MD 20814-3991
301-634-7164
http://www.the-aps.org/awards/student.htm
Fellowship Name: Explorations in Biomedicine Undergraduate Summer Research Fellowship for Native Americans. *Academic Area: Physiology. *Age Group: Undergraduate students. *Eligibility: Applicants must be Native American undergraduate students with little or no research experience in the life sciences, but who are interested in finding out more about biomedical research. *Application Process: Applicants should submit a completed application form along with transcripts, a personal statement, and two letters of recommendation. Visit the society's Web site to download an application. *Amount: $3,500 to $4,000 (work and living expenses); $1,000 (travel expenses for Experimental Biology annual conference). *Deadline: February 3.

American Physiological Society
9650 Rockville Pike
Bethesda, MD 20814-3991
301-634-7164
http://www.the-aps.org/awards/student.htm
Fellowship Name: Minority Travel Fellowship Award. *Academic Area: Physiology. *Age Group: Undergraduate students, graduate students, post-doctoral scholars. *Eligibility: Applicants must demonstrate financial need and be members of one of the following underrepresented minority groups: African Americans, Native Americans, Hispanic Americans, or Pacific Islanders. *Application Process: Applicants should submit a completed application along with a current curriculum vitae, letter of recommendation from their advisor, and a summary of estimated expenses. Visit the association's Web site to download an application. *Amount: Awards vary. *Deadline: November 9.

American Physiological Society
9650 Rockville Pike
Bethesda, MD 20814-3991
301-634-7164
http://www.the-aps.org/awards/student.htm
Fellowship Name: Porter Physiology Fellowship for Minorities. *Academic Area: Physiology. *Age Group: Graduate students. *Eligibility: Applicants must be African American, Hispanic American, Native American, Native Alaskan, or Native Pacific Islander; U.S. citizens or permanent residents; and accepted into or currently enrolled in a graduate program in physiology. *Application Process: Applicants should submit a completed application form along with supporting materials. Visit the society's Web site to download an application. *Amount: $18,000. *Deadline: January 15.

American Planning Association
122 South Michigan Avenue, Suite 1600
Chicago, IL 60603
312-431-9100
awardsprogram@planning.org
http://www.planning.org/institutions/scholarship.htm
Fellowship Name: American Planning Association Planning Fellowship Program. *Academic Area: Planning. *Age Group: Graduate students. *Eligibility: Applicants must be African American, Hispanic American, or Native American first- or second-year graduate students who are citizens of the United States and enrolled in an approved Planning

Accreditation Board graduate planning program. Applicants must also demonstrate financial need. *Application Process: Applicants should submit a completed application along with a personal statement, two letters of recommendation, transcripts, a resume (optional), and a notarized statement of financial independence. Visit the association's Web site to download an application. *Amount: $1,000 to $5,000. *Deadline: April 30.

American Political Science Association (APSA)

1527 New Hampshire Avenue, NW
Washington, DC 20036-1206
202-483-2512
apsa@apsanet.org
http://www.apsanet.org/section_427.cfm
Fellowship Name: APSA Minority Fellows Program. *Academic Area: Political science. *Age Group: Graduate students. *Eligibility: Applicants must members of one of the following racial/ethnic minority groups: African Americans, Latinos/as, or Native Americans (federal- and state-recognized tribes). They must demonstrate an interest in teaching and potential for research in political science; be U.S. citizens at time of award; demonstrate financial need; and be entering a doctoral program for the first time. *Application Process: Applicants should submit a completed application along with a personal statement (maximum 500 words), official transcripts, three letters of recommendation, and GRE scores. Visit the association's Web site to download an application. *Amount: $4,000. *Deadline: October 31.

American Psychological Association

HIV/AIDS Application
750 First Street, NE
Washington, DC 20002-4242
202-336-6127
mfp@apa.org
http://www.apa.org/mfp
Fellowship Name: HIV/AIDS Research Fellowship. *Academic Area: Psychology. *Age Group: Graduate students. *Eligibility: Applicants must be American citizens or permanent resident aliens, demonstrate a strong commitment to a career in HIV/AIDS research related to ethnic minorities, enrolled full time in a doctoral program, and be members of one of the following ethnic minorities: African American, Alaskan Native, American Indian, Asian American, Hispanic/Latino, Native Hawaiian, or Pacific Islander.

*Application Process: Applicants should submit a completed application along with a cover letter, two essays, a curriculum vita, three recommendations, transcripts, and GRE scores. Visit the association's Web site to download an application. *Amount: Awards vary. *Deadline: January 15.

American Psychological Association

MHSAS Application
750 First Street, NE
Washington, DC 20002-4242
202-336-6127
mfp@apa.org
http://www.apa.org/mfp
Fellowship Name: Mental Health and Substance Abuse Services (MHSAS) Fellowship. *Academic Area: Psychology. *Age Group: Graduate students. *Eligibility: Applicants must be American citizens or permanent resident aliens, demonstrate a strong commitment to a career in ethnic minority mental health and substance abuse services, be enrolled full time in an APA-accredited doctoral program, and be members of one of the following ethnic minority groups: African American, Alaskan Native, American Indian, Asian American, Hispanic/Latino, Native Hawaiian, or Pacific Islander. *Application Process: Applicants should submit a completed application along with a cover letter, two essays, a curriculum vita, three recommendations, transcripts, and GRE scores. Visit the association's Web site to download an application. *Amount: Awards vary. *Deadline: January 15.

American Psychological Association

MHR Application
750 First Street, NE
Washington, DC 20002-4242
202-336-6127
mfp@apa.org
http://www.apa.org/mfp
Fellowship Name: Mental Health Research (MHR) Fellowship. *Academic Area: Psychology. *Age Group: Graduate students. *Eligibility: Applicants must be American citizens or permanent resident aliens, demonstrate a strong commitment to a career in mental health research related to ethnic minorities, be enrolled full time in a doctoral program, and be members of one of the following ethnic minority groups: African American, Alaskan Native, American Indian, Asian American, Hispanic/Latino, Native Hawaiian, or Pacific Islander. *Application Process: Applicants should submit a completed application along with a cover letter, two

essays, a curriculum vita, three recommendations, transcripts, and GRE scores. Visit the association's Web site to download an application. *Amount: Awards vary. *Deadline: January 15.

American Society for Microbiology
Education Board
1752 N Street, NW
Washington, DC 20036
202-942-9283
fellowships-careerinformation.asmusa.org
http://www.asm.org/Awards/index.asp?bid=14956
Fellowship Name: Microbiology Undergraduate Research Fellowship (MURF). *Academic Area: Microbiology. *Age Group: Undergraduate students. *Eligibility: Applicants must be U.S. citizens or permanent U.S. residents, enrolled as full-time matriculating undergraduate students during the 2006–07 academic year at an accredited U.S. institution; be a member of an underrepresented group in microbiology; have taken introductory courses in biology, chemistry, and, preferably, microbiology prior to submission of the application; have a strong interest in obtaining a Ph.D., or M.D./Ph.D. in the microbiological sciences; and have lab research experience. *Application Process: Applicants should submit a completed application along with supporting materials. Applications are available to download from the society's Web site in September of each year. *Amount: $3,500, plus travel and lodging expenses. *Deadline: February 1.

American Society for Microbiology
Education Board
1752 N Street, NW
Washington, DC 20036
202-942-9283
fellowships-careerinformation.asmusa.org
http://www.asm.org/Awards/index.asp?bid=14956
Fellowship Name: Robert D. Watkins Graduate Research Fellowship. *Academic Area: Microbiology. *Age Group: Graduate students. *Eligibility: Applicants must be formally admitted to a doctoral program in the microbiological sciences at an accredited U.S. institution; have successfully completed the first year of the graduate program; be student members of the society; mentored by a society member; U.S. citizens or a permanent residents; members of an underrepresented group in microbiology; and not have funding OR have funding that will expire by

the start date of the fellowship. *Application Process: Applicants must apply online via the society's Web site. Three letters of recommendation and official transcripts must also be submitted. *Amount: $57,000 (over three years). *Deadline: May 1.

American Society of Mechanical Engineers (ASME)
Attn: Maisha Phillips
Three Park Avenue
New York, NY 10016
212-591-8131
phillipsm@asme.org
http://www.asme.org/education/enged/aid/fellow.htm?IMAGE.X=16\&IMAGE.Y=14
Fellowship Name: ASME Graduate Teaching Fellowship. *Academic Area: Engineering (mechanical). *Age Group: Graduate students. *Eligibility: Applicant must be a Ph.D. student in mechanical engineering, with a demonstrated interest in a teaching career and must be a U.S. citizen or permanent resident, have an undergraduate degree from an Accreditation Board for Engineering and Technology-accredited program, and be a student member of ASME. Preference is given to women and minority applicants. *Application Process: Applicants should submit a completed application along with undergraduate GPA, GRE scores, a current resume or vitae, two letters of recommendation from faculty or M.S. committee, transcripts of all academic work, and a statement about their interest in a faculty career. Visit the society's Web site to download an application. *Amount: $5,000. *Deadline: October 21.

American Sociological Association (ASA)
ASA Minority Affairs Program
1307 New York Avenue, NW, Suite 700
Washington, DC 20005-4701
202-383-9005
minority.affairs@asanet.org
http://www.asanet.org/page.ww?section=Funding&name=Minority+Fellowship+Program
Fellowship Name: ASA Minority Fellowship. *Academic Area: Sociology. *Age Group: Graduate students. *Eligibility: Applicants must be graduate minority students entering or continuing in a doctoral program in sociology. Applicants must be applying to or enrolled in sociology departments that have strong mental illness research programs and/or faculty who are currently engaged in research focusing on mental health issues. Applicants must demonstrate a

commitment to research in mental illness, academic achievement, scholarship, writing ability, research potential, and financial need. *Application Process: Applicants should submit a completed application along with essays, three letters of recommendation, transcripts, and options documents (resume, published papers). Visit the association's Web site to download an application. *Amount: $20,772. *Deadline: January 31.

Asian Cultural Council (ACC)
437 Madison Avenue, 37th Floor
New York, NY 10022-7001
212-812-4300
acc@accny.org
http://www.asianculturalcouncil.org/programs.html
Fellowship Name: ACC Fellowships. *Academic Area: Performing arts (general), visual arts (general). *Age Group: Open. *Eligibility: Applicants must be Asian, wishing to pursue research, training, and a creative program in the United States. *Application Process: Applicants should send a brief description of the activity for which assistance is being sought to the council. If the proposed activity falls within the ACC's guidelines, application materials requesting more detailed information will be provided by the ACC, and applicants will be informed as to when their proposals can be presented to the trustees of the council for formal review. Visit the council's Web site for further information. *Amount: Awards vary. *Deadline: February 1.

Asian Pacific American Women's Leadership Institute
PO Box 2330
La Mesa, CA 91943-2330
619-698-3746
info@apawli.org
http://www.apawli.org/fellowship.asp
Fellowship Name: The Leadership Training Program is a year-long fellowship program that provides comprehensive training (with guest speakers, activities, readings, and other learning tools) to women in three, one-week sessions. *Academic Area: Open. *Age Group: Professionals. *Eligibility: Asian and Pacific American women leaders are selected to participate in the program. *Amount: Approximately 75 percent of costs for this program are paid by foundation, corporate, and individual contributions. Participants are asked to cover the remaining tuition, but this tuition is based on the fellow's ability to pay. *Deadline: Varies. Contact the institute for more information.

Association on American Indian Affairs
Attn: Lisa Wyzlic
966 Hungerford Drive, Suite 12-B
Rockville, MD 20850
240-314-7155
lw.aaia@verizon.net
http://www.indian-affairs.org
Fellowship Name: Florence Young Memorial Fellowship. *Academic Area: Performing arts (general), visual arts (general). *Age Group: Graduate students. *Eligibility: Applicants should have certification proving at least 1/4 Indian blood and demonstrate financial need and academic merit. *Application Process: Applicants should submit an application along with a copy of transcripts, a current financial aid award letter, two recommendations, an essay detailing their educational goals, a certificate proving Native American heritage, and a financial needs analysis. Visit the association's Web site to download an application. *Amount: $5,000. *Deadline: August 1.

Association on American Indian Affairs
Attn: Lisa Wyzlic
966 Hungerford Drive, Suite 12-B
Rockville, MD 20850
240-314-7155
lw.aaia@verizon.net
http://www.indian-affairs.org
Fellowship Name: Sequoyah Graduate Fellowship. *Academic Area: Open. *Age Group: Graduate students. *Eligibility: Applicants should have certification proving at least 1/4 Indian blood and demonstrate financial need and academic merit. *Application Process: Applicants should submit an application along with a copy of transcripts, a current financial aid award letter, two recommendations, an essay detailing their educational goals, a certificate proving Native American heritage, and a financial needs analysis. Visit the association's Web site to download an application. *Amount: $1,500. *Deadline: August 1.

Bell Labs
Attn: Lucent Technologies Foundation
600 Mountain Avenue, Room 6F4
Murray Hill, NJ 07974
908-582-7906

foundation@lucent.com

http://www.lucent.com/news/foundation/blgrfp

Fellowship Name: The Bell Labs Graduate Research Fellowship Program seeks to increase the number of women and minorities pursuing Ph.D.'s in science, math, engineering, and technology. Fellows will be exposed to a variety of research environments by participating in ongoing research activities at Bell Laboratories. The fellowship is renewable up to four years. *Academic Area: Communications science, computer science, engineering (computer), engineering (electrical), engineering (general), engineering (mechanical), information science, mathematics, physics, statistics. *Age Group: Graduate students. *Eligibility: Women and/or minorities pursuing full-time doctoral studies in chemical engineering, chemistry, communications science, computer science, computer engineering, electrical engineering, information science, materials science, mathematics, mechanical engineering, operations research, physics, or statistics are eligible to apply. Candidates are selected based on their academic achievement and their potential as research scientists. The fellowship is geared toward graduating college seniors, but is also open to first-year graduate students. *Application Procedure: Contact the foundation for guidelines.*Amount: The fellowships provide an annual stipend of $17,000, a $250 book allotment per semester, and $1,000 annually for travel expenses to conferences. *Deadline: Contact the foundation for more information.

Congressional Black Caucus Foundation Leadership Institute for Public Service

Congressional Fellows Program
1720 Massachusetts Avenue, NW
Washington, DC 20036
202-263-2800
jlubin@cbcfinc.org
http://www.cbcfinc.org/Leadership%20Education/
   Fellowships/congressional.html

Fellowship Name: The Congressional Fellows Program helps African Americans gain experience in government. *Academic Area: Government, political science. *Age Group: Professionals. *Eligibility: African-American professionals with an interest in the public policy process and the empowerment of Blacks in American politics may apply for this program. Applicants may be persons with graduate or professional degrees, professionals with a minimum of five years experience pursuing graduate studies,

and junior faculty. Applicants must also be willing to live in Washington, D.C., metropolitan area for the duration of the nine-month fellowship. *Application Procedure: Applicants must submit a current resume, a five- to 10-page writing sample, official transcripts, three essays on topics picked by the institute, and a completed application (available for download at the organization's Web site). *Amount: The program covers costs for relocation, housing, transportation costs, and health benefits, as well as provides a stipend. *Deadline: April 2.

Congressional Black Caucus Foundation Leadership Institute for Public Service

Louis Stokes Urban Health Policy Fellows Program
1720 Massachusetts Avenue, NW
Washington, DC 20036
202-263-2800
jlubin@cbcfinc.org
http://www.cbcfinc.org/Leadership%20Education/
   Fellowships/index.html

Fellowship Name: The Louis Stokes Urban Health Policy Fellows Program is a leadership development program that seeks to increase the number of qualified ethnic health policy professionals and reduce or eliminate health disparities in the United States and abroad. *Academic Area: Medical (general). *Age Group: Professionals. *Eligibility: African-American health policy professionals may apply for this program. Applicants must have a master's degree in a health-related field (behavioral science, social sciences, biological sciences, and health professions), a graduate GPA of at least 3.5, and strong communication skills. Preferred applicants also have experience in minority HIV/AIDS issues, the Healthy Peoples 2010 Initiative, the health professions training industry, health insurance coverage, and international experience and/or fluency in a foreign language. *Application Procedure: Applicants must submit a current resume, a five- to 10-page writing sample, official transcripts, three essays on topics picked by the institute, and a completed application (available for download at the organization's Web site).*Amount: $35,000, plus health insurance.*Deadline: April 1.

Congressional Hispanic Caucus Institute (CHCI)

CHCI Public Policy Fellowship
911 Second Street, NE
Washington, DC 20002
800-392-3532
http://www.chci.org/chciyouth/fellowship/fellowship.htm

Fellowship Name: CHCI Public Policy Fellowship. *Academic Area: Public policy. *Age Group: Graduate students. *Eligibility: Applicants must demonstrate high academic achievement, remarkable participation in public service oriented activities, leadership skills and potential for growth, and superior analytical and communication skills. Applicants must also be of Hispanic descent. *Application Process: Applicants should submit a completed application along with supporting materials. Visit the organization's Web site to download an application. *Amount: $2,061 monthly stipend. *Deadline: March 1.

Consortium for Graduate Study in Management

5585 Pershing, Suite 240
St. Louis, MO 63112-4621
314-877-5500, 888-658-6814
frontdesk@cgsm.org
http://www.cgsm.org

Fellowship Name: Consortium for Graduate Study in Management. *Academic Area: Business. *Age Group: Graduate students. *Eligibility: Applicants must be U.S. citizens or U.S. permanent residents from an underrepresented group: African Americans, Hispanic Americans, or Native Americans. Applicants must hold a bachelor's degree. *Application Process: Applicants must apply to the consortium by submitting an application. Once a person is admitted to the consortium, he or she becomes eligible for fellowships. Along with a completed application, send two letters of recommendation, transcripts, GMAT scores, answers to essay questions, and a resume. An interview with a local consortium representative will also be required. Visit the consortium's Web site to download an application. *Amount: Awards vary. *Deadline: January 15.

Entomological Society of America

10001 Derekwood Lane, Suite 100
Lanham, MD 20706-4876
301-731-4535
esa@entsoc.org
http://www.entsoc.org/awards/student/beck.htm

Fellowship Name: Stan Beck Fellowship. *Academic Area: Entomology. *Age Group: Undergraduate students, graduate students. *Eligibility: Applicants should have some sort of need, either based on physical limitations or economic, minority, or environmental considerations. *Application Process: Applicants should submit their curriculum vita via a template on the organization's Web site. Additional required

items include a letter of nomination, a description of their academic studies, transcripts, a statement of applicant's need or challenge, and three letters of recommendation or support. Visit the organization's Web site for further instructions. *Amount: Awards vary. *Deadline: July 1.

Fund for Theological Education

Attn: Nikol Reed
825 Houston Mill Road, Suite 250
Atlanta, GA 30329
404-727-1451
http://www.thefund.org/programs

Fellowship Name: FTE Dissertation Fellowship. *Academic Area: Religion. *Age Group: Graduate students. *Eligibility: African-American students who are pursuing religion or theology graduate studies and who are in the final writing stage of their dissertations may apply. Their dissertation committee must have approved the dissertation research proposal and writing plan and given permission to proceed before the applicant submits the application for the Dissertation Fellows Program. Applicants must be able to write full time during the fellowship year. *Application Process: Applicants should submit a completed application along with a curriculum vitae, dissertation prospectus and one-page abstract, transcripts, list of dissertation advisor and committee members, two letters of recommendation, budget statement form, and documentation from their school showing financial aid received. Visit the fund's Web site to download an application. *Amount: $15,000 stipend, plus full tuition scholarship. *Deadline: February 1.

Fund for Theological Education (FTE)

Attn: Nikol Reed
825 Houston Mill Road, Suite 250
Atlanta, GA 30329
404-727-1451
http://www.thefund.org/programs

Fellowship Name: FTE Doctoral Fellowship. *Academic Area: Religion. *Age Group: Graduate students. *Eligibility: Applicants must be African-American students preparing to enter their first year of an accredited Ph.D. or Th.D. program in religion or theology. They must be committed to becoming a leader within theological education, and be giving strong consideration to teaching or conducting research in a theological school. Applicants must also be U.S. citizens. *Application Process: Applicants should submit a completed application along with a curriculum vitae, two-page essay, transcripts, GRE scores (copies acceptable), two letters of recommendation, budget statement form, and documentation from school showing financial aid received. Visit the fund's Web site to download an application. *Amount: $15,000 stipend, plus full tuition scholarship. *Deadline: March 1.

Health Resources and Services Administration

U.S. Department of Health and Human Services
Attn: Daniel Reed
5600 Fishers Lane, Parklawn Building, Room 14-45
Rockville, MD 20857
301-443-2982
DReed1@hrsa.gov
http://bhpr.hrsa.gov/diversity/mffp/default.htm
Fellowship Name: Minority Faculty Fellowship Program. *Academic Area: Medicine (general). *Age Group: Open. *Eligibility: Applicants must be racial and ethnic minorities underrepresented in the health professions who are interested in teaching, administration, or research positions at a health professions institution. *Application Process: Applicants should contact the organization for further information on the application process. *Amount: Awards vary. *Deadline: Contact the organization for deadline information.

Hispanic-Serving Health Professions Schools

1120 Connecticut Avenue, NW, Suite 260
Washington, DC 20036
202-293-2701
hshps@hshps.org
http://www.hshps.com/fellowship.html
Fellowship Name: Hispanic-Serving Health Professions Schools/Office of Minority Health Fellowship Program. *Academic Area: Biology, medicine (physicians), public health. *Age Group: Graduate students, medical students. *Eligibility: Applicants must have completed all of the courses for a doctoral degree, received a nomination from the president or dean of their institution, and have a demonstrated interest in Hispanic health. *Application Process: Applicants must submit a completed application along with two letters of recommendation, current curriculum vitae, letter of support, personal statement, proof of citizenship or eligibility to work in the United States, and a development training prospectus. Visit the association's Web site to download an application. *Amount: Awards vary. *Deadline: Deadlines vary.

Investigative Reporters and Editors Inc.

Attn: John Green
University of Missouri School of Journalism
138 Neff Annex
Columbia, MO 65211
573-882-2722
jgreen@ire.org
http://www.ire.org/training/fellowships.html
Fellowship Name: Minority Fellowship. *Academic Area: Journalism. *Age Group: Open. *Eligibility: Applicants must identify themselves with one of the following minority groups: Black/African American, American Indian/Alaskan, Native American, Asian American, Native Hawaiian/Pacific Islander, or Hispanic/Latino. Applicants should contact the organization by e-mail or phone for additional eligibility requirements. *Application Process: Applicants can obtain applications by contacting the organization. *Amount: Awards vary, covering the costs of conference attendance. *Deadline: Contact the organization for deadline information.

Minami, Lew & Tamaki LLP

Attn: Dale Minami
360 Post Street, 8th Floor
San Francisco, CA 94108
http://www.takasugifellowship.com
Fellowship Name: Robert M. Takasugi Public Interest Fellowship. *Academic Area: Law. *Age Group: Law students, professionals. *Eligibility: All fellows must work at a public interest "sponsoring" organization in either the San Francisco Bay area or the Greater Los Angeles Metropolitan area, subject to approval by the fellowship. Applicants should be members of an underrepresented minority group, including women, and may be law students or graduates. *Application Process: Applicants should submit a cover letter, resume; three references (without letters); and answers to several questions listed on the organization's Web site. Visit the organization's Web site for further information. *Amount: Up to $5,000. *Deadline: March 18.

Mystic Seaport Museum

75 Greenmanville Avenue, PO Box 6000
Mystic, CT 06355-0990
860-572-5359
munson@mysticseaport.org
http://www.mysticseaport.org/index.cfm?fuseaction=
home.viewpage&page_id=BA0F6A5D-D0B2-1CEA-
5778CABEA131F76E

Fellowship Name: The Paul Cuffe Memorial Fellowship is offered to encourage research that considers the participation of Native and African Americans in the maritime activities of New England, primarily its southeastern shores. Fellowships support research and writing, a portion of which should normally be carried out in the Mystic area. *Academic Area: Maritime studies. *Age Group: Open. *Eligibility: Applicants should have a proposed research project and be members of an ethnic or racial minority. *Application Process: Applicants should send a curriculum vita or resume, a full description of the proposed project, a preliminary bibliography, brief project budget, and contact information for three references. Visit the museum's Web site for further information. *Amount: Up to $2,400. *Deadline: March 30.

National Academy of Sciences
Fellowships Office, GR 346A
500 Fifth Street, NW
Washington, DC 20001
202-334-2872
infofell@nas.edu
http://www.nationalacademies.org/grantprograms.html
Fellowship Name: The Ford Foundation Diversity Fellowships-Dissertation Awards provide one year of financial support for students working to complete a dissertation leading to a Doctor of Philosophy or Doctor of Science degree. *Academic Area: Anthropology, archaeology, astronomy, chemistry, communications science, computer science, earth science, economics, engineering (general), English/literature, foreign languages, geography, history, linguistics, mathematics, philosophy, physics, planning, political science, psychology, religion, sociology, visual arts (history). *Age Group: Graduate students. *Eligibility: Applicants must be U.S. citizens, have excellent academic achievement, and be committed to a career in teaching and research. The Fellowship is available to people of all races, although special consideration will be given to Alaska Natives (Eskimo or Aleut), Black/African Americans, Mexican Americans/Chicanas/Chicanos, Native American Indians, Native Pacific Islanders (Polynesian/Micronesian), and Puerto Ricans. *Application Process: Applicants should submit academic transcripts, a statement detailing their previous research, an annotated bibliography, an essay that explains their plan and timeline for completing the dissertation, a personal statement, letters of recommendation, a completed application (available at the organization's Web site), and other documentation. *Amount: $21,000. *Deadline: December 1.

National Academy of Sciences
Fellowships Office, GR 346A
500 Fifth Street, NW
Washington, DC 20001
202-334-2872
infofell@nas.edu
http://www.nationalacademies.org/grantprograms.html
Fellowship Name: The Ford Foundation Diversity Fellowships-Postdoctoral Awards provide one year of financial support for students engaged in postdoctoral study after the attainment of the Ph.D. or Sc.D. degree. *Academic Area: Anthropology, archaeology, astronomy, chemistry, communications science, computer science, earth science, economics, engineering (general), English/literature, foreign languages, geography, history, linguistics, mathematics, philosophy, physics, planning, political science, psychology, religion, sociology, visual arts (history). *Age Group: Post-doctoral scholars. *Eligibility: Applicants must be U.S. citizens, have excellent academic achievement, and be committed to a career in teaching and research. The fellowship is available to people of all races, although special consideration will be given to Alaska Natives (Eskimo or Aleut), Black/African Americans, Mexican Americans/Chicanas/Chicanos, Native American Indians, Native Pacific Islanders (Polynesian/Micronesian), and Puerto Ricans. *Application Process: Applicants should submit an abstract of their dissertation, an abstract of their proposed plan of study or research, an annotated bibliography, a personal statement, a completed application (available at the organization's Web site), and other documentation. *Amount: $40,000. *Deadline: December 15.

National Academy of Sciences
Fellowships Office, GR 346A
500 Fifth Street, NW
Washington, DC 20001
202-334-2872
infofell@nas.edu
http://www.nationalacademies.org/grantprograms.html
Fellowship Name: The Ford Foundation Diversity Fellowships-Predoctoral Awards provide three years of financial support for students pursuing graduate study leading to a Doctor of Philosophy or Doctor of Science

degree. The fellowship is available to people of all races, although special consideration will be given to Alaska Natives (Eskimo or Aleut), Black/African Americans, Mexican Americans/Chicanas/Chicanos, Native American Indians, Native Pacific Islanders (Polynesian/Micronesian), and Puerto Ricans. *Academic Area: Anthropology, archaeology, astronomy, chemistry, communications science, computer science, earth science, economics, engineering (general), English/literature, foreign languages, geography, history, linguistics, mathematics, philosophy, physics, planning, political science, psychology, religion, sociology, visual arts (history). *Age Group: Graduate students. *Eligibility: Applicants must be U.S. citizens, have excellent academic achievement, and be committed to a career in teaching and research. Applicants may be college seniors, students who have completed undergraduate study, students who have completed some graduate study, and those already enrolled in a Ph.D. or Sc.D. program that can prove that they will benefit from a three-year fellowship. *Application Process: Applicants should submit academic transcripts, a maximum four-page essay that describes their proposed plan of graduate study and research, a personal statement, letters of recommendation, a completed application (available at the organization's Web site), and other documentation. *Amount: $19,000 per year. *Deadline: November 17.

National Asian Pacific American Bar Association Foundation
Attn: Parkin Lee, Esq.
New York Life Investment Management, LLC
51 Madison Avenue, Room 1104
New York, NY 10010
foundation@napaba.org
http://www.napaba.org/napaba/showpage.asp?code=scholarships
Fellowship Name: Law Partners Community Law Fellowship. *Academic Area: Law. *Age Group: Law students. *Eligibility: Applicants must be Asian American law students who are committed to serving and contributing to the Asian Pacific American community. *Application Process: Contact the foundation for information on the application process. *Amount: Varies. *Deadline: Varies.

National Association of Black Journalists
8701-A Adelphi Road
Adelphi, MD 20783
301-445-7100
http://www.nabj.org/media_institute/fellowships/index.html
Fellowship Name: The Ethel Payne Fellowship allows African-American journalists to gain experience in international reporting through self-conceived assignments in Africa. Winners spend up to three weeks in Africa and provide reports to the association. *Academic Area: Broadcasting, journalism. *Age Group: Professionals. *Eligibility: African-American journalists who are members of the association may apply. Applicants must be full-time journalists or freelancers with five years of experience. *Application Process: Applicants must submit an 800-word project proposal, a 300-word essay detailing their journalism experience, three samples of published or aired work, two letters of recommendation, and a completed application. *Amount: $5,000. *Deadline: Varies.

National Association of Black Journalists (NABJ)
8701-A Adelphi Road
Adelphi, MD 20783
301-445-7100
http://www.nabj.org/media_institute/fellowships/index.html
Fellowship Name: The NABJ/United Nations Fellowship allows African-American journalists the opportunity to cover international summits in Africa. *Academic Area: Journalism. *Age Group: College students, professionals. *Eligibility: African-American journalists who are members of the NABJ may apply. Past applicants have been between the ages of 18 and 30. *Application Process: Contact the NABJ for information on the application process. *Amount: Varies. *Deadline: Varies.

National Black MBA Association (NBMBAA)
Attn: Ph.D. Fellowship Program
180 North Michigan Avenue, Suite 1400
Chicago, IL 60601
312-236-2622, ext. 8086
scholarship@nbmbaa.org
http://www.nbmbaa.org/scholarship.cfm
Fellowship Name: NBMBAA Ph.D. Fellowship Program. *Academic Area: Business, management. *Age Group: Graduate students. *Eligibility: African-American students who are enrolled in a full-time doctoral business or management program or related major may apply. The program must be accredited by the AACSB: The International Association for Management Education. *Application Process: Applicants must submit official transcripts, a completed application, a current curriculum vita or a resume, a 5 X 7 black-

and-white photograph for use in public relations, and a competitive research paper that answers the following questions: What is one of the major questions in your field that needs to be addressed? and What unique perspective can Black scholars provide to this discussion? They must also agree to become lifetime members of the association. *Amount: $13,000 for those who have successfully completed their comprehensive exams; $7,000 for all other applicants. *Deadline: May 16.

National Consortium for Graduate Degrees for Minorities in Engineering and Science (GEM)

PO Box 537
Notre Dame, IN 46556
574-631-7771
http://was.nd.edu/gem/gemwebapp/public/gem_01_100.htm
Fellowship Name: MS Engineering Fellowship Program. *Academic Area: Biochemistry, chemistry, computer science, engineering (general), environmental science, information technology, mathematics, pharmaceutical sciences, physics. *Age Group: Graduate students. *Eligibility: Minority college juniors and seniors, as well as graduate students, with an interest in engineering and science may apply. *Application Process: Contact GEM for information on application guidelines. *Amount: $10,000 stipend, plus full tuition and fees at a GEM member university. *Deadline: Varies.

National Consortium for Graduate Degrees for Minorities in Engineering and Science (GEM)

PO Box 537
Notre Dame, IN 46556
574-631-7771
http://was.nd.edu/gem/gemwebapp/public/gem_01_100.htm
Fellowship Name: Ph.D. Engineering Fellowship Program. *Academic Area: Engineering (general). *Age Group: Graduate students. *Eligibility: Underrepresented minority students who have completed or are currently enrolled in a master's program in engineering or a related field may apply. *Application Process: Contact GEM for information on application guidelines. *Amount: $14,000 stipend, plus full tuition and fees at a GEM member university. *Deadline: Varies.

National Consortium for Graduate Degrees for Minorities in Engineering and Science (GEM)

PO Box 537
Notre Dame, IN 46556
574-631-7771
http://was.nd.edu/gem/gemwebapp/public/gem_01_100.htm
Fellowship Name: Ph.D. Science Fellowship Program. *Academic Area: Biology, chemistry, computer science, earth science, mathematics, physics. *Age Group: Graduate students. *Eligibility: Minority college juniors and seniors and graduate students who plan to or who are currently pursuing doctoral degrees in the natural sciences may apply. *Application Process: Contact GEM for information on application guidelines. *Amount: $14,000 stipend, plus full tuition and fees at a GEM member university. *Deadline: Varies.

National Medical Fellowships

Gerber Fellowship in Pediatric Nutrition
Five Hanover Square, 15th Floor
New York, NY 10004
http://www.nmf-online.org/Programs/Fellowships/fellowships.htm
Fellowship Name: Gerber Foundation Fellowship in Pediatric Nutrition. *Academic Area: Medicine (physicians). *Age Group: Medical students. *Eligibility: African American, mainland Puerto Rican, Mexican American, Native Hawaiian, Alaska Native, and American Indian medical students or residents who are conducting research in pediatric nutrition may apply. Applicants must be U.S. citizens and demonstrate strong academic achievement and an interest in pursuing careers in pediatric nutrition research. *Application Process: Applicants must submit a letter of recommendation from their medical school dean or director of graduate education, a letter of commitment from their mentor or principal investigator detailing the research project they will conduct, an official academic transcript, a curriculum vitae, a statement of their career goals and how the fellowship will help them achieve these goals, a two-page description of the research project (written by the applicant), and a completed application (available for download online at the organization's Web site). *Amount: $3,000. *Deadline: Typically in October.

National Medical Fellowships

W.K. Kellogg Foundation in Health Research
1627 K Street, NW, Suite 1200
Washington, DC 20006-1702
http://www.nmf-online.org/Programs/Fellowships/fellowships.htm

Fellowship Name: W.K. Kellogg Foundation Doctoral Fellowship in Health Policy. *Academic Area: Medicine (general). *Age Group: Graduate students. *Eligibility: African Americans, Asian Americans, Hispanic Americans, and Native Americans enrolled in graduate programs in public health, health policy, or social policy may apply. Applicants must be accepted for admission into one of the following academic institutions: Heller Graduate School of Brandeis University, Mailman School of Public Health at Columbia University, Harvard School of Public Health, Johns Hopkins School of Hygiene and Public Health, RAND Graduate School, University of California-Los Angeles School of Public Health, University of Michigan School of Public Health, or University of Pennsylvania. They must also be U.S. citizens and committed to working with underserved populations upon completion of their doctorate. *Application Process: Applicants must submit official academic transcripts; a resume or curriculum vitae; a 500- to 1,000-word essay detailing their qualifications, their interest in one of the fellowship focus areas, and how the fellowship will help support their career goals; copies of published articles or abstracts; and a completed application (available for download online at the organization's Web site). *Amount: Tuition, fees, and a partial living stipend. *Deadline: Typically in June.

National Organization of Black Law Enforcement Executives (NOBLE)
4609 Pinecrest Office Park Drive, Suite F
Alexandria, VA 22312-1442
703-658-1529
noble@noblenatl.org
http://www.noblenatl.org/displaycommon.cfm?an=1&s ubarticlenbr=62
Fellowship Name: The NOBLE Fellowship Program is geared to increase the number of minority law enforcement officials in administrative, management, and research and training positions. *Academic Area: Criminal justice. *Age Group: Professionals. *Eligibility: Full-time minority law enforcement officials who hold a college degree may apply. Members of NOBLE will receive special consideration. The college degree requirement may be waived for professionals who have considerable experience in law enforcement. *Application Process: Applicants should submit a completed application, which includes a statement detailing their proposed project/activity for the fellowship period. Although applications are accepted throughout the year, applicants should include a proposed starting date

for the fellowship on their application. *Amount: Contact NOBLE for details. *Deadline: Applications are accepted throughout the year.

National Physical Science Consortium (NPSC)
Attn: Program Administrator
3716 South Hope, Suite 348
Los Angeles, CA 90007-4344
800-952-4118
npschq@npsc.org
http://npsc.org
Fellowship Name: National Physical Science Consortium Fellowship. *Academic Area: Biochemistry, computer science, engineering (general), physical sciences, science. *Age Group: Graduate students, professionals. *Eligibility: Students and professionals, especially women and underrepresented minorities, who are interested in earning a Ph.D. are eligible to apply. Applicants must be U.S. citizens who plan to or who are currently pursuing graduate work at an NPSC member institution. *Application Procedure: Applicants should apply online at the consortium's Web site. Required documents include academic transcripts and three to five letters of recommendation from professors and employers. *Amount: Up to $21,000. *Deadline: November 5. Contact the consortium for details.

National Urban Fellows
102 West 38th Street, Suite 700
New York, NY 10018
212-730-1700
http://www.nuf.org
Fellowship Name: The National Urban Fellows Program is a full-time graduate program comprised of two semesters of academic course work and a nine-month mentorship, leading to a Master of Public Administration degree from Bernard M. Baruch College, School of Public Affairs, City University of New York. *Academic Area: Open. *Age Group: Graduate students, early career professionals. *Eligibility: Applicants must be U.S. citizens from diverse backgrounds, have a bachelor's degree, have three to five years of experience in a management capacity, demonstrate leadership abilities and high personal standards, meet the admission requirements of Baruch College, and be committed to helping solve urban and rural problems through public service. *Application Process: Applicants should submit a completed application (available for download at the organization's Web site), an autobiographical

statement, a statement of career goals, a resume, academic transcripts, and three letters of recommendation. A $50 nonrefundable application fee is also required. *Amount: A $25,000 stipend, full tuition, a $500 relocation allowance, reimbursement for travel associated with the program, and a $500 book allowance. *Deadline: Last Friday in February.

Native American Journalists Association (NAJA)
555 Dakota Street
Al Neuharth Media Center
Vermillion, SD 57069
605-677-5282
info@naja.com
http://www.naja.com/programs/professional/fellowships
Fellowship Name: Professional Development Fellowship. *Academic Area: Journalism. *Age Group: Professionals. *Eligibility: Native American journalists who are members of the NAJA may apply. Applicant must have worked as a journalist for at least two years and earn more than 50 percent of his or her income from journalism. *Application Process: Applicants should submit a current resume; a detailed budget and description of the class or seminar they would like to take and how it will be useful to their career, and a letter of recommendation from the applicant's supervisor stating why this educational opportunity would be useful. (Note: funds are also available for one-time equipment purchase; applicants should submit a detailed explanation of how this equipment will help them advance in their careers.)*Amount: $500 and $1,000. *Deadline: January 1, June 1.

The Newberry Library
60 West Walton Street
Chicago, IL 60610-7324
312-255-3666
research@newberry.org
http://www.newberry.org/research/L3rfellowships.html
Fellowship Name: Frances C. Allen Fellowship (a one-month to one-year fellowship that encourages Native American women to pursue advanced study). *Academic Area: Open (special emphasis on the humanities and social sciences). *Age Group: Graduate students. *Eligibility: Women of Native American heritage are eligible to apply. Allen Fellows are expected to spend a large part of their tenure at the Newberry's D'Arcy McNickle Center for American Indian History. *Application Procedure: Applicants should submit a cover sheet, a project description, a curriculum vitae, and letters of reference. Visit the Newberry's Web site for more information. *Amount: Up to $8,000 (may include travel expenses). *Deadline: March 1.

The Newberry Library
60 West Walton Street
Chicago, IL 60610-7324
312-255-3666
research@newberry.org
http://www.newberry.org/research/L3rfellowships.html
Fellowship Name: The Susan Kelly Power and Helen Hornbeck Tanner Fellowship is provided for two months of residential research at the Newberry Library. *Academic Area: Humanities. *Age Group: Graduate students, post-doctoral scholars. *Eligibility: Native American Ph.D. candidates and post-doctoral scholars may apply. *Application Process: Applicants should submit a project description of 1,500 words, a curriculum vitae, three letters of reference, and a cover sheet (available at the Newberry's Web site), which details their personal and professional background. *Amount: $2,400. *Deadline: March 1.

Newspaper Association of America (NAA)
NAA Diversity Department
1921 Gallows Road, Suite 600
Vienna, VA 22182-3900
703-902-1727
dukem@naa.org
http://www.naa.org/artpage.cfm?AID=6233&SID=1018
Fellowship Name: The Marketing Fellowship is provided to help a minority early career professional attend the NAA annual conference, which features educational programs on advertising, circulation, promotion, and market development. *Academic Area: Journalism. *Age Group: Early career professionals. *Eligibility: Minority marketing, advertising and circulation non-managerial staff, managers, and executives who have worked three or fewer years in their current positions may apply. Applicants must be attending an NAA conference for the first time. *Application Process: Contact the NAA for information on the application process. *Amount: Cost of travel and accommodations for the NAA annual conference. *Deadline: Varies.

Newspaper Association of America
Attn: Angela Winters
1921 Gallows Road, Suite 600
Vienna, VA 22182-3900
703-902-1727
angela.winters@naa.org

http://www.naa.org/artpage.cfm?AID=1212&SID=1018

Fellowship Name: The Minority Fellowship was created to increase the number of minority professionals entering or advancing in newspaper management. Fellows in the six-month program attend seminars in business, leadership, editorial, design, and production. *Academic Area: Journalism. *Age Group: Early career professionals. *Eligibility: Minority journalism professionals who are in the early stages of their careers may apply. *Application Process: Candidates are nominated by newspaper executives and journalism educators. An application and recommendation forms are available at the association's Web site. *Amount: Cost of seminar registration fees, travel, meals, and hotel expenses during the fellowship. *Deadline: October 31.

Organization of Black Airline Pilots (OBAP)
8630 Fenton Street, Suite 126
Silver Spring, MD 20910
800-538-6227
nationaloffice@obap.org
http://www.obap.org/Programs/programs-fellowship.asp

Fellowship Name: The OBAP Fellowship Program provides funding for OBAP members to obtain advanced pilot ratings. *Academic Area: Aviation. *Age Group: Early career professionals. *Eligibility: Minority aviation professionals in their second year of active membership with the OBAP may apply. *Application Process: Contact the OBAP for information on application requirements. *Amount: Typically less than $1,500. *Deadline: Applications are accepted throughout the year.

Paul and Daisy Soros Fellowships for New Americans
400 West 59th Street
New York, NY 10019
212-547-6926
pdsoros_fellows@sorosny.org
http://www.pdsoros.org

Fellowship Name: The Paul and Daisy Soros Fellowship for New Americans provides graduate education opportunities for new immigrants. *Academic Area: Open. *Age Group: Graduate students. *Eligibility: Resident aliens who are 30 years of age or younger as of November 1 of the year of application may apply. *Application Process: Applicants should submit two essays on specified topics, three recommendation letters, a one- to two-page resume, and a completed application (available at the organization's Web site). *Amount: A maintenance grant of $20,000 and a tuition grant of one-half the tuition cost of the U.S. graduate program attended by the fellow (up to a maximum of $16,000 per academic year) are provided. *Deadline: November 1.

Radio and Television News Directors Foundation
Attn: Irving Washington
1600 K Street, NW, Suite 700
Washington, DC 20006-2838
202-467-5218
irvingw@rtndf.org
http://www.rtnda.org/asfi/fellowships/minority.shtml

Fellowship Name: Michele Clark Fellowship. *Academic Area: Broadcasting. *Age Group: Early career professionals. *Eligibility: Early career minority journalists in television or radio news may apply. *Application Process: Contact the RTND Foundation for information on application requirements. *Amount: $1,000, plus an expenses-paid trip to the Radio-Television News Directors Association International Conference. *Deadline: Varies.

Radio and Television News Directors (RTND) Foundation
Attn: Irving Washington
1600 K Street, NW, Suite 700
Washington, DC 20006-2838
202-467-5218
irvingw@rtndf.org
http://www.rtnda.org/asfi/fellowships/minority.shtml

Fellowship Name: $2,500 N.S. Bienstock Fellowship. *Academic Area: Broadcasting. *Age Group: Early career professionals. *Eligibility: Early career minority journalists in radio or television news management may apply. *Application Process: Contact the RTND Foundation for information on application requirements. *Amount: $2,500, plus an expenses-paid trip to the Radio-Television News Directors Association International Conference. *Deadline: Varies.

Robert Toigo Foundation
Attn: Gabriela Snyder, Fellowship Program Administrator
1230 Preservation Park Way
Oakland, CA 94612
application@toigofoundation.org
http://www.toigofoundation.org/fellows/process.html

Fellowship Name: Robert Toigo Fellowship. *Academic Area: Business, finance. *Age Group: Graduate students. *Eligibility: Minority students who have been accepted into an MBA program may apply. Applicants must be U.S. citizens or permanent residents and planning to pursue a career in finance (including, but not limited to investment management, investment banking, corporate finance [non-investment banking], real estate, private equity, venture capital, sales and trading, research, or financial services consulting). *Application Process: An application is available at the foundation's Web site. *Amount: $5,000 toward two years of graduate school tuition. *Deadline: Varies.

Robert Wood Johnson Foundation
Amos Medical Faculty Development Program
8701 Georgia Avenue, Suite 411
Silver Spring, MD 20910
301-565-4080
amfdp@starpower.net
http://www.amfdp.org
Fellowship Name: The Foundation's Amos Medical Faculty Development Program seeks to "increase the number of faculty from historically disadvantaged backgrounds who can achieve senior rank in academic medicine." The program provides four-year postdoctoral research awards to physicians. *Academic Area: Medicine (physicians). *Age Group: Medical students, professionals. *Eligibility: Applicants must be historically disadvantaged physicians, U.S. citizens or permanent residents of the United States, currently completing or have completed their formal clinical training, and planning to pursue academic careers. They must also be willing to conduct four consecutive years of formal research, work to improve health care for the underserved, and serve as role models for faculty and students and faculty from disadvantaged backgrounds. Physicians who have recently completed their formal clinical training will receive priority in the selection process. *Application Process: Applicants should submit a completed proposal and application, which includes information on their academic background, research experiences and interests, and career objectives, as well as professional references and a plan for working with a mentor during the program. Semifinalists will be picked from the initial group of applicants and participate in an interview with a selection committee. Finalists will be chosen from this group. *Amount: $65,000 a year, plus a $26,350 annual grant toward support of research activities. *Deadline: Typically in March.

School of American Research
PO Box 2188
Santa Fe, NM 87504-2188
505-954-7200
scholar@sarsf.org
http://www.sarweb.org/home/nativeprograms.htm
Fellowship Name: The Katrin H. Lamon Resident Scholar Fellowship Program provides Native American scholars the opportunity to complete a book-length manuscript or doctoral dissertation during a nine-month residential tenure. *Academic Area: Humanities, science. *Age Group: Graduate students, professionals. *Eligibility: Native American scholars may apply. *Application Process: Contact the school for information on the application process. *Amount: Fellows receive an apartment, office, stipend, and other benefits. *Deadline: Varies.

School of American Research
PO Box 2188
Santa Fe, NM 87504-2188
505-954-7200
info@sarsf.org
http://www.sarweb.org/home/nativeprograms.htm
Fellowship Name: The School of American Research offers several Artist Fellowships for Native American artists. *Academic Area: Visual arts (general). *Age Group: Professionals. *Eligibility: Native American artists may apply. *Application Process: Contact the school for information on the application process. *Amount: Varies by fellowship. *Deadline: Varies.

Smithsonian Institution
Office of Fellowships
MRC 902, PO Box 37012, Victor Building, Suite 9300
Washington, DC 20013-7012
202-275-0655
siofg@si.edu
http://www.si.edu/ofg/Applications/SIFELL/SIFELLapp.htm
Fellowship Name: The Smithsonian Institution offers a variety of scholarships to minority students. *Academic Area: Open. *Age Group: Graduate students, post-doctoral scholars. *Eligibility: Minority students may apply. Contact the Smithsonian for eligibility guidelines for specific fellowships. *Application Process: Application requirements vary by fellowships, but all applicants will be required to submit a research proposal, a curriculum vitae, academic transcripts, and letters of reference.

*Amount: Fellowships range from $4,500 to $40,000. *Deadline: January 15.

Society for Advancement of Chicanos and Native Americans in Science (SACNAS)

Attn: Pixan Serna
PO Box 8526
Santa Cruz, CA 95061-8526
831-459-0170, ext. 238
pixan@sacnas.org
http://www.sacnas.org/genomicopportunity.html

Fellowship Name: The Student/Mentor Summer Workshop Fellowship allows fellows to attend SACNAS National Conference and other genomics/bioinformatics conferences and workshops with their faculty mentor. *Academic Area: Science. *Age Group: Graduate students. *Eligibility: Applicants, as well as their faculty mentors, must be members of the society. They must also be enrolled in a graduate program in bioinformatics or genomics. *Application Process: Applicants should submit an essay detailing why they deserve the fellowship, information on their educational background and experiences, information on their mentor, and a completed application (available at the society's Web site). *Amount: Payment for travel and lodging costs for the SACNAS National Conference and other related opportunities. *Deadline: February 28.

Zeta Phi Beta Sorority Inc.

National Educational Foundation
1734 New Hampshire Avenue, NW
Washington, DC 20009
202-387-3103
IHQ@zphib1920.org
http://www.zphib1920.org/nef/schapp.pdf

Fellowship Name: Deborah Partridge Wolfe International Fellowship. *Academic Area: Open. *Age Group: Undergraduate students, graduate students. *Eligibility: African-American students who are pursuing undergraduate or graduate education in any discipline may apply. This fellowship is available to U.S. students studying abroad and foreign students studying in the United States. Applicants do not need to be members of Zeta Phi Beta Sorority to be eligible for this fellowship. *Application Process: Applicants should submit three letters of recommendation, academic transcripts, a brief overview of their

academic plans, a completed application (available at the sorority's Web site), and a 150-word+ essay that details their academic goals and why they should receive the award. *Amount: $500 to $1,000. *Deadline: February 1.

Zeta Phi Beta Sorority Inc.

National Educational Foundation
1734 New Hampshire Avenue, NW
Washington, DC 20009
202-387-3103
IHQ@zphib1920.org
http://www.zphib1920.org/nef/schapp.pdf

Fellowship Name: Mildred Cater Bradham Social Work Fellowship. *Academic Area: Social work. *Age Group: Graduate students. *Eligibility: Members of Zeta Phi Beta Sorority (an African-American service organization) who are pursuing a graduate or professional degree in social work may apply. Students must plan to study full time. *Application Process: Applicants should submit three letters of recommendation, academic transcripts, a completed application (available at the sorority's Web site), and a 150-word+ essay that details their academic goals and why they should receive the award. *Amount: $500 to $1,000. *Deadline: February 1.

Zeta Phi Beta Sorority Inc.

National Educational Foundation
1734 New Hampshire Avenue, NW
Washington, DC 20009
202-387-3103
IHQ@zphib1920.org
http://www.zphib1920.org/nef/schapp.pdf

Fellowship Name: Nancy B. Woolridge McGee Graduate Fellowship. *Academic Area: Open. *Age Group: Graduate students. *Eligibility: Members of Zeta Phi Beta Sorority (an African-American service organization) who are pursuing a graduate or professional degree may apply. Students must plan to study full time. *Application Process: Applicants should submit three letters of recommendation, academic transcripts, proof of enrollment, a completed application (available at the sorority's Web site), and a 150-word+ essay that details their academic goals and why they should receive the award. *Amount: $500 to $1,000. *Deadline: February 1.

GRANTS

Grants are similar to fellowships, although they may be given at any level, and are generally given for work on a specific project, such as research or for travel expenses to a professional conference.

Alabama Commission on Higher Education

PO Box 302000
Montgomery, AL 36130-2000
334-242-1998
http://www.ache.state.al.us
Grant Name: The Alabama Student Grant Program provides need-based educational grants to students, including minorities. *Academic Area: Open. *Age Group: Undergraduate students. *Eligibility: Applicants must be planning to attend one of the following Alabama postsecondary institutions full or part time: Birmingham-Southern College, Concordia College, Faulkner University, Huntingdon College, Judson College, Miles College, Oakwood College, Samford University, Selma University, Southeastern Bible College, Southern Vocational College, Spring Hill College, Stillman College, or the University of Mobile. The grant is not need-based. *Application Process: Applications are available at the financial aid offices of the aforementioned colleges. *Amount: Up to $1,200. *Deadline: Varies.

Alaska Commission on Postsecondary Education

707 A Street, Suite 206
Anchorage, AK 99501-3625
800-441-2962
customer_service@acpe.state.ak.us
http://alaskaadvantage.state.ak.us/page/225
Grant Name: The AlaskAdvantage Education Grant provides need-based educational grants to students, including minorities. *Academic Area: Open. *Age Group: Undergraduate students. *Eligibility: Individuals planning to attend postsecondary institutions in Alaska may apply. Applicants must also demonstrate academic achievement, be U.S. citizens, and demonstrate financial need of at least $500. *Application Process: Contact the commission for information on application requirements. *Amount: $500 to $2,000. *Deadline: April 15.

American Academy of Child and Adolescent Psychiatry

Attn: Earl Magee
3615 Wisconsin Avenue, NW
Washington, DC 20016-3007
202-966-7300, ext. 115
emagee@aacap.org
http://www.aacap.org/awards/index.htm
Grant Name: Jeanne Spurlock Minority Medical Student Clinical Fellowship in Child and Adolescent Psychiatry. *Academic Area: Medicine (psychiatry). *Age Group: Medical students. *Eligibility: Applicants must be in good academic standing at an accredited U.S. medical school and be African American, Asian American, Native American, Alaskan Native, Mexican American, Hispanic American, or Pacific Islander. *Application Process: Applicants should submit a completed application along with a two-page personal statement, a resume, a letter verifying good standing in medical school, and a letter of support from the student's mentor. Visit the academy's Web site to download an application. *Amount: $3,000. *Deadline: March 15.

American Association of University Women (AAUW)

AAUW Educational Foundation
Career Development Grants
301 ACT Drive, PO Box 4030
Iowa City, IA 52245-4030
319-337-1716, ext. 60
aauw@act.org
http://www.aauw.org/fga/fellowships_grants/career_development.cfm
Grant Name: Career Development Grant. *Academic Area: Open. *Age Group: Graduate students. *Eligibility: Applicants must be women who hold a bachelor's degree and are preparing to advance their careers, change careers, or re-enter the work force. Special consideration is given to AAUW members, women of color, and women pursuing their first advanced degree or credentials in nontraditional fields. Course work must be taken at an accredited two- or four-year college or university, or at a technical school that is fully licensed or accredited by an agency recognized by the U.S. Department of Education. Applicants pursing doctoral-level work are not eligible. *Application Process: Applicants should submit a completed application along with a proposal narrative, budget, recommendation form, and filing fee. Visit the organization's Web site to download an application. *Amount: $2,000 to $8,000. *Deadline: December 15.

American Philosophical Society

Phillips Fund Grant for Native American Research
Attn: Linda Musumeci
104 South Fifth Street
Philadelphia, PA 19106-3386
215-440-3429
Lmusumeci@amphilsoc.org
http://www.amphilsoc.org/grants/phillips.htm
Grant Name: Phillips Fund Grant for Native America Research. *Academic Area: History, linguistics. *Age Group: Graduate students, recent Ph.D.'s. *Eligibility: Applicants must plan to conduct research in the area of Native American linguistics, ethnohistory, or the history of studies of Native Americans in the continental United States and Canada. *Application Process: Applicants should submit a completed application. Applications are available for download from the society's Web site. *Amount: Up to $3,000. *Deadline: March 1.

American Society of Mechanical Engineers

Attn: Mary James Legatski
103 South Newport Way
Dagsboro, DE 19939-9219
legatskim@asme.org
http://www.asme.org/communities/diversities/bdo/dag.html
Grant Name: Diversity Action Grant. *Academic Area: Engineering (mechanical). *Age Group: College students. *Eligibility: Applicants must be interested in promoting diversity and inclusion within their own section, within the society membership, and within the engineering community at large. *Application Process: Applicants should submit a detailed budget plan, including the amount of money requested; information on groups with which their section will be partnering or collaborating; and the project objectives, methodology, and evaluation plan. *Amount: $500 to $1,500. *Deadline: November 1.

Arkansas Department of Higher Education

114 East Capitol Avenue
Little Rock, AR 72201
501-371-2013
finaid@adhe.arknet.edu
http://www.arkansashighered.com/minoritygrant.html
Grant Name: Freshman/Sophomore Minority Grant Program. *Academic Area: Education. *Age Group: Undergraduate students. *Eligibility: African American, Hispanic American, and Asian American college freshmen and sophomores majoring in education at select Arkansas schools may apply. Applicants must also be residents of Arkansas, planning to or currently attending select postsecondary institutions in Arkansas, demonstrate financial need, and sign a statement of interest that establishes their interest in teaching. *Application Process: Applicants should contact the department for information on application requirements. *Amount: $1,000. *Deadline: Applications are accepted throughout the year.

Asian Cultural Council

437 Madison Avenue, 37th Floor
New York, NY 10022-7001
212-812-4300
acc@accny.org
http://www.asianculturalcouncil.org/programs.html
Grant Name: Japan-United States Arts Program. *Academic Area: Performing arts (general), visual arts (general). *Age Group: Open. *Eligibility: Applicants must have the desire to study and understand Japanese art and culture. Japanese artists, scholars, and specialists travel to the United States for research, observation, and creative work, and their American counterparts visit Japan for similar purposes. *Application Process: Interested candidates should contact the council for further application information. *Amount: Awards vary. *Deadline: Contact the council for deadline information.

Association of American Geographers (AAG)

AAG Dissertation Research Grants
Attn: Ehsan M. Khater
1710 16th Street, NW
Washington, DC 20009-3198
202-234-1450
ckhater@aag.org
http://www.aag.org/grantsawards/dissertationresearch.html
Grant Name: Paul Vouras Fund. *Academic Area: Geography. *Age Group: Graduate students. *Eligibility: Applicants should demonstrate high standards of scholarship and propose relevant doctoral dissertation research in geography. Preference is given to applicants who are minorities. *Application Process: Applicants should submit a completed application along with a proposal describing the problem they hope to solve, outlining the methods and data they intend to use, and

summarizing the results they expect. Budget items should be included within the body of the proposal. Visit the association's Web site to download an application. *Amount: $500. *Deadline: December 31.

California Student Aid Commission

PO Box 419027
Rancho Cordova, CA 95741-9027
888-224-7268
http://www.csac.ca.gov
Grant Name: The Cal Grant Program provides need-based educational grants to students, including minorities. *Academic Area: Open. *Age Group: Undergraduate students. *Eligibility: Applicants must be from an underrepresented minority group, residents of California, planning to or currently attending a postsecondary institution in California, and demonstrate financial need. *Application Process: Contact the commission for information on application requirements. *Amount: Varies. *Deadline: Varies.

Colorado Commission on Higher Education

1380 Lawrence Street, Suite 1200
Denver, CO 80204
303-866-2723
CCHE@state.co.us
http://www.state.co.us/cche/finaid/index.html
Grant Name: Colorado Diversity Grant. *Academic Area: Open. *Age Group: Undergraduate students. *Eligibility: Applicants must be from an underrepresented minority group, residents of Colorado, planning to or currently attending select postsecondary institutions in Colorado, and demonstrate financial need. *Application Process: Contact the commission for information on application requirements. *Amount: Varies. *Deadline: Varies.

Conference of Minority Public Administrators (COMPA)

Chris Snead, Chair
COMPA Awards Committee
22 Lincoln Street
Hampton, VA 23669
757-727-6377
csnead@hampton.gov
http://www.natcompa.org
Grant Name: The Conference of Minority Public Administrators Travel Grant provides funding for students to travel to the COMPA's annual conference. *Academic Area: Government. *Age Group: Undergraduate students, graduate students. *Eligibility: Applicants must be students who are not employed full time and aspire to attend the conference for the purpose of networking, presenting theses or dissertations, and/or participating as a panelist for various student/practitioner/academia tracks. *Application Process: Applicants should visit the conference's Web site to download an application form. *Amount: $500. *Deadline: December 16.

Connecticut Department of Higher Education

Minority Teacher Incentive Grant Program
61 Woodland Street
Hartford, CT 06105-2326
860-447-1855
http://www.ctdhe.org/SFA/pdfs/MTIP%20Brochure%20and%20Form.pdf
Grant Name: Minority Teacher Incentive Grant. *Academic Area: Education. *Age Group: Undergraduate students. *Eligibility: Applicants must be minorities, college juniors or seniors, residents of Connecticut, and currently pursuing an education-related major at a select postsecondary institution in Connecticut. *Application Process: Applicants must be nominated by the dean of education at their school. *Amount: Up to $5,000 a year, plus up to $2,500 to repay college loans. *Deadline: October 1.

Delaware Higher Education Commission

820 North French Street
Wilmington, DE 19801
302-577-3240, 800-292-7935
dhec@doe.k12.de.us
http://www.doe.state.de.us/high-ed/scholarships.htm
Grant Name: The Delaware Higher Education Commission offers several need-based educational grants to students, including minorities. *Academic Area: Open. *Age Group: Undergraduate students, graduate students. *Eligibility: Applicants must demonstrate financial need, be legal residents of Delaware and U.S. citizens, and be enrolled full time at select Delaware colleges. *Application Process: Contact the commission for information on application requirements. *Amount: Varies. *Deadline: April 15

First Nations Development Institute

First Nations Grantmaking
Attn: Michael Roberts
2300 Fall Hill Avenue, Suite 412

Fredericksburg, VA 22401
540-371-5615
mroberts@firstnations.org
http://www.firstnations.org/grants.asp
Grant Name: First Nations Grantmaking Program.
  *Academic Area: Open. *Age Group: Open.
  *Eligibility: These funds are awarded for the purpose
  of providing both financial and technical resources to
  Native American tribes and nonprofit organizations
  to support asset-based development efforts that
  fit within the culture and that are sustainable.
  *Application Process: Applicants should visit the
  institute's Web site to review the criteria for each
  of the individual funds. Contact the institute with
  questions regarding application procedures.
  *Amount: Awards vary. *Deadline: Deadlines vary.

Florida Department of Education

Office of Student Financial Assistance
1940 North Monroe Street, Suite 70
Tallahassee, FL 32303-4759
888-827-2004
http://www.firn.edu/doe/bin00065/jmfactsheet.htm
Grant Name: José Martí Scholarship Challenge Grant
  Fund. *Academic Area: Open. *Age Group: High
  school seniors, undergraduate students, graduate
  students. *Eligibility: Applicants must be Hispanic
  American, residents of Florida, planning to or
  currently attending select postsecondary institutions
  in Florida, have a GPA of at least 3.0, and demonstrate
  financial need. Priority will be given to applicants who
  are high school seniors. *Application Process: Contact
  the department for information on application
  requirements. *Amount: $2,000. *Deadline: Varies.

Georgia Student Finance Commission

2082 East Exchange Place
Tucker, GA 30084
770-724-9000, 800-505-4732
http://www.gsfc.org/Main/dsp_main.cfm
Grant Name: The commission offers several need-
  based educational grants to students, including
  minorities. *Academic Area: Open. *Age Group:
  Undergraduate students. *Eligibility: Applicants
  must demonstrate financial need, be legal residents
  of Georgia and U.S. citizens, and be enrolled at
  select Georgia colleges. *Application Process:
  Varies; contact the commission for information on
  application requirements. *Amount: Varies by grant.
  *Deadline: Varies by grant.

Hawaii Department of Education

PO Box 2360
Honolulu, HI 96804
808-586-3230
doe_info@notes.k12.hi.us
http://doe.k12.hi.us/college_financialaid.htm
Grant Name: The department offers several need-based
  educational grants to students, including minorities.
  *Academic Area: Open. *Age Group: Undergraduate
  students. *Eligibility: Applicants must demonstrate
  financial need, be legal residents of Hawaii and U.S.
  citizens, and be enrolled at select Hawaii colleges.
  *Application Process: Varies; contact the department
  for information on application requirements.
  *Amount: Varies by grant. *Deadline: Varies by grant.

Health Resources and Services Administration

U.S. Department of Health and Human Services
Attn: Karen Smith
Parklawn Building
5600 Fishers Lane
Rockville, MD 20857
301-443-1438
ksmith1@hrsa.gov
http://bhpr.hrsa.gov/diversity/hcop/default.htm
Grant Name: Health Careers Opportunity Program
  Grant. *Academic Area: Medicine (general). *Age
  Group: High school seniors, undergraduate students,
  graduate students. *Eligibility: Applicants must come
  from a disadvantaged background, which is defined
  as an environment that has inhibited the individual
  from obtaining the knowledge, skills, and abilities to
  succeed in a health professions school or program
  and/or a student from a family with an annual income
  below a level based on low-income thresholds.
  Applicants must be U.S. citizens or possess a visa
  permitting permanent U.S. residence. High school
  seniors and college students may apply. *Application
  Process: Applicants should contact the administration
  for information about application procedures.
  *Amount: Awards vary. *Deadline: Contact the
  administration for deadline information.

Hispanic Theological Initiative

12 Library Place
Princeton, NJ 08540
609-252-1721
hti@ptsem.edu
http://www.htiprogram.org/scholarships/doctoral.htm
Grant Name: Hispanic Theological Initiative Doctoral

Grant. *Academic Area: Religion. *Age Group: Graduate students. *Eligibility: Applicant must be full-time Latino/a doctoral student. The student's institution must partner with the initiative in providing the student with a tuition scholarship, as well. *Application Process: Applicants should submit a completed application along with transcripts and recommendations by professors and Latino/a community members. Visit the initiative's Web site to download an application. *Amount: $15,000, renewable for a second year. *Deadline: December 7.

Illinois Student Assistance Commission

1755 Lake Cook Road
Deerfield, IL 60015-5209
800-899-4722, 800-526-0844 (TDD)
collegezone@isac.org
http://www.collegezone.com/studentzone/416_855.htm
Grant Name: The Monetary Award Program offers need-based educational grants to students, including minorities. *Academic Area: Open. *Age Group: Undergraduate students. *Eligibility: Applicants must demonstrate financial need, be legal residents of Illinois and U.S. citizens, and be enrolled full or part time at select Illinois colleges. *Application Process: Contact the commission for information on application requirements. *Amount: Varies depending on financial need. *Deadline: Varies.

Iowa College Student Aid Commission

200 - 10th Street, 4th Floor
Des Moines, IA 50309-2036
515-242-3388
info@iowacollegeaid.org
http://www.iowacollegeaid.org/scholarshipsandgrants/grantlist.html
Grant Name: The commission offers several need-based educational grants to students, including minorities. *Academic Area: Open. *Age Group: Undergraduate students. *Eligibility: Applicants must demonstrate financial need, be legal residents of Iowa and U.S. citizens, and plan to or be currently enrolled at select Iowa colleges. *Application Process: Varies by grant; contact the commission for information on application requirements. *Amount: $1,000 to $4,000. *Deadline: Varies by grant.

Kansas Board of Regents

1000 SW Jackson Street, Suite 520
Topeka, KS 66612-1368
785-296-3421
http://www.kansasregents.org/financial_aid
Grant Name: Kansas Comprehensive Grants are available to students, including minorities. *Academic Area: Open. *Age Group: Undergraduate students. *Eligibility: Applicants must demonstrate financial need, be legal residents of Kansas and U.S. citizens, and plan to or be currently enrolled at select Kansas colleges. *Application Process: Varies; contact the board for information on application requirements. *Amount: $200 to $1,100. *Deadline: Varies.

Kentucky Higher Education Assistance Authority

PO Box 798
Frankfort, KY 40602-0798
800-928-8926
http://www.kheaa.com
Grant Name: The authority offers several need-based educational grants to students, including minorities. *Academic Area: Open. *Age Group: Undergraduate students. *Eligibility: Applicants must demonstrate financial need, be legal residents of Kentucky and U.S. citizens, and plan to or be currently enrolled at select Kentucky colleges. *Application Process: Varies; contact the authority for information on application requirements. *Amount: $200 to $2,800. *Deadline: Varies by grant.

Maryland Higher Education Commission

Office of Student Financial Assistance
839 Bestgate Road, Suite 400
Annapolis, MD 21401-3013
800-974-1024, 800-735-2258 (TTY)
osfamail@mhec.state.md.us
http://www.mhec.state.md.us/financialAid
Grant Name: The commission offers several need-based educational grants to students, including minorities. *Academic Area: Open. *Age Group: Undergraduate students. *Eligibility: Applicants must demonstrate financial need, be legal residents of Maryland and U.S. citizens, and plan to or be currently enrolled at select Maryland colleges. *Application Process: Varies; contact the commission for information on application requirements. *Amount: $200 to $17,800. *Deadline: Varies by grant.

Massachusetts Office of Student Financial Assistance

454 Broadway, Suite 200
Revere, MA 02151
617-727-9420

osfa@osfa.mass.edu
http://www.osfa.mass.edu
Grant Name: The office offers several need-based educational grants to students, including minorities. *Academic Area: Open. *Age Group: Undergraduate students. *Eligibility: Applicants must demonstrate financial need, be legal residents of Massachusetts and U.S. citizens, and plan to or be currently enrolled at select Massachusetts colleges. *Application Process: Varies; contact the office for information on application requirements. *Amount: $200 to $7,500. *Deadline: Varies by grant.

Michigan Bureau of Student Financial Assistance
PO Box 30047
Lansing, MI 48909-7547
800-642-5626, ext. 37054
sfs@michigan.gov
http://www.michigan.gov/mistudentaid
Grant Name: The bureau offers several need-based educational grants to students, including minorities. *Academic Area: Open. *Age Group: Undergraduate students. *Eligibility: Applicants must demonstrate financial need, be legal residents of Michigan and U.S. citizens, and plan to or be currently enrolled at select Michigan colleges. *Application Process: Varies; contact the bureau for information on application requirements. *Amount: $600 to $1,000. *Deadline: Varies by grant.

Minnesota Office of Higher Education
1450 Energy Park Drive, Suite 350
St. Paul, MN 55108-5227
651-642-0567, 800-657-3866
http://www.getreadyforcollege.org/gPg.cfm?pageID=1296
Grant Name: The Minnesota Office of Higher Education provides several need-based educational grants to students from families with low or moderate incomes. *Academic Area: Open. * Age Group: Undergraduate students. *Eligibility: Applicants must be from low- or moderate-income families and plan to attend a postsecondary institution in Minnesota. *Application Process: Contact the office for information on application requirements. *Amount: Varies. *Deadline: Varies by grant; contact the office for details.

Mississippi Office of Student Financial Aid
3825 Ridgewood Road
Jackson, MS 39211-6453
800-327-2980

sfa@ihl.state.ms.us
http://www.ihl.state.ms.us/financialaid/default.asp
Grant Name: The office offers several need-based educational grants to students, including minorities. *Academic Area: Open. *Age Group: Undergraduate students. *Eligibility: Applicants must demonstrate financial need, be legal residents of Mississippi and U.S. citizens, and plan to or be currently enrolled at select Mississippi colleges. *Application Process: Varies; contact the office for information on application requirements. *Amount: $500 to $2,500. *Deadline: September 15.

Missouri Department of Higher Education
3515 Amazonas Drive
Jefferson City, MO 65109
573-751-2361
info@dhe.mo.gov
http://www.dhe.mo.gov
Grant Name: The department offers several need-based educational grants to students, including minorities. *Academic Area: Open. *Age Group: Undergraduate students. *Eligibility: Applicants must demonstrate financial need, be legal residents of Missouri and U.S. citizens, and plan to or be currently enrolled at a Missouri college. *Application Process: Varies; contact the department for information on application requirements. *Amount: Varies by grant. *Deadline: Varies by grant.

Montana Guaranteed Student Loan Program
PO Box 203101
Helena, MT 59620-3101
800-537-7508
http://www.mgslp.state.mt.us
Grant Name: The program offers several need-based educational grants to students, including minorities. *Academic Area: Open. *Age Group: Undergraduate students. *Eligibility: Applicants must demonstrate financial need, be legal residents of Montana and U.S. citizens, and plan to or be currently enrolled at select Montana colleges. *Application Process: Varies; contact the program for information on application requirements. *Amount: Varies by grant. *Deadline: Varies by grant.

National Alliance of Black School Educators Foundation
310 Pennsylvania Avenue, SE
Washington, DC 20003
202-608-6310

Eguidugli@nabse.org

http://www.nabse.org/foundation.htm

Grant Name: Research Grant. *Academic Area: Education. *Age Group: Graduate students. *Eligibility: Applicants must be African-American students. Contact the organization for further eligibility requirements. *Application Process: Applicants should contact the foundation for information on application procedures. *Amount: Awards vary. *Deadline: Contact the foundation for deadline information.

National Asian American Telecommunications Association (NAATA)

NAATA Media Fund

145 Ninth Street, Suite 350

San Francisco, CA 94103

415-863-0814, ext.106

mediafund@naatanet.org

http://www.naatanet.org/community/filmmaker/ mediafund/index.html

Grant Name: National Asian American Telecommunications Association Media Fund Grant. *Academic Area: Journalism. *Age Group: Open. *Eligibility: Applicants should be independent media producers addressing contemporary issues, growth, and change in our communities. Works should bring light to underrepresented or unheard voices, place Asian Americans in the context of an increasingly multicultural society, and look at issues of national interest, but from a unique Asian American perspective. *Application Process: Visit the association's Web site to download an application and guidelines. *Amount: $10,000 to $50,000. *Deadline: Rolling.

New Hampshire Postsecondary Education Commission

Three Barrell Court, Suite 300

Concord, NH 03301-8543

603-271-2555, 800-735-2964 (TDD)

http://www.state.nh.us/postsecondary/fin.html

Grant Name: The commission offers several need-based educational grants to students, including minorities. *Academic Area: Open. *Age Group: Undergraduate students, veterinary students. *Eligibility: Applicants must demonstrate financial need, be legal residents of New Hampshire and U.S. citizens, and plan to or be currently enrolled at select New Hampshire colleges. *Application Process: Varies; contact the commission for information on application requirements. *Amount: $125 to $12,000. *Deadline: Varies by grant.

New Jersey Higher Education Student Assistance Authority

PO Box 540

Trenton, NJ 08625

800-792-8670

http://www.nj.gov/highereducation/njhesaa.htm

Grant Name: The authority offers several need-based educational grants to students, including minorities. *Academic Area: Open. *Age Group: Undergraduate students. *Eligibility: Applicants must demonstrate financial need, be legal residents of New Jersey and U.S. citizens, and plan to or be currently enrolled at select New Jersey colleges. *Application Process: Varies; contact the authority for information on application requirements. *Amount: Varies by grant. *Deadline: Varies by grant.

New Mexico Higher Education Department

1068 Cerrillos Road

Santa Fe, NM 87505

505-476-6500

cordy.medina@state.nm.us

http://hed.state.nm.us/index.asp

Grant Name: The department offers several need-based educational grants to students, including minorities. *Academic Area: Open. *Age Group: Undergraduate students. *Eligibility: Applicants must demonstrate financial need, be legal residents of New Mexico and U.S. citizens, and plan to or be currently enrolled at select New Mexico colleges. *Application Process: Varies; contact the department for information on application requirements. *Amount: Varies by grant. *Deadline: Varies by grant.

New York State Higher Education Services Corporation

99 Washington Avenue

Albany, NY 12255

888-697-4372

http://www.hesc.state.ny.us

Grant Name: The corporation's New York State Tuition Assistance Program offers need-based educational grants to students, including minorities. *Academic Area: Open. *Age Group: Undergraduate students. *Eligibility: Applicants must demonstrate financial need, be legal residents of New York and U.S. citizens, and plan to or be currently enrolled at select New York colleges. *Application Process: Varies; contact the corporation for information on application requirements. *Amount: Up to $5,000. *Deadline: Varies.

North Carolina State Education Assistance Authority
PO Box 14103
Research Triangle Park, NC 27709
919-549-8614
information@ncseaa.edu
http://www.ncseaa.edu
Grant Name: The authority offers several need-based educational grants to students, including minorities. *Academic Area: Open. *Age Group: Undergraduate students. *Eligibility: Applicants must demonstrate financial need, be legal residents of North Carolina and U.S. citizens, and plan to or be currently enrolled at select North Carolina colleges. *Application Process: Varies; contact the authority for information on application requirements. *Amount: Varies by grant. *Deadline: Varies by grant.

Ohio Board of Regents
State Grants and Scholarships Department
30 East Broad Street, 36th Floor
Columbus, OH 43215-34114
888-833-1133
http://www.regents.state.oh.us/sgs/financialaid.html
Grant Name: The board offers several need-based educational grants to students, including minorities. *Academic Area: Open. *Age Group: Undergraduate students. *Eligibility: Applicants must demonstrate financial need, be legal residents of Ohio and U.S. citizens, and plan to or be currently enrolled at select Ohio colleges. *Application Process: Varies; contact the board for information on application requirements. *Amount: $174 to $5,466. *Deadline: Varies by grant.

Oklahoma State Regents for Higher Education (OSRHE)
655 Research Parkway, Suite 200
Oklahoma City, OK 73104
405-225-9100
rstokes@osrhe.edu
http://www.okhighered.org/student%2Dcenter/financial%2Daid
Grant Name: The OSRHE offers several need-based educational grants to students, including minorities. *Academic Area: Open. *Age Group: Undergraduate students. *Eligibility: Applicants must demonstrate financial need, be legal residents of Oklahoma and U.S. citizens, and plan to or be currently enrolled at select Oklahoma colleges. *Application Process: Varies; contact the OSRHE for information on

application requirements. *Amount: Varies by grant. *Deadline: Varies by grant.

Oregon Student Assistance Commission
1500 Valley River Drive, Suite 100
Eugene, OR 97401
541-687-7400
awardinfo@mercury.osac.state.or.us
http://www.getcollegefunds.org/ong.html
Grant Name: State Opportunity Grants are available to students, including minorities. *Academic Area: Open. *Age Group: Undergraduate students. *Eligibility: Applicants must demonstrate financial need, be legal residents of Oregon and U.S. citizens, and plan to or be currently enrolled at select Oregon colleges. *Application Process: Varies; contact the commission for information on application requirements. *Amount: $1,164 to $3,606. *Deadline: Varies.

Pennsylvania Higher Education Assistance Agency
1200 North Seventh Street
Harrisburg, PA 17102-1444
800-692-7392
http://www.pheaa.org
Grant Name: The agency offers several need-based educational grants to students, including minorities. *Academic Area: Open. *Age Group: Undergraduate students. *Eligibility: Applicants must demonstrate financial need, be legal residents of Pennsylvania and U.S. citizens, and plan to or be currently enrolled at select Pennsylvania colleges. *Application Process: Varies; contact the agency for information on application requirements. *Amount: Varies by grant. *Deadline: Varies by grant.

Playwrights' Center
Many Voices Residency
2301 Franklin Avenue East
Minneapolis, MN 55406-1099
612-332-7481
info@pwcenter.org
http://www.pwcenter.org/fellowships_MV.asp
Grant Name: Many Voices Residency. *Academic Area: Performing arts (theatre), writing. *Age Group: Open. *Eligibility: Applicants should be artists of color pursuing the opportunity to develop new work in the field of playwriting. Many Voices is designed to increase cultural diversity in the contemporary theater, both locally and nationally. Applicants must be U.S. citizens or permanent residents and

recipients must maintain residency in Minnesota or within 100 miles of the Twin Cities during the grant year. *Application Process: Applicants should submit a completed application form along with a one-page personal statement and/or resume, a writing sample of any length, and a one-page description of goals for the residency. Application packets should be submitted in four collated, bound packets. Visit the center's Web site to download an application. *Amount: Awards vary. *Deadline: July 30.

Presbyterian Church USA

Attn: Laura Bryan
100 Witherspoon Street
Louisville, KY 40202
888-728-7228, ext. 5776
Lbryan@ctr.pcusa.org
http://www.pcusa.org/financialaid/graduate.htm
Grant Name: Native American Supplemental Grant. *Academic Area: Religion. *Age Group: Graduate students. *Eligibility: Applicants must be Native Americans preparing to serve in a Presbyterian Church USA congregation. Applicants must be members of the Presbyterian Church, U.S. citizens or permanent residents, demonstrate financial need, and be pursuing a first professional degree in preparation for a church occupation. *Application Process: Applicants should submit a completed application along with supporting documents. Visit the organization's Web site to download an application. *Amount: $500 to $1,500. *Deadline: October 15.

Presbyterian Church USA

Attn: Laura Bryan
100 Witherspoon Street
Louisville, KY 40202
888-728-7228, ext. 5667
Lbryan@ctr.pcusa.org
http://www.pcusa.org/financialaid/graduate.htm
Grant Name: Racial Ethnic Supplemental Grant. *Academic Area: Religion. *Age Group: Graduate students. *Eligibility: Applicants must be African American, Alaska Native, Asian American, Hispanic American, or Native American students who have been awarded the Presbyterian Study Grant (a grant that is available to all ethnic groups) and have remaining need. Applicants must be preparing to serve in a Presbyterian Church USA congregation, and must currently be members of the Presbyterian Church USA, U.S. citizens or permanent residents, demonstrate financial

need, and be pursuing a first professional degree in preparation for a church occupation. *Application Process: Applicants should submit a completed application along with supporting documents. Visit the organization's Web site to download an application. *Amount: $500 to $1,000. *Deadline: October 15.

Professional Women of Color (PWC)

Dream Grant
PO Box 5196
New York, NY 10185
212-714-7190
TLawr64783@aol.com
http://www.pwcnetwork.org/dreamgrant.html
Grant Name: The Professional Women of Color Dream Grant helps minority women start a business, attend an educational program, finish a research project, or introduce a new product. *Academic Area: Open. *Age Group: Undergraduate students, graduate students, professionals. *Eligibility: Current members of PWC are eligible to apply. *Application Procedure: Applicants should submit a 300- to 1,000-word essay that details their project/venture, a resume, a one-page bio, and a 3 1/2 x 5 black and white head shot. An application fee of $50 is required. *Amount: Grants range from $3,000 to $5,000. *Deadline: Varies. Contact PWC for more information.

Rhode Island Higher Education Assistance Authority

560 Jefferson Boulevard
Warwick, RI 02886
800-922-9855, 401-734-9481 (TDD)
info@riheaa.org
http://www.riheaa.org/borrowers/grants
Grant Name: The Rhode Island State Grant Program provides grants to students, including minorities. *Academic Area: Open. *Age Group: Undergraduate students. *Eligibility: Applicants must demonstrate financial need, be legal residents of Rhode Island and U.S. citizens, and plan to or be currently enrolled at select Rhode Island colleges. *Application Process: Varies; contact the authority for information on application requirements. *Amount: $300 to $1,400. *Deadline: March 1.

South Carolina Higher Education Tuition Grants Commission

101 Business Park Boulevard, Suite 2100
Columbia, SC 29203-9498
803-896-1120

info@sctuitiongrants.org
http://www.che.sc.gov/StudentServices/NeedBased/
   NBG.htm
Grant Name: The commission's Need-Based Grant
   Program provides grants to students, including
   minorities. *Academic Area: Open. *Age Group:
   Undergraduate students. *Eligibility: Applicants must
   demonstrate financial need, be legal residents of
   South Carolina and U.S. citizens, and plan to or be
   currently enrolled at select South Carolina colleges.
   *Application Process: Contact the commission for
   information on application requirements. *Amount:
   Up to $2,500. *Deadline: Varies.

State Council of Higher Education for Virginia
101 North 14th Street, James Monroe Building
Richmond, VA 23219
804-225-2600
http://www.schev.edu/Students/Students.
   asp?from=students
Grant Name: The Tuition Assistance Grant Program
   provides grants to students, including minorities.
   *Academic Area: Open. *Age Group: Undergraduate
   students, graduate students. *Eligibility: Applicants
   must demonstrate financial need, be legal residents of
   Virginia, and plan to or be currently enrolled at select
   Virginia colleges. *Application Process: Contact the
   council for information on application requirements.
   *Amount: $1,900 to $2,500. *Deadline: July 31.

State Student Assistance Commission of Indiana
150 West Market Street, Suite 500
Indianapolis, IN 46204
317-232-2350
grants@ssaci.in.gov
http://www.in.gov/ssaci
Grant Name: The commission offers several need-based
   educational grants to students, including minorities.
   *Academic Area: Open. *Age Group: Undergraduate
   students. *Eligibility: Applicants must demonstrate
   financial need, be legal residents of Indiana and U.S.
   citizens, and plan to or be currently enrolled at select
   Indiana colleges. *Application Process: Varies; contact
   the commission for information on application
   requirements. *Amount: Varies by grant. *Deadline:
   Varies by grant.

Studio Museum in Harlem
AIR Program
144 West 125th Street

New York, NY 10027
212-864-4500
http://www.studiomuseum.org/air_overview.html
Grant Name: Artists-In-Residence Program. *Academic
   Area: Visual arts (general). *Age Group: Open.
   *Eligibility: Applicants must be artists of African
   descent, able to demonstrate at least three years of
   professional commitment, and currently engaged in
   studio work. Applicants may not attend school during
   the residency or produce art as a hobby. *Application
   Process: Applicants should submit a completed
   application along with a resume, an artist statement,
   10 slides or one video, a slide list, supplementary
   materials (reviews, catalogues, brochures), a self-
   addressed stamped postcard and envelope, and two
   letters of recommendation. Visit the museum's Web
   site to download an application. *Amount: $15,000,
   plus $1,000 for materials. *Deadline: April 1.

Tennessee Student Assistance Corporation
404 James Robertson Parkway, Suite 1950, Parkway
   Towers
Nashville, TN 37243-0820
615-741-1346
http://www.state.tn.us/tsac
Grant Name: The Tennessee Student Assistance Award
   Program provides grants to students, including
   minorities. *Academic Area: Open. *Age Group:
   Undergraduate students. *Eligibility: Applicants
   must demonstrate financial need, be legal
   residents of Tennessee, and plan to or be currently
   enrolled at select Tennessee colleges. *Application
   Process: Contact the corporation for information
   on application requirements. *Amount: Varies.
   *Deadline: Varies.

Texas Higher Education Coordinating Board
PO Box 12788
Austin, TX 78711-2788
512-427-6101
http://www.collegefortexans.com
Grant Name: The board offers several need-based
   educational grants to students, including minorities.
   *Academic Area: Open. *Age Group: Undergraduate
   students. *Eligibility: Applicants must demonstrate
   financial need, be legal residents of Texas, and plan
   to or be currently enrolled at select Texas colleges.
   *Application Process: Varies; contact the board for
   information on application requirements. *Amount:
   Varies by grant. *Deadline: Varies by grant.

United States Bureau of Indian Affairs

Office of Indian Education
1849 C Street, NW
MS-3512 MIB
Washington, DC 20240-0001
202-208-6123
http://www.oiep.bia.edu

Grant Name: Higher ED Grant. *Academic Area: Open. *Age Group: High school seniors, undergraduate students. *Eligibility: Applicants must be at least 1/4 degree Indian blood, accepted for admission to a nationally accredited institution of higher education that provides a course of study conferring the associate of arts or bachelor's degree, and demonstrate financial need. High school seniors and undergraduate students may apply. *Application Process: Applicants should contact their tribe for application information. The grant application is available from the education office of the tribe they are affiliated with or possess membership. Visit the bureau's Web site for more information. *Amount: Awards vary. *Deadline: Deadlines vary.

United States Department of Agriculture

Cooperative State Research, Education, and Extension Service
Attn: Audrey Trotman
1400 Independence Avenue, SW, Stop 2201
Washington, DC 20250-2201
202-720-2193
atrotman@csrees.usda.gov
http://www.csrees.usda.gov/fo/fundview.cfm?
fonum=1110

Grant Name: Higher Education Multicultural Scholars Program. *Academic Area: Agriculture, food sciences. *Age Group: Open. *Eligibility: These grants are awarded to U.S. public or private nonprofit colleges/universities that offer baccalaureate degree or first professional degree programs in at least one discipline of food and agricultural sciences; land-grant colleges/universities, including those in insular areas; colleges/universities with significant minority enrollment and a demonstrable capacity to teach food and agricultural sciences; and other colleges/universities with a demonstrable capacity to teach food and agricultural sciences. The grants are then awarded to minority students at the institutions. *Application Process: Institutions interested in applying should visit the service's Web site to download an application. *Amount: $40,000 to $100,000. *Deadline: June 1.

United States Department of Education

Federal Student Aid Information Center
PO Box 84
Washington, DC 20044-0084
800-433-3243
http://studentaid.ed.gov/students/publications/
student_guide/index.html

Grant Name: Federal Supplemental Educational Opportunity Grants are available to all students, including minorities. *Academic Area: Open. *Age Group: Undergraduate students. *Eligibility: Applicants must demonstrate financial need, be U.S. citizens, be high school graduates, have a valid Social Security number, and plan to or be currently enrolled in accredited postsecondary program in the United States. *Application Process: Contact the Federal Student Aid Information Center for information on application requirements. *Amount: $100 to $4,000. *Deadline: Varies.

United States Department of Education

Federal Student Aid Information Center
PO Box 84
Washington, DC 20044-0084
800-433-3243
http://studentaid.ed.gov/students/publications/
student_guide/index.html

Grant Name: Pell Grants are available to all students, including minorities. *Academic Area: Open. *Age Group: Undergraduate students. *Eligibility: Applicants must demonstrate financial need, be U.S. citizens, be high school graduates, have a valid Social Security number, and plan to or be currently enrolled in accredited postsecondary program in the United States. *Application Process: Contact the Federal Student Aid Information Center for information on application requirements. *Amount: $400 to $4,050. *Deadline: Varies.

Utah Higher Education Assistance Authority

60 South 400 West
Salt Lake City, UT 84101-1284
877-336-7378
http://www.uheaa.org

Grant Name: The authority offers several need-based educational grants to students, including minorities. *Academic Area: Open. *Age Group: Undergraduate students. *Eligibility: Applicants must demonstrate financial need, be legal residents of Utah and U.S. citizens, and plan to or be currently enrolled at select

Utah colleges. *Application Process: Varies; contact the authority for information on application requirements. *Amount: Varies by grant. *Deadline: Varies by grant.

Vermont Student Assistance Corporation

PO Box 999
Winooski, VT 05404
800-798-8722
info@vsac.org
http://services.vsac.org/ilwwcm/connect/VSAC

Grant Name: The corporation offers several need-based educational grants to students, including minorities. *Academic Area: Open. *Age Group: Undergraduate students. *Eligibility: Applicants must demonstrate financial need, be legal residents of Vermont and U.S. citizens, and plan to or be currently enrolled at select Vermont colleges. *Application Process: Varies; contact the corporation for information on application requirements. *Amount: Varies by grant. *Deadline: Varies by grant.

Washington Higher Education Coordinating Board

917 Lakeridge Way, PO Box 43430
Olympia, WA 98504-3430
360-753-7800
info@hecb.wa.gov
http://www.hecb.wa.gov/paying

Grant Name: The board offers several need-based educational grants to students, including minorities. *Academic Area: Open. *Age Group: Undergraduate students. *Eligibility: Applicants must demonstrate financial need, be legal residents of Washington, and plan to or be currently enrolled at select Washington colleges. *Application Process: Varies; contact the board for information on application requirements. *Amount: $2,328 to $5,008. *Deadline: Varies by grant.

West Virginia Higher Education Policy Commission

1018 Kanawha Boulevard East, Suite 700
Charleston, WV 25301
304-558-4614
http://www.hepc.wvnet.edu/students

Grant Name: The commission offers several need-based educational grants to students, including minorities. *Academic Area: Open. *Age Group: Undergraduate students. *Eligibility: Applicants must demonstrate financial need, be legal residents of West Virginia and U.S. citizens, and plan to or be currently enrolled at select West Virginia colleges. *Application Process: Varies; contact the commission for information on application requirements. *Amount: Varies by grant. *Deadline: Varies by grant.

Wisconsin Higher Educational Aids Board

PO Box 7885
Madison, WI 53707-7885
608-266-0888
sandy.thomas@heab.state.wi.us
http://www.heab.state.wi.us

Grant Name: Indian Student Assistance Grant. *Academic Area: Open. *Age Group: Undergraduate students, graduate students. *Eligibility: Applicants must be at least 25 percent Native American, demonstrate financial need, be legal residents of Wisconsin, and plan to or be currently enrolled at select Wisconsin colleges. *Application Process: An application is available at the board's Web site. *Amount: $250 to $1,100. *Deadline: Varies.

Wisconsin Higher Educational Aids Board

PO Box 7885
Madison, WI 53707-7885
608-267-2212
mary.kuzdas@heab.state.wi.us
http://www.heab.state.wi.us

Grant Name: Minority Undergraduate Retention Grant. *Academic Area: Open. *Age Group: Undergraduate students. *Eligibility: Applicants must be African American, American Indian, Hispanic American, or Southeast Asian from Laos, Cambodia, or Vietnam; demonstrate financial need, be legal residents of Wisconsin, and be college sophomores, juniors, or seniors at select Wisconsin colleges. *Application Process: Contact the board for information on application requirements. *Amount: $250 to $2,500. *Deadline: Varies.

LOANS

Loans for minority-owned businesses are available from lenders around the country. Your local Small Business Administration office can get you connected with specialized lenders.

First Nations Oweesta Corporation

2300 Fall Hill Avenue, Suite 412
Fredericksburg, VA 22401
540-371-5615
info@firstnations.org
http://www.oweesta.org

Loan Name: First Nations Oweesta Corporation, a subsidiary of First Nations Development Institute, offers loans and other assistance to Native American tribes, businesses, and individuals. *Academic Area: Open. *Age Group: Open. *Eligibility: Native Americans may apply. *Application Process: Contact the First Nations Oweesta Corporation for information on specific loan programs. *Amount: Varies. *Loan Repayment Deadline: Varies by loan. *Application Deadline: Applications are accepted throughout the year.

Health Resources and Services Administration

U.S. Department of Health and Human Services
5600 Fishers Lane
Rockville, MD 20857
http://bhpr.hrsa.gov/dsa/lds.htm

Loan Name: Loan for Disadvantaged Students. *Academic Area: Medicine (dentistry), medicine (general), medicine (physicians), pharmaceutical sciences. *Age Group: Open. *Eligibility: Disadvantaged students, including minorities, who are interested in pursuing careers in the health sciences may apply. Applicants must be citizens, nationals, or lawful permanent residents of the United States or the District of Columbia, the Commonwealths of Puerto Rico or the Marianas Islands, the Virgin Islands, Guam, the American Samoa, the Trust Territory of the Pacific Islands, the Republic of Palau, the Republic of the Marshall Islands, or the Federated State of Micronesia. *Application Process: Students should contact the financial aid office of their school to see if the loan program is available. *Amount: Not to exceed the cost of attendance (tuition, reasonable educational expenses, and reasonable living expenses). *Loan Repayment Deadline: Varies. *Application Deadline: Varies.

Hispanic Association of Colleges and Universities/ National Education Loan Network

8415 Datapoint Drive, Suite 400
San Antonio, TX 78229
866-866-7372

http://www.nelnet.net/hacu

Loan Name: The Hispanic Association of Colleges and Universities (HACU), in cooperation with the National Education Loan Network, offers loans to parents of Hispanic students via its Educational Loan Program. *Academic Area: Open. *Age Group: Open. *Eligibility: Parents of Hispanic students who are attending HACU-member colleges and universities may apply. *Application Process: Contact either organization for details. *Amount: Varies. *Loan Repayment Deadline: Varies. *Application Deadline: Contact either organization for details.

Hispanic Association of Colleges and Universities/ National Education Loan Network

8415 Datapoint Drive, Suite 400
San Antonio, TX 78229
866-866-7372
http://www.nelnet.net/hacu

Loan Name: The Hispanic Association of Colleges and Universities (HACU), in cooperation with the National Education Loan Network, offers loans to Hispanic students via its Educational Loan Program. *Academic Area: Open. *Age Group: Open. *Eligibility: Hispanic students who are attending HACU-member colleges and universities may apply. *Application Process: Contact either organization for details. *Amount: Varies. *Loan Repayment Deadline: Varies. *Application Deadline: Contact either organization for details.

Minority Business Development Agency (MBDA)

U.S. Department of Commerce
1401 Constitution Avenue, NW
Washington, DC 20230
888-324-1551
http://www.mbda.gov

Loan Name: The MBDA does not provide funding, but helps minorities locate financial resources, including loans. *Academic Area: Open.*Age Group: Open. *Eligibility: Minorities may contact the MBDA for assistance and referral. *Application Process: N/A. *Amount: Varies by loan program.*Loan Repayment Deadline: N/A.*Application Deadline: N/A.

National Education Loan Network (Nelnet)
888-486-4722
campussolutions@nelnet.net
http://www.nelnet.net
Loan Name: Nelnet, one of the leading education finance companies in the nation, provides loans to students, including minorities. *Academic Area: Open. *Age Group: Open. *Eligibility: College students at all levels may apply. *Application Process: Contact Nelnet for information on specific loan programs. *Amount: Varies. *Loan Repayment Deadline: Varies by loan. *Application Deadline: Applications are accepted throughout the year.

National Minority Business Council (NMBC)
25 West 45th Street, Suite 301
New York, NY 10036
212-997-4753
http://www.nmbc.org
Loan Name: The NMBC offers minority business owners short-term loans for working capital via its NMBC Micro-Loan Fund. *Academic Area: Open. *Age Group: Open. *Eligibility: Minority business owners who are members of the NMBC may apply. *Application Process: Contact the NMBC for information on specific loan programs. *Amount: $1,500 to $25,000. *Loan Repayment Deadline: Varies by loan. *Application Deadline: Applications are accepted throughout the year.

National Minority Supplier Development Council
Business Consortium Fund Inc.
305 Seventh Avenue, 20th Floor
New York, NY 10001
212-243-7360
http://www.bcfcapital.com
Loan Name: The Business Consortium Fund Inc. was created by the National Minority Supplier Development Council, a minority business membership organization. It offers several loan and financial assistance programs to minority business owners. *Academic Area: Open. *Age Group: Open. *Eligibility: Applicants must be minorities who own at least 51 percent of a for-profit business in the United States. Businesses must be certified by a National Minority Supplier Development Council (NMSDC)-affiliated regional council and have a supplier/vendor relationship with a corporate member of the NMSDC or an affiliate regional council of the NMSDC. *Application Process: Loan applicants should submit information on why they need the loan and how they will repay it, a history of their business, recent (last three years) financial statements, a schedule of term debts, signed personal and corporate income tax returns for the most recent two years, and other documentation. *Amount: Up to $750,000. *Loan Repayment Deadline: No more than four years from the date of issue. *Application Deadline: Applications are accepted throughout the year.

Native American Business Development Center
Attn: National Center for American Indian Enterprise Development
953 East Juanita Avenue
Mesa, AZ 85204
480-545-1298
http://www.ncaied.org/gsp/nabdc.html
Loan Name: The Native American Business Development Center provides loans and financial assistance to Native Americans. It has regional locations throughout the United States. *Academic Area: Open. *Age Group: Open. *Eligibility: Native Americans who need funds to operate or expand their businesses are eligible to apply. *Application Process: Contact the center for information. *Amount: Varies. *Loan Repayment Deadline: Varies by loan. *Application Deadline: Applications are accepted throughout the year.

P.E.O. International
3700 Grand Avenue
Des Moines, IA 50312
515-255-3153
http://www.peointernational.org/projects/overview.php
Loan Name: The P.E.O. Educational Loan Fund is a revolving loan fund established in 1907 to lend money to worthy women students (including those who are minorities) to assist them in securing a higher education. *Academic Area: Open. *Age Group: Undergraduate students, graduate students. *Eligibility: Applicants must be citizens or legal permanent residents of the United States or Canada, high school graduates, enrolled in an accredited school, and recommended by a local P.E.O. chapter. *Application Process: Applications are mailed from the P.E.O. Executive Office upon receipt of the recommendation from the local P.E.O. chapter. *Amount: Up to $9,000 at 2 percent interest. *Loan Repayment Deadline: Due six years from the date of issue. *Application Deadline: Applications are accepted throughout the year.

Sallie Mae

PO Box 59012
Panama City, FL 32412-9012
http://www.salliemae.com
Loan Name: Sallie Mae, which calls itself "the nation's No. 1 paying-for-college company", provides federally guaranteed student loans to students, including minorities. *Academic Area: Open. *Age Group: Open. *Eligibility: College students at all levels may apply. *Application Process: Contact Sallie Mae for information on specific loan programs. *Amount: Varies. *Loan Repayment Deadline: Varies by loan. *Application Deadline: Applications are accepted throughout the year.

Small Business Administration (SBA)

409 Third Street, SW
Washington, DC 20416
800-827-5722
http://www.sba.gov
Loan Name: The Small Business Administration (SBA) provides several loan programs, including the 8(a) Minority Program, to entrepreneurs. *Academic Area: Open. *Age Group: Open. *Eligibility: Minority entrepreneurs with a viable business plan are eligible to apply. *Application Process: Contact the SBA for details. *Amount: Varies. *Loan Repayment Deadline: Varies. *Application Deadline: Contact the SBA for details.

United States Department of Education

400 Maryland Avenue, SW
Washington, DC 20202
800-433-3243
http://studentaid.ed.gov/PORTALSWebApp/students/english/index.jsp
Loan Name: The U.S. Department of Education's Federal Student Aid Program provides students (including minorities) with $60 billion a year in loans, grants, and work-study assistance. *Academic Area: Open. *Age Group: Open. *Eligibility: College students at all levels may apply. *Application Process: Contact the U.S. Department of Education for information on specific programs. *Amount: Varies. *Loan Repayment Deadline: Varies by loan. *Application Deadline: Varies.

Wells Fargo

Women/Minority Services
800-869-3557
http://www.wellsfargo.com/biz/intentions/women_minority_services.jhtml
Loan Name: Wells Fargo, a financial services company, provides a variety of loans and other financial resources to minority business owners. *Academic Area: Open. *Age Group: Open. *Eligibility: Minority business owners may apply. *Application Process: Contact Wells Fargo for information on specific loan programs. *Amount: $10,000 to $100,000. *Loan Repayment Deadline: Varies by loan. *Application Deadline: Applications are accepted throughout the year.

Wells Fargo Education Financial Services

Student Loans
PO Box 5185
Sioux Falls, SD 57117-5185
800-658-3567
http://www.wellsfargo.com/student/loans/undergrad/index.jhtml
Loan Name: Wells Fargo, a financial services company, provides a variety of loans to students, including minorities. *Academic Area: Open. *Age Group: Undergraduate students, graduate students, medical students. *Eligibility: College students at all levels may apply. *Application Process: Contact Wells Fargo for information on specific loan programs. *Amount: Varies. *Loan Repayment Deadline: Varies by loan. *Application Deadline: Applications are accepted throughout the year.

Women's World Banking (WWB)

Eight West 40th Street, 9th Floor
New York, NY 10018
212-768-8513
http://www.swwb.org
Loan Name: WWB and its member organizations provides loans to women entrepreneurs of limited economic means in Africa, Asia, Latin America, North America, Europe, and the Middle East. *Academic Area: Open. *Age Group: Open. *Eligibility: Women entrepreneurs are eligible to apply. *Application Process: Applicants must obtain these loans from one of WWB's 26 women-led affiliates and affiliates-in-formation. Contact WWB for details. *Amount: Up to $1 million. *Loan Repayment Deadline: Varies. *Application Deadline: Contact WWB for more information.

SCHOLARSHIPS

Scholarships are offered at all levels, from high school through postdoctoral to working men and women.

Alpha Delta Kappa International
1615 West 92nd Street
Kansas City, MO 64114-3296
816-363-5525, 800-247-2311
dfrost@alphadeltakappa.org
http://www.alphadeltakappa.org
Scholarship Name: International Teacher Education Scholarship. *Academic Area: Education. *Age Group: College students between the ages of 20 and 35. *Eligibility: Applicants must be female non-U.S. citizens (including minorities) living outside of the United States, must maintain that residency status from the time of application to awarding of the scholarship, must be single with no dependents, and must rank academically in the top 25 percent of their class. Applicants must have completed at least one year of college and agree to purchase health insurance as well as fund her own travel expenses. Must maintain full-time student status. *Application Process: Submit completed application. Visit Alpha Delta Kappa's Web site to download an application. *Amount: $10,000 per year, divided into installments at designated intervals according to the college/university attended. Can apply for up to two years. *Deadline: January 1.

Alpha Kappa Alpha Educational Advancement Foundation
Attn: Scholarship Application Enclosed
5656 South Stoney Island Avenue
Chicago, IL 60637
773-947-0026
akaeaf@aol.com
http://www.akaeaf.org
Scholarship Name: This African-American service sorority offers a variety of merit-based and need-based scholarships. *Academic Area: Open. *Age Group: Undergraduate students, graduate students. *Eligibility: Applicants need not be members of Alpha Kappa Alpha to apply. The sorority supports students without regard to sex, race, creed, color, ethnicity, religion, sexual orientation, or disability. *Application Process: Undergraduate applicants should submit a completed application (available for download each November), a personal statement, three letters of recommendation, and official transcripts. Graduate students should also include a current resume and

documentation of project and/or research plans. All applications should have the applicant's Social Security number on each page. Visit the sorority's Web site to download an application. *Amount: $750 to $1,500. *Deadline: January 15.

American Association of Blacks in Energy (AABE)
927 15th Street, NW, Suite 200
Washington, DC 20005
800-466-0204
aabe@aabe.org
http://www.aabe.org
Scholarship Name: AABE Scholarships. Academic Area: Engineering (general), mathematics, physical sciences. *Age Group: High school seniors. *Eligibility: Applicants must be African Americans, Hispanic Americans, or Native Americans who have applied to one or more accredited colleges/universities, plan to major in engineering, mathematics, or the physical sciences, and have a minimum of a "B" average, both overall and in math and science courses. *Application Process: Applicants should submit a completed application form, high school transcripts, two letters of recommendation (one academic and one non-academic), and a copy of their parent(s) or guardian(s) signed tax return for the previous year (or a verified FAFSA form). Applications should be submitted to the regional AABE office nearest the applicant. Do not submit applications to the national office. Visit the organization's Web site to download an application and to locate your regional office. *Amount: $1,500 to $3,000. *Deadline: March 4.

American Association of Critical-Care Nurses (AACN)
101 Columbia
Aliso Viejo, CA 92656-4109
800-899-2226
info@aacn.org
http://www.aacn.org
Scholarship Name: BSN Educational Advancement Scholarship. *Academic Area: Nursing (critical care). Age Group: College juniors and seniors. *Eligibility: Applicant must be an AACN member in good standing, have an active RN license, maintain a cumulative GPA of at least 3.0, and must also be currently working in critical care or have worked in critical care for at least one year in the last three years. Also must currently

be enrolled in an accredited nursing program and have junior or upper division status. Twenty percent of scholarship funds will be awarded to ethnic minorities. *Application Process: Applicants must submit a completed application by mail, followed by final grade reports. Letters of verification from your place of employment and school must also be sent. Visit the association's Web site to download an application. *Amount: $1,500. Deadline: April 1 for application, July 1 for final grade reports.

American Association of Critical-Care Nurses (AACN)
101 Columbia
Aliso Viejo, CA 92656-4109
800-899-2226
info@aacn.org
http://www.aacn.org
Scholarship Name: Graduate Educational Advancement Scholarship. *Academic Area: Nursing (critical care). Age Group: Graduate students. *Eligibility: Applicant must be an AACN member in good standing, have an active RN license, maintain a cumulative GPA of at least 3.0, and must also be currently working in critical care or have worked in critical care for at least one year in the last three years. Also must be a graduate of a baccalaureate degree program and be currently enrolled in a graduate program leading to a master's or doctorate in nursing. Alternately, may also be enrolled in a faculty supervisor's clinical practicum leading to eligibility for the CCNS exam. Twenty percent of total scholarship funds are awarded to ethnic minorities. *Application Process: Applicants must submit a completed application by mail, followed by final grade reports. Letters of verification from your place of employment and schools must also be sent. *Amount: $1,500. Deadline: April 1 for application, July 1 for final grade reports.

American Association of Law Libraries
Chair, Scholarships Committee
53 West Jackson, Suite 940
Chicago, IL 60604
312-939-4764
membership@aall.org
http://www.aallnet.org/services/sch_strait.asp
Scholarship Name: George A. Strait Minority Scholarship Endowment. *Academic Area: Law. *Age Group: College students. *Eligibility: Minority college students who plan to pursue a career in law librarianship are eligible to apply. Applicants

must demonstrate financial need. *Application Process: Application packets should include an official transcript, verification of acceptance or attendance at a postsecondary program, three letters of recommendation, and a personal statement describing the applicant's reasons for applying for the scholarship and his or her interest in law librarianship. *Amount: Varies. *Deadline: April 1.

American Association of University Women
International Fellowships
PO Box 4030
Iowa City, IA 52243-4030
319-337-1716, ext. 60
aauw@act.org
http://www.aauw.org
Scholarship Name: International Fellowships. *Academic Area: Open. *Age Group: Graduate students. *Eligibility: Applicants must be full-time students who are not U.S. citizens or permanent residents. Both graduate and postgraduate study at accredited institutions are supported. *Application Process: Applications are available on the Association's Web site between August 1 and December 1. *Amount: $18,000 to $30,000. *Deadline: December 1.

American Bar Association (ABA)
ABA Legal Opportunity Scholarship Fund-Application
321 North Clark Street
Chicago, IL 60610-4714
312-988-5415
mastronardi@staff.abanet.org
http://www.abanet.org/fje/allenbroussard.html
Scholarship Name: Allen E. Broussard Scholarship. *Academic Area: Law. *Age Group: College students. *Eligibility: Minority college students who plan to attend California Bay Area law schools are eligible to apply. Applicants must demonstrate financial need. *Application Process: Applicants may complete the ABA Legal Opportunity Scholarship Fund (another scholarship offered by the ABA) application. Application packets should include an official transcript, verification of acceptance by a law program, two letters of recommendation (with at least one from a professor), and a personal statement (no longer than 1,000 words) describing the applicant's interest in studying law, potential financial need, and personal activities, such as community service. *Amount: $5,000. *Deadline: March 1.

American Bar Association (ABA)
ABA Legal Opportunity Scholarship Fund-Application
321 North Clark Street
Chicago, IL 60610-4714
312-988-5415
mastronardi@staff.abanet.org
http://www.abanet.org/fje/losfpage.html
Scholarship Name: The Legal Opportunity Scholarship Fund provides financial assistance to encourage minorities to pursue careers in law. *Academic Area: Law. *Age Group: College students. *Eligibility: Minority college students who are citizens or permanent residents of the United States and who are entering students at an American Bar Association-accredited law school are eligible to apply. Applicants must also have a cumulative GPA of 2.5 on a 4.0 scale. *Application Process: Application packets should include an official transcript, verification of acceptance by a law program, two letters of recommendation (with at least one from a professor), and a personal statement (no longer than 1,000 words) describing the applicant's interest in studying law, potential financial need, and personal activities, such as community service. *Amount: $5,000. *Deadline: March 1.

American Dental Association Foundation
211 East Chicago Avenue
Chicago, IL 60611
312-440-2547
adaf@ada.org
http://www.ada.org/ada/prod/adaf/prog_scholarship_prog.asp
Scholarship Name: Minority Dental Student Scholarship. *Academic Area: Medicine (dentistry). *Age Group: Undergraduate students. *Eligibility: African American, Hispanic American, and Native American students who are entering their second year of dental education may apply. Applicants must have a GPA of at least 3.0. *Application Process: Applicants should obtain an application from their dental schools and allied dental health programs. *Amount: Up to $2,500. *Deadline: July 31.

American Geological Institute (AGI)
Attn: Scholarship Coordinator
4220 King Street
Alexandria, VA 22302-1502
703-379-2480
http://www.agiweb.org/education/mpp.html
Scholarship Name: AGI Minority Geoscience Student Scholarships. *Academic Area: Geosciences. *Age Group: Undergraduate students, graduate students. *Eligibility: Applicants must be U.S. citizens and verifiable members of a minority group. They must also demonstrate financial need and be enrolled full time in an academic program leading to a degree in one of the geosciences. Applicable majors include the following: geology, geophysics, geochemistry, hydrology, meteorology, physical oceanography, planetary geology, or earth-science education. *Application Process: Applicants should submit a completed application along with a 250-word personal statement, official transcripts and ACT/SAT/GRE scores, and three letters of recommendation. Visit the association's Web site to download an application. *Amount: $500 to $3,000. *Deadline: March 1.

American Health and Beauty Aids Institute
Fred Luster, Sr. Education Foundation
401 North Michigan Avenue, Suite 2200
Chicago, IL 60611
312-644-6610
ahbai@sba.com
http://www.ahbai.org
Scholarship Name: Fred Luster, Sr. Education Foundation-College-Bound Student Scholarships. *Academic Area: Business, chemistry, engineering (general). *Age Group: High school seniors. *Eligibility: Candidates must be college-bound high school seniors enrolled at a four-year college with a minimum 3.0 grade point average. Applicants must demonstrate scholastic achievement, financial need, and participation in extracurricular activities. *Application Process: Applicants must submit a completed application form, two letters of recommendation, official high school transcript, proof of income (W2), and a black and white photograph (for publicity purposes). Visit the organization's Web site to download an application. *Amount: $250 to $500. *Deadline: April 15.

American Health and Beauty Aids Institute
Fred Luster, Sr. Education Foundation
401 North Michigan Avenue, Suite 2200
Chicago, IL 60611
312-644-6610
ahbai@sba.com
http://www.ahbai.org
Scholarship Name: Fred Luster, Sr. Education Foundation-Scholarship for Basic Cosmetology Students.

*Academic Area: Cosmetology. *Age Group: Open. *Eligibility: Applicants must be currently enrolled in or have been accepted by a state-approved cosmetic art training facility prior to applying for scholarship. Applicants must also have completed an initial 300 hours before funds are approved or disbursed to the facility, and they must have maintained a minimum of 85 percent passing grade and 85 percent attendance. Applications will be rated based on scholastic record, attendance record, participation in extracurricular activities, and awards and honors received. *Application Process: Applicants must submit a completed application form, copy of high school diploma or GED equivalent, official transcript from cosmetology training facility, two letters of recommendation, and a black and white photograph (for publicity purposes). Visit the organization's Web site to download an application. *Amount: $250 to $500. *Deadline: November 8.

American Indian College Fund

Citigroup Scholarship and Career Exploration Program
8333 Greenwood Boulevard
Denver, CO 80221
800-776-3863
kjewett@collegefund.org
http://www.collegefund.org
Scholarship Name: Citigroup Scholarship and Career Exploration Program. *Academic Area: Open. *Age Group: College students. *Eligibility: Applicants must be attending one of four tribal colleges in South Dakota and must be attending school full time. They must have attained and will maintain a 3.0 cumulative grade point average (students who have not yet completed a year of college will be required to achieve a 3.0 in the first year of the scholarship program); commit to organizing and participating in the Citigroup Career Exploration Day; have demonstrated leadership, service and commitment to the American Indian community; and be of American Indian or Alaskan Native decent. Scholarships are need based and students majoring in business, information technology, and computer science are highly encouraged to apply. *Application Process: Applicants should submit a completed application form and packet including a signed authorization form for release of information, official college transcripts, completed FAFSA, a 500-word personal statement, two letters of recommendation, tribal enrollment information or proof of descendancy, and

a small color photograph. Visit the association's Web site to download an application. *Amount: $2,500. *Deadline: May 1.

American Indian College Fund

Ford Motor Company/American Indian College Fund Corporate Scholars Program
8333 Greenwood Boulevard
Denver, CO 80221
800-776-3863
kjewett@collegefund.org
http://www.collegefund.org
Scholarship Name: Ford/American Indian College Fund Corporate Scholars Program. *Academic Area: Business, education, engineering (general), mathematics, science. *Age Group: College sophomores and above. *Eligibility: Applicants must have achieved sophomore status; declared a major in one of the aforementioned fields; have at least a 3.0 grade point average; demonstrate leadership and commitment to the American Indian community; be American Indian, Alaska Native, or Hawaii Native; have submitted a Federal Application for Federal Student Aid; and attend one of the 34 tribal colleges. *Application Process: Applicants should submit a completed application form, a one-page personal essay, a leadership evaluation form, a financial need analysis, proof of tribal enrollment or descendancy, a recommendation letter from a faculty member, and a small color photograph. Visit the association's Web site to download an application. *Amount: $2,000. *Deadline: May 1.

American Indian College Fund

General Mills Tribal College Scholarship Program
8333 Greenwood Boulevard
Denver, CO 80221
800-776-3863
kjewett@collegefund.org
http://www.collegefund.org
Scholarship Name: General Mills Tribal College Scholarship Program. *Academic Area: Open. *Age Group: College students. *Eligibility: Applicants must be enrolled in a tribal college or university in the states of California, Minnesota, or New Mexico. Applicants must be full-time students in either an associate or bachelor's degree program, have demonstrated exceptional academic achievement and financial need, and demonstrated leadership, service and commitment to the American Indian community. Applicants must be of American Indian

or Alaskan Native decent. *Application Process: Applicants should submit a completed application form and packet including a completed FAFSA. Visit the association's Web site to download an application. *Amount: $2,000. *Deadline: May 1.

American Indian College Fund
Lockheed Martin/American Indian College Fund
Scholars Program
8333 Greenwood Boulevard
Denver, CO 80221
800-776-3863
kjewett@collegefund.org
http://www.collegefund.org
Scholarship Name: Lockheed Martin/American Indian College Fund Scholarship. *Academic Area: Engineering (general). *Age Group: College sophomores and above. *Eligibility: Applicants must have achieved sophomore status and have declared a major in pre-engineering at a tribal college, with plans to graduate or transfer to an Accreditation Board for Engineering and Technology (ABET)-accredited institution, have at least a 3.0 grade point average, plan to complete a bachelor's degree in engineering at an ABET-accredited university or college, demonstrate leadership and commitment to the American Indian community, and be American Indian or Alaska Native with proof of descendancy. *Application Process: Applicants should submit a completed application form and packet including a signed authorization form for release of information, letter of acceptance from ABET-accredited institution if transferring, official college transcripts, a 500-word personal statement, two letters of recommendation, tribal enrollment information or proof of descendancy, a small color photograph, and a copy of their resume. Visit the association's Web site to download an application. *Amount: $5,000. *Deadline: August 1.

American Indian College Fund
Morgan Stanley/American Indian College Fund
Scholarship and Career Development Program
8333 Greenwood Boulevard
Denver, CO 80221
800-776-3863
kjewett@collegefund.org
http://www.collegefund.org
Scholarship Name: Morgan Stanley Tribal College Scholars Program. *Academic Area: Business, finance.

*Age Group: College students. *Eligibility: Applicants must be enrolled full time in an associate or bachelor's degree program at an accredited tribal college or university, have at least a 3.0 grade point average, demonstrate leadership and commitment to the American Indian community, and be an American Indian or Alaska Native. *Application Process: Applicants should submit a completed application form and packet, including proof of tribal enrollment or descendancy. Visit the association's Web site to download an application. *Amount: $2,500. *Deadline: May 1.

American Indian College Fund
Nissan North America Inc.
Tribal College Transfer Program
8333 Greenwood Boulevard
Denver, CO 80221
800-776-3863
kjewett@collegefund.org
http://www.collegefund.org
Scholarship Name: Nissan North America Scholars Program *Academic Area: Open. *Age Group: College sophomores. *Eligibility: Applicants must be college sophomores by the fall semester and enrolled full time in an associate degree program at a tribal college or university. Applicants should have demonstrated general academic achievement and plan to transfer to a bachelor's degree program at a tribal college or at a mainstream institution. Applicants must also have demonstrated leadership, service, and commitment to the American Indian community and be American Indian or Alaska Native with proof of descendancy. *Application Process: Applicants should submit a completed application form and packet including a signed authorization form for release of information, official college transcripts, 500-word personal statement, two letters of recommendation, tribal enrollment information or proof of descendancy, and a small color photograph. Visit the association's Web site to download an application. *Amount: $2,000. *Deadline: May 1.

American Indian Education Foundation
10029 SW Nimbus Avenue, Suite 200
Beaverton, OR 97008
866-866-8642
bcantor@nrc1.org
http://www.aiefprograms.org
Scholarship Name: Freshman Scholarship. *Academic

Area: Open. *Age Group: High school seniors. *Eligibility: Native American high school seniors are eligible to apply. Applicants must have an ACT score of at least 14 and attend school full time. *Application Process: Applicants should submit academic transcripts, a copy of their SAT or ACT scores, verification of acceptance into a university, a completed application, and an essay that details their personal, academic, and career interests; financial need; and service to the community (including the Native American community). Visit the foundation's Web site to download an application. *Amount: $3,000. *Deadline: May 4.

American Indian Education Foundation
10029 SW Nimbus Avenue, Suite 200
Beaverton, OR 97008
866-866-8642
bcantor@nrc1.org
http://www.aiefprograms.org
Scholarship Name: Paul Francis and Josephine Nipper Memorial Scholarship. *Academic Area: Open. *Age Group: High school seniors, undergraduate students. *Eligibility: Native American students who plan to or who are currently attending an accredited two- or four-year postsecondary institution may apply. Applicants must have an ACT score of at least 14, attend school full time, and show a strong commitment to improving their community. *Application Process: Applicants should submit academic transcripts, a copy of their SAT or ACT scores, verification of acceptance into a university, a completed application, and an essay that details their personal, academic, and career interests; financial need; and service to the community (including the Native American community). Visit the foundation's Web site to download an application. *Amount: Up to $2,500. *Deadline: May 4.

American Indian Education Foundation
10029 SW Nimbus Avenue, Suite 200
Beaverton, OR 97008
866-866-8642
bcantor@nrc1.org
http://www.aiefprograms.org
Scholarship Name: Undergraduate Scholarship. *Academic Area: Open. *Age Group: Undergraduate students. *Eligibility: Native American students who plan to return or who are currently attending an accredited two- or four-year postsecondary

institution may apply. Applicants must have an ACT score of at least 14 and attend school full time. *Application Process: Applicants should submit academic transcripts, a copy of their SAT or ACT scores, verification of acceptance into a university, a completed application, and an essay that details their personal, academic, and career interests; financial need; and service to the community (including the Native American community). Visit the foundation's Web site to download an application. *Amount: $1,500. *Deadline: May 4.

American Indian Graduate Center
4520 Montgomery Boulevard, NE, Suite 1B
Albuquerque, NM 87109
505-881-4584, 800-628-1920
http://www.aigc.com
Scholarship Name: The center, in cooperation with the United Negro College Fund and the Bill and Melinda Gates Foundation, offers the Gates Millennium Scholarship. *Academic Area: Open. *Age Group: High school seniors. *Eligibility: Minority students (including Native Americans) planning to enroll full time in a postsecondary institution are eligible to apply. Applicants must also have a GPA of at least 3.3 on a 4.0 scale, demonstrate leadership abilities, show financial need, and be citizens or legal permanent residents or nationals of the United States. *Application Process: Visit the center's Web site for information on application requirements. *Amount: Varies. *Deadline: January 13.

American Indian Science and Engineering Society (AISES)
2305 Renard, SE, Suite 200, PO Box 9828
Albuquerque, NM 87119-9828
505-765-1052
info@aises.org
http://www.aises.org
Scholarship Name: A.T. Anderson Memorial Scholarship. *Academic Area: Engineering (general), mathematics, medicine (general), natural resources, physical science, science. *Age Group: High school seniors, undergraduate students, graduate students. *Eligibility: Applicants must be enrolled as full-time students at an accredited four-year college or university or a two-year college or university. Applicants must also be current AISES members with a minimum GPA of 2.0. Proof of membership in an American Indian tribe is required (or proof

of 1/4 American Indian or Alaskan native blood). *Application Process: Applicants should submit a completed application form, a 500-word personal statement, two letters of recommendation, official transcripts, a resume, and proof of tribal enrollment. Visit the association's Web site for membership information and to download an application. *Amount: $1,000 for undergraduate students; $2,000 for graduate students. *Deadline: June 15.

American Indian Science and Engineering Society (AISES)

2305 Renard, SE, Suite 200, PO Box 9828
Albuquerque, NM 87119-9828
505-765-1052
info@aises.org
http://www.aises.org
Scholarship Name: Burlington Northern Santa Fe Foundation Scholarship. *Academic Area: Business, engineering (general), mathematics, medicine (general), science, technology. *Age Group: High school seniors. *Eligibility: Applicants must currently be high school seniors residing in one of the following states serviced by the Burlington Northern and Santa Fe Pacific Corporation and its affiliated companies: Arizona, California, Colorado, Kansas, Minnesota, Montana, New Mexico, North Dakota, Oklahoma, Oregon, South Dakota, and Washington. Applicants must also be current AISES members with a minimum 2.0 GPA. Proof of membership in an American Indian tribe is required (or proof of 1/4 American Indian or Alaskan native blood). *Application Process: Applicants should submit a completed application form, a 500-word personal statement, two letters of recommendation, official transcripts, a resume, and proof of tribal enrollment. Visit the association's Web site for membership information and to download an application. *Amount: $2,500. *Deadline: April 15.

American Indian Science and Engineering Society (AISES)

2305 Renard, SE, Suite 200, PO Box 9828
Albuquerque, NM 87119-9828
505-765-1052
info@aises.org
http://www.aises.org
Scholarship Name: EPA Tribal Lands Environmental Science Scholarship. *Academic Area: Engineering (environmental), science. *Age Group: Undergraduate students, graduate students. *Eligibility: Applicant

must be a full-time junior or senior or a full-time graduate student at an accredited four-year college or university or graduate college or university. Applicants must also be current AISES members with a minimum 2.7 GPA. Applicants must also be U.S. citizens or permanent U.S. residents. *Application Process: Applicants should submit a completed application form, a 500-word personal statement, two letters of recommendation, official transcripts, a resume, and proof of tribal enrollment. Visit the association's Web site for membership information and to download an application. *Amount: $4,000. *Deadline: June 15.

American Indian Science and Engineering Society (AISES)

2305 Renard, SE, Suite 200, PO Box 9828
Albuquerque, NM 87119-9828
505-765-1052
info@aises.org
http://www.aises.org
Scholarship Name: General Motors Engineering Scholarship. *Academic Area: Engineering (general). *Age Group: High school seniors, undergraduate students, graduate students. *Eligibility: Applicants must be enrolled as full-time students at an accredited college or university and must be current AISES members. Applicants must have a minimum cumulative GPA of 3.0. General Motors gives preference to electrical, industrial, or mechanical engineering majors. Applicants must provide proof of at least 1/4 American Indian blood or at least 1/4 Alaskan Native blood. *Application Process: Applicants should submit a completed application form, a 500-word personal statement, two letters of recommendation, official transcripts, a resume, and proof of tribal enrollment. Visit the association's Web site for membership information and to download an application. *Amount: $3,000. *Deadline: June 15.

American Indian Science and Engineering Society (AISES)

2305 Renard, SE, Suite 200, PO Box 9828
Albuquerque, NM 87119-9828
505-765-1052
info@aises.org
http://www.aises.org
Scholarship Name: Henry Rodriguez Reclamation College Scholarship and Internship. *Academic Area: Engineering (general), science. *Age Group: High school seniors, undergraduate students. *Eligibility:

Applicants must be enrolled as full-time students at an accredited college or university, current AISES members, and U.S. citizens or permanent residents. Applicants must have a minimum cumulative GPA of 2.50 and must be enrolled members of a federally recognized Indian tribe. They must also agree to serve an eight- to 10-week paid internship with the Bureau of Reclamation prior to graduation in either Washington, D.C., or Denver, Colorado. *Application Process: Applicants should submit a completed application form, a 500-word personal statement, two letters of recommendation, official transcripts, a resume, and proof of tribal enrollment. Visit the association's Web site for membership information and to download an application. *Amount: $5,000. *Deadline: June 15.

American Institute of Certified Public Accountants (AICPA)

AICPA Minority Initiatives Committee
1211 Avenue of the Americas
New York, NY 10036-8775
212-596-6200
http://www.aicpa.org/members/div/career/mini/smas.htm
Scholarship Name: Scholarship for Minority Accounting Students. *Academic Area: Accounting. *Age Group: Undergraduate students, graduate students. *Eligibility: Undergraduate minority students at regionally accredited institutions who have completed at least 30 semester hours of study (including six hours of accounting work) are eligible to apply. Applicants must also have a GPA of at least 3.3, be attending school full time, and be U.S. citizens. The scholarship is also available to graduate students who meet certain educational criteria. Contact the institute for more information. *Application Process: Application packets should include a letter of recommendation from either a faculty member or a certified public accountant, an official transcript, and a completed financial aid worksheet (included with the application form). Visit the institute's Web site to download an application. *Amount: $5,000. *Deadline: June 1.

American Library Association (ALA)

Scholarship Committee
50 East Huron Street
Chicago, IL 60611
800-545-2433, ext. 4277
scholarships@ala.org
http://www.ala.org/hrdr/scholarship
Scholarship Name: LITA/LSSI Minority Scholarship. *Academic Area: Library sciences. *Age Group: Graduate students. *Eligibility: Applicants must be U.S. or Canadian citizens currently enrolled in an ALA-accredited master's program who are qualified members of a principal minority group (American Indian or Alaskan native, Asian or Pacific Islander, African American, or Hispanic). Candidates must not have earned more than 12 hours toward a Master of Library Science degree. Economic need is considered when all other criteria are equal. This scholarship is awarded annually by the Library and Information Technology Association, a division of the American Library Association, and Library Systems and Services, Inc. *Application Process: An online application must be submitted, which includes a personal statement and three references. Official transcripts from your undergraduate university must be submitted by mail. Visit the association's Web site to submit an application. *Amount: $2,500. *Deadline: March 1.

American Library Association (ALA)

Scholarship Committee
50 East Huron Street
Chicago, IL 60611
800-545-2433, ext. 4277
scholarships@ala.org
http://www.ala.org/hrdr/scholarship
Scholarship Name: LITA/OCLC Minority Scholarship. *Academic Area: Library sciences. *Age Group: Graduate students. *Eligibility: Applicants must be U.S. or Canadian citizens currently enrolled in an ALA accredited master's program who are qualified members of a principal minority group (American Indian or Alaskan native, Asian or Pacific Islander, African-American, or Hispanic). Candidates must not have earned more than 12 hours toward a Master of Library Science degree. Economic need is considered when all other criteria are equal. The scholarship, awarded jointly annually by OCLC, Inc. and the Library and Information Technology Association, is designed to encourage the entry of qualified persons into the library and automation field who have a strong commitment to the use of automated systems in libraries. *Application Process: An on-line application must be submitted, which includes a personal statement and three references. Official transcripts from your undergraduate university must be submitted

by mail. Visit the association's Web site to submit an application. *Amount: $3,000. *Deadline: March 1.

American Library Association (ALA)

Attn: Wendy Prellwitz, ALA Office for Diversity
50 East Huron Street
Chicago, IL 60611
800-545-2433, ext. 5048
spectrum@ala.org
http://www.ala.org/hrdr/scholarship

Scholarship Name: Spectrum Scholarship. *Academic Area: Library sciences. *Age Group: Graduate students. *Eligibility: Applicants must be U.S. or Canadian citizens currently enrolled in an ALA-accredited program who are members of one of the following ethnic minorities: American Indian/Alaska Native, Asian, Black/African American, Hispanic/Latino, or Native Hawaiian/Other Pacific Islander. Applicant shall have completed no more than a third of the credit requirements toward her or his Master's of Library Information Science or school library media degree. *Application Process: An online application must be submitted, which includes a personal statement and three references. Official transcripts from your undergraduate university must be submitted by mail. Visit the association's Web site to submit an application. *Amount: $5,000. *Deadline: March 1.

American Meteorological Society (AMS)

Attn: Minority Scholarship
45 Beacon Street
Boston, MA 02108
617-227-2426, ext. 246
dfernand@ametsoc.org
http://www.ametsoc.org/amsstudentinfo/scholfeldocs

Scholarship Name: AMS/Industry Minority Scholarships. *Academic Area: Meteorology. *Age Group: High school seniors. *Eligibility: Applicants must be entering their freshman year of college in the fall and belong to a traditionally underrepresented minority group in the sciences—Hispanic, Native American, or Black/African American. Applicants must plan to pursue careers in the atmospheric or related oceanic and hydrologic sciences. *Application Process: Applicants should submit a completed application along with an official high school transcript, a copy of SAT or ACT scores, a 500-word essay, and a letter of recommendation from a high school teacher or guidance counselor. All originals must be mailed to the closest AMS local chapter listed at the bottom of

the application. Photocopies should be mailed to the AMS main office in Boston. Visit the association's Web site to download an application. *Amount: $3,000. *Deadline: February 11.

American Physical Society (APS)

Attn: APS Minority Scholarship
One Physics Ellipse
College Park, MD 20740
301-209-3232
http://www.aps.org/educ/com/scholars/index.cfm

Scholarship Name: American Physical Society Minority Scholarship for Undergraduate Physics Majors. *Academic Area: Physics. *Age Group: High school seniors, college freshmen and sophomores. *Eligibility: Applicants must be an African American, Hispanic American, or Native American U.S. citizen or permanent resident who is majoring in or planning to major in physics. *Application Process: Applications will be available for download from the society's Web site on November 1. Interested candidates may also write to the American Physical Society for more information. *Amount: $2,000 for the first year, $3,000 for renewal years. *Deadline: First Friday in February.

American Planning Association (APA)

Attn: Kriss Blank, Leadership Affairs Associate
APA Judith McManus Scholarship
122 South Michigan Avenue, Suite 1600
Chicago, IL 60603-6107
312-431-9100
kblank@planning.org
http://www.planning.org/institutions/scholarship.htm

Scholarship Name: Judith McManus Scholarship. *Academic Area: Planning. *Age Group: High school seniors, undergraduate students, graduate students. *Eligibility: Applicants must be women, U.S. citizens, and members of one of the following minority groups: African American, Hispanic American, or Native American. Applicants must demonstrate a commitment to planning, strong academic achievement and/or improvement, professional presentation, and financial need. *Application Process: Applicants must submit a completed application along with a two- to five-page personal background statement describing the student's career goals, two letters of recommendation, official transcripts of college work completed, written verification from the student's school of the average cost per academic year, a resume (optional), a copy of the student's acceptance letter (incoming students only), and a notarized statement of financial independence signed by the student's parent(s), also optional. Visit the APA's Web site to download an application. *Amount: $2,000 to $4,000. *Deadline: April 30.

American Speech-Language-Hearing Association

Attn: Emily Diaz
10801 Rockville Pike
Rockville, MD 20852
800-638-8255, ext. 4314
ediaz@asha.org
http://www.ashfoundation.org/foundation/grants

Scholarship Name: International Student Scholarship. *Academic Area: Medicine (general). *Age Group: Graduate students. *Eligibility: Applicants must be full-time international/minority students who demonstrate outstanding academic achievement. *Application Process: Interested candidates should write to the association for more information. Applications are available for download from the association's Web site. *Amount: $2,000 to $4,000. *Deadline: Contact the association for information.

American Speech-Language-Hearing Association

Attn: Emily Diaz
10801 Rockville Pike
Rockville, MD 20852
800-638-8255, ext. 4314
ediaz@asha.org
http://www.ashfoundation.org/foundation/grants
301-897-5700

Scholarship Name: Minority Student Scholarship. *Academic Area: Medicine (general). *Age Group: Graduate students. *Eligibility: Applicants must be racial/ethnic minority students who are U.S. citizens and who have been accepted into a graduate program. *Application Process: Interested candidates should write to the association for more information. Applications are available for download from the association's Web site. *Amount: $2,000 to $4,000. *Deadline: Contact the association for information.

American Water Works Association

Scholarship Committee
6666 West Quincy Avenue
Denver, CO 80235
303-347-6206
swheeler@awwa.org
http://www.awwa.org
303-347/6206

Scholarship Name: Holly A. Cornell Scholarship. *Academic Area: Engineering (water supply and treatment). *Age Group: Graduate students. *Eligibility: Applicants must be female and/or minority master's degree students in pursuit of advanced training in the field of water supply and treatment, must demonstrate a quality academic record, and have potential to provide leadership in the field of water supply and treatment. *Application Process: Applicants must submit a completed application, official transcripts of all university education, official copies of GRE scores (required), three letters of recommendation, a proposed curriculum of study, and a one- to two-page statement describing the student's career objectives. Visit the association's Web site to download an official application. *Amount: $5,000. *Deadline: January 15.

Asian American Journalists Association (AAJA)

Attn: Scholarship Committee
1182 Market Street, Suite 320
San Francisco, CA 94102
415-346-2051, ext. 102
brandons@aaja.org
http://www.aaja.org

Scholarship Name: AAJA/Cox Foundation Scholarship. *Academic Area: Broadcasting, journalism. *Age Group: High school seniors, undergraduate students, graduate students. *Eligibility: Applicants must be full-time students with a commitment to the field of journalism, possess sensitivity to Asian American and Pacific Islander issues as demonstrated by community involvement, have journalistic ability, and demonstrate financial need. *Application Process: Applicants should submit a completed application, resume, official transcripts (two copies), a 500-word personal essay, and work samples (which will not be returned). Three copies of the completed packet are required. Visit the association's Web site to download an application. *Amount: Up to $2,500. *Deadline: April 8.

Asian American Journalists Association (AAJA)

Attn: Scholarship Committee
1182 Market Street, Suite 320
San Francisco, CA 94102
415-346-2051, ext. 102
brandons@aaja.org
http://www.aaja.org

Scholarship Name: AAJA/S.I. Newhouse Foundation Scholarships. *Academic Area: Journalism. *Age Group: High school seniors, undergraduate students, graduate students. *Eligibility: Applicants must be full-time students with a commitment to the field of journalism, possess sensitivity to Asian American and Pacific Islander issues as demonstrated by community involvement, have journalistic ability, and demonstrate financial need. While the scholarship is open to all students, the AAJA especially encourages applicants from historically underrepresented Asian Pacific American groups, including Vietnamese, Cambodians, Hmong, and other Southeast Asians, South Asians, and Pacific Islanders. S.I. Newhouse scholarship winners will be eligible for summer internships with a Newhouse publication. *Application Process: Applicants should submit a completed application, resume, official transcripts (and two copies), a 500-word personal essay, and work samples (which will not be returned). Three copies of the completed packet are required. Visit the association's Web site to download an application. *Amount: Up to $5,000. *Deadline: April 8.

Asian American Journalists Association
Attn: Scholarship Committee
1182 Market Street, Suite 320
San Francisco, CA 94102
415-346-2051, ext. 102
brandons@aaja.org
http://www.aaja.org
Scholarship Name: Mary Moy Quan Ing Memorial Scholarship. *Academic Area: Journalism. *Age Group: High school seniors. *Eligibility: Applicants must plan on being full-time students with a commitment to the field of journalism, possess sensitivity to Asian American and Pacific Islander issues as demonstrated by community involvement, have journalistic ability, and demonstrate financial need. *Application Process: Applicants should submit a completed application, resume, official transcripts (two copies), a 500-word personal essay, and work samples (which will not be returned). Three copies of the completed packet are required. Visit the association's Web site to download an application. *Amount: $2,000. *Deadline: April 8.

Asian American Journalists Association
Attn: Scholarship Committee
1182 Market Street, Suite 320
San Francisco, CA 94102

415-346-2051, ext. 102
brandons@aaja.org
http://www.aaja.org
Scholarship Name: Minoru Yasui Memorial Scholarship. *Academic Area: Broadcasting, journalism. *Age Group: High school seniors, undergraduate students, graduate students. *Eligibility: Applicants must be full-time students with a commitment to the field of journalism, possess sensitivity to Asian American and Pacific Islander issues as demonstrated by community involvement, have journalistic ability, and demonstrate financial need. This scholarship is awarded to a promising male Asian American broadcaster. *Application Process: Applicants should submit a completed application, resume, official transcripts (two copies), a 500-word personal essay, and work samples (which will not be returned). Three copies of the completed packet are required. Visit the association's Web site to download an application. *Amount: $2,000. *Deadline: April 8.

Association for Women Geoscientists (AWG)
Attn: Minority Scholarship
PO Box 30645
Lincoln, NE 68503-0645
651-426-3316
minorityscholarship@awg.org
http://www.awg.org/eas/scholarships.html
Scholarship Name: AWG Minority Scholarship. *Academic Area: Geosciences. *Age Group: High school seniors, undergraduate students. *Eligibility: Applicants must be African American, Hispanic American, or Native American women pursuing or planning to pursue a degree in geology, geophysics, geochemistry, hydrology, meteorology, physical oceanography, planetary geology, or earth science education at an accredited college or university. *Application Process: Applicants must submit a completed application, a statement of their academic and career goals, two letters of recommendation, high school and college transcripts, and SAT or ACT scores. Visit the association's Web site to download an application as well as to find information about additional scholarships in geoscience available in select regional areas. *Amount: $5,000. *Deadline: May 15.

Association of Black Women Historians
Attn: Wanda A. Hendricks, Ph.D.
Attn: University of South Carolina
204 Flinn Hall

Columbia, SC 29208
803-777-4007
nationaldirector@abwh.org
http://www.abwh.org
Scholarship Name: Drusilla Dunjee Houston Memorial
Scholarship Award. *Academic Area: History. *Age
Group: Graduate students. *Eligibility: Candidates
must be African-American females. *Application
Process: Candidates must be nominated for the award.
*Amount: $300. *Deadline: August 31.

Association of Black Women Historians

Attn: Wanda A. Hendricks, Ph.D.
Attn: University of South Carolina
204 Flinn Hall
Columbia, SC 29208
803-777-4007
nationaldirector@abwh.org
http://www.abwh.org
Scholarship Name: Lillie M. Newton Hornsby Memorial
Award. *Academic Area: History. *Age Group: College
juniors and seniors. *Eligibility: Candidate must be an
African-American female with an accomplishment in
historical research. *Application Process: Candidates
must be nominated for the award. *Amount: $250.
*Deadline: September 1.

Association of Latino Professionals in Finance and Accounting (ALPFA)

Attn: Hispanic Scholarship Fund
510 West Sixth Street, Suite 400
Los Angeles, CA 90014
800-644-4223
HCF-Info@hispanicfund.org
http://www.alpfa.org/index.cfm?fuseaction=Page.
viewPage&pageId=354
Scholarship Name: The association, in conjunction
with the Hispanic College Fund, offers the ALPFA
Scholarship Program. *Academic Area: Accounting,
finance, information technology. *Age Group:
Undergraduate students, graduate students.
*Eligibility: Hispanic students who plan to enroll as
full-time undergraduate or graduate students in an
accounting, finance, information technology, or a
related field are eligible to apply. Applicants must be
also be U.S. citizens and have a minimum cumulative
3.0 GPA on a 4.0 scale. *Application Process: Visit the
Hispanic Scholarship Fund's Web site to download an
application. *Amount: Awards range from $1,000 to
$5,000. *Deadline: Typically at the end of March.

Association of Latino Professionals in Finance and Accounting (ALPFA)

510 West Sixth Street, Suite 400
Los Angeles, CA 90014
800-644-4223
http://www.alpfa.org/index.cfm?fuseaction=Page.
viewPage&pageId=354
Scholarship Name: The association, in conjunction with
the Bentley McCallum Graduate School of Business,
offers the Bentley Graduate Merit Scholarship.
*Academic Area: Accounting, finance. *Age Group:
Graduate students. *Eligibility: Hispanic students who
are active ALPFA members who have been accepted
to a graduate program at Bentley are eligible to
apply. *Application Process: Visit http://www.bentley.
edu/graduate/grad_app.pdf to download a graduate
school application, which includes information on the
scholarship. *Amount: Varies. *Deadline: April 15.

Association on American Indian Affairs

Attn: Lisa Wyzlic, Director of Scholarship Programs
966 Hungerford Drive, Suite 12-B
Rockville, MD 20850
240-314-7155
lw.aaia@verizon.net
http://www.indian-affairs.org
Scholarship Name: This association offers a variety of
scholarships for Native Americans. *Academic Area:
Open. *Age Group: Undergraduate students, graduate
students. *Eligibility: Applicants must show proof
of being at least 1/4 American Indian and proof of
tribal enrollment. Applicants must also be full-time
students, show financial need, and demonstrate
academic achievement. *Application Process:
Applicants should submit a completed application
form and packet including a financial need analysis
form with signature from their financial aid office,
a certificate of Indian blood and proof of tribal
enrollment, an essay addressing their educational
goals and life experiences (not to exceed three
pages), two letters of recommendation, most recent
transcripts, and current financial aid award letter. Visit
the association's Web site to download an application.
*Amount: Awards vary. *Deadline: August 1. Do not
mail applications prior to May 1.

Biophysical Society

Attn: Yvonne Cissel
9650 Rockville Pike
Bethesda, MD 20814

301-634-7114
ycissel@biophysics.org
http://www.biophysics.org
Scholarship Name: Herman R. Branson Summer Mini Course in Biophysics Scholarship. *Academic Area: Biophysics. *Age Group: College students. *Eligibility: Applicants must belong to an ethnic/racial minority and must have completed two semesters of calculus-based introductory general physics. *Application Process: Applicants must submit a completed application, a copy of their college transcripts, one letter of recommendation from a faculty member, and a 750-word essay detailing their career aspirations. Visit the association's Web site to download an application. *Amount: Full tuition, room and board, and a grant toward travel and living expenses for the five-week course. *Deadline: March 7

Black Caucus of the American Library Association
Attn: Michael Walker
E. J. Josey Scholarship Committee
849 West Wythe Street
Petersburg, VA 23803
http://www.bcala.org
Scholarship Name: E. J. Josey Scholarship Award. *Academic Area: Library sciences. *Age Group: Undergraduate students, graduate students. *Eligibility: Applicants must be African-American students enrolled in, or accepted to, ALA-accredited programs. *Application Process: Applicants must submit a cover letter providing their name, address, phone number, and graduate program; the name of their school; and their anticipated date of graduation. Applicants must also submit an essay of 1,000 to 1,200 words discussing the current theme chosen for each year. Essays will be judged on the basis of good argument development and critical analysis, clear language, conciseness, and creativity. Visit the organization's Web site for information about current essay topics. *Amount: $2,000. *Deadline: February 28.

Black Women Lawyers Association of Greater Chicago
321 South Plymouth Court, Suite 600
Chicago, IL 60604
312-554-2088
scholarshipbd@bwla.org
http://www.bwla.org
Scholarship Name: Black Women Lawyers Association of Greater Chicago Scholarship. *Academic Area: Law. *Age Group: Law students. *Eligibility: Applicants must be enrolled in an accredited law school in Illinois and be in good academic standing. *Application Process: Applicants must submit one official law school transcript, one letter of recommendation from a law school professor or staff member, a resume detailing their contact information and community service involvement, and a 1,000-word essay on a specific topic. Visit the association's Web site for further information on current essay questions. *Amount: Awards vary. *Deadline: March 4.

Black Women Lawyers Association of Los Angeles
Attn: Karen E. Pointer
Scholarship Selection Committee
PO Box 8179
Los Angeles, CA 90008
213-538-0137
kpointer@lpclawyers.com
http://www.blackwomenlawyersla.org
Scholarship Name: Black Women Lawyers Association of Los Angeles Scholarship. *Academic Area: Law. *Age Group: Law students. *Eligibility: Applicants must be second or third-year full-time law students or fourth-year night-program law students in attendance at an accredited law school or have passed the California first year student's examination. They must demonstrate financial need, be involved in community service projects, and exhibit strong academic achievement as well as legal writing ability. *Application Process: Applicants must submit a completed application along with required documents. Visit the association's Web site to request an application and instructions. *Amount: Awards vary. *Deadline: April 9.

Black Women Lawyers Association of New Jersey
PO Box 22524
Trenton, NJ 08607
abwlnj@yahoo.com
http://www.abwlnj.org
Scholarship Name: Black Women Lawyers Association of New Jersey Scholarship. *Academic Area: Law. *Age Group: Law students. *Eligibility: Contact the association for eligibility requirements. *Application Process: Contact the association for information on current scholarship opportunities. *Amount: Awards vary. *Deadline: Deadlines vary.

Catching the Dream Inc.
Attn: Scholarship Affairs Office
8200 Mountain Road, NE, Suite 203
Albuquerque, NM 87110

505-262-2351, ext. 116

NScholarsh@aol.com

http://www.catchingthedream.org/wst_page4.html

Scholarship Name: MESBEC Scholarship Program. *Academic Area: Business, computer science, education, engineering (general), mathematics, and science. *Age Group: High school seniors, undergraduate students, graduate students. *Eligibility: Applicants must be 1/4 Native American; enrolled in a federally recognized, state recognized, or terminated tribe; and plan to or be currently attending school full time. They should also have high ACT or SAT scores, excellent grades, work experience, leadership skills, and a commitment to their Native American community. *Application Process: Applicants must submit proof of high school completion, college admission, and tribal enrollment; an essay detailing their career plans; and a completed application, which is available for download at the organization's Web site. *Amount: $500 to $5,000. *Deadline: Varies.

Catching the Dream Inc.

Attn: Scholarship Affairs Office

8200 Mountain Road, NE, Suite 203

Albuquerque, NM 87110

505-262-2351, ext. 116

NScholarsh@aol.com

http://www.catchingthedream.org/wst_page4.html

Scholarship Name: The Native American Leadership Education Scholarship Program is open to Native Americans who are paraprofessionals in Indian schools. *Academic Area: Counseling, education. *Age Group: High school seniors, undergraduate students, graduate students. *Eligibility: Applicants must be 1/4 Native American; enrolled in a federally recognized, state recognized, or terminated tribe; and plan to or be currently attending school full time. They should also have high ACT or SAT scores, excellent grades, work experience, leadership skills, and a commitment to their Native American community. *Application Process: Applicants must submit proof of high school completion, college admission, and tribal enrollment; an essay detailing their career plans; and a completed application, which is available for download at the organization's Web site. *Amount: $500 to $5,000. *Deadline: Varies.

Catching the Dream Inc.

Attn: Scholarship Affairs Office

8200 Mountain Road, NE, Suite 203

Albuquerque, NM 87110

505-262-2351, ext. 116

NScholarsh@aol.com

http://www.catchingthedream.org/wst_page4.html

Scholarship Name: Tribal Business Management Scholarship. *Academic Area: Business, economics, finance, management. *Age Group: High school seniors, undergraduate students, graduate students. *Eligibility: Applicants must be 1/4 Native American; enrolled in a federally recognized, state recognized, or terminated tribe; and plan to or be currently attending school full time. They should also have high ACT or SAT scores, excellent grades, work experience, leadership skills, and plan to work in economic development for tribes. *Application Process: Applicants must submit proof of high school completion, college admission, and tribal enrollment; an essay detailing their career plans; and a completed application, which is available for download at the organization's Web site. *Amount: $500 to $5,000. *Deadline: Varies.

Chi Eta Phi Sorority Inc.

3029 13th Street, NW

Washington, DC 20009

202-232-3858

chietaphi@erols.com

http://www.chietaphi.com

Scholarship Name: Aliene Carrington Ewell Scholarship. *Academic Area: Nursing (general). *Age Group: Undergraduate students. *Eligibility: Applicants must currently be pursuing a nursing degree and demonstrate scholastic ability, financial need, and leadership potential. Although a large number of sorority members are African American, this scholarship is open to students of all races. *Application Process: Contact the sorority via e-mail for information on application availability. *Amount: Awards vary. *Deadline: Deadlines vary.

Chi Eta Phi Sorority Inc.

3029 13th Street, NW

Washington, DC 20009

202-232-3858

chietaphi@erols.com

http://www.chietaphi.com

Scholarship Name: Mabel Keaton Staupers Scholarship. *Academic Area: Nursing (general). *Age Group: Undergraduate students, graduate students. *Eligibility: Applicants must be pursuing a baccalaureate, master's, or doctoral degree in nursing. Applicants should have contributed to the recruitment and retention of minorities into nursing and the advancement of minority nurses in education and nursing and have demonstrated leadership skills. Applicants must also be members of both Chi Eta Phi and the American Nurses Association. *Application Process: Contact the sorority via e-mail for information on application availability. *Amount: Awards vary. *Deadline: Deadlines vary.

Chinese American Medical Society (CAMS)

Attn: David Y. Wang, M.D.
Chairman, CAMS Scholarship Committee
171 East 84th Street, Apartment 33B
New York, NY 10028
212-744-1646
dwang007@yahoo.com
http://www.camsociety.org
Scholarship Name: CAMS Scholarships. *Academic Area: Medicine (dentistry), Medicine (general), science. *Age Group: Undergraduate students, graduate students. *Eligibility: Applicants must demonstrate either academic excellence and/or financial need. *Application Process: Applicants should submit a completed application form along with a letter from the dean of students verifying good standing, two letters of recommendation, transcripts, a personal statement, and current vitae. Since some scholarships are allotted for merit and others financial hardship, those with financial hardship should also submit a personal letter stating these hardships as well as a letter from the dean or a teacher corroborating this statement. Visit the organization's Web site to download an application. *Amount: Inquire by e-mail for information about the awards. *Deadline: March 31.

Conference of Minority Public Administrators (COMPA)

Attn: Chris Snead, COMPA Awards Committee
22 Lincoln Street
Hampton, VA 23669
757-727-6377
csndad@hampton.gov
http://www.natcompa.org
Scholarship Name: Ronald H. Brown Memorial Scholarship. *Academic Area: Open. *Age Group: High school seniors. *Eligibility: Minorities who attend a public high school in the city where the Conference of Minority Public Administrators holds its annual conference (which varies by year) may apply. Applicants must also have a minimum GPA of 3.25 on a 4.0 scale and a minimum ACT/SAT score of 22 or 1000. *Application Process: Applicants should submit

an application along with an acceptance letter to a four-year institution of higher learning, official high school transcripts and ACT/SAT scores, and a two-page essay describing how the student's future goals align with Ronald H. Brown's philosophy of fighting to create opportunities for people of every race, social class, and nationality. Visit the association's Web site to find the applicable city for each given year as well as to download an application form. *Amount: $1,000. *Deadline: Contact the organization for further information.

Conference of Minority Transportation Officials (COMTO)

Attn: Paralee Shivers, National Scholarship Chairperson
COMTO National Scholarship Program
818 18th Street, NW, Suite 850
Washington, DC 20006
202-530-0551
pcheatham@comto.org
http://www.comto.org/start.htm
Scholarship Name: This organization offers numerous scholarships to minorities. *Academic Area: Transportation. *Age Group: High school seniors, undergraduate students, graduate students. *Eligibility: Applicants should visit the organization's Web site for specific eligibility requirements for individual awards. *Application Process: Applicants should submit a completed application along with two letters of recommendation, an acceptance letter from their university/college (where applicable), official transcripts, a resume, a 500-word cover letter with introduction and career goals, and a head-shot (3 x 5) photo. Winners must agree to attend an award luncheon or send a videotape of their acceptance of the award. *Amount: $1,500 to $10,000. *Deadline: March 31.

Congressional Black Caucus Foundation (CBCF)

1720 Massachusetts Avenue, NW
Washington, DC 20036
202-263-2800
http://www.cbcfinc.org
Scholarship Name: CBC Spouses Education Scholarship. *Academic Area: Education. *Age Group: High school seniors, undergraduate students, graduate students. *Eligibility: Applicants must be academically talented and highly motivated students who intend to pursue full-time undergraduate, graduate, or doctoral degrees. Applicants must have a minimum 2.5 GPA, demonstrate academic achievement, exhibit

leadership ability, and participate in community service activities. All applicants must reside or attend school in a congressional district represented by a Congressional Black Caucus member. *Application Process: Applicants should submit a completed application form and packet including a resume, high school or college transcripts, two letters of recommendation, a 500-word personal essay, and a recent photo. Visit the foundation's Web site to download an application. Applications should be mailed to the applicant's local CBCF office; visit the foundation's Web site to determine the address of your local office. *Amount: Awards vary. *Deadline: May 31.

Congressional Black Caucus Foundation

1720 Massachusetts Avenue, NW
Washington, DC 20036
202-263-2800
http://www.cbcfinc.org

Scholarship Name: CBC Spouses Performing Arts Scholarship. *Academic Area: Performing arts (general). *Age Group: High school seniors, undergraduate students, graduate students. *Eligibility: Applicants must be academically talented and highly motivated students who intend to pursue full-time undergraduate, graduate, or doctoral degrees. Applicants must have a minimum 2.5 GPA, demonstrate academic achievement, exhibit leadership ability, and participate in community service activities. All applicants must reside or attend school in a congressional district represented by a Congressional Black Caucus member. *Application Process: Applicants should submit a completed application form and packet including a resume, high school or college transcripts, two letters of recommendation, a 500-word personal essay, and a recent photo. Applicants must also submit a video recording of their most recent performance. Applications and videos must be submitted to the Local Scholarship Selection Committee for review. Visit the foundation's Web site to download an application and to determine the address of your local office. *Amount: $3,000 *Deadline: May 31.

Congressional Black Caucus Foundation

1720 Massachusetts Avenue, NW
Washington, DC 20036
202-263-2800
http://www.cbcfinc.org

Scholarship Name: CBC Spouses Cheerios Brand Health Initiative Scholarship. *Academic Area:

Medicine (general). *Age Group: High school seniors, undergraduate students, graduate students. *Eligibility: Applicants must be academically talented and highly motivated students who intend to pursue full-time undergraduate, graduate, or doctoral degrees. Applicants must have a minimum 2.5 GPA, demonstrate academic achievement, exhibit leadership ability, and participate in community service activities. All applicants must reside or attend school in a congressional district represented by a Congressional Black Caucus member. *Application Process: Applicants should submit a completed application form and packet including a resume, high school or college transcripts, two letters of recommendation, a 500-word personal essay, and a recent photo. Visit the foundation's Web site to download an application. Applications should be mailed to the applicant's local CBCF office; visit the foundation's Web site to determine the address of your local office. *Amount: Awards vary. *Deadline: May 31.

Congressional Black Caucus Foundation (CBCF)

1720 Massachusetts Avenue, NW
Washington, DC 20036
202-263-2800
http://www.cbcfinc.org

Scholarship Name: CBCF Vivien Thomas Scholarship for Medical Science and Research. *Academic Area: Medicine (general), science. *Age Group: High school seniors, undergraduate students. *Eligibility: Applicants must intend to focus on improving human health, exemplify high academic standards, and demonstrate need of financial assistance to realize their dreams of earning a college degree. *Application Process: Applicants should submit a completed application form and packet including a resume, high school or college transcripts, two letters of recommendation, a 500-word personal essay, and a recent photo. Visit the foundation's Web site to download an application. Applications should be mailed to the applicant's local CBCF office; visit the foundation's Web site to determine the address of your local office. This award is sponsored by GlaxoSmithKline. *Amount: Awards vary. *Deadline: May 31.

Congressional Hispanic Caucus Institute (CHCI)

CHCI Scholarship Awards
911 Second Street, NE
Washington, DC 20002
800-392-3532
rcasas@chci.org

http://www.chci.org

Scholarship Name: CHCI Scholarship Award. *Academic Area: Open. *Age Group: High school students, undergraduate students, graduate students. *Eligibility: Applicants should be U.S. citizens or legal permanent residents with a history of consistent active participation in public service-oriented activities. Applicants should be accepted into an accredited community college, four-year university, or a graduate/professional program and must be enrolled as full-time students. Applicants should also demonstrate financial need and have good writing skills. *Application Process: Applicants should submit a completed application along with two letters of recommendation in sealed and signed envelopes, a resume outlining all extracurricular activities, responses to two essay questions, a copy of their Student Aid Report, and a self-addressed stamped postcard. Visit the organization's Web site to download an application. *Amount: $2,500 (to attend a four-year university or graduate school); $1,000 (to attend a two-year community college). *Deadline: April 15.

Eddie Robinson Foundation

Attn: Christina DeMesquita
3391 Peachtree Road, NE, Suite 105
Atlanta, GA 30326
404-475-8408, ext. 205
info@eddierobinson.com
http://www.eddierobinson.com

Scholarship Name: Eddie Robinson Eighth Grade and High School Senior Scholarship. *Academic Area: Open. *Age Group: Eighth grade students, high school seniors. *Eligibility: Applicants must have distinguished themselves as leaders among their peers in the school and community, excel in the athletic arena while maintaining excellence in the classroom, and display a can-do attitude despite obstacles. *Application Process: Applicants should submit a typed list of scholastic achievements, athletic accomplishments, community involvement activities, and extracurricular activities, a 500-word typed essay about how they will mirror the values of Eddie Robinson, official transcripts, ACT or SAT scores (high school students), and two letters of recommendation. Awards are distributed once a student can prove enrollment in an institution of higher education. *Amount: Awards vary. *Deadline: Contact the foundation for deadlines.

Health Resources and Services Administration

U.S. Department of Health and Human Services
200 Independence Avenue, SW
Washington, DC 20201
202-619-0257, 877-696-6775
http://bhpr.hrsa.gov/dsa/sds.htm

Scholarship Name: Scholarship for Disadvantaged Students. *Academic Area: Medicine (general), nursing (general). *Age Group: College students. *Eligibility: Disadvantaged students, including minority students, who are enrolled in health professions and nursing programs are eligible to apply. Applicants must demonstrate financial need and be citizens, nationals, or lawful permanent residents of the United States. *Application Process: Applicants should apply for this scholarship at the student financial aid office of the school they plan to attend. *Amount: Varies. *Deadline: Varies.

Hispanic Association of Colleges and Universities (HACU)

HACU Scholarship Program
One Dupont Circle, NW, Suite 605
Washington, DC 20036
202-467-0893
hnip@hacu.net
http://www.hacu.net/hacu/Student_Resources1_
EN.asp?SnID=1721883662

Scholarship Name: HACU Scholarship. *Academic Area: Open. *Age Group: High school seniors, undergraduate, graduate students. *Eligibility: Applicants should be attending a HACU member or partner college or university and meet all additional criteria for the scholarship for which they are applying. Scholarship requirements vary. Visit the association's Web site for a complete listing of scholarship and their eligibility requirements. *Application Process: Scholarship materials are to be sent to the financial aid office at HACU-member and -partner colleges and universities. Applications are available for download during the early months of each year. Visit the organization's Web site for more information or send inquiries via e-mail. Amount: $500 to $2,000. *Deadline: May 27.

Hispanic College Fund (HCF)

HCF Scholarship Selection Committee
1717 Pennsylvania Avenue, NW, Suite 460
Washington, DC 20006
800-644-4223
hcf-info@hispanicfund.org

http://www.hispanicfund.org

Scholarship Name: El Nuevo Constructor Scholarship. *Academic Area: Construction. *Age Group: High school seniors, undergraduate students. *Eligibility: Hispanic students who are pursuing a bachelor's or associate degree in a construction-related field may apply. Applicants must also have a GPA of at least 3.0; be U.S. citizens; and attend school full time. *Application Process: Visit the HCF's Web site to apply online. *Amount: Awards range from $500 to $5,000. *Deadline: April 15.

Hispanic College Fund (HCF)

HCF Scholarship Selection Committee
1717 Pennsylvania Avenue, NW, Suite 460
Washington, DC 20006
800-644-4223
hcf-info@hispanicfund.org
http://www.hispanicfund.org

Scholarship Name: Lockheed Martin Scholarship. *Academic Area: Computer science, engineering (general). *Age Group: High school seniors, undergraduate students. *Eligibility: Hispanic students who are pursuing a bachelor's degree in computer science, engineering, or a related major may apply. Applicants must have a GPA of at least 3.0, be U.S. citizens, and attend school full time. *Application Process: Visit the HCF's Web site to apply online. *Amount: Awards range from $500 to $5,000. *Deadline: April 15.

Hispanic College Fund (HCF)

HCF Scholarship Selection Committee
1717 Pennsylvania Avenue, NW, Suite 460
Washington, DC 20006
800-644-4223
hcf-info@hispanicfund.org
http://www.hispanicfund.org

Scholarship Name: M&T Bank Scholarship. *Academic Area: Business, computer science, engineering (general). *Age Group: High school seniors, undergraduate students. *Eligibility: Hispanic students residing in Maryland, Virginia, Pennsylvania, or New York are eligible to apply. Applicants must have a GPA of at least 3.0; be pursuing a bachelor's degree in business, computer science, engineering, or a business-related major; be U.S. citizens; and attend school full time. *Application Process: Visit the HCF's Web site to apply online. *Amount: Awards range from $500 to $5,000. *Deadline: April 15.

Hispanic College Fund (HCF)

HCF Scholarship Selection Committee
1717 Pennsylvania Avenue, NW, Suite 460
Washington, DC 20006
800-644-4223
hcf-info@hispanicfund.org
http://www.hispanicfund.org

Scholarship Name: Sallie Mae Fund First in My Family Scholarship. *Academic Area: Open. *Age Group: High school seniors, undergraduate students. *Eligibility: Hispanic students who are the first person in their families to attend college may apply. Applicants must have a GPA of at least 3.0; be U.S. citizens; and attend school full time. *Application Process: Visit the HCF's Web site to apply online. *Amount: Awards range from $500 to $5,000. *Deadline: April 15.

Hispanic Dental Association

1224 Centre West, Suite 400B
Springfield, IL 62704
800-852-7921
HispanicDental@hdassoc.org
http://www.hdassoc.org

Scholarship Name: Colgate-Palmolive Company and Hispanic Dental Association Foundation Scholarship. *Academic Area: Medicine (dentistry), public health. *Age Group: Graduate students. *Eligibility: Applicants must be accepted to or currently enrolled in a Master's in Public Health or a Dental Public Health program, be of Hispanic origin (at least one parent of Hispanic descent), be a permanent resident of the United States, have credentials in a dental profession either in the United States or abroad, and show evidence of commitment and dedication to serve the Hispanic community. *Application Process: Applicants should submit a completed application along with a curriculum vitae, an advanced education verification form, and two letters of recommendation. Visit the association's Web site to download an application. *Amount: $10,000. *Deadline: August 1.

Hispanic Dental Association (HDA)

1224 Centre West, Suite 400B
Springfield, IL 62704
800-852-7921
HispanicDental@hdassoc.org
http://www.hdassoc.org

Scholarship Name: Dr. Genaro Romo, Jr. & HDA Foundation Scholarship. *Academic Area: Medicine (dentistry) *Age Group: Undergraduate students.

*Eligibility: Applicants must be accepted to or currently enrolled at the University of Illinois Chicago School of Dentistry, Dental and Dental Hygiene. *Application Process: Applicants should submit a completed application along with supporting documents. Contact the association for further information about the application process. *Amount: $500 to $1,000. *Deadline: Varies.

Hispanic Dental Association (HDA)
1224 Centre West, Suite 400B
Springfield, IL 62704
800-852-7921
HispanicDental@hdassoc.org
http://www.hdassoc.org
Scholarship Name: Dr. Juan D. Villarreal & HDA Foundation Scholarship. *Academic Area: Medicine (dentistry). *Age Group: Dental students. *Eligibility: Applicants must be accepted to or currently enrolled in an accredited dental school in the state of Texas. Applicants must demonstrate scholastic achievement, a commitment to community service, leadership skill, and a commitment to improving health in the Hispanic community. *Application Process: Applicants should submit a completed application along with supporting documents. Contact the association for further information about the application process. *Amount: $500 to $1,000. *Deadline: Contact the association for deadline information.

Hispanic Dental Association (HDA)
1224 Centre West, Suite 400B
Springfield, IL 62704
800-852-7921
HispanicDental@hdassoc.org
http://www.hdassoc.org
Scholarship Name: Procter & Gamble Oral Care & HDA Foundation Scholarship. *Academic Area: Medicine (dental hygiene), medicine (dentistry). *Age Group: Undergraduate students, dental students. *Eligibility: Applicants must be accepted to or currently enrolled in an accredited dental, dental hygiene, dental assisting, or dental technician program. They must demonstrate scholastic achievement, a commitment to community service, leadership skill, and a commitment to improving health in the Hispanic community. *Application Process: Applicants should submit a completed application along with supporting documents. Contact the association for further information about the application process. *Amount: $500 to $1,000. *Deadline: Varies.

Hispanic National Bar Association Foundation
Attn: Duard Bradshaw, President
815 Connecticut Avenue, NW, Suite 500
Washington, DC 20006
330-434-3000
dbradshaw@rodericklinton.com
http://www.hnba.com
Scholarship Name: This foundation offers scholarships for law students administered through the Hispanic Scholarship Fund. *Academic Area: Law. *Age Group: Law students. *Eligibility: Students interested in being considered for this program must be graduate students accepted to an accredited law school in the United States. Students must have a 3.0 GPA or higher and be enrolled as full-time students. Applicants should visit the Hispanic Scholarship Fund's Web site at http://www.hsf.net for further information about specific eligibility requirements for individual scholarships. *Application Process: Applications are available beginning August 1 through October 15. Visit the Hispanic Scholarship Fund's Web site to download applications. *Amount: Awards vary. *Deadline: October 15.

Hispanic Public Relations Association (HPRA)
Attn: Susie Gonzalez
College Outreach Committee Director
660 S. Figueroa Street, Suite 1140
Los Angeles, CA 90017
sgonzalez_hpra@yahoo.com
http://www.hprala.org
Scholarship Name: HPRA Scholarship. *Academic Area: Public relations. *Age Group: College juniors and seniors. *Eligibility: Applicants must be deserving Hispanic students attending four-year colleges and universities in Southern California. Applicants must have at least a 2.7 cumulative GPA and a 3.0 GPA in their major. Preference is given to students majoring in public relations. *Application Process: Applicants should submit a completed application form, one letter of recommendation from an academic professor, a letter of recommendation from an employer or internship supervisor (if available), official university transcripts, a one- to two-page personal statement explaining the applicant's career and educational aspirations as well as his or her involvement in the Hispanic community, a one-page resume, and a writing sample (press kits, newspaper clips, short stories, research papers). Contact Susie Gonzalez via e-mail with questions. *Amount: Awards vary. *Deadline: July 15.

Hispanic Scholarship Fund

55 Second Street, Suite 1500
San Francisco, CA 94105
877-473-4636
scholar1@hsf.net
http://www.hsf.net

Scholarship Name: The fund offers a variety of scholarships to Hispanic students. Since 1975, it has awarded more than 68,000 scholarships in excess of $144 million. *Academic Area: Open. *Age Group: High school seniors, undergraduate students, graduate students. *Eligibility: Applicants must be U.S. citizens or permanent residents, be of Hispanic heritage, apply for federal financial aid using the FAFSA, be completing their first undergraduate or graduate degree, and attend school full time. *Application Process: Applicants must submit a completed transcript, an enrollment verification form, recommendations, and a completed application (including essays). *Amount: Varies by scholarship. *Deadline: Varies.

Hispanic-Serving Health Professions Schools

1120 Connecticut Avenue, NW, Suite 260
Washington, DC 20036
202-293-2701
hshps@hshps.org
http://www.hshps.com

Scholarship Name: Hispanic-Serving Health Professions Schools is the only national organization representing Hispanic-serving health professions schools. It provides information on scholarships offered by corporations, federal agencies, and other nonprofit organizations *Academic Area: Medicine (general). *Age Group: Varies by scholarship. *Eligibility: Varies by scholarship. *Application Process: Varies by scholarship. *Amount: Varies by scholarship. *Deadline: Varies by scholarship.

Indian Health Service

Division of Health Professions Support
801 Thompson Avenue, Suite 120
Rockville, MD 20852
301-443-6197
http://www.ihs.gov/JobsCareerDevelop/DHPS/
   Scholarships/Scholarship_index.asp

Scholarship Name: Health Professions Pregradate Scholarship. *Academic Area: Medicine (dentistry), medicine (general). *Age Group: High school seniors, undergraduate students. *Eligibility: Applicants must be American Indian or Alaska Native, be enrolled or plan to enroll in a bachelor degree program, and plan to serve Native American people at the completion of their training. *Application Process: The applicant should submit two faculty/employer recommendations, a completed application, an official transcript, and documentation of Native American heritage. An application is available at the service's Web site. *Amount: Full tuition and related fees, plus a stipend for daily living needs. *Deadline: March 28.

Indian Health Service

Division of Health Professions Support
801 Thompson Avenue, Suite 120
Rockville, MD 20852
301-443-6197
http://www.ihs.gov/JobsCareerDevelop/DHPS/
   Scholarships/Scholarship_index.asp

Scholarship Name: Health Professions Preparatory Scholarship. *Academic Area: Medicine (general), nursing (general). *Age Group: High school seniors, undergraduate students. *Eligibility: Applicants must be American Indian or Alaska Native, be enrolled or plan to enroll in a preprofessional postsecondary education program, and plan to serve Native American people at the completion of their training. *Application Process: The applicant should submit two faculty/employer recommendations, a completed application, an official transcript, and documentation of Native American heritage. An application is available at the service's Web site. *Amount: Full tuition and related fees, plus a stipend for daily living needs. *Deadline: March 28.

Indian Health Service

Division of Health Professions Support
801 Thompson Avenue, Suite 120
Rockville, MD 20852
301-443-6197
http://www.ihs.gov/JobsCareerDevelop/DHPS/
   Scholarships/Scholarship_index.asp

Scholarship Name: Health Professions Scholarship. *Academic Area: Medicine (dental hygiene), medicine (dentistry), medicine (general), medicine (sonography), nursing (general), psychology, social work. *Age Group: College juniors and seniors, graduate students. *Eligibility: Applicants must be American Indian or Alaska Native, be enrolled or plan to enroll in an undergraduate or graduate program, and plan to serve Native American people at the completion of their training. Applicants must also be willing to work for the Indian Health Service one year for every year of financial aid that they receive *Application Process: The applicant should submit two faculty/employer recommendations, a completed application, an official transcript, and documentation of Native American heritage. An application is available at the service's Web site. *Amount: Full tuition and related fees, plus a stipend for daily living needs. *Deadline: March 28.

Intel Corporation
Corporate U.S. Headquarters
2200 Mission College Boulevard, PO Box 58119
Santa Clara, CA 95052-8119
408-765-8080
http://www.intel.com/community
Scholarship Name: This company offers scholarships to women, including minorities. *Academic Area: Computer science, engineering (electrical), engineering (computer), information technology. *Age Group: High school seniors. *Eligibility: Intel awards renewable scholarships for women and underrepresented minority students at a number of collaborating universities at Intel sites in the United States. These scholarship programs are administered at the relevant Intel sites and are available only for study at the designated collaborating universities. Visit the company's Web site for more information. *Application Process: Applicants must apply for scholarships through the collaborating universities. Applications should be requested from these organizations. Visit Intel's Web site for a complete list of participating institutions in the United States and abroad. *Amount: Awards vary. *Deadline: Deadlines vary.

Intertribal Timber Council
Attn: Education Committee
1112 NE 21st Avenue
Portland, OR 97232
503-282-4296
itc1@teleport.com
http://www.itcnet.org
Scholarship Name: Truman D. Picard Scholarship. *Academic Area: Natural resources. *Age Group: High school seniors, undergraduate students. *Eligibility: Applicants should be planning to pursue or pursuing a career in natural resources and demonstrate financial need, as well as academic achievement. *Application Process: Applicants should submit a letter, not to exceed two pages, demonstrating

their interest in natural resources, commitment to education, community and culture, academic merit, and financial need. Applicants should also submit a resume, three letters of reference, and validated enrollment in a federally recognized tribe or Native Alaska Corporation as established by the U.S. government. High school seniors should provide documented proof of application to an institution to study in the area of natural resources as well as high school transcripts. College students should provide documented proof of studying in the area of natural resources along with college transcripts. *Amount: $1,200 for high school students; $1,800 for students already attending college. *Deadline: Contact the council for deadlines.

Japanese American Citizens League (JACL)
1765 Sutter Street
San Francisco, CA 94115
415-921-5225
jacl@jacl.org
http://www.jacl.org
Scholarship Name: JACL Scholarship. *Academic Area: Open. *Age Group: High school seniors, undergraduate students, graduate students. *Eligibility: Applicants must be active National JACL members at either the individual or student/youth level. For membership applications, visit the league's Web site. Also visit the JACL's Web site for eligibility requirements for specific scholarships. *Application Process: Applicants should submit a personal statement, letter of recommendation, official transcripts including SAT and/or ACT test scores, and documentation of work experience and community involvement. Visit the league's Web site to download an application or request one by sending a self addressed and stamped size #10 envelope to the organization. *Amount: Awards vary. *Deadline: March 1 entering freshmen. April 1 for everyone excluding entering freshmen.

Kappa Phi Iota Sorority
kappa_phi_iota@hotmail.com
http://www.angelfire.com/nj/kappaphiiota
Scholarship Name: This historically black sorority with a strong literary focus offers scholarships to women. *Academic Area: English/literature, writing. *Age Group: Students (of all ages). *Eligibility: Applicants must be members of Kappa Phi Iota and exhibit excellence and potential in writing. *Application

Process: Applicants should contact their local chapters for more information about scholarship funds available. Or, contact the national office by e-mail for application information. *Amount: Awards vary. *Deadline: Deadlines vary.

Korean-American Scientists and Engineers Association (KSEA)

1952 Gallows Road, Suite 300
Vienna, VA 22182
703-748-1221
sejong@ksea.org
http://www.ksea.org/index.asp

Scholarship Name: This association offers numerous scholarships for students of Korean heritage. *Academic Area: Engineering (general), science. *Age Group: Varies by scholarship. *Eligibility: Applicants must be undergraduate or graduate students in the United States; of Korean heritage, majoring in science, engineering, or a related field; and members of the KSEA. Students may apply for KSEA membership at the time of scholarship application. *Application Process: Applicants should submit a completed application form, a curriculum vitae that includes work experience and extracurricular activities, official transcripts, test scores (relevant SAT or GRE scores), a 500-word essay on either their career goals and their contributions to society or the meaning of Korean heritage in their life, and three letters of recommendation. Visit the association's Web site to download an application. *Amount: $1,000. *Deadline: February 15.

KPMG Foundation

Attn: Anita C. English, Scholarship Administrator
Three Chestnut Ridge Road
Montvale, NJ 07645
acenglish@kpmg.com
http://www.kpmgfoundation.org/index.asp

Scholarship Name: Minority Accounting Doctoral Scholarship. *Academic Area: Accounting. *Age Group: Graduate students. *Eligibility: African American, Hispanic American, or Native American students who have been accepted into a full time doctoral program are eligible to apply. Applicants must be citizens of the United States and be enrolled full time. *Application Process: Applicants should submit the following materials: a cover letter detailing their reasons for pursuing a Ph.D. in accounting, a copy of their most current resume, copies of their

undergraduate and graduate transcripts, and a completed application. *Amount: Up to $10,000. *Deadline: May 1.

Lambda Alpha Upsilon Fraternity

Attn: Orlando Ortiz
29 John Street, PMB 181
New York, NY 10038
programming@lambdas.com
http://www.lambdas.com

Scholarship Name: Jose Chiu Scholarship. *Academic Area: Open. *Age Group: Undergraduate students. *Eligibility: Applicant should be a member of Lambda Alpha Upsilon. The award's purpose is to cover the cost of books for a deserving, qualified brother pursing undergraduate studies. *Application Process: Applicants should contact Orlando Ortiz via e-mail for an application and for further information. *Amount: Awards vary. *Deadline: Contact the organization for deadlines.

Lambda Alpha Upsilon Fraternity

Attn: Orlando Ortiz
29 John Street, PMB 181
New York, NY 10038
programming@lambdas.com
http://www.lambdas.com

Scholarship Name: Lambda Way Scholarship Fund. *Academic Area: Education. *Age Group: College students. *Eligibility: Applicant should not have a previous affiliation with the Hispanic-interest fraternity, Lambda Alpha Upsilon, and should have achieved a GPA of 3.0 or better. *Application Process: Applicants should contact Orlando Ortiz via e-mail for an application and for further information. *Amount: Awards vary. *Deadline: Contact the organization for deadlines.

Lambda Theta Nu Sorority

1220 Rosecrans, #543
San Diego, CA 92106
communications@lamdathetanu.org
http://www.lambdathetanu.org

Scholarship Name: Lambda Scholarships are available at the local chapter level. *Academic Area: Open. *Age Group: High school seniors. *Eligibility: Applicants must be females of Latino heritage with a dedication to community service and empowerment of the Latino community. Applicants also must be planning to attend an accredited community college, university, or technical or vocational school. *Application Process: Applicants must submit a completed application to the appropriate local chapter (which can be found on the sorority's Web site). A personal statement addressing family background, scholastic achievements, educational and career goals, commitment to Latin community, and financial need should also be enclosed, along with one letter of recommendation from a high school administrator, teacher, or community leader and official high school transcripts. Visit the sorority's Web site to download an application. *Amount: Awards vary. *Deadline: May 1.

Latin American Educational Foundation (LAEF)

Scholarship Selection Committee
904 West Colfax Avenue, Suite 103
Denver, CO 80204
303-446-0541
carmen@laef.org
http://www.laef.org
Scholarship Name: LAEF Scholarship. *Academic Area: Open. *Age Group: High school seniors, undergraduate students. *Eligibility: Applicants must be residents of the state of Colorado; of Hispanic heritage and/or actively involved in the Hispanic community; accepted to an accredited college, university, or vocational school; maintain a minimum 3.0 cumulative grade point average; and fulfill at least 10 hours of community service during the year of funding. Applicants must also demonstrate financial need. *Application Process: Applicants should submit a completed application, your most recent federal income tax returns (or your parents' return if you are under age 24), a one-page personal essay, a list of community service and extracurricular activities, two letters of recommendation, relevant high school or college transcripts, and verification of SAT and/or ACT scores. Visit the organization's Web site to download the application. *Amount: Awards vary. *Deadline: February 15. Applications should not be mailed before September 1.

Latin American Professional Women's Association

Attn: Ms. Magdalena Duran
3514 North Broadway, PO Box 31532
Los Angeles, CA 90031
213-227-9060
Scholarship Name: Latin American Professional Women's Association Scholarship. *Academic Area: Open. *Age Group: Age 23 and up. *Eligibility: Applicant must be a female of Hispanic decent who is returning to school. *Applicsilon Process: Applicants should contact the association by mail for an application. *Amount: $500. *Deadline: April 1.

Latino Medical Student Association

2550 Corporate Place, Suite C202
Monterey Park, CA 91754
lmsaregional@lmsa.net
http://www.lmsa.net
Scholarship Name: Janine Gonzalez MCAT Scholarship. *Academic Area: Medicine (general). *Age Group: Premedical students. *Eligibility: Applicants must demonstrate financial need, academic, and extracurricular achievement. *Application Process: Applications are available for download from the association's Web site in September. Visit the association's Web site to fill out a membership registration form to be updated regarding current and new scholarship opportunities. *Amount: Awards vary. *Deadline: January 8.

Latino Professional Network

PO Box 6019
Boston, MA 02209
617-247-1818
info@lpn.org
http://www.lpn.org
Scholarship Name: This organization offers scholarship opportunities for Hispanic Americans. *Academic Area: Open. *Age Group: Varies by scholarship. *Eligibility: Candidates should contact the network for eligibility requirements and information. Scholarships offered are in partnership with Harvard University and Bentley College. *Application Process: Contact the network regarding the availability of scholarships and the application process. *Amount: Awards vary. *Deadline: Varies.

La Unidad Latina Foundation

Lambda Upsilon Lambda Fraternity
359 Prospect Avenue
Brooklyn, NY 11215
foundation@launidadlatina.org
http://foundation.launidadlatina.org
Scholarship Name: La Unidad Latina Foundation Scholarship. *Academic Area: Open. *Age Group: College students. *Eligibility: Contact the foundation for information about eligibility requirements. *Application Process: Contact the foundation for

information about application procedures. *Amount: $250 to $1,000. *Deadline: Varies.

League of United Latin American Citizens (LULAC)

2000 L Street, NW, Suite 610
Washington, DC 20036
202-833-6130
Lnescaaward@aol.com
http://www.lulac.org

Scholarship Name: GE Foundation/LULAC Scholarships. *Academic Area: Business, engineering. *Age Group: College sophomores through seniors. *Eligibility: Applicants must be full-time students pursuing a bachelor's degree at an accredited college or university in the United States, have a college grade point average of at least 3.25 on a 4.0 scale, and must be a U.S. citizen or legal resident. *Application Process: Applicants should submit a completed and signed application, college transcript, letters of reference from three adults, and a typed personal statement of not more than 300 words describing their professional and career goals. Visit the league's Web site to download an application. *Amount: $5,000. *Deadline: July 15.

League of United Latin American Citizens (LULAC)

2000 L Street, NW, Suite 610
Washington, DC 20036
202-833-6130
Lnescaaward@aol.com
http://www.lulac.org

Scholarship Name: General Motors/LULAC Scholarships. *Academic Area: Engineering (general). *Age Group: High school seniors, undergraduate students. *Eligibility: Applicants must be full-time students pursuing a bachelor's degree at an accredited college or university in the United States. *Application Process: Applicants should submit a completed application packet. Visit the league's Web site to download an application. *Amount: $2,000. *Deadline: Contact the league for deadline information.

Los Angeles Council of Black Professional Engineers

Attn: AL-BEN Scholarship Committee
PO Box 881029
Los Angeles, CA 90009
310-635-7734
corettak@earthlink.net
http://www.lablackengineers.org

Scholarship Name: The AL-BEN Scholarship Awards and Incentives Program. *Academic Area: Computer science, engineering (general), mathematics, science. *Age Group: High school seniors, undergraduate students. *Eligibility: Applicants should demonstrate academic achievement and a commitment to community service. While there are no restrictions on where applicants are from, preference is given to Southern California residents. *Application Process: Applicants should submit a completed application, two letters of recommendation, a two-page essay, and official transcripts. Visit the association's Web site to download an application. *Amount: $500 to $1,000. *Deadline: March 5.

Magic Johnson Foundation

9100 Wilshire Boulevard, Suite 700 East
Beverly Hills, CA 90212
310-256-4400
scholars@magicjohnson.org
http://www.magicjohnson.org

Scholarship Name: Taylor Michaels Scholarship. *Academic Area: Open. *Age Group: High school seniors. *Eligibility: Applicants must be planning to attend a four-year college or university, have a GPA of at least 2.5, and be a resident of Atlanta, Cleveland, Houston, Los Angeles, or New York. Applicants should also be involved in extracurricular activities or community service activities. Recipients will be required to participate in Life and Practical Skills classes conducted by the Magic Johnson Foundation and must attend the annual week-long Leadership Conference. Graduating scholars are required to become peer mentors to incoming scholarship recipients as well as to volunteer for the organization. *Application Process: The downloadable application is not available from the Web site. Contact the foundation by e-mail for application information. *Amount: $1,000 to full scholarships. *Deadline: Contact the foundation for deadline information.

Media Action Network for Asian Americans (MANAA)

MANAA Scholarship
PO Box 11105
Burbank, CA 91510
manaaletters@yahoo.com
http://www.manaa.org

Scholarship Name: MANAA Media Scholarship. *Academic Area: Film/video, writing. *Age Group: Undergraduate students, graduate students.

*Eligibility: Applicants must desire to advance a positive and enlightened understanding of the Asian Pacific American experience in the mainstream media. Applicants must exhibit strong academic achievement and personal merit. Financial need is also considered. *Application Process: Applicants should submit a copy of all official transcripts, completed financial aid documents, two letters of recommendation, and a double-spaced essay of not more than 1,000 words. A work sample consisting of a short film or screenplay is highly recommended. *Amount: $1,000. *Deadline: June 1.

Mexican American Legal Defense and Educational Fund (MALDEF)

MALDEF Law School Scholarship Program
634 South Spring Street, 11th Floor
Los Angeles, CA 90014
213-629-2512
http://www.maldef.org
Scholarship Name: MALDEF Law School Scholarship. *Academic Area: Law. *Age Group: Law students. *Eligibility: Applicants can be entering their first, second, or third year of law school, but must be attending full-time for the upcoming school year to qualify. Applicants must demonstrate involvement in and commitment to service in the Latino community through the legal profession, academic and professional achievement, and financial need. *Application Process: Applicants should submit a completed and signed MALDEF application, a current resume, a typed 750-word personal statement, an official undergraduate transcript (or photocopy), official law school transcripts (if the applicant has already completed some law school), a letter of recommendation describing involvement in the Latino community, a letter of recommendation from a professor, a completed financial need statement, and a copy of the LSDAS Report with LSAT scores. Visit the fund's Web site to download an application. *Amount: $3,000 to $7,000. *Deadline: October 1.

National Action Council for Minorities in Engineering (NACME)

440 Hamilton Avenue, Suite 302
White Plains, NY 10601-1813
914-539-4010
scholarships@nacme.org
http://www.nacme.org
Scholarship Name: This association offers scholarship funding for minority students. *Academic Area: Engineering (general). *Age Group: Varies by scholarship. *Eligibility: Applicants must be African American, American Indian, or Latino Americans. *Application Process: This association has partnered with 32 universities to create the NACME Scholars (Block Grant) Program. Applicants should visit the association's Web site to view the participating colleges and universities and to discover the application process for each one. Contact NACME for additional information. *Amount: Awards vary. *Deadline: Deadlines vary.

National Alliance of Black School Educators (NABSE)

310 Pennsylvania Avenue, SE
Washington, DC 20003
202-608-6310
debharvil@aol.com
http://www.nabse.org
Scholarship Name: This association offers scholarships to minorities. *Academic Area: Education. *Age Group: Varies by scholarship. *Eligibility: Contact the foundation of the NABSE for further information. *Application Process: Contact the foundation of the NABSE for information on the availability of funds and the process for applying. This association also lists links to more than 30 other sources of scholarship aid for minority students in a variety of disciplines. *Amount: Awards vary. *Deadline: Varies.

National Asian Pacific American Bar Association (NAPABA) Foundation

Attn: Parkin Lee, Esq.
New York Life Investment Management, LLC
51 Madison Avenue, Room 1104
New York, NY 10010
foundation@napaba.org
http://www.napaba.org
Scholarship Name: Anheuser-Busch NAPABA Law Foundation Presidential Scholarship. *Academic Area: Law. *Age Group: Law students. *Eligibility: Applicants must be enrolled as a law degree candidate at an accredited law school in the United States at least half-time. *Application Process: Applicant should submit a completed application form along with an official copy of the applicant's most recent law school transcript (or for first-year law students, a statement from their law school certifying that they are law degree candidates enrolled at least half-time), a resume, and two letters of recommendation from

persons not related to the applicant. Applicants who wish to demonstrate financial need may also submit a copy of their law school application for financial assistance. Visit the foundation's Web site to download an application. *Amount: $5,000. *Deadline: September 13.

National Asian Pacific American Bar Association (NAPABA) Foundation

Attn: Parkin Lee, Esq.
New York Life Investment Management, LLC
51 Madison Avenue, Room 1104
New York, NY 10010
foundation@napaba.org
http://www.napaba.org
Scholarship Name: Diane Yu Loan Repayment Assistance Program. *Academic Area: Law. *Age Group: Early career professionals. *Eligibility: Applicants must be recent law graduates who are working in Asian Pacific American legal service organizations. *Application Process: Applicants should submit a completed application form along with an official copy of their law school transcripts, a resume, a 500-word essay, and two letters of recommendation from persons not related to the applicant. Applicants who wish to demonstrate financial need may also submit a copy of their law school application for financial assistance. This award is paid toward a student's student loan debt. Visit the foundation's Web site to download an application. *Amount: $5,000, for each of two years. *Deadline: September 13.

National Asian Pacific American Bar Association (NAPABA) Foundation

Attn: Parkin Lee, Esq.
New York Life Investment Management, LLC
51 Madison Avenue, Room 1104
New York, NY 10010
foundation@napaba.org
http://www.napaba.org
Scholarship Name: NAPABA Law Foundation Scholarship. *Academic Area: Law. *Age Group: Law students. *Eligibility: Applicants must be enrolled as a law degree candidate at an accredited law school in the United States at least half-time. *Application Process: Applicant should submit a completed application form along with an official copy of the applicant's most recent law school transcript (or for first-year law students, a statement from their law school certifying that they are law degree candidates

enrolled at least half-time), a resume, and two letters of recommendation from persons not related to the applicant. Applicants who wish to demonstrate financial need may also submit a copy of their law school application for financial assistance. Visit the foundation's Web site to download an application. *Amount: $2,500. *Deadline: September 13.

National Association for Black Geologists and Geophysicists (NABGG)

Attn: Scholarship Committee
4212 San Felipe, Suite 420
Houston, TX 77027-2902
nabgg_us@hotmail.com
http://www.nabgg.com
Scholarship Name: NABGG Scholarship. *Academic Area: Geosciences. *Age Group: Undergraduate students, graduate students. *Eligibility: Applicants must be members of a minority group, U.S. citizens (or possess a valid student visa), and maintain a 2.5 GPA. *Application Process: Applicants should submit a completed application along with a personal statement, official transcripts, and two letters of recommendation. Visit the association's Web site to download an application. *Amount: Awards vary. *Deadline: April 30.

National Association for Equal Opportunity in Higher Education (NAFEO)

NAFEO Member Services and Program Office
8701 Georgia Avenue, Suite 200
Silver Spring, MD 20910
301-650-2240
http://www.nafeo.org
Scholarship Name: This organization offers scholarships to minorities. *Academic Area: Mathematics. *Age Group: College students. *Eligibility: Varies by scholarship. This organization offers scholarships to students to attend summer math programs at select universities. *Application Process: Visit the association's Web site for links to specific programs at select universities. *Amount: Awards vary. *Deadline: Deadlines vary.

National Association of Black Accountants (NABA)

7249-A Hanover Parkway
Greenbelt, MD 20770
301-474-6222
http://www.nabainc.org
Scholarship Name: NABA Scholarship Fund. *Academic

Area: Accounting, business, finance. *Age Group: Undergraduate students, graduate students. *Eligibility: Applicants must be members of an ethnic minority and be currently enrolled full time as an undergraduate freshman, sophomore, junior, or first-year senior or as a graduate student enrolled or accepted into a Master's of Accountancy program. Applicants must be paid NABA members. Dues can be submitted with a scholarship application. Applicants must have a 2.5 minimum overall GPA. *Application Process: Applicants must submit a completed application form along with official transcripts, financial aid transcripts, a Student Aid Report, a resume, and a 500-word personal biography discussing the applicant's career objectives, leadership abilities, and community involvement. Applicants may also include information about how they have overcome a personal, family, or financial hardship. Applications are available by contacting the national office directly. *Amount: $500 to $6,000. *Deadline: December 31.

National Association of Black Journalists

8701-A Adelphi Road
Adelphi, MD 20783-1716
301-445-7100, ext. 108
http://www.nabj.org
Scholarship Name: This association offers numerous scholarships to minorities. *Academic Area: Journalism. *Age Group: Undergraduate students, graduate students. *Eligibility: Applicants must be attending an accredited four-year institution in the United States or be candidates for graduate school. Applicants should contact the association for further eligibility requirements for specific scholarships. *Application Process: Applicants should submit four copies of a completed application, two letters of recommendation, samples of work, resume, transcripts, and a 500- to 800-word essay. Applicants can apply for up to two separate scholarship awards and should contact the association for further information on individual scholarships. *Amount: Up to $5,000. *Deadline: April 1.

National Association of Black Scuba Divers

PO Box 91630
Washington, DC 20090-1630
800-521-6227
secy@nabsdivers.org
http://www.nabsdivers.org

Scholarship Name: This organization offers scholarship funds to minority students. *Academic Area: Science. *Age Group: Open. *Eligibility: Applicants should contact the organization about the specific eligibility requirements and availability of scholarship funds. *Application Process: Applicants should contact the association to receive information about application procedures and scholarship funds available. *Amount: Varies. *Deadline: Varies.

National Association of Black Telecommunications Professionals

Attn: Cynthia Newman
2020 Pennsylvania Avenue, NW
PO Box 735
Washington, DC 20006
800-946-6228
http://www.nabtp.org
Scholarship Name: This organization traditionally offers scholarships to minorities. *Academic Area: Business, communications science, computer science, engineering (general). *Age Group: Students. *Eligibility: Applicants must be majoring in a telecommunications-related field (computer science, business, engineering, mass communication), and show notable achievements through academics, extracurricular, and community activities. *Application Process: Applicants should contact the organization for updated application procedures and scholarship availability. *Amount: $2,000. Deadline: Contact the organization for deadlines.

National Association of Health Services Executives (NAHSE)

NAHSE Educational Assistance Program
8630 Fenton Street, Suite 126
Silver Spring, MD 20910
202-628-3953
http://www.nahse.org
Scholarship Name: This organization offers several scholarships to minorities. *Academic Area: Medicine (general). *Age Group: High school seniors, undergraduate students, graduate students. *Eligibility: Applicants must be able to demonstrate financial need and must have a minimum GPA of 2.5 (for undergraduates) and 3.0 (for graduate students). Applicants must also be NAHSE members. *Application Process: Applicants should submit a completed application along with as essay as described in the application materials,

resume, transcripts (all that are applicable), three reference letters, two pictures (3 x 5), and a NAHSE student membership application (if dues have not already been paid). Visit the association's Web site to download an application. *Amount: Awards vary. *Deadline: July 1.

National Association of Hispanic Journalists
1000 National Press Building
529 14th Street, NW
Washington, DC 20045-2001
202-662-7145
nahj@nahj.org
http://www.nahj.org
Scholarship Name: This organization offers numerous scholarships to students of Hispanic descent. *Academic Area: Broadcasting, journalism. *Age Group: High school seniors, undergraduate students, graduate students. *Eligibility: Applicants should visit the organization's Web site to view a complete listing of individual scholarship in their respective categories since each scholarship has different requirements for eligibility. *Application Process: Applicants should submit a completed (typed) application along with most recent W-2 forms (parents/guardians or the applicants if they are independent), a one-page resume, work samples (limit four), two letters of recommendation, official transcripts (in sealed envelopes), and a typed autobiographical essay written in the third person as a news story. Visit the organization's Web site to download an application as well as to review any additional application items necessary for specific scholarships. *Amount: $1,000 to $10,000. *Deadline: January 28.

National Association of Hispanic Nurses
Awards/Scholarship Committee Chair
1501 16th Street, NW
Washington, DC 20036
202-387-2477
latinanrse@socal.rr.com
http://www.thehispanicnurses.org
Scholarship Name: AETNA/National Coalition Of Ethnic Minority Nurse Associations Scholars Program. *Academic Area: Nursing (general). *Age Group: Undergraduate students, graduate students. *Eligibility: Hispanic nursing students who are currently enrolled in four-year or master's degree nursing programs may apply. Applicants must also have a GPA of at least 3.0 and be members of the

National Association of Hispanic Nurses. *Application Process: Applicants should submit two letters of recommendation that support their ability to perform research to help eliminate disparities in health care, an official sealed transcript, a completed application, and a three- to four-page statement that details their qualifications and their leadership in the Hispanic community. *Amount: $2,000. *Deadline: April 15.

National Association of Hispanic Nurses
Awards/Scholarship Committee Chair
1501 16th Street, NW
Washington, DC 20036
202-387-2477
latinanrse@socal.rr.com
http://www.thehispanicnurses.org
Scholarship Name: Juanita Robles-Lopez/Pampers Parenting Institute and Proctor and Gamble Scholarship. *Academic Area: Nursing (midwifery), nursing (neonatal). *Age Group: Undergraduate students. *Eligibility: Hispanic nursing students who are currently enrolled in a graduate maternal child nursing program may apply. Applicants must also have a GPA of at least 3.0 and be members of the National Association of Hispanic Nurses. *Application Process: Applicants should submit two letters of recommendation, an official sealed transcript, a completed application, and a three- to four-page statement detailing the maternal child needs affecting the Hispanic community and their potential leadership in this area. *Amount: $2,000. *Deadline: April 15.

National Association of Hispanic Nurses
Awards/Scholarship Committee Chair
1501 16th Street, NW
Washington, DC 20036
202-387-2477
latinanrse@socal.rr.com
http://www.thehispanicnurses.org
Scholarship Name: National Scholarship. *Academic Area: Nursing (general). *Age Group: Undergraduate students. *Eligibility: Hispanic nursing students who are currently enrolled in an accredited school of nursing and who are U.S. citizens or legal residents of the United States may apply. Applicants must also have a GPA of at least 3.0, show potential for leadership in nursing, demonstrate financial need, and be members of the National Association of Hispanic Nurses. *Application Process: Applicants should submit one letter of recommendation, an official

sealed transcript, a completed application, and other documentation. *Amount: Varies. *Deadline: April 15.

National Association of Negro Business and Professional Women's Clubs (NANBPWC)
1806 New Hampshire Avenue, NW
Washington, DC 20009
202/483-4206
nanbpwc@aol.com
http://www.nanbpwc.org
Scholarship Name: Dr. Julianne Malveaux Scholarship. *Academic Area: Economics, journalism. *Age Group: College sophomores or juniors. *Eligibility: Applicants must be African-American women who are United States citizens and have a 3.0 GPA. *Application Process: Applicants should submit a completed application. Visit the association's Web site to download an application, or request application information by e-mail. *Amount: $1,000. *Deadline: March 1.

National Association of Negro Business and Professional Women's Clubs (NANBPWC)
1806 New Hampshire Avenue, NW
Washington, DC 20009
202/483-4206
nanbpwc@aol.com
http://www.nanbpwc.org
Scholarship Name: NANBPWC, Inc. Scholarship. *Academic Area: Business. *Age Group: High school seniors. *Eligibility: Applicants must aspire to business or professional education at the college or university level, Applicants should have a 3.0 GPA and must be referred by a NANBPWC club member. *Application Process: Applicants should submit a completed application along with a 300-word minimum essay addressing the topic, "Why is education important to me?" Visit the association's Web site to download an application, or request application information by e-mail. *Amount: $1,000. *Deadline: March 1.

National Black Association for Speech-Language and Hearing
Attn: Dr. Elise Davis-McFarland
Trident Technical College
PO Box 118067
Charleston, SC 29423-8067
honors@nbaslh.org
http://www.nbaslh.org
Scholarship Name: This association offers scholarships for minorities. *Academic Area: Medicine (general).

*Age Group: Varies by scholarship. *Eligibility: Candidates should contact the organization by e-mail for information on eligibility. *Application Process: Candidates should contact the organization by e-mail for application information. *Amount: Awards vary. *Deadline: Varies.

National Black Law Student Association (NBLSA)
1225 11th Street, NW
Washington, DC 20001-4217
education@nblsa.org
http://www.nblsa.org
Scholarship Name: This organization offers three essay-based scholarships for minorities. *Academic Area: Law. *Age Group: Varies by scholarship. *Eligibility: Applicants must be members of the NBLSA. *Application Process: The directions, criteria, and essays for the scholarships are posted on the NBLSA Web site each September 1. *Amount: $500 to $1,000. *Deadline: October 15.

National Black MBA Association (NBMBAA)
Attn: Lori Johnson
180 North Michigan Avenue
Chicago, IL 60601
312-236-2622, ext. 8086
scholarship@nbmbaa.org
http://www.nbmbaa.org
Scholarship Name: MBA Scholarship. *Academic Area: Business. *Age Group: Graduate students. *Eligibility: Applicants must be attending graduate school full time in the United States and must be members of a minority group. *Application Process: Applicants should submit a two-page, typed essay that addresses one of the topics listed on the association's Web site. Essays should have a cover page with essay title and author's name. To accommodate blind review, ONLY the cover page should contain the author's name. Applicants should also submit a resume, and sealed transcripts of all college coursework. In addition to the scholarship award, recipients are required to attend the Association's Annual Conference and Exposition, which is paid for (registration, housing, and travel) by the organization. *Amount: $7,000 to $12,500. *Deadline: May 13.

National Black MBA Association (NBMBAA)
Attn: Lori Johnson
180 North Michigan Avenue
Chicago, IL 60601
312-236-2622, ext. 8086

scholarship@nbmbaa.org
http://www.nbmbaa.org
Scholarship Name: NBMBAA Undergraduate
Scholarship. *Academic Area: Business. *Age Group:
Undergraduate students. *Eligibility: Applicants
must be minority students. *Application Process: This
scholarship is implemented at the local chapter level
only. Applicants should visit the organization's Web
site for a listing of local chapters. Applicants should
contact their local chapter directly. *Amount: $1,000.
*Deadline: Deadlines vary by chapter.

National Black Nurses' Association (NBNA)
Scholarship Committee
8630 Fenton Street, Suite 330
Silver Springs, MD 20910-3803
800-575-6298
NBNA@erols.com
http://www.nbna.org
Scholarship Name: This organization offers scholarships
for minorities. *Academic Area: Nursing (general).
*Age Group: Undergraduate students. *Eligibility:
Applicant must be currently enrolled in a nursing
program (BSN, AD, diploma, LPN, or LVN) and in good
scholastic standing. Applicant must also be a member
of the NBNA, including a local-chapter member, and
must have at least one full year of school remaining.
*Application Process: Applicants should submit
a completed application form, official transcripts
from an accredited school or nursing, a two-page
essay, and two letters of recommendation—one
from the applicant's school of nursing and one from
the applicant's local chapter. Applicants may also
choose to send supporting materials that document
participation in student nurse activities and
involvement in the African-American community. Visit
the association's Web site to download an application.
*Amount: $500 to 2,000. *Deadline: April 15.

National Black Police Association (NBPA)
NBPA Scholarship Award
3251 Mt. Pleasant Street, NW, 2nd Floor
Washington, DC 20010-2103
202-986-2070
nbpanatofc@worldnet.att.net
http://www.blackpolice.org/Scholarship.html
Scholarship Name: Alphonso Deal Scholarship Award.
*Academic Area: Criminal justice. *Age Group: High
school seniors. *Eligibility: Applicants must be
United States citizens, of good character, and be
accepted by a college or university (two-year colleges

are acceptable). *Application Process: Applicant
should submit a completed application, high school
transcript, and a recommendation from his or her
principal, counselor, or teacher. Visit the association's
Web site to download an application. *Amount:
Awards vary. *Deadline: June 1.

**National Center for American Indian Enterprise
Development (NCAIED)**
NCAIED Scholarship Committee
953 East Juanita Avenue
Mesa, AZ 85204
800-462-2433, ext. 234
events@ncaied.org
http://www.ncaied.org/fundraising/scholar.html
Scholarship Name: American Indian Fellowship in
Business Scholarship. *Academic Area: Business. *Age
Group: College juniors and seniors, graduate students.
*Eligibility: Native Americans who are studying
business at the postsecondary level are eligible to
apply. *Application Process: Applicants must submit
academic transcripts, documentation of tribal
enrollment, a completed application (available for
download at the center's Web site), a statement that
details their reasons for pursuing higher education
and post-college career plans, and separate essays
(250 words each) that specifically address their
community involvement, personal challenges, and
business experience (paid or volunteer). *Amount:
Varies. *Deadline: August 4.

National Medical Fellowships Inc.
Need-Based Scholarship Program
Five Hanover Square, 15th Floor
New York, NY 10004
212-483-8880
http://www.nmf-online.org/Programs/Scholarships/
scholarships.htm
Scholarship Name: Need-Based Scholarship Program.
*Academic Area: Medicine (physicians). *Age Group:
Medical students. *Eligibility: Students from ethnic
groups that are underrepresented in the medical
profession (specifically, African Americans, Mexican
Americans, Native Americans, Alaska Natives,
Native Hawaiians, and mainland Puerto Ricans)
may apply. Applicants must be U.S. citizens who
have been accepted to an accredited U.S. medical
school. *Application Process: The application packet
should include a completed application, a signed
personal statement, financial aid transcripts, a letter
of recommendation, and copies of federal tax forms.

Visit the organization's Web site to download an application. *Amount: Awards range from $500 to $10,000. *Deadline: June 30.

National Newspaper Publishers Association
3200 13th Street, NW
Washington, DC 20010
202-588-8764
blackpressusa@nnpa.org
http://www.nnpa.org
Scholarship Name: This organization has scholarship funds for minorities. *Academic Area: Journalism. *Age Group: College students. *Eligibility: For eligibility requirements, contact the association by e-mail. *Application Process: Applicants should contact the organization by e-mail for information about available scholarship and the application process. *Amount: Awards vary. *Deadline: Varies.

National Society of Black Engineers
1454 Duke Street
Alexandria, VA 22314
703-549-2207, ext. 305
scholarships@nsbe.org
http://www.nsbe.org
Scholarship Name: This organization offers many corporate scholarships for minorities. *Academic Area: Engineering (general). *Age Group: Varies by scholarship. *Eligibility: All scholarships require academic excellence. However, some do not require as high of a GPA as others. Visit the society's Web site after September 15 for complete eligibility requirements for individual scholarships. *Application Process: Applicants can download applications and instructions from the society's Web site. *Amount: $500 to $7,500. *Deadline: Deadlines vary.

National Society of Black Physicists (NSBP)
NSBP Scholarship
6704G Lee Highway
Arlington, VA 22205
703-536-4207
scholarship@nsbp.org
http://www.nsbp.org
Scholarship Name: Elmer S. Imes and Robert A. Ellis Memorial Scholarship. *Academic Area: Physics. *Age Group: College students. *Eligibility: Contact the society by e-mail for specific eligibility requirements. *Application Process: Applicants should visit the society's Web site after August 15 to download an application. *Amount: Varies. *Deadline: January 14.

National Society of Black Physicists (NSBP)
NSBP Scholarship
6704G Lee Highway
Arlington, VA 22205
703-536-4207
scholarship@nsbp.org
http://www.nsbp.org
Scholarship Name: National Society of Black Physicists/ American Astronomical Society Commemorative Scholarship. *Academic Area: Physics. *Age Group: College students. *Eligibility: Applicants should be physics majors with an emphasis in astronomy, astrophysics, or space science. Contact the organization by e-mail for specific eligibility requirements. *Application Process: Applicants should visit the organization's Web site after August 15 to download an application. *Amount: $1,000. *Deadline: January 14.

National Society of Black Physicists (NSBP)
NSBP Scholarship
6704G Lee Highway
Arlington, VA 22205
703-536-4207
scholarship@nsbp.org
http://www.nsbp.org
Scholarship Name: National Society of Black Physicists/ Black Enterprise Magazine Commemorative Scholarships. *Academic Area: Physics. *Age Group: College sophomores or juniors. *Eligibility: Applicants must be declared physics majors approaching their junior or senior year of college. *Application Process: Applicants should visit the society's Web site after August 15 to download an application. *Amount: $1,000. *Deadline: January 14.

National Society of Black Physicists (NSBP)
NSBP Scholarship
6704G Lee Highway
Arlington, VA 22205
703-536-4207
scholarship@nsbp.org
http://www.nsbp.org
Scholarship Name: National Society of Black Physicists and Lawrence Livermore National Laboratory Undergraduate Scholarship. *Academic Area: Physics. *Age Group: High school seniors, undergraduate students. *Eligibility: Applicants must be U.S. citizens. The recipient will be required to participate in a summer internship at Lawrence Livermore National Laboratory for at least one summer during his or

her undergraduate education. The scholarship winner also receives full travel support to attend the Annual Conference of the National Society of Black Physicists and Black Physics Students and receive the award. Recipients must maintain a "B" average for the scholarship to be renewable. *Application Process: Visit the society's Web site to download an application. *Amount: $5,000. *Deadline: January 7.

National Society of Hispanic MBAs (NSHMBA)
Attn: Julie Aretz, Scholarship America
One Scholarship Way, PO Box 297
Saint Peter, MN 56082
507-931-1682
scholarships@nshmba.org
http://www.nshmba.org
Scholarship Name: NSHMBA Scholarship. *Academic Area: Business. *Age Group: Graduate students. *Eligibility: Applicants must be enrolled in an MBA program at an accredited college or university for the fall semester. Applicants must be members of the NSHMBA (registration available on the Web site for non-members), be U.S. citizens or legal permanent residents, have at least a 3.0 GPA, and come from a Hispanic background where at least one parent is Hispanic or both parents are half Hispanic. *Application Process: Applicants must submit all undergraduate and graduate transcripts, two letters of recommendation, a Student Aid Report, and a copy of the first page of the previous year's IRS form 1040 on which the student is claimed as an exemption. Applicants must also complete an application which is either available after April 5 to be downloaded from the organization's Web site or can be requested by e-mail. *Amount: $2,500 to $5,000 for full-time students; $1,500 for part-time students. *Deadline: Varies.

National Society of Professional Engineers
Educational Foundation
1420 King Street
Alexandria, VA 22314-2794
703-684-2800
ed@nspe.org
http://www.nspe.org
Scholarship Name: Maureen L. & Howard N. Blitman, P.E. Scholarship to Promote Diversity in Engineering. *Academic Area: Engineering (general). *Age Group: High school seniors. *Eligibility: Applicants must be members of an ethnic minority underrepresented in the field of engineering (African American, Hispanic American, or Native American) and must enroll in

a program that is accredited by the Engineering Accreditation Commission of the Accreditation Board for Engineering and Technology. Applicants are judged on their grade point averages, internship experience or community involvement, faculty recommendations, honors and awards received, and their answers to four questions on the application. *Application Process: Applicant must submit a completed application, high school transcripts, two teacher recommendations, and a copy of either the SAT or ACT scores. Visit the society's Web site to download an application. *Amount: $5,000. *Deadline: March 1.

National Technical Association
26100 Brush Avenue, Suite 315
Cleveland, OH 44132
216-289-4682
http://www.ntaonline.org
Scholarship Name: The National Technical Association is dedicated to encouraging minority youth and women to choose careers in science and technology, and recognizing, honoring, and preserving the legacy of minority pioneers in technological fields. It offers scholarships to minorities when funds are available. *Academic Area: Science, technology. *Age Group: Varies by scholarship. *Eligibility: Applicants must be members of the organization, demonstrate financial need, and excel academically. *Application Process: Most scholarships require essays, letters of recommendation, and transcripts to be submitted. Contact the association for scholarship availability and application procedures. An online information request form is available. *Amount: Varies by scholarship. *Deadline: Contact the association for specific deadlines.

National Trust for Historic Preservation
Attn: Mildred Colodny Scholarship Committee
1785 Massachusetts Avenue, NW
Washington, DC 20036-2117
800-944-6847
david_field@nthp.org
http://www.nationaltrust.org/help/colodny.html
Scholarship Name: The Mildred Colodny Scholarship for the Study of Historic Preservation was created to increase diversity and multiculturalism in the field of preservation. *Academic Area: History. *Age Group: College students. *Eligibility: Minority students interested in the field of historic preservation are eligible to apply. *Application Process: The application

packet should include a completed application (available for download at the trust's Web site), a resume (detailing work, internship, or volunteer experience), academic transcripts, and two letters of recommendation. *Amount: Varies. *Deadline: February 28.

National Urban League
120 Wall Street
New York, NY 10005
212-558-5300
info@nul.org
http://www.nul.org
Scholarship Name: This organization offers more than 50 scholarships for minorities. *Academic Area: Varies by scholarship. *Age Group: Varies by scholarship. *Eligibility: Visit the league's Web site for links to more than 50 scholarships available to African American and minority students. *Application Process: Applicants should visit the league's Web site for more information on application procedures or request further information from the organization by e-mail. *Amount: Awards vary. *Deadline: January 31.

National Women's Studies Association (NWSA)
Attn: Dr. Pat Washington
4537 Alamo Drive
San Diego, CA 92115
619-582-5383
TheMorganGirl@aol.com
http://www.nwsa.org
Scholarship Name: NWSA Women of Color Caucus Student Essay Award. *Academic Area: Women's studies. *Age Group: Undergraduate students, graduate students. *Eligibility: Applicants must be women of Latina/o, Asian/Asian American/Pacific Islander, or Native American/American Indian/Alaskan Native descent. Candidates should visit the association's Web site for specific eligibility requirements for individual awards (there are several awards in this category). *Application Process: Applicants must submit an original and published essay, between 15 and 25 pages (excluding bibliography), on white, letter quality paper, with clearly legible text (do not submit work on onion skin paper). Essays must be in 12-point font, double-spaced, with one-inch margins on all sizes, and page numbers centered at the bottom of each page. Include in the upper right corner of the title page only the writer's name, address, phone number, e-mail

address, college or university affiliation, and student status. *Amount: $400. *Deadline: February 15.

Native American Journalists Association (NAJA)
555 Dakota Street
Al Neuharth Media Center
Vermillion, SD 57069
605-677-5282
info@naja.com
http://www.naja.com
Scholarship Name: NAJA Scholarship. *Academic Area: Broadcasting, education, journalism. *Age Group: High school seniors, college students. *Eligibility: Applicants must be Native American students who are current paid members of the organization ($10 for high school students, $20 for college students). Applicants must demonstrate financial need, academic achievement, and a desire to work in journalism. *Application Process: Applicants must submit a completed application; a cover letter stating financial need, area of interest (print, broadcast, photojournalism, new media, journalism education), and reasons for pursuing a career in journalism; a brief description of any college courses taken; a copy of their FAFSA application or report; one copy of school transcripts; three letters of recommendation; work samples (if available); and a financial profile. Proof of enrollment in a federal- or state-recognized tribe may be requested. Visit the organization's Web site to download an application. *Amount: $500 to $5,000. *Deadline: April 14.

Native American Women's Health Education Resource Center
PO Box 572
Lake Andes, SD 57356-0572
605-487-7072
http://www.nativeshop.org/nawherc.html
Scholarship Name: This organization offers scholarships to minorities. *Academic Area: Open. *Age Group: Varies by scholarship. *Eligibility: Applicants must be female Native Americans. *Application Process: Applicants should contact the organization to inquire about current, available scholarship funds. *Amount: Awards vary. *Deadline: Contact the center for more information about deadlines.

Omega Delta Phi Fraternity
Attn: Daniel Hyliard, National Director of Scholastics
2413 Maple Drive
Jackson, MI 49203

dan.hyliard@omegadeltaphi.com
http://www.omegadeltaphi.com
Scholarship Name: Brother of the Year "Untouchable" Undergraduate Scholarship. *Academic Area: Open. *Age Group: Undergraduate students. *Eligibility: Members of this Hispanic fraternity who have provided an exceptional number of service hours to their organization may apply. Applicants should demonstrate a high level of academic achievement as well as hard work and dedication to Omega Delta Phi. *Application Process: Applicants should submit a completed application form, including the signatures of chapter/colony president and committee chair verifying hours served, two letters of recommendation, transcripts, and personal statement. Visit the fraternity's Web site to download an application. *Amount: $1,000. *Deadline: June 20.

Omega Delta Phi Fraternity

Attn: Daniel Hyliard, National Director of Scholastics
2413 Maple Drive
Jackson, MI 49203
dan.hyliard@omegadeltaphi.com
http://www.omegadeltaphi.com
Scholarship Name: "Carlos Contreras" Brother of the Year Graduate Scholarship. *Academic Area: Open. *Age Group: Graduate students. *Eligibility: Members of this Hispanic fraternity who have demonstrated significant leadership contributions to their organization may apply. Applicants should also demonstrate a high level of academic achievement as well as a commitment to community service. *Application Process: Applicants should submit a completed application form, two letters of recommendation, transcripts, and personal statement. Visit the fraternity's Web site to download an application. *Amount: $1,000. *Deadline: June 20.

Omega Phi Beta Sorority

Attn: Director of Reach for the Gold Book Scholarship
Grand Central Station, PO Box 3352
New York, NY 10163
reachforgold@omegaphibeta.org
http://www.omegaphibeta.org
Scholarship Name: Reach for the Gold Book Scholarship (Academic). *Academic Area: Open. *Age Group: High school seniors. *Eligibility: Applicants must be female students of color graduating from high school in May/June and accepted to a full-time college or university program for the fall semester. Applicants must also be U.S. citizens or legal residents with a high school

academic average of 3.7/4.0 and a minimum ACT score of 23 or SAT score of 900. *Application Process: Applicants must submit an official high school transcript; a copy of their ACT or SAT scores; one letter of recommendation from a teacher, guidance counselor, or school official; a 500-word personal essay; and a business size, self-addressed stamped envelope. *Amount: $500, to cover the cost of books. *Deadline: Must be postmarked between April 1 and May 15.

Omega Phi Beta Sorority

Attn: Director of Reach for the Gold Book Scholarship
Grand Central Station, PO Box 3352
New York, NY 10163
reachforgold@omegaphibeta.org
http://www.omegaphibeta.org
Scholarship Name: Reach for the Gold Book Scholarship (Community Service). *Academic Area: Open. *Age Group: High school seniors. *Eligibility: Applicants must be female students of color graduating from high school in May/June and accepted to a full-time college or university program for the fall semester. They must also be U.S. citizens or legal residents with a high school academic average of 2.7/4.0 and a demonstrated involvement in community service projects. *Application Process: Applicants must submit an official high school transcript; one letter of recommendation from a teacher, guidance counselor, or school official; one letter of recommendation from a community service agency verifying involvement; a 500-word personal essay; and a business size, self-addressed stamped envelope. *Amount: $500, to cover the cost of books. *Deadline: Must be postmarked between April 1 and May 15.

Omega Psi Phi Fraternity

Charles R. Drew Scholarship Commission
International Headquarters
3951 Snapfinger Parkway
Decatur, GA 30035
404-284-5533
http://www.omegapsiphifraternity.org
Scholarship Name: Founders' Memorial Scholarship and District and National Scholar of the Year Award. *Academic Area: Open. *Age Group: Varies by scholarship. *Eligibility: Members of Omega Psi Phi Fraternity (an African-American service organization) may apply. Applicants must maintain at least a "B" average, participate in extra curricular activities, and

demonstrate community or campus involvement. *Application Process: These scholarships all begin the process by requiring nomination at the chapter and then district levels. Each chapter can submit one nomination to the district scholarship committee. Fraternity members should contact their local chapter president for additional information on being nominated. *Amount: Varies by scholarship. *Deadline: Varies by district.

Omega Psi Phi Fraternity
Charles R. Drew Scholarship Commission
International Headquarters
3951 Snapfinger Parkway
Decatur, GA 30035
404-284-5533
http://www.omegapsiphifraternity.org
Scholarship Name: George E. Meares Memorial Scholarship. *Academic Area: Criminal justice, social sciences, social work. *Age Group: Graduate students. *Eligibility: Applicants must be U.S. citizens and members of Omega Psi Phi Fraternity (an African-American service organization). *Application Process: Applicants should request an application from the Charles R. Drew Scholarship Commission of the Fraternity or from the George E. Meares Scholarship Fund. Completed applications should be sent directly to the George E. Meares Scholarship Fund. Contact the fraternity for further information. *Amount: Up to $1,000. *Deadline: April 1.

Omega Psi Phi Fraternity
Charles R. Drew Scholarship Commission
International Headquarters
3951 Snapfinger Parkway
Decatur, GA 30035
404-284-5533
http://www.omegapsiphifraternity.org
Scholarship Name: Herman S. Dreer Scholarship/ leadership Award. *Academic Area: Open. *Age Group: College sophomores, juniors, and seniors. *Eligibility: Members of Omega Psi Phi Fraternity (an African-American service organization) may apply. Applicants must have completed their first year at a four-year college; exemplify the cardinal principles of manhood, scholarship perseverance, and uplift; and maintain a 2.7 or higher GPA. *Application Process: Applicants should submit their credentials to their district representatives for consideration to the International Scholarship Commission. Only one

applicant per district can be nominated. *Amount: Awards vary. *Deadline: 30 days following the close of the annual district meeting.

Omega Psi Phi Fraternity
Charles R. Drew Scholarship Commission
International Headquarters
3951 Snapfinger Parkway
Decatur, GA 30035
404-284-5533
http://www.omegapsiphifraternity.org
Scholarship Name: Ronald E. McNair Scientific Achievement Award. *Academic Area: Biology, chemistry, mathematics, physics. *Age Group: College juniors and seniors. *Eligibility: Applicants must maintain at least a 3.5 GPA and be members of Omega Psi Phi Fraternity (an African-American service organization) in good financial standing. *Application Process: Applicants should inquire at the chapter level regarding application procedures. Contact the national office with additional questions about obtaining an application. *Amount: $500. *Deadline: June 30.

Organization of Black Airline Pilots (OBAP)
Attn: William Davis
OBAP/Delta Scholarship
8630 Fenton Street, Suite 126
Silver Spring, MD 20910
800-538-6227
http://www.obap.org
Scholarship Name: Delta Air Lines Boeing B737-800 Type Rating Certificate Scholarship. *Academic Area: Aviation. *Age Group: Undergraduate students, early career professionals. *Eligibility: Applicants must be pursuing or hold a baccalaureate degree, have a minimum GPA of 2.5 (on a 4.0 scale), possess leadership potential, and be a current OBAP member in good standing (dues paid). Applicants must hold commercial, instrument and multiengine land certificates, have a minimum of 500 hours total time, and a current first class FAA medical certificate. Application Process: Applicants should submit resumes that include all certifications/ratings, total flying time, all schools attended, academic honors, scholarships, awards, special achievements, and any military history (if applicable). Applicant should include in the application package a copy of his or her driver's license, driving record for the past seven years (including dates and locations of any moving

violations) as well as any convictions of any type of violations of the law (moving or not), with dates and locations. Applicants should also submit a copy of his or her current passport. *Amount: *$35,000 (value of six-week program and paid expenses). *Deadline: June 15.

Organization of Black Airline Pilots (OBAP)
8630 Fenton Street, Suite 126
Silver Spring, MD 20910
800-538-6227
http://www.obap.org
Scholarship Name: OBAP Scholarship Program. *Academic Area: Aviation. *Age Group: Open. *Eligibility: Some scholarships may require OBAP membership, while others will not. *Application Process: There is no reliable schedule that identifies when scholarship offers will be available. Notice of available scholarships will be provided to OBAP members through its Web site, newsletter, and the NewsFlash@obap.org e-mail list. *Amount: Awards vary. *Deadline: Deadlines vary by scholarship.

Pacific Islanders in Communications
Attn: Gus Cobb Adams
Scholarship Committee
1221 Kapi'olani Boulevard, Suite 6A-4
Honolulu, HI 96814-3513
808-591-0059
gcobb-adams@piccom.org
http://www.piccom.org
Scholarship Name: Pacific Islanders in Communications Scholarship Fund. *Academic Area: Broadcasting, communications science. *Age Group: High school seniors, undergraduate students, graduate students. *Eligibility: Applicants must be at least 18 years of age; be pursuing a degree, certificate, and/or other certification in media and/or communications at the undergraduate, graduate, and unclassified levels of study; demonstrate academic proficiency and/or have demonstrated experience in media and/or communications or a related field; demonstrate commitment to the Pacific Islander community; and demonstrate a need for financial assistance. *Application Process: Applicants should submit a completed application form, a 500-word essay, a copy of the U.S. Department of Education's Free Application for Federal Student Aid, three letters of recommendation from nonfamily members, and current transcripts. Visit the organization's Web site

to download an application. *Amount: Up to $5,000. *Deadline: March 4.

Phi Beta Sigma Fraternity
Attn: Brother Michael W. Hines, International Director of Education
Two Belmonte Circle
Atlanta, GA 30311
404-752-1210
mhines@pbseducation1914.org
http://www.pbseducation1914.org
Scholarship Name: Phi Beta Sigma Scholarships. *Academic Area: Open. *Age Group: Undergraduate students, graduate students. *Eligibility: Applicants must be active members of Phi Beta Sigma (an African-American service organization) in good standing and maintain at least a 3.0 GPA. *Application Process: Applicants should submit a completed application along with official transcripts, three letters of recommendation, a resume, list of involvement with national programs and special events, an essay outlining career ambitions and goals, and a picture (head-shot). Visit the fraternity's Web site to download an application. *Amount: Awards vary. *Deadline: April 1.

Phi Delta Psi Fraternity
Memorial Scholarship Program
8200 East Jefferson, Suite 907
Detroit, MI 48214
pdpsi@phideltapsifraternity.org
http://www.phideltapsifraternity.org
Scholarship Name: This fraternity offers scholarship funding through its Memorial Scholarship Fund. *Academic Area: Open. *Age Group: College students. *Eligibility: Applicants must be members of Phi Delta Psi Fraternity (an African-American service organization). *Application Process: Applicants should contact the fraternity for further information about the availability of scholarship funds and the application process. Members should contact their chapter president for further information or contact the national office by e-mail. *Amount: Awards vary. *Deadline: Varies.

Pi Delta Psi Fraternity
Church Street Station
PO Box 2920
New York, NY 10008-2920
917-421-3900

president@pideltapsi.com
http://www.pideltapsi.com
Scholarship Name: Pi Delta Psi Academic Award.
*Academic Area: Open. *Age Group: Undergraduate students. *Eligibility: Applicants must be members of Pi Delta Psi Fraternity (an Asian American service organization) who have achieved the highest academic excellence. Candidates must be full-time students. *Application Process: Applicants must be nominated by the president of his school's chapter who must submit a letter of intent for his nominee at the end of each year. Each school must include documentation and an explanation as to why each of these individuals should be considered. The applicant must also supply an original copy of his current semester transcript. Applicants should request further information from their local chapter president. *Amount: $250. *Deadline: Contact the fraternity for deadline information.

Pi Delta Psi Fraternity
Church Street Station
PO Box 2920
New York, NY 10008-2920
917-421-3900
president@pideltapsi.com
http://www.pideltapsi.com
Scholarship Name: Pi Delta Psi Award (aka The Odie Award). *Academic Area: Open. *Age Group: Undergraduate students. *Eligibility: Applicants must be members of Pi Delta Psi Fraternity (an Asian American service organization) who have shown exceptional dedication to the fraternity as well as outstanding contribution to the community. Applicants will have shown exemplary conduct as honorable men and the poise of a great role model. *Application Process: The president must state why this nominee should be considered a candidate by either his leadership skills or his dedications and contributions to the fraternity and the community. Applicants should request further information from their local chapter president. *Amount: $250. *Deadline: Contact the fraternity for deadline information.

Presbyterian Church USA
Financial Aid for Studies
100 Witherspoon Street
Louisville, KY 40202
888-728-7228, ext. 5776
http://www.pcusa.org/financialaid/undergraduate.htm

Scholarship Name: Student Opportunity Scholarship.
*Academic Area: Open. *Age Group: High school seniors. *Eligibility: Minority students (African American, Alaska Native, Asian American, Hispanic American, Native American, and Middle Easterners) who are members of the Presbyterian Church USA and U.S. citizens or permanent residents of the United States are eligible to apply. Applicants must also demonstrate financial need and attend college full time. *Application Process: Contact the Presbyterian Church USA for information. *Amount: Scholarships range from $200 to $1,500. *Deadline: May 1.

Professional Hispanics in Energy
20505 Yorba Linda Boulevard, Suite 324
Yorba Linda, CA 92886-7109
714-777-7729
http://www.phie.org
Scholarship Name: This organization offers scholarships for Hispanic students. *Academic Area: Geosciences. *Age Group: Varies by scholarship. *Eligibility: Applicants must be deserving students of Hispanic descent. *Application Process: Contact the organization by phone or e-mail (visit the Web site to submit a question) for further information about the scholarship application process. *Amount: Awards vary. *Deadline: Contact the organization for deadline information.

Radio and Television News Directors Foundation (RTNDF)
1600 K Street, NW, Suite 700
Washington, DC 20006-2838
202-467-5218
irvingw@rtndf.org
http://www.rtnda.org/asfi/scholarships/minority.shtml
Scholarship Name: Carole Simpson Scholarship.
*Academic Area: Broadcasting, journalism. *Age Group: High school seniors, undergraduate students. *Eligibility: Minority students whose career objective is electronic journalism (radio or television) and have at least one full year of college remaining are eligible to apply. Applicants must also attend college full time. *Application Process: Contact the foundation for details. *Amount: $2,000. *Deadline: Varies.

Radio and Television News Directors Foundation (RTNDF)
1600 K Street, NW, Suite 700
Washington, DC 20006-2838
202-467-5218

irvingw@rtndf.org

http://www.rtnda.org/asfi/scholarships/minority.shtml

Scholarship Name: Ed Bradley Scholarship. *Academic Area: Broadcasting, journalism. *Age Group: High school seniors, undergraduate students. *Eligibility: Minority students whose career objective is electronic journalism (radio or television) and have at least one full year of college remaining are eligible to apply. Applicants must also attend college full time. *Application Process: Contact the RTNDF for details. *Amount: $10,000. *Deadline: Varies.

Radio and Television News Directors Foundation (RTNDF)

1600 K Street, NW, Suite 700

Washington, DC 20006-2838

202-467-5218

irvingw@rtndf.org

http://www.rtnda.org/asfi/scholarships/minority.shtml

Scholarship Name: Ken Kashiwahara Scholarship. *Academic Area: Broadcasting, journalism. *Age Group: High school seniors, undergraduate students. *Eligibility: Minority students whose career objective is electronic journalism (radio or television) and have at least one full year of college remaining are eligible to apply. Applicants must also attend college full time. *Application Process: Contact the foundation for details. *Amount: $2,500. *Deadline: Varies.

REFORMA

Reforma Scholarship Committee

Ramona Grijalva

PO Box 7453

Tucson, AZ 85725

480-471-7452

http://www.reforma.org/scholarship.htm

Scholarship Name: REFORMA Scholarship. *Academic Area: Library sciences. *Age Group: Graduate students. *Eligibility: Applicants must qualify for graduate study in library science and be citizens or permanent residents of the United States. *Application Process: Applicants should submit a completed application, two recommendations, transcripts, a personal statement, and a current resume. Visit the association's Web site to download an application form. *Amount: $1,500. *Deadline: March 15.

Ron Brown Scholar Program

1160 Pepsi Place, Suite 206

Charlottesville, VA 22901

434-964-1588

http://www.ronbrown.org

Scholarship Name: Ron Brown Scholar Program. *Academic Area: Open. *Age Group: High school seniors. *Eligibility: African-American students who plan to attend college full time may apply. Applicants must be U.S. citizens or permanent residents. *Application Process: Visit the program's Web site for information. *Amount: Varies. *Deadline: January 9.

Society for Advancement of Chicanos and Native Americans in Science (SACNAS)

Attn: Genome Scholars Program

PO Box 8526

Santa Cruz, CA 95061-8526

831-459-0170, ext. 238

pixan@sacnas.org

http://www.sacnas.org

Scholarship Name: SACNAS Genome Scholars Program. *Academic Area: Bioinformatics. *Age Group: College seniors, graduate students. *Eligibility: Applicants should be graduating seniors who are accepted into a graduate program or students who are already enrolled in a graduate program. Applicants must be current SACNAS members who are U.S. citizens or permanent residents. *Application Process: Applicants should submit a completed application along with GRE test scores, a letter of reference, a personal statement, a faculty mentor personal profile, a faculty mentor personal statement, a supporting essay, and official transcripts. Visit the society's Web site to download an application. *Amount: $25,000. *Deadline: January 15.

Society of Hispanic Professional Engineers

Attn: Rafaela Schwan

AHETEMS Scholarship Program

University of Texas at Arlington

College of Engineering, Box 19019

Arlington, TX 76019-0019

817-272-1116

rschawan@shpe.org

http://www.shpe.org

Scholarship Name: SHPE/AHETEMS Scholarship. *Academic Area: Engineering (general), mathematics, science. *Age Group: High school seniors, undergraduate students, graduate students. *Eligibility: Applicants must be U.S. citizens or legal residents who have graduated from an accredited U.S. high school, are accepted into or attending an accredited two-year or four-year college or university in the United States or Puerto Rico, enrolled full time, maintain a minimum GPA of 2.5 on a 4.0 (for high school seniors and undergraduates) and 3.25 on a 4.0 scale (for graduate students), and are society members in good standing. Scholarships are both merit and need based. *Application Process: Applicants should submit a completed application, personal statement, transcripts, and a recommendation letter. Visit the society's Web site to download an application. *Amount: $1,000 to $3,000. *Deadline: April 1.

Society of Manufacturing Engineers Education Foundation
Scholarship Review Committee
One SME Drive, PO Box 930
Dearborn, MI 48121
313-425-3300
foundation@sme.org
http://www.sme.org/cgi-bin/smeefhtml.pl?/foundation/scholarships/schl_briefly.html&&&SEF&
Scholarship Name: Edward S. Roth Manufacturing Engineering Scholarship. *Academic Area: Engineering (manufacturing). *Age Group: High school seniors, undergraduate students, graduate students. *Eligibility: Minority students planning to or currently enrolled full time in a degree program in manufacturing engineering in the United States or Canada are eligible to apply. Applicants must have a GPA of at least 3.0 on a 4.0 scale, be U.S. citizens, and plan to attend one of the following schools: Boston University, Bradley University, Brigham Young University, California Polytechnic State University, Central State University, University of Massachusetts, University of Miami, Miami University, St. Cloud State University, University of Texas-Pan American, Utah State University, and Worcester Polytechnic Institute. Preference will be given to students demonstrating financial need. *Application Process: Applicants must submit a maximum 300-word statement detailing their career objectives, a student resume, an official transcript, two recommendation letters, and a completed application (available at the foundation's Web site).*Amount: Varies. *Deadline: December 5.

Society of Manufacturing Engineers Education Foundation
Scholarship Review Committee
One SME Drive, PO Box 930
Dearborn, MI 48121

313-425-3300
foundation@sme.org
http://www.sme.org/cgi-bin/smeefhtml.pl?/foundation/scholarships/schl_briefly.html&&&SEF&
Scholarship Name: Caterpillar Scholars Award. *Academic Area: Engineering (manufacturing). *Age Group: High school seniors, undergraduate students. *Eligibility: Minority students planning to or currently enrolled full time in a degree program in manufacturing engineering in the United States or Canada are eligible to apply. Applicants must have a GPA of at least 3.0 on a 4.0 scale. *Application Process: Applicants must submit a maximum 300-word statement detailing their career objectives, a student resume, an official transcript, two recommendation letters, and a completed application (available at the foundation's Web site). *Amount: Varies. *Deadline: December 5.

Society of Mexican American Engineers and Scientists
Attn: Scholarship Committee
711 West Bay Area Boulevard, Suite 206
Webster, TX 77598-4051
281-557-3677
execdir@maes-natl.org
http://www.maes-natl.org
*Scholarship Name: This association offers five types of scholarships—Padrino, Founders, Presidential, Graduate Student, and General Scholarships—for Hispanic students. *Academic Area: Engineering (general), science. *Age Group: Undergraduate students, graduate students. *Eligibility: All applicants must be current society student members who are enrolled as full-time students in an accredited college or university in the United States prior to submission of the application. Community college applicants must be enrolled in transferable majors to a four-year institution offering a baccalaureate degree. Applicants will be evaluated for all scholarship awards including the top awards of Padrino, Founders, and Presidential Scholarships. Selection is based on financial need, academic achievement, personal qualities, strengths, and leadership abilities. *Application Process: Applicants should submit a completed application and an additional three copies of the scholarship application packet to the national office. Also required are at least one recommendation form and school transcripts. Recommendation letters should be in a sealed envelope and do not need to be copied. Visit

the society's Web site to download an application. *Amount: $1,000 to $3,000. *Deadline: October 6.

Thurgood Marshall Scholarship Fund (TMSF)
90 William Street, Suite 1203
New York, NY 10038
212-573-8888
pallen@tmsf.org
http://www.thurgoodmarshallfund.org
Scholarship Name: Sidney B. Williams, Jr. Intellectual Property Law School Scholarship. *Academic Area: Law. *Age Group: Law students, early career professionals. *Eligibility: Sponsored by the American Intellectual Property Law Education Foundation, this scholarship is awarded to minority students developing a career in intellectual property law or holding a past or present, full- or part-time position in an area related to intellectual property law. Applicants must also have a demonstrated financial need and outstanding academic performance in the undergraduate level and law school level (if applicable). All applicants must be U.S. citizens. *Application Process: Applicants should submit a completed application form, a FAFSA report, all academic transcripts, and two letters of recommendation. Visit the fund's Web site to download an application. *Amount: $10,000 per school year, renewable upon reapplication, for up to three academic years. *Deadline: February 25.

Thurgood Marshall Scholarship Fund (TMSF)
90 William Street, Suite 1203
New York, NY 10038
212-573-8888
pallen@tmsf.org
http://www.thurgoodmarshallfund.org
Scholarship Name: Thurgood Marshall Scholarship Fund. *Academic Area: Open. *Age Group: Varies by scholarship. *Eligibility: Applicants must be enrolled, accepted, or planning to enroll in one of the 47 Thurgood Marshall Scholarship Fund member schools. *Application Process: Applicants must contact their campus TMSF scholarship coordinator for an application. Application packages consist of a general information form, enrollment/certification of academic standing, acceptance form, financial aid information, high school transcripts (for incoming freshmen), undergraduate transcripts (for graduate and law school), resume or personal information form, recommendation letters, an essay, and a personal photograph/head-shot. These materials are submitted to the scholarship coordinator on campus. Applicants should consult their schools concerning the selection process. *Amount: $2,200 per semester (average). *Deadline: Deadlines vary.

Urban Financial Services Coalition
Attn: Herbert W. Whiteman, Jr. Scholarship
2121 K Street, NW, Suite 800
Washington, DC 20037
202-261-3569
ufscf@ufscfoundation.org
http://www.ufscfoundation.org
Scholarship Name: Herbert W. Whiteman, Jr. Scholarship. *Academic Area: Business, finance. *Age Group: Undergraduate students, graduate students. *Eligibility: Applicants must exhibit academic excellence (maintain at least a 3.0 GPA) and demonstrate leadership ability. *Application Process: Applicants should submit a completed application, a letter of reference, a current resume, an acceptance letter from a college or a registration invoice, and a 400- to 500-word essay on "Excellence in Leadership- How Do You Personally Exemplify the Quality?" Visit the coalition's Web site to download an application. *Amount: Awards vary. *Deadline: April 16.

Zeta Phi Beta Sorority Inc.
National Educational Foundation
1734 New Hampshire Avenue, NW
Washington, DC 20009
202-387-3103
IHQ@zphib1920.org
http://www.zpbnef1975.org
Scholarship Name: Isabel M. Herson Scholarship in Education. *Academic Area: Education. *Age Group: Undergraduate students, graduate students. *Eligibility: This African-American sorority's scholarship does not require sorority membership. Applicants must be female, full-time students. *Application Process: Applicants must submit a completed application, 150-word personal essay describing their educational goals and professional aspirations, and three letters of recommendation. Visit the foundation's Web site to download an application. *Amount: $500 to $1,000. *Deadline: February 1.

Zeta Phi Beta Sorority Inc.
National Educational Foundation
1734 New Hampshire Avenue, NW

Washington, DC 20009
202-387-3103
IHQ@zphib1920.org
http://www.zpbnef1975.org
Scholarship Name: Lullelia W. Harrison Scholarship
in Counseling. *Academic Area: Counseling.
*Age Group: Undergraduate students, graduate
students. *Eligibility: This African-American sorority's
scholarship does not require sorority membership.
Applicants must be female full-time students.
*Application Process: Applicants must submit a
completed application, 150-word personal essay
describing their educational goals and professional
aspirations, and three letters of recommendation. Visit
the foundation's Web site to download an application.
*Amount: $500 to $1,000. *Deadline: February 1.

Zeta Phi Beta Sorority Inc.
National Educational Foundation
1734 New Hampshire Avenue, NW
Washington, DC 20009
202-387-3103
IHQ@zphib1920.org
http://www.zpbnef1975.org
Scholarship Name: S. Evelyn Lewis Memorial Scholarship
in Medical Health Sciences. *Academic Area: Medicine
(general). *Age Group: Undergraduate students,
graduate students. *Eligibility: This African-American
sorority's scholarship does not require sorority
membership. Applicants must be female, full-time
students. *Application Process: Applicants must submit
a completed application, 150-word personal essay
describing their educational goals and professional
aspirations, and three letters of recommendation. Visit
the foundation's Web site to download an application.
*Amount: $500 to $1,000. *Deadline: February 1.

Zeta Phi Beta Sorority Inc.
National Educational Foundation
1734 New Hampshire Avenue, NW
Washington, DC 20009
202-387-3103
IHQ@zphib1920.org
http://www.zpbnef1975.org
Scholarship Name: Zeta Phi Beta General Graduate
Scholarship. *Academic Area: Open. *Age Group:
Graduate students. *Eligibility: This African-American
sorority's scholarship does not require sorority
membership. Applicants must be female, full-time

students pursuing a master's, doctoral, or post-
doctoral degree. *Application Process: Applicants
must submit a completed application, 150-word
personal essay describing their educational goals
and professional aspirations, and three letters of
recommendation. Visit the foundation's Web site to
download an application. *Amount: Up to $2,500.
*Deadline: February 1.

Zeta Phi Beta Sorority Inc.
National Educational Foundation
1734 New Hampshire Avenue, NW
Washington, DC 20009
202-387-3103
IHQ@zphib1920.org
http://www.zpbnef1975.org
202-387-3103
Scholarship Name: Zeta Phi Beta General Undergraduate
Scholarship. *Academic Area: Open. *Age Group: High
school seniors, undergraduate students. *Eligibility:
This African-American sorority's scholarship does not
require sorority membership. Applicants must be
full-time students or enrolled as full-time students
for the upcoming fall semester. *Application Process:
Applicants must submit a completed application,
150-word personal essay describing their educational
goals and professional aspirations, and three letters
of recommendation. Visit the foundation's Web site to
download an application. *Amount: $500 to $1,000.
*Deadline: February 1.

Zeta Phi Beta Sorority Inc.
National Educational Foundation
1734 New Hampshire Avenue, NW
Washington, DC 20009
202-387-3103
IHQ@zphib1920.org
http://www.zpbnef1975.org
Scholarship Name: Zora Neale Hurston Scholarship.
*Academic Area: Anthropology. *Age Group: Graduate
students. *Eligibility: This African-American sorority's
scholarship does not require sorority membership.
Applicants must be female, full-time students.
*Application Process: Applicants must submit a
completed application, 150-word personal essay
describing their educational goals and professional
aspirations, and three letters of recommendation. Visit
the foundation's Web site to download an application.
*Amount: $500 to $1,000. *Deadline: February 1.

UNITED NEGRO COLLEGE FUND SCHOLARSHIPS

United Negro College Fund
8260 Willow Oaks Corporate Drive, PO Box 10444
Fairfax, VA 22031-8044
800-331-2244
http://www.uncf.org
The United Negro College Fund (UNCF) is the nation's oldest and most successful African American higher education assistance organization. It is a consortium of 39 private, accredited historically black colleges and universities. UNCF offers programs designed to enhance the quality of education for America's brightest young minds, and is committed to providing financial assistance to deserving students, raising operating funds for member colleges and universities, and supplying technical assistance to member institutions. UNCF oversees more than 450 scholarship programs; visit its Web site for a listing of opportunities and application information. A sampling of UNCF scholarships is listed below.

Abercrombie and Fitch Scholarship Program
Scholarship Name: Abercrombie and Fitch Scholarship Program. *Academic Area: Open. *Age Group: College freshmen. *Eligibility: Applicants must be enrolled in an accredited four-year college or university and maintain a 3.0 GPA. *Application Process: Applicants must submit a completed application along with a one-page essay, official transcripts, two letters of recommendation, and a head-shot photo. *Amount: $3,000. *Deadline: October 28.

Alliant Techsystems Internship/Scholarship
Scholarship Name: Alliant Techsystems Internship/Scholarship. *Academic Area: Accounting. *Age Group: College sophomores and juniors. *Eligibility: Applicants must have a 3.0 GPA and be attending one of the 39 UNCF member colleges and universities. Application Process: Applicants must participate in a paid summer internship prior to receiving a scholarship the following academic year. Visit the UNCF's Web site to connect to the sponsor's Web site to download an application. *Amount: $5,000. *Deadline: Deadlines vary.

Alton and Dorothy Higgins MD Scholarship
Scholarship Name: Alton and Dorothy Higgins MD Scholarship. *Academic Area: Medicine (general). *Age Group: College juniors and seniors, graduate students. *Eligibility: Applicants must maintain a 3.0 GPA, show financial need, and be attending one of the UNCF member colleges or universities. *Application Process: Applicants should submit a completed application along with two letters of recommendation, an essay, transcripts, a financial need statement, and a small head-shot photo. Visit the UNCF Web site to download an application. *Amount: $5,000 to $10,000. *Deadline: June 4.

American Hotel Foundation Scholarship
Scholarship Name: American Hotel Foundation Scholarship. *Academic Area: Management. *Age Group: Undergraduate students, graduate students. *Eligibility: Applicants must maintain a 2.5 GPA and attend one of the 39 UNCF member colleges or universities. *Application Process: Applicants must have unmet need as verified by the university financial aid office, complete the Free Application for Federal Student Aid, and must request that the Student Analysis Report be sent to the financial aid office at their college or university. Students should complete their online student profiles at the UNCF Web site. *Amount: $1,500. *Deadline: Deadlines vary.

Athena Group L.L.C. Scholarship
Scholarship Name: Athena Group, L.L.C. Scholarship. *Academic Area: Finance. *Age Group: College sophomores and juniors. *Eligibility: Applicants must be female residents of the New York City metropolitan area, attending one of the 39 UNCF member colleges or universities. Applicants must have a 3.0 GPA and have a declared finance major. *Application Process: Applicants should submit a completed application along with two nomination letters, a 500-word essay, undergraduate school transcripts, a resume, and a small head-shot photograph. Visit the UNCF Web site to download an application. *Amount $7,000. *Deadline: March 4.

AXA Foundation Fund Achievement Scholarship
Scholarship Name: AXA Foundation Fund Achievement Scholarship. *Academic Area: Business. *Age Group: High school seniors, undergraduate students, graduate students. *Eligibility: Applicants must be residents of New York who are attending or planning to attend one of the UNCF member colleges or universities. Applicants must also maintain a 3.0 GPA, show unmet financial need, demonstrate a commitment to community service, and exhibit high academic achievement and leadership ability. *Application Process: Applicants should contact the sponsoring organization directly for application materials. *Amount: $2,00 to $5,000. *Deadline: Deadlines vary.

Bank of America Scholarship
Scholarship Name: Bank of America Scholarship. *Academic Area: Business, computer science, education, finance, information technology, marketing. *Age Group: Undergraduate students, graduate students. *Eligibility: Applicants must maintain a 2.5 GPA and attend one of the following UNCF colleges or universities located in one of the Bank of America core states: Benedict College, Bennett College for Women, Bethune-Cookman College, Claflin University, Clark Atlanta University, Edward Waters College, Fisk University, Florida Memorial College, Huston-Tillotson College, Jarvis Christian College, Johnson C. Smith University, Lane College, LeMoyne-Owen College, Livingstone College, Morehouse College, Morris College, Paine College, Paul Quinn College, Philander Smith College, Saint Augustine's College, Saint Paul's College, Shaw University, Spelman College, Virginia Union University, Voorhees College, or Wiley College. *Application Process: Applicants should contact the sponsoring company directly for application information. *Amount: $1,000. *Deadline: Deadlines vary.

Benice Michaelson Diamond Fund
Scholarship Name: Benice Michaelson Diamond Fund. *Academic Area: Open. *Age Group: Undergraduate students, graduate students. *Eligibility: Applicants must be attending one of the 39 UNCF member colleges or universities, maintain a 2.5 GPA, and demonstrate unmet financial need. Applicants also must be able to prove that their parents are or were members of a trade union. *Application Process: Applicants should submit a completed application,

one letter of recommendation, and a personal statement detailing their career goals. Visit the UNCF Web site to download an application. *Amount: Awards vary. *Deadline: September 17.

Best Buy Scholarship Programs
Scholarship Name: Best Buy Scholarship Program. *Academic Area: Accounting, advertising, business, communications science, computer science, finance, marketing. *Age Group: Undergraduate students. *Eligibility: Applicants must be attending one of the 39 UNCF member colleges or universities or Florida A&M, maintain a 3.0 GPA, and show unmet financial need. Of the two types of scholarships offered (employee and non-employee), the employee scholarship requires the student to have worked at Best Buy for at least six months. *Application Process: Applicants should submit a completed application along with a resume, official transcripts, two letters of recommendation, and a 500-word essay. Visit the UNCF Web site to download an application. *Amount: $2,500 (employee); $5,000 (non-employee). *Deadline: November 5.

Cardinal Health Scholarship
Scholarship Name: Cardinal Health Scholarship. *Academic Area: Accounting, chemistry, computer science, engineering (computer), engineering (general), finance, information technology, marketing, pharmaceutical sciences. *Age Group: College freshmen, sophomores, and juniors. *Eligibility: Applicants must be attending accredited four-year colleges or universities, maintain a 3.0 GPA, demonstrate non-collegiate leadership experience, and unmet financial need. *Application Process: Applicants should submit a completed application along with official transcripts and a personal statement. Visit the UNCF's Web site to download an application. *Amount: $5,000. *Deadline: October 30.

Carolyn Bailey Thomas Scholarship
Scholarship Name: Carolyn Bailey Thomas Scholarship. *Academic Area: Open. *Age Group: High school seniors, undergraduate students, graduate students. *Eligibility: Applicants must maintain a 3.0 GPA, demonstrate financial need, and attend or plan to attend one of the 39 UNCF member colleges or universities. *Application Process: Applicants should contact the sponsoring institution directly for information on application

procedures. *Amount: Awards vary, based on need. *Deadline: Deadlines vary.

Castle Rock Foundation Scholarship

Scholarship Name: Castle Rock Foundation Scholarship. *Academic Area: Business, engineering (general). *Age Group: High school seniors, undergraduate students, graduate students. *Eligibility: Applicants must be attending or planning to attend one of the following participating schools: Bethune-Cookman College, LeMoyne-Owen College, Morehouse College, Shaw University, Spelman College, Tuskegee University, Xavier University. Applicants must also maintain a 2.5 GPA. *Application Process: Applicants should contact the scholarship sponsor directly for application information. *Amount: $3,600. *Deadline: Deadlines vary.

Catherine W. Pierce Scholarship

Scholarship Name: Catherine W. Pierce Scholarship. *Academic Area: History, visual arts (general). *Age Group: Undergraduate students, graduate students. *Eligibility: Applicants must maintain a 3.0 GPA and demonstrate financial need. *Application Process: Applicants should submit an application along with supporting materials. Visit the UNCF Web site to download an application. *Amount: Up to $5,000. *Deadline: Deadlines vary.

CDM Scholarship/Internship

Scholarship Name: CDM Scholarship/Internship. *Academic Area: Engineering (general). *Age Group: Undergraduate students, graduate students. *Eligibility: Applicants must be attending one of the 39 participating UNCF colleges or universities, maintain a 3.0 GPA, and be willing to accept a paid summer internship with the sponsoring company. *Application Process: Applicants should submit a completed application along with two letters of recommendation, official transcripts, and an updated resume. Visit the UNCF Web site to download the application. *Amount: $5,000, plus a $2,000 living expenses stipend for the internship. *Deadline: March 1.

ChevronTexaco Scholars Program

Scholarship Name: ChevronTexaco Scholars Program. *Academic Area: Engineering (general). *Age Group: College sophomores and juniors. *Eligibility: Applicants must be attending one of the following participating UNCF schools: Clark Atlanta University, Morehouse College, Spelman College, or Tuskegee

University. Applicants must also maintain a 2.5 GPA, demonstrate financial need, exhibit leadership skills, and have a commitment to community service. *Application Process: Applicants should submit a completed application along with transcripts, resume, a nomination letter from a faculty member, two personal references, and a one-page statement of career interest. Visit the UNCF Web site to download an application. *Amount: Up to $3,000. *Deadline: March 21.

Chrysler Corporation Scholarship

Scholarship Name: Chrysler Corporation Scholarship. *Academic Area: Open. *Age Group: High school seniors, undergraduate students, graduate students. *Eligibility: Applicants must be attending or planning to attend one of the 39 UNCF member colleges or universities and maintain a 2.5 GPA. *Application Process: Applicants should download an application from the UNCF Web site and submit it along with supporting materials. *Amount: $3,900. *Deadline: Deadlines vary.

Cisco/United Negro College Fund Scholars Program

Scholarship Name: Cisco/United Negro College Fund Scholars Program. *Academic Area: Computer science, engineering (electrical). *Age Group: College sophomores. *Eligibility: Applicants must be attending one of the following UNCF member schools: Claflin University, Clark Atlanta University, Dillard University, Jarvis Christian College, Johnson C. Smith University, Livingstone College, Morehouse College, Paul Quinn College, Rust College, Saint Augustine's College, Shaw University, Spelman College, Wiley College, or Xavier University. Applicants also most maintain a 3.2 GPA and agree to participate in an internship with the sponsoring company. Preference is given to women and those who demonstrate a commitment to community service. *Application Process: Applicants should contact the scholarship sponsor for application information. *Amount: $4,000. *Deadline: Deadlines vary.

C. R. Bard Scholarship and Internship Program

Scholarship Name: C. R. Bard Scholarship and Internship Program. *Academic Area: Business. *Age Group: College sophomores. *Eligibility: Applicants must be residents of New Jersey who are attending one of the 39 UNCF member colleges or universities and must maintain a 3.0 GPA. Applicants also must accept a paid summer internship at the C. R. Bard headquarters in Murray Hill, New Jersey. *Application Process: Applicants should contact the scholarship sponsor directly for application information. *Amount: $4,000. *Deadline: Deadlines vary.

C-SPAN Scholarship Program

Scholarship Name: C-SPAN Scholarship Program. *Academic Area: Broadcasting, communication sciences, English/literature, film/video, history, political science. *Age Group: College sophomores or juniors. *Eligibility: Applicants must be attending one of the 39 UNCF member colleges or universities, maintain a 3.0 GPA, and demonstrate unmet financial need. Accepting an internship with the sponsoring company is part of this scholarship opportunity. *Application Process: Applicants should submit a completed application along with two nomination letters from faculty members, transcripts, resume, a 300-word essay, and a small head-shot photo. Visit the UNCF Web site to download an application. *Amount: $2,000 (one time), plus a $200 weekly stipend. *Deadline: April 8.

Doris and John Carpenter Scholarship

Scholarship Name: Doris and John Carpenter Scholarship. *Academic Area: Open. *Age Group: High school seniors, undergraduate students. *Eligibility: Applicants must be attending or planning to attend one of the 39 UNCF member colleges or universities, maintain a 2.5, and demonstrate financial need. The scholarship is awarded to students who demonstrate the greatest financial need. *Application Process: Applicants should contact the scholarship sponsor directly for application information. *Amount: $2,000 to $5,000. *Deadline: Deadlines vary.

Dorothy N. McNeal Scholarship

Scholarship Name: Dorothy N. McNeal Scholarship. *Academic Area: Open. *Age Group: High school seniors, undergraduate students, graduate students. *Eligibility: Applicants must maintain a 2.5 GPA, demonstrate unmet financial need, and attend or plan to attend one of the 39 UNCF member colleges or universities. Applicants should be interested in pursuing careers related to community service. *Application Process: Applicants should contact the sponsoring institution for application procedures. *Amount: Awards vary, based on need. *Deadline: Deadlines vary.

Dr. James M. Rosin Scholarship

Scholarship Name: Dr. James M. Rosin Scholarship. *Academic Area: Medical (general). *Age Group: Undergraduate students, graduate students. *Eligibility: Applicants must maintain a 3.0 GPA, demonstrate financial need, and be committed to personal growth, to helping others, and to their education. *Application Process: Applicants should contact the sponsoring institution directly for information about application procedures. *Amount: $5,000. *Deadline: Deadlines vary.

Earl and Patricia Armstrong Scholarship

Scholarship Name: Earl and Patricia Armstrong Scholarship. *Academic Area: Biology, medicine (general). *Age Group: Undergraduate students, graduate students. *Eligibility: Applicants must maintain a 3.0 GPA, have unmet need as verified by their university's financial aid office, complete the Free Application for Federal Student Aid, and request that the Student Analysis Report be sent to their school's financial aid office. Students also must be attending one of the 39 UNCF member colleges or universities. Students can begin the application process by completing their online student profiles on the UNCF Web site. *Amount: Up to $3,000. *Deadline: Deadlines vary.

Ella Fitzgerald Charitable Foundation Scholarship

Scholarship Name: Ella Fitzgerald Charitable Foundation Scholarship. *Academic Area: Performing arts (music-general). *Age Group: High school seniors, undergraduate students, graduate students. *Eligibility: Applicants must maintain a 2.5 GPA, show unmet financial need, and attend or be planning to attend one of the 39 UNCF member colleges or universities. *Application Process: Applicants should contact the sponsoring institution directly for application procedures. *Amount: Awards vary. *Deadline: Deadlines vary.

ESSENCE Scholars Program

Scholarship Name: ESSENCE Scholars Program. *Academic Area: Open. *Age Group: College sophomores and juniors. *Eligibility: Applicants must be females attending one of the following UNCF member colleges or universities: Howard University or Hampton University. Applicants must also maintain a 3.0 GPA. *Application Process: Applicants should apply online via the UNCF Web site. *Amount: $10,000. *Deadline: October 15.

Fannie Mae Foundation Scholarship

Scholarship Name: Fannie Mae Foundation Scholarship. *Academic Area: Open. *Age Group: College juniors. *Eligibility: Applicants must maintain a 3.0 GPA and be attending one of the following colleges or universities: Benedict College, Bethune-Cookman College, Johnson C. Smith University, LeMoyne-Owen College, and other UNCF participating schools. Applicants also must demonstrate financial need and be involved in community development programs. *Application Process: Applicants should submit a completed application along with a 500-word essay on their community service work, transcripts, two letters of recommendation, and a small head-shot photograph. Visit the UNCF Web site to download an application. *Amount: Awards vary. *Deadline: November 5.

Financial Services Institution

Scholarship Name: Financial Services Institution Scholarship. *Academic Area: Finance. *Age Group: High school seniors, undergraduate students, graduate students. *Eligibility: Applicants must maintain a 2.5 GPA, have unmet financial need, and be attending or planning to attend one of the 39 UNCF member colleges or universities. *Application Process: Applicants should contact the scholarship sponsor directly for application procedures. *Amount: Varies, based on need. *Deadline: Deadlines vary.

GAP Foundation Scholarship

Scholarship Name: GAP Foundation Scholarship. *Academic Area: Fashion, management. *Age Group: High school seniors, undergraduate students, graduate students. *Eligibility: Applicants must maintain a 3.0 GPA, show unmet financial need, and attend or be planning to attend one of the 39 UNCF member colleges or universities. *Application Process: Applicants should submit a completed application along with transcripts, a resume, two nomination letters, a one-page essay on their career goals, and a financial need statement. Visit the UNCF Web site to download an application. *Amount: Up to $10,000. *Deadline: October 15.

Gates Millennium Scholarship

Scholarship Name: Gates Millennium Scholarship. *Academic Area: Mathematics, science. *Age Group: High school seniors. *Eligibility: Applicants must have at least a 3.3 GPA, show unmet financial need, and be entering freshman who are planning to attend one of the 39 UNCF member colleges or universities. The scholarship is open to African Americans, American Indians/Native Alaskans, Asian Pacific Islander Americans, and Hispanic Americans. *Application Process: Applicants should contact the scholarship sponsor directly for application procedures. *Amount: Awards vary. *Deadline: Deadlines vary.

General Mills Technology Scholars Award

Scholarship Name: General Mills Technology Scholars Award. *Academic Area: Engineering (general), food science. *Age Group: College juniors and seniors. *Eligibility: Applicants must maintain a 3.0 GPA, show unmet financial need, and be attending one of the UNCF member colleges and universities or selected HBCUs and majority institutions. Applicants must also show demonstrated leadership skills and academic achievement. *Application Process: Applicants should submit a completed application along with transcripts, resume, two recommendation letters, and a 500-word essay. Visit the UNCF Web site to download an application. *Amount: $5,000. *Deadline: November 5.

General Motors Sullivan Fellowship

Scholarship Name: General Motors Sullivan Fellowship. *Academic Area: Engineering (general). *Age Group: College freshmen, sophomores, and juniors. *Eligibility: Applicant must maintain a 3.0 GPA, show unmet financial need, and attend or plan to attend one of the following schools: Clark Atlanta University, Morehouse College, Spelman College, Tuskegee University. *Application Process: Applicants should contact the sponsoring institution directly for application procedures. *Amount: $5,000. *Deadline: Deadlines vary.

GlaxoSmithKline Company Science Achievement Award

Scholarship Name: GlaxoSmithKline Company Science Achievement Award. *Academic Area: Science. *Age Group: Graduate students. *Eligibility: Applicants must maintain a 3.0 GPA. Applicants can be attending any graduate school in the United States, but they must have graduated from a UNCF school. *Application Process: Applicants should submit a completed application along with an essay, transcripts, graduate school admission letter, two letters of recommendation, and a small head-shot photo. Visit the UNCF Web site to download an application. *Amount: $3,000. *Deadline: December 2.

Houghton Mifflin Company Fellows Program/ Internship

Scholarship Name: Houghton Mifflin Company Fellows Program/Internship. *Academic Area: Publishing. *Age Group: College juniors. *Eligibility: Applicants must maintain a 3.0 GPA, attend one of the 39 UNCF member colleges or universities, and have an interest in learning about the field of publishing. This scholarship is awarded in combination with a paid summer internship in publishing. *Application Process: Applicants should contact the sponsoring institution directly for application procedures. *Amount: $3,700 (scholarship), $3,300 (internship). *Deadline: Deadlines vary.

Intel Scholars Program

Scholarship Name: Intel Scholars Program. *Academic Area: Computer science, engineering (general). *Age Group: College sophomores. *Eligibility: Applicants must maintain a 3.0 GPA, demonstrate financial need, and be attending one of the UNCF member colleges or universities or one of the following additional institutions: North Carolina A&T State University, North Carolina State University, Georgia Institute of Technology, or Tennessee State University. *Application Process: Applicants should apply online through a link on the UNCF Web site. *Amount: Up to $5,000. *Deadline: March 31.

Jack and Jill of America Foundation Scholarship

Scholarship Name: Jack and Jill of America Foundation Scholarship. *Academic Area: Open. *Age Group: High school seniors. *Eligibility: Applicants must maintain a 3.0 GPA, have financial need, demonstrate leadership qualities, and agree to complete 60 hours of community service in the year following the awarding of the scholarship. *Application Process: Applicants should submit a completed application along with a resume, high school transcripts, an essay, and two letters of recommendation. Visit the UNCF Web site to download an application. *Amount: $1,500 to $2,500. *Deadline: March 14.

Jeffry and Barbara Picower Foundation Scholarship

Scholarship Name: Jeffry and Barbara Picower Foundation Scholarship. *Academic Area: Open. *Age Group: High school seniors, undergraduate students, graduate students. *Eligibility: Applicants must maintain a 3.0 GPA, demonstrate financial need, and attend or plan to attend one of the 39 UNCF member colleges or universities. *Application Process: Applicants should contact the sponsoring institution directly for application procedures. *Amount: $5,000. *Deadline: Deadlines vary.

Jesse Jones Jr. Scholarship

Scholarship Name: Jesse Jones, Jr. Scholarship. *Academic Area: Business. *Age Group: High school seniors, undergraduate students. *Eligibility: Applicants must maintain a 2.5 GPA, demonstrate unmet financial need, and attend or be planning to attend one of the 39 UNCF member colleges or universities. *Application Process: Applicants should contact the sponsoring institution directly for application procedures. *Amount: $2,000 to $5,000. *Deadline: Deadlines vary.

Jimi Hendrix Endowment Fund Scholarship

Scholarship Name: Jimi Hendrix Endowment Fund Scholarship. *Academic Area: Performing arts (music-general). *Age Group: High school seniors, undergraduate students. *Eligibility: Applicants must maintain a 2.5 GPA, show unmet financial need, and attend or be planning to attend one of the 39 UNCF member colleges or universities. *Application Process: Applicants should contact the sponsoring institution directly for application procedures. *Amount: $2,000 to $5,000. *Deadline: Deadlines vary.

John Lennon Scholarship

Scholarship Name: John Lennon Scholarship. *Academic Area: Performing arts (music-general). *Age Group: High school seniors, undergraduate students. *Eligibility: Applicants must maintain a 3.0 GPA, demonstrate financial need, and attend or plan to attend one of the 39 UNCF member colleges or universities. *Application Process: Applicants should submit a completed application along with transcripts, two references, an autobiographical essay, financial need statement, and a small head-shot photo. Visit the UNCF Web site to download an application. *Amount: $5,000. *Deadline: March 14.

Mae Maxey Memorial Scholarship

Scholarship Name: Mae Maxey Memorial Scholarship. *Academic Area: Open. *Age Group: High school seniors, undergraduate students. *Eligibility: Applicants must maintain a 2.5 GPA and be attending or planning to attend one of the 39 UNCF member colleges or universities. While the scholarship is open to all, students who express an interest in poetry are given priority. *Application Process: Applicants should contact the sponsoring institution directly for application procedures. *Amount: $1,000 to $5,000. *Deadline: Deadlines vary.

Malcolm X Scholarship for Exceptional Courage

Scholarship Name: Malcolm X Scholarship for Exceptional Courage. *Academic Area: Open. *Age Group: High school seniors, undergraduate students. *Eligibility: Applicants must maintain a 2.5 GPA, demonstrate financial need, and attend or plan to attend one of the 39 UNCF member colleges or universities. Applicants who have overcome tremendous obstacles, hardships, or special circumstances are encouraged to apply. *Application Process: Applicants should submit a completed application along with an essay, transcripts, two recommendation letters, and a small head-shot photo. Visit the UNCF Web site to download an application. *Amount: $4,000. *Deadline: March 7.

Mary E. Scott Memorial Scholarship

Scholarship Name: Mary E. Scott Memorial Scholarship. *Academic Area: Open. *Age Group: High school seniors, undergraduate students. *Eligibility: Applicants must maintain a 2.5 GPA, demonstrate financial need, and attend or plan to attend one of the 39 UNCF member colleges or universities. *Application Process: Applicants should contact the sponsoring institution directly to obtain application procedures. *Amount: $1,500 to $5,000. *Deadline: Deadlines vary.

Maytag Company Scholarship

Scholarship Name: Maytag Company Scholarship. *Academic Area: Business, computer science, engineering (general), information technology. *Age Group: Undergraduate students, graduate students. *Eligibility: Applicants must maintain a 2.5 GPA, demonstrate unmet financial need, and attend one of the following schools: Benedict College, Claflin University, Lane College, Morris College, Paine College, Philander Smith College, Voorhees College, Wilberforce University, or Historically Black Colleges and Universities. *Application Process: Applicants should contact the sponsoring institution for application procedures. *Amount: $1,250. *Deadline: Deadlines vary.

Medtronic Foundation Internship/Scholarship

Scholarship Name: Medtronic Foundation Internship/ Scholarship. *Academic Area: Engineering (general), science. *Age Group: College sophomores and juniors. *Eligibility: Applicants must maintain have a minimum 3.3 GPA and attend one of the 39 UNCF member colleges or universities. *Application Process: Applicants should submit a completed application along with transcripts, a resume, two letters of recommendation, an autobiographical essay including career aspirations, and a small head-shot photograph. Visit the UNCF Web site to download an application. *Amount: $5,000. *Deadline: March 15.

Mike and Stephanie Bozic Scholarship

Scholarship Name: Mike and Stephanie Bozic Scholarship. *Academic Area: Open. *Age Group: High school seniors, undergraduate students. *Eligibility: Applicants must be attending or planning to attend one of the 39 UNCF member colleges or universities, maintain a 2.5 GPA, and demonstrate unmet financial need. *Application Process: Applicants should contact the sponsor directly for application information. *Amount: Awards vary. *Deadline: Deadlines vary.

Mitsubishi Motors U.S.A. Foundation Leadership Awards

Scholarship Name: Mitsubishi Motors U.S.A. Foundation Leadership Award. *Academic Area: Open. *Age Group: High school seniors, undergraduate students. *Eligibility: Applicants must maintain a 2.5 GPA, demonstrate unmet financial need, and attend or plan to attend one of the 39 UNCF member colleges or universities. Applicants should also have community service experience that demonstrates their leadership in community activities. *Application Process: Applicants should submit a completed application along with transcripts, two letters of recommendation, a financial need statement, and answers to two short essay questions listed on the application. Visit the UNCF Web site to download an application. *Amount: $2,000. *Deadline: October 29.

Nathalia Bowser Scholarship

Scholarship Name: Nathalia Bowser Scholarship. *Academic Area: Open. *Age Group: Undergraduate students, graduate students. *Eligibility: Applicants must be African-American males attending Morris College or Voorhees College in South Carolina. Applicants also must maintain a 2.5 GPA. *Application

Process: Applicants should contact the sponsor directly for application information. *Amount: $1,500. *Deadline: Deadlines vary.

National Association for the Advancement of Colored People/Agnes Jones Jackson Scholarship
Scholarship Name: National Association for the Advancement of Colored People (NAACP)/Agnes Jones Jackson Scholarship. *Academic Area: Open. *Age Group: Undergraduate and graduate students under the age of 25. *Eligibility: Applicants must be current (verifiable) NAACP members, U.S. citizens, full-time students in an accredited college (A graduate student may be full- or part-time student), possess a 3.0 GPA (graduate students) or a 2.5 GPA (undergraduates), and demonstrate financial need. *Application Process: Applicants should submit a completed application along with three letters of recommendation, transcripts, a financial verification letter, evidence of enrollment, and a one-page essay. Visit the UNCF Web site to download an application. *Amount: $1,500 (undergraduate); $2,500 (graduate). *Deadline: March 25.

National Association for the Advancement of Colored People/Earl G. Graves Scholarship
Scholarship Name: National Association for the Advancement of Colored People (NAACP)/Earl G. Graves Scholarship. *Academic Area: Business. *Age Group: College junior and seniors, graduate students. *Eligibility: Applicants must be full-time students in good academic standing at an accredited college and must be in the top 20 percent of their class. *Application Process: Applicants should submit a completed application along with three letters of recommendation, transcripts, evidence of full-time enrollment, and a one-page essay. Visit the UNCF Web site to download an application. *Amount: $5,000. *Deadline: March 25.

National Association for the Advancement of Colored People/Historically Black College and University Scholarship Fund
Scholarship Name: National Association for the Advancement of Colored People (NAACP)/Historically Black College and University Scholarship Fund. *Academic Area: Open. *Age Group: High school seniors. *Eligibility: Applicants must be incoming freshmen planning to attend a Historically Black College or University. Applicants must also maintain a 2.5 GPA and demonstrate financial need. *Application Process: Applicants should submit a completed

application along with transcripts, three letters of recommendation, financial verification information, an essay, and evidence of full-time enrollment. Visit the UNCF Web site to download an application. *Amount: $2,000. *Deadline: March 25.

National Association for the Advancement of Colored People/Lillian and Samuel Sutton Education Scholarship
Scholarship Name: National Association for the Advancement of Colored People (NAACP)/Lillian and Samuel Sutton Education Scholarship. *Academic Area: Education. *Age Group: High school seniors, undergraduate students, and graduate students. *Eligibility: Applicants must be U.S. citizens, full-time students in an accredited college in the United States (a graduate student may be a full- or part-time student), possess a 3.0 GPA (graduate students) or a 2.5 GPA (undergraduate students), and demonstrate financial need. NAACP membership and participation is desirable. *Application Process: Applicants must submit a completed application along with two letters of recommendation, evidence of enrollment, transcripts, financial verification information, and a one-page essay. Visit the UNCF Web site to download an application. *Amount: $1,000 (undergraduate); $2,000 (graduate). *Deadline: March 25, 2005.

National Association for the Advancement of Colored People/Roy Wilkins Educational Scholarship
Scholarship Name: National Association for the Advancement of Colored People (NAACP)/Roy Wilkins Educational Scholarship. *Academic Area: Open. *Age Group: High school seniors. *Eligibility: Applicants must have a 2.5 GPA (high school) and demonstrate financial need. NAACP membership and participation is desirable. *Application Process: Applicants should submit a completed application along with transcripts, a letter verifying acceptance to college, a financial need statement, and proof of NAACP membership, if applicable. Visit the UNCF Web site to download an application. *Amount: $1,000. *Deadline: March 25.

National Association for the Advancement of Colored People/Willems, Hubertus W. V. Scholarship for Male Students
Scholarship Name: National Association for the Advancement of Colored People (NAACP)/Willems, Hubertus W. V. Scholarship for Male Students. *Academic Area: Chemistry, engineering (general),

mathematics, science. *Age Group: High school seniors, undergraduate students, graduate students. *Eligibility: Applicant must be male U.S. citizens who are attending an accredited college as full-time students (graduate students may be part-time students). They must also have a 2.5 GPA (undergraduates) or a 3.0 GPA (graduate students) and demonstrate financial need. NAACP membership and participation is highly desirable. *Application Process: Applicants should submit a completed application along with transcripts, evidence of enrollment, financial verification information, and a one-page essay. Visit the UNCF Web site to download an application. *Amount: $2,000 (undergraduates); $3,000 (graduate students). *Deadline: March 25.

Nelnet Scholarship

Scholarship Name: Nelnet Scholarship. *Academic Area: Open. *Age Group: High school seniors, undergraduate students. *Eligibility: Applicants must maintain a 2.5 GPA, demonstrate unmet financial need, and attend or plan to attend one of the 39 UNCF member colleges or universities. *Application Process: Applicants should contact the sponsoring institution directly for application procedures. *Amount: $1,000. *Deadline: Deadlines vary.

Nicholas H. Noyes Jr. Memorial Foundation Scholarship

Scholarship Name: Nicholas H. Noyes Jr. Memorial Foundation Scholarship. *Academic Area: Open. *Age Group: High school seniors, undergraduate students. *Eligibility: Applicants must possess a 2.5 GPA, demonstrate financial need, and attend or plan to attend one of the 39 UNCF member colleges or universities. *Application Process: Applicants should submit a completed application and supporting materials. Visit the UNCF Web site to download an application. *Amount: Awards vary, based on need. *Deadline: Deadlines vary.

Nissan/United Negro College Fund

Scholarship Name: Nissan/United Negro College Fund. *Academic Area: Business, engineering (general), finance, marketing. *Age Group: High school seniors. *Eligibility: Applicants must be students enrolled in a Los Angeles Unified School District school and must be planning to attend a Historically Black College or University (HBCU). Applicants must also have a 3.0 GPA. *Application Process: Applicants should submit a completed application along with

two recommendations, an essay (subject listed on application), high school transcripts, and a letter of acceptance from an HBCU. Visit the UNCF Web site to download an application. *Amount: $10,000. *Deadline: June 6.

Northrop Grumman Diversity Scholarship

Scholarship Name: Northrop Grumman Diversity Scholarship. *Academic Area: Computer science, engineering (computer), engineering (electrical), engineering (mechanical), and mathematics. *Age Group: College sophomores, juniors and seniors, graduate students. *Eligibility: Applicants should have a 3.0 GPA and attend or plan to attend selected HBCUs and majority institutions. This scholarship supports females and minorities in the technical disciplines. *Application Process: Applicants should submit a resume along with transcripts, resume, two letters of recommendation, and answers to a few short essays (listed on application). Visit the UNCF Web site to download an application. *Amount: $1,500 and up. *Deadline: February 28.

Principal Financial Group Scholarship

Scholarship Name: Principal Financial Group Scholarship. *Academic Area: Business, finance, information technology. *Age Group: High school seniors, undergraduate students. *Eligibility: Applicants must maintain a 3.0 GPA, demonstrate financial need, and attend or plan to attend one of the 39 UNCF member colleges or universities. Applicants must be residents of Iowa who value community involvement and academic achievement. *Application Process: Applicants should submit an application along with transcripts, a personal statement, two letters of recommendation, a letter of acceptance from a UNCF school, and their most recent tax return. Visit the UNCF Web site to download an application. *Amount: Up to $12,000, based on need. *Deadline: March 1.

Raymond W. Cannon Memorial Scholarship

Scholarship Name: Raymond W. Cannon Memorial Scholarship. *Academic Area: Law, pharmaceutical sciences. *Age Group: College juniors. *Eligibility: Applicants must be attending one of the 39 UNCF member colleges or universities, maintain a 2.5 GPA, and possess demonstrated leadership skills in high school and college. *Application Process: Applicants should contact the scholarship sponsor directly for application information. *Amount: $2,000 to $5,000. *Deadline: Deadlines vary.

Reader's Digest Scholarship

Scholarship Name: Reader's Digest Scholarship.
  *Academic Area: Communication sciences, English/
  literature, journalism. *Age Group: College juniors and
  seniors. *Eligibility: Applicants must maintain a 3.0
  GPA, demonstrate financial need, attend one of the
  39 UNCF member colleges or universities, and have
  an interest in print journalism. *Application Process:
  Applicants should submit a completed application
  along with transcripts, recommendations, a published
  writing sample, a personal statement, a financial
  need statement, and a small head-shot photograph.
  Visit the UNCF Web site to download an application.
  *Amount: $5,000. *Deadline: November 18.

Robert Dole Scholarship

Scholarship Name: Robert Dole Scholarship. *Academic
  Area: Open. *Age Group: High school seniors,
  undergraduate students. *Eligibility: Applicants must
  be attending or planning to attend one of the 39
  UNCF member colleges or universities, maintain a
  2.5 GPA, prove unmet financial need, and be either
  physically or mentally challenged. *Application
  Process: Applicants should submit a completed
  application along with a nomination letter from a
  faculty member, transcripts, a 500-word essay, and
  a financial need statement. Visit the UNCF Web
  site to download an application. *Amount: $3,000.
  *Deadline: October 31.

Robert Half International Scholarship

Scholarship Name: Robert Half International. *Academic
  Area: Accounting, business. *Age Group: High
  school seniors, undergraduate students. *Eligibility:
  Applicants must maintain a 2.5 GPA, show unmet
  financial need, and be attending or planning to attend
  one of the 39 UNCF member colleges or universities.
  *Application Process: Applicants should contact
  the sponsoring institution directly for application
  procedures. *Amount: $1,000 to $1,750. *Deadline:
  Deadlines vary.

Sallie Mae Fund American Dream Scholarship

Scholarship Name: Sallie Mae Fund American Dream
  Scholarship. *Academic Area: Open. *Age Group: High
  school seniors, undergraduate students. *Eligibility:
  Applicants must maintain a minimum 2.5 GPA and
  demonstrate financial need. *Application Process:
  Applicants should apply online via a link at the UNCF
  Web site. *Amount: $500 to $5,000. *Deadline: April 15.

Samuel Newhouse Scholarship

Scholarship Name: Samuel Newhouse Scholarship.
  *Academic Area: Open. *Age Group: High school
  seniors, undergraduate students. *Eligibility:
  Applicants must maintain a 3.0 GPA, demonstrate
  financial need, and attend or plan to attend one of the
  following schools: Dillard University, Miles College,
  Oakwood College, Stillman College, Talladega College,
  Tuskegee University, or Xavier University. *Application
  Process: Applicants should contact the sponsoring
  institution directly for information on the application
  procedure. *Amount: Awards vary, based on need.
  *Deadline: Deadlines vary.

SBC Foundation Scholarship

Scholarship Name: SBC Foundation Scholarship.
  *Academic Area: Business, computer science,
  economics, engineering (general), finance,
  information technology. *Age Group: College juniors.
  *Eligibility: Applicants must maintain a 3.0 GPA,
  demonstrate financial need, and attend one of the
  39 UNCF member colleges or universities. Applicants
  must also be permanent residents of one of the
  following states: Arkansas, California, Illinois, Indiana,
  Kansas, Michigan, Missouri, Oklahoma, Ohio, Texas, or
  Wisconsin. *Application Process: Applicants should
  submit a completed application along with two
  nominating letters, a one-page personal statement,
  transcripts, a resume, and a small head-shot photo.
  Visit the UNCF Web site to download an application.
  *Amount: $5,000. *Deadline: January 17.

Sodexho Scholarship

Scholarship Name: Sodexho Scholarship. *Academic
  Area: Medicine (general), political science, social
  work. *Age Group: High school seniors, college
  freshmen. Eligibility: Applicants must maintain a 3.0
  GPA, demonstrate financial need, and attend or plan
  to attend one of the 39 UNCF member colleges or
  universities or a HBCU school. Applicants should have
  an interest in careers that focus on health disciplines,
  government, or combating homelessness or other
  social welfare programs. *Application Process:
  Applicants should contact the sponsoring institution
  directly for application procedures. *Amount: Up to
  $3,500. *Deadline: Deadlines vary.

SouthTrust Scholarship/Internship

Scholarship Name: SouthTrust Scholarship/Internship.
  *Academic Area: Business. *Age Group: College

sophomores and juniors. *Eligibility: Applicants must maintain a 3.0 GPA, demonstrate financial need, and attend one of the 39 UNCF member colleges or universities. Applicants must also be willing to commit to a six- to eight-week summer internship. *Application Process: Applicants should submit a completed application along with transcripts, a 500-word essay, two letters of recommendation, a financial need statement, and a small head-shot photograph. Visit the UNCF Web site to download an application. *Amount: $6,250. *Deadline: March 30.

Sterling Bank Scholarship
Scholarship Name: Sterling Bank Scholarship. *Academic Area: Open. *Age Group: High school seniors, undergraduate students. *Eligibility: Applicants must maintain a 2.5 GPA, demonstrate financial need, and attend or plan to attend one of the 39 UNCF member colleges or universities. *Application Process: Applicants should contact the sponsoring institution directly to obtain application information. *Amount: Awards vary, based on need. *Deadline: Deadlines vary.

Terex/United Negro College Fund Scholarship
Scholarship Name: Terex/United Negro College Fund Scholarship. *Academic Area: Open. *Age Group: Undergraduate students, graduate students. *Eligibility: Applicants must be employees or children of employees of Terex Corporation. Applicants must also maintain a 3.0 GPA. *Application Process: Applicants should submit a completed application along with supporting materials. Visit the UNCF Web site to download an application. *Amount: $2,500. *Deadline: Deadlines vary.

Time Warner Scholars Program
Scholarship Name: Time Warner Scholars Program. *Academic Area: Open. *Age Group: College sophomores. *Eligibility: Applicants should maintain a 3.0 GPA, demonstrate financial need, and attend one of the following participating Historically Black Colleges and Universities: Benedict College, Bennett College for Women, Bethune-Cookman College, Claflin University, Clark Atlanta University, Dillard University, Edward Waters College, Fisk University, Florida A&M University, Florida Memorial College, Huston-Tillotson College, Johnson C. Smith University, Lane College, LeMoyne-Owen College,

Livingstone College, Miles College, Morehouse College, Morris College, Norfolk State University, Oakwood College, Paine College, Paul Quinn College, Philander Smith College, Rust College, Saint Augustine's College, Saint Paul's College, Shaw University, Spelman College, Stillman College, Talladega College, Tougaloo College, Tuskegee University, Virginia Union University, Voorhees College, Wilberforce University, Wiley College, or Xavier University. *Application Process: Applicants should apply online via a link on the UNCF Web site. *Amount: $2,500. *Deadline: October 15.

Toyota/United Negro College Fund Scholarship
Scholarship Name: Toyota/United Negro College Fund Scholarship. *Academic Area: Business, communications science, computer science, engineering (general), English/literature, information technology. *Age Group: High school seniors or college freshmen. *Eligibility: Applicants must maintain a 3.0 GPA, demonstrate financial need, and attend one of the following schools: Bethune-Cookman College, Clark Atlanta University, Morehouse College, Spelman College, Tuskegee University, or Xavier University. *Application Process: Applicants should submit a completed application along with recommendations, transcripts, one-page personal statement, resume, and a small head-shot photograph. Visit the UNCF Web site to download an application. *Amount: $7,500, renewable through senior year. *Deadline: October 28.

TRW Information Technology Minority Scholarship
Scholarship Name: TRW Information Technology Minority Scholarship. *Academic Area: Computer science. *Age Group: College sophomores and juniors. *Eligibility: Applicants must maintain a 3.0 GPA, demonstrate financial need, and attend one of the following schools: George Mason University, Howard University, Morgan State, Pennsylvania State, or Virginia Polytechnic Institute. *Application Process: Applicants should contact the sponsoring institution directly for application procedures. *Amount: $3,000. *Deadline: Deadlines vary.

UBS/PaineWebber Scholarship
Scholarship Name: UBS/PaineWebber Scholarship. *Academic Area: Business. *Age Group: College sophomores and juniors. *Eligibility: Applicants

must maintain a 3.0 GPA, have unmet financial need, and attend one of the 39 UNCF member colleges or universities. *Application Process: Applicants should submit a completed application along with two letters of nomination, a three-page essay that describes their leadership abilities, resume, transcripts, and a head-shot photograph. Visit the UNCF Web site to download an application. *Amount: $8,000. *Deadline: March 18.

United Negro College Fund/Foot Locker Foundation, Inc. Scholarship

Scholarship Name: United Negro College Fund/Foot Locker Foundation Inc. Scholarship. *Academic Area: Open. *Age Group: Undergraduate students, graduate students. *Eligibility: Applicants must maintain a 2.5 GPA, demonstrate financial need, and attend one of the 39 UNCF member colleges or universities. *Application Process: Applicants should submit a completed application along with transcripts, two nomination letters, a financial need statement, and a one-page autobiographical essay. Visit the UNCF Web site to download an application. *Amount: $5,000. *Deadline: April 1.

United Parcel Service Foundation

Scholarship Name: United Parcel Service Foundation Scholarship. *Academic Area: Open. *Age Group: Undergraduate students, graduate students. *Eligibility: Applicants must maintain a 2.5 GPA, demonstrate unmet financial need, and attend one of the 39 UNCF member colleges or universities. *Application Process: Applicants should submit a completed application along with supporting materials. Visit the UNCF Web site to download an application. *Amount: Awards vary, based on need. *Deadline: Deadlines vary.

USENIX Association Scholarship

Scholarship Name: USENIX Association Scholarship. *Academic Area: Computer science, information technology. *Age Group: Undergraduate students, graduate students. *Eligibility: Applicants must maintain a 3.5 GPA, demonstrate unmet financial need, and attend one of the 39 UNCF member colleges or universities. *Application Process: Applicants should contact the sponsoring institution directly for information about application procedures. *Amount: Up to $10,000. *Deadline: Deadlines vary.

ORGANIZATIONS

This section includes professional organizations, minority colleges, fraternities and sororities, and other groups that assist individuals with the pursuit of career, education, and community. In the section on professional organizations, you will find nonprofit associations composed of individuals working together to further minorities and students within their particular professions: the section on minority colleges includes those two-year and four-year institutions that have historically demonstrated a commitment to furthering minority students; the section on fraternities and sororities provides a list of some of the national organizations, and their chapters, serving minority college students and alumni; and the section on other organizations includes foundations, Native American tribes, job banks, employment services, and other groups that assist minorities.

PROFESSIONAL ORGANIZATIONS

African Scientific Institute
PO Box 12153
Oakland, CA 94604
510-653-7027
asi@QuixNet.net
http://www.asi-org.net
The institute helps enhance the awareness and
participation of African Americans in science
and technology. It also seeks to acquaint youth
with opportunities in scientific fields and helps
them prepare for careers in those fields. The
institute offers consulting and research services.
Through conferences and workshops, it allows for
professionals to network while developing their skills.
The institute also sponsors community and youth
programs.

American Association of Blacks in Energy
927 15th Street, NW, Suite 200
Washington, DC 20005
202-371-9530
http://www.aabe.org
This national association of energy professionals is
dedicated to serving as a resource for discussion
of the economic, social, and political impact of
environmental and energy policies on African
Americans and other minorities. The association also
encourages students to pursue careers in energy-
related fields by offering scholarships and other
financial aid.

American Health and Beauty Aids Institute (AHBAI)
401 North Michigan Avenue
Chicago, IL 60611
312-644-6610
ahbai@sba.com
http://www.ahbai.org
AHBAI represents the ethnic health and beauty aids (HBA)
industry. AHBAI consists of 17 member companies
with more than 100 associate members in a variety
of fields. AHBAI assists those in the industry with
job searches, scholarships, internships, and training.
Among its services, AHBAI helps to strengthen the link
between professionals and product manufacturers,
sponsors a trade show, conducts workshops, and
offers scholarship opportunities.

American Indian Library Association
http://www.nativeculturelinks.com/aila.html
This affiliate of the American Library Association serves
Native American library professionals through
conferences, newsletters, and other services.

**American Indian Science and Engineering Society
(AISES)**
PO Box 9828
Albuquerque, NM 87119-9828
505-765-1052
info@aises.org
http://www.aises.org
The AISES sponsors a national conference, a student
science fair, college scholarships, internships, and
publishes a magazine, Winds of Change. AISES is
composed of both professional and college chapters.

Asian American Journalists Association
1182 Market Street, Suite 320
San Francisco, CA 94102
415-346-2051
national@aaja.org
http://www.aaja.org
The Asian American Journalists Association (AAJA) was
formed in 1981 and seeks to: increase employment
of Asian American print and broadcast journalists;
assist high school and college students of Asian
heritage pursuing journalism careers; encourage
fair, sensitive, and accurate news coverage of Asian
American issues; and provide support for Asian
American journalists. The AAJA hosts a national
convention, sponsors scholarships and fellowships,
offers a newsletter and other publications, provides
job services, offers national awards, and maintains an
informative Web site.

Asian American Law Enforcement Association
aaleachgo@aol.com
http://www.aalea.org
This not-for-profit organization represents Asian
Americans in law enforcement agencies in Chicago,
the greater Chicagoland area, and Midwestern
states. It encourages the recruitment, hiring,
and promotion of Asians in all areas of law
enforcement.

Asian American MultiTechnology Association

3300 Zanker Road, Maildrop SJ2F8
San Jose, CA 95134
408-955-4505
aama@aamasv.com
http://www.aamasv.com
This association of corporations and individuals
promotes the growth and success of U.S. technology
manufacturing and related enterprises throughout
the Pacific Rim.

Asian American Psychological Association (AAPA)

PMB #527
5025 North Central Avenue
Phoenix, AZ 85012
602-230-4257
http://www.aapaonline.org
Among its purposes, the AAPA seeks to advance the
welfare of Asian Americans by encouraging, assisting,
and advocating research on and service to Asian
Americans. The AAPA also offers student membership,
conducts meetings, issues publications and other
educational materials, and informs others of
sociopsychological issues facing Asian Americans.

Asian Professional Exchange (APEX)

207 East Franklin Avenue, Suite B
El Segundo, CA 90245
http://www.apex.org
The Asian Professional Exchange is a nonprofit
community-based organization with goals and
purposes that are charitable, cultural, and educational
in nature. APEX is generally comprised of Asian
Americans in their 20s and 30s, who are professionals,
entrepreneurs, and graduate students in the Southern
California area. APEX serves as a medium to bring
increased awareness about and to Asian Americans
through community service, fellowship, charitable
fund-raisers, cultural events, professional networking,
and educational seminars.

Association for the Advancement of Creative Musicians (AACM)

410 South Michigan Avenue, Suite 943
Chicago, IL 60680
312-922-1900
greatblackmusic@aacmchicago.org
http://aacmchicago.org
The association is a collective of musicians and
composers dedicated to nurturing, performing,
and recording serious, original music. The AACM
pays homage to the diverse styles of expression
within the body of Black music in the United States,
Africa, and throughout the world. It sponsors public
concerts and a free music-training program for city
youth.

Association of African American Web Developers

http://www.aaawd.net
This is a professional association for African Americans in
all phases of Web development. Student members are
also welcome.

Association of African Women Scholars

aaws@iupui.edu
http://www.iupui.edu/~aaws
This worldwide organization is dedicated to promoting
and encouraging scholarship on African women in
African studies and forming networks with scholars,
activists, students, and policy makers inside and
outside Africa.

Association of American Indian Physicians

1225 Sovereign Row, Suite 103
Oklahoma City, OK 73108
405-946-7072
aaip@aaip.com
http://www.aaip.com
This association seeks to increase the recruitment and
retention of Native American high school and college
students into the medical and health professions
(including the allied health professions, such as
dentistry, veterinary medicine, optometry, and
pharmacy). It offers preadmission workshops, job
shadowing, and a mentoring program.

Association of Black Cardiologists (ABC)

6849 B-2 Peachtree Dunwoody Road, NE
Atlanta, GA 30328
800-753-9222
abcardio@abcardio.org
http://www.abcardio.org
Representing African-American cardiologists and
medical professionals, the ABC sponsors a number of
programs including training and legislative programs.
Its Cardiologists-In-Training Program offers seminars
such as "Searching for a Job" and "Post-Residency/
Fellowship Employment Contracts: Negotiating
Your Life After Training," as well as fellowships and
mentoring opportunities to medical students.

Association of Black Psychologists

PO Box 55999
Washington, DC 20040-5999
202-722-0808
http://www.abpsi.org
The association works to address the psychological needs of African Americans through research publications and assessment techniques. It is currently working to establish professional certification, training, and development programs. The association offers membership to African-American undergraduate and graduate students who are studying psychology.

Association of Hispanic Advertising Agencies (AHAA)

8201 Greensboro Drive, 2nd Floor
McLean, VA 22102
703-610-9014
info@ahaa.org
http://www.ahaa.org
The mission of the AHAA is to promote the growth, strength, and professionalism of the Hispanic marketing and advertising industry to a diverse audience of business, government, and educational institutions. It offers a semiannual conference and continuing education opportunities and research data at its Web site.

Association of Hispanic Healthcare Executives

PO Box 230832, Ansonia Station
New York, NY 10023
212-877-1615
ahheinnyc@aol.com
http://www.ahhe.org
This organization works to increase the presence of Hispanics in health administration professions. It offers an internship/mentorship program for undergraduate students, and undergraduate and graduate fellowships.

Association of Latino Professionals in Finance and Accounting (ALPFA)

510 West Sixth Street, Suite 400
Los Angeles, CA 90014
213-243-0004
info@national.alpfa.org
http://www.alpfa.org
The ALPFA is a national organization (formerly known as the American Association of Hispanic Certified Public Accountants) that is dedicated to helping Hispanic students, accountants, CPAs, and finance professionals enhance their professional capabilities while expanding Hispanic representation in the nation's work force. The ALPFA works to increase enrollment of Hispanic accounting students and to promote the hiring and retention of Hispanic accounting and finance graduates throughout the Big Three accounting firms, other major international and national firms, and regional and local firms. It also assists these firms in the recruiting, developing, and promoting of Hispanic professionals, provides networking and career opportunities for its members, and expands business relationships between Hispanic CPA firms, the corporate sector, and major accounting firms. The ALPFA is open to all Hispanic CPAs, accountants, and finance-related professionals and students. Each year, the ALPFA holds a national convention and offers its participants quality continuing professional education, along with networking and career opportunities.

Association of Mexican Professionals of Silicon Valley

1169 South Tenth Street
San Jose, CA 95112
http://www.mexpro.org
The association represents Mexican professionals in the technology industry and works to strengthen Mexico-United States relations.

Black Americans in Publishing

PO Box 6275
FDR Station
New York, NY 10150
212-772-5951
http://aalbc.com/writers/black2.htm
This organization, (formerly known as Black Women in Publishing), is an employee-based trade association. It works to increase the presence of African-American professionals in the publishing industry. Through meetings and publications, it creates networking forums, assists with career growth and entrepreneurial opportunities, and recognizes those successful in the industry. Members work in many different areas of the publishing industry, including human resources, editorial and management, finance and production, art and design, marketing and sales, and wholesale and retail. They are writers, publishers, freelancers, agents, attorneys, CEOs, VPs, and business owners.

Black Business Expo and Trade Show

3683 Crenshaw Boulevard, Suite 502
Los Angeles, CA 90016

323-290-4743
info@blackbusinessexpo.com
http://www.blackbusinessexpo.com
The Black Business Expo and Trade Show is an event in
    Los Angeles showcasing the products and services of
    Black-owned businesses in such areas as health care,
    manufacturing, technology, and commerce.

Black Career Women (BCW)
PO Box 19332
Cincinnati, OH 45219-0332
513-531-1932
http://www.bcw.org
This organization is devoted to the professional
    development of African-American women. With
    nationwide contacts, BCW gives the working
    African-American woman a forum for learning and
    for enriching her career. BCW hosts workshops and
    seminars. Its Web site features career information, job
    listings, and a variety of other useful resources.

Black Caucus of the American Library Association
PO Box 1738
Hampton, VA 23669
http://www.bcala.org
This national organization of librarians promotes African
    Americans in the profession. It holds semi-annual
    meetings and conferences, publishes a newsletter,
    and awards scholarships. It provides information on
    education and careers (including a Career Bibliography)
    at its Web site.

Black Coaches Association
Pan American Plaza
201 South Capitol Avenue, Suite 495
Indianapolis, IN 46225
317-829-5600
http://www.bcasports.org
BCA focuses on the concerns of minority coaches within
    the NCAA, the NAIA, and in the junior college, high
    school, and professional ranks. Projects include
    conventions and workshops. Its Web site offers job
    listings and information on postgraduate scholarships.

Black Culinarian Alliance (BCA)
55 West 116th Street, Suite 234
New York, NY 10026
800-308-8188
info@thebca.net
http://www.blackculinarians.com

BCA addresses issues of multiculturalism within the
    hospitality industry. It hosts annual events and
    provides networking opportunities.

Black Data Processing Associates (BDPA)
6301 Ivy Lane, Suite 700
Greenbelt, MD 20770
800-727-2372
info@bdpa.org
http://www.bdpa.org
BDPA serves to strengthen the link between the
    information technology industry and African-
    American communities. The organization consists of
    more than 55 local chapters across the country, and
    it offers many services including: career counseling,
    technological assistance, networking opportunities,
    workshops, and computer competitions. BDPA serves
    students and IT professionals seeking advancement.
    Through educational and executive programs, an
    annual conference, and online resources, BDPA assists
    its members with career development.

Blacks in Government
3005 Georgia Avenue, NW
Washington, DC 20001-3807
202-667-3280
http://www.bignet.org
Blacks in Government is an organization that provides
    employee support, advocacy, and resources for
    African-American civil servants. It sponsors a national
    training conference and networking opportunities.

California Chicano News Media Association (CCNMA)
USC Annenberg School of Journalism
One California Plaza
300 South Grand Avenue, Suite 3950
Los Angeles, CA 90071-8110
213-437-4408
ccnmainfo@ccnma.org
http://www.ccnma.org
The CCNMA serves media professionals and employers
    nationwide. It works to promote diversity in print and
    broadcast newsrooms and news coverage. CCNMA
    achieves this through internship and scholarship
    programs, networking opportunities for students and
    professionals, and job placement services.

California Librarians Black Caucus (CLBC)
PO Box 2906
Los Angeles, CA 90078-2906

310-835-3350
information@clbc.org
http://www.clbc.org
The California Librarians Black Caucus is a statewide organization with branches in Northern and Southern California. It works to increase the numbers of African Americans in the library workplace and to assist them in their professional development. It also speaks on behalf of African-American communities regarding the provision of library and information services, and promotes literature and information by and about African Americans.

Center for the Advancement of Hispanics in Science and Engineering Education
8100 Corporate Drive, Suite 401
Landover, MD 20785
301-918-1014
http://www.cahsee.org
This organization seeks to overcome the underrepresentation of Hispanics in the engineering and scientific community by offering resources, opportunities, and program for Hispanic youth in science and engineering education. Visit its Web site for details.

Chinese American Medical Society (CAMS)
281 Edgewood Avenue
Teaneck, NJ 07666
hw5@columbia.edu
http://www.camsociety.org
This nonprofit organization works to promote medical professionals of Chinese descent through such activities as annual meetings, scientific research, and a scholarship program. CAMS also provides endowments to medical schools and hospitals. Members include physicians in primary care as well as various specialties in academic and research institutions, and medical students.

Conference of Minority Public Administrators (COMPA)
22 Lincoln Street
Hampton, VA 23669
757-727-6377
http://www.natcompa.org
The Conference of Minority Public Administrators is unique in that it is the only national entity devoted primarily to providing professional development opportunities for all America's minority public administrators. COMPA works to eliminate the institutional and social barriers to the professional development and employment of minority public administrators. Specific goals are to provide leadership in the elimination of discriminatory practices in the public sector; promote recruitment of minorities for leadership positions at all levels of government; provide a forum to promote, upgrade, and refine skills of minority administrators; and develop and maintain a roster of skilled minority professionals in public administration. COMPA sponsors an annual national symposium, publishes a journal and newsletter for its members, and awards scholarships to deserving students of public administration, public affairs, and public policy.

Conference of Minority Transportation Officials
818 18th Street, NW, Suite 850
Washington, DC 20006
202-530-0551
comto@comto.org
http://www.comto.org/start.htm
The conference represents those working in all areas of transportation. It maintains a job bank and offers opportunities in networking, training, education, and research. It also provides scholarships and a youth internship program.

Congressional Hispanic Caucus Institute (CHCI)
911 Second Street, NE
Washington, DC 20002
800-392-3532
http://www.chci.org
The Congressional Hispanic Caucus was established to monitor legislative and other government activity that affects Hispanics. It sponsors educational and internship programs, scholarships and fellowships, and other activities to increase the opportunities for Hispanics to participate in and contribute to the American political system. The board of directors includes influential Hispanic business persons from the private sector and community leaders from across the country who, in conjunction with the Hispanic members of Congress, bring to the institute policy-related knowledge and experience at the local, state, and national levels. The CHCI offers programs designed to afford leadership development training for talented young Hispanics, as well as the opportunity to enter a wider range of professional areas.

Emma L. Bowen Foundation

1299 Pennsylvania Avenue, NW, 11th Floor

Washington, DC 20004

202-637-4494

http://www.emmabowenfoundation.com

The Emma L. Bowen Foundation offers a multi-year work/study program for rising minority high school seniors who are interested in media careers. Students participate in the program throughout their college careers, learning industry-specific skills via mentorship and training programs with participating corporations. Many participants are offered positions after graduation. Contact the foundation for more information.

Hispanic Dental Association

188 West Randolph Street, Suite 415

Chicago, IL 60601

800-852-7921

HispanicDental@hdassoc.org

http://www.hdassoc.org

The Hispanic Dental Association is a national membership organization of Hispanic and non-Hispanic dental professionals including dentists, dental hygienists, dental assistants, dental technologists, academic and practicing professionals, students, and researchers. Its Web site features job listings and information on scholarships, membership for dental students, and issues of importance to dental professionals.

Hispanic Employment Program Managers (HEPM)

PO Box 230294

Centreville, VA 20120-0294

hepm@aol.com

866-437-3247

hepm@aol.com

http://www.hepm.org

HEPM focuses on the needs of Hispanic Americans in all areas of federal employment. It provides information about job opportunities, Hispanic culture, and multicultural events. Visit its Web site for job listings.

Hispanic National Bar Association (HNBA)

815 Connecticut Avenue, NW, Suite 500

Washington, DC 20006

202-223-4777

http://www.hnba.com

The HNBA works to advance Hispanics in the legal profession. It encourages Hispanics to enter the legal profession, promotes the appointment of Hispanics to positions of leadership, and promotes the appointment of Hispanic judges. The HNBA hosts networking opportunities, seminars, and provides information on employment opportunities. It also publishes a newsletter, offers scholarships, and assists the Hispanic community in obtaining legal services. Visit its Web site for job listings.

Hispanic Public Relations Association (HPRA)

660 South Figueroa Street, Suite 1140

Los Angeles, CA 90017

http://www.hprala.org

This professional membership organization of Hispanics working in public relations sponsors educational programs and provides assistance to students interested in careers in public relations. It also offers scholarships for students who are pursuing careers in public relations and related communications fields and who plan to attend a postsecondary institution in Southern California.

Hispanic-Serving Health Professions Schools

1120 Connecticut Avenue, NW, Suite 260

Washington, DC 20036

202-293-2701

hshps@hshps.com

http://www.hshps.com

This nonprofit organization represents more than 20 medical schools and three schools of public health across the United States. Its mission is to "improve the health of Hispanics through academic development, research initiatives and training." Visit its Web site for detailed information on public health careers, scholarship links, and details on the Health Careers Opportunity Program.

International Association of Black Professional Fire Fighters (IABPFF)

1020 North Taylor Avenue

St. Louis, MO 63113

786-229-6914

execdir411@hotmail.com

http://www.iabpff.org

The IABPFF serves fire fighters across the country through its many committees and local area chapters. It hosts an annual convention and lists job opportunities at its Web site.

International Black Buyers and Manufacturers Expo and Conference
http://www.ibbmec.com
This conference allows business owners to meet with African-American manufacturers, retailers, booksellers, importers/exporters, clothiers, fine artists/craftspeople, technology professionals, and service providers.

International Black Writers and Artists (IBWA)
PO Box 43576
Los Angeles, CA 90043
ibwa_la@yahoo.com
http://members.tripod.com/~IBWA/home.htm
IBWA/LA's vision is to expose and recognize writers and artists of color to ensure they are published, read, seen, and sought as a viable pool of talent. As a publishing group, IBWA solicits, critiques, selects, edits, and publishes manuscripts and visual arts in various forms. In addition, aid is offered to literary artists in their quests to prepare works for publication by themselves or others. IBWA provides visibility, information, education, and entertainment through a significant network of professionals and emerging faces. Benefits of membership include *Black Expressions*, the newsletter of the International Black Writers and Artists (which features job listings and internship opportunities); discounts on activities, services, and products of IBWA; priority consideration for UCLA Extension Scholarships; option of being listed in the *IBWA Directory of Artists and Writers*; and connection with professionals who share similar goals.

International Society of African Scientists (ISAS)
PO Box 9209
Wilmington, DE 19809
http://www.dca.net/isas
The ISAS sponsors annual technical conferences, offers a quarterly newsletter, maintains a directory of technical professionals of African descent, and provides assistance to educational and research institutions in Africa and the Caribbean.

Korean-American Scientists and Engineers Association (KSEA)
1952 Gallows Road, Suite 300
Vienna, VA 22182
703-748-1221
sejong@ksea.org

http://www.ksea.org/index.asp
The KSEA helps members develop their full career potential by providing professional opportunities in the areas of science, technology, and entrepreneurship. KSEA hosts an annual meeting and technical conference, offers scholarships and summer internships, sponsors youth programs, gives job referrals, and provides many other services.

Latin Business Association (LBA)
120 South San Pedro Street, Suite 530
Los Angeles, CA 90012
213-628-8510
http://www.lbausa.com
This nonprofit organization serves Hispanic-owned businesses across the United States. It supports the LBA Institute, which provides research, technical assistance, and access to capital for Latino entrepreneurs. Benefits of membership include a subscription to the LBA Business Review, monthly networking opportunities, and access to health care plans. It also hosts the National Latino Business Expo, one of the largest gatherings of Latino business owners in the United States.

Latino Professional Network (LPN)
PO Box 6019
Boston, MA 02209
617-247-1818
info@lpn.org
http://www.lpn.org
The Latino Professional Network is a membership organization for Hispanic professionals in Massachusetts and the nation. In cooperation with academic institutions such as Harvard University and Bentley College, the LPN also offers scholarships for high school and college students. At its Web site, visitors can post their resumes, learn about job opportunities, and read articles about issues currently affecting the Hispanic business community.

Law Enforcement Association of Asian Pacifics
905 East Second Street, Suite 200
Los Angeles, CA 90012
amerasia@starmail.com
http://members.tripod.com/~amerasia2
This is a professional association of law enforcement officers in federal, municipal, state, county, and other agencies.

Los Angeles Council of Black Professional Engineers (LACBPE)
PO Box 881029
Los Angeles, CA 90009
310-635-7734
secy1@successnet.net
http://www.lablackengineers.org
The LACBPE works to enhance the educational, employment, and business opportunities of minority engineers. The Council offers programs for students at all levels (such as EXCELL, which provides PSAT and SAT prep classes for minorities), consults with colleges and universities and employers regarding issues of importance to minorities, and offers scholarships. Visit its Web site for further information.

Minnesota American Indian Chamber of Commerce
1508 East Franklin Avenue, Suite 100
Minneapolis, MN 55404
612-870-4533
info@maicc.org
http://www.maicc.org
This organization supports American Indian entrepreneurs and the Native American community in Minnesota through programs and services. It provides education, training, and employment services to Native American youth and adults.

National Action Council for Minorities in Engineering (NACME)
440 Hamilton Avenue, Suite 302
White Plains NY 10601-1813
914-539-4010
webmaster@nacme.org
http://www.nacme.org
The NACME is a not-for-profit organization whose mission is to increase the representation of successful African Americans, Latinos, and American Indians in engineering. It conducts research, analyzes and advances public policies; develops and operates precollege and university programs, as well as awareness and training programs; and disseminates information through publications, conferences, and electronic media. NACME is best known for its national scholarship program. It also offers a Web site (http://www.guidemenacme.org/guideme) for students interested in learning more about engineering.

National Alliance of Black Interpreters
PO Box 5630
Evanston, IL 60204-5630
http://www.naobi.org
This organization promotes African Americans in the profession of sign language interpreting. Visit its Web site for information on educational opportunities, careers, and its annual conference.

National Alliance of Black School Educators (NABSE)
310 Pennsylvania Avenue, SE
Washington, DC 20003
800-221-2654
http://www.nabse.org
The NABSE is a nonprofit organization that serves as a network of African-American educators. The organization develops instructional methods to improve the education of African-American youth. It focuses on professional development programs that strengthen the skills of teachers, principals, and other educators, and on advocacy for high standards in education. The NABSE hosts conferences, awards scholarships and grants, and sponsors research programs.

National Alliance of Market Developers (NAMD)
620 Sheridan Avenue
Plainfield, NJ 07060
908-561-4062
http://www.namdntl.org
Membership of this organization consists of African-American professionals in marketing, management, advertising, sales, public relations, urban affairs, and related fields. In addition to offering professional support, the NAMD offers education and guidance programs.

National Asian Pacific American Bar Association (NAPABA)
910 17th Street, NW, Suite 315
Washington, DC 20006
202-775-9555
ed@napaba.org
http://www.napaba.org
This is a national association of Asian Pacific American attorneys, judges, law professors, and law students. NAPABA advocates for the legal needs and interests of the Asian Pacific American community. It offers scholarships to law students who show a commitment

to serve or contribute to the Asian Pacific American community.

National Association for Black Geologists and Geophysicists (NABGG)

4212 San Felipe, Suite 420
Houston, TX 77027-2902
nabgg_us@ hotmail.com
http://www.nabgg.com
The NABGG was organized to inform students of career opportunities that exist in the fields of geology and geophysics, and to encourage them to take advantage of scholarship programs, grants, and loans that are established for minority students. The association also aids minority students in the search for summer employment and aids corporate members interested in obtaining summer employees for positions that will enhance the students' background and marketability. Visit its Web site for more information.

National Association for Multi-Ethnicity in Communications (NAMIC)

336 West 37th Street, Suite 302
New York, NY 10018
212-594-5985
info@ namic.com
http://www.namic.com
The association promotes diversity in the telecommunications industry, focusing on the urban cable marketplace. Membership is comprised of 17 chapters throughout the United States. Members include cable operators, programmers, hardware suppliers, telecommunication and news media professionals, and entrepreneurs. The NAMIC publishes a membership directory and a newsletter, and hosts conferences. It also sponsors mentoring programs and an online job bank.

National Association of Black Accountants (NABA)

7429-A Hanover Parkway
Greenbelt, MD 20770
301-474-6222
http://www.nabainc.org
The NABA works to expand the influence of minority professionals in the fields of accounting and finance. In addition to helping members promote and develop their professional skills, this association helps minority students enter the accounting profession. The association offers undergraduate and graduate

scholarships, hosts conferences, publications, and maintains an online career center.

National Association of Black Journalists (NABJ)

University of Maryland
8701-A Adelphi Road
Adelphi, MD 20783-1716
301-445-7100
nabj@nabj.org
http://www.nabj.org
The National Association of Black Journalists is the largest media organization for people of color in the world. Its mission is to strengthen ties among African-American journalists, promote diversity in newsrooms, honor excellence and outstanding achievement in the media industry, expand job opportunities and recruiting activities for established African-American journalists and students interested in the journalism field, and expand and balance the media's coverage of the African-American community and experience. Each year, the NABJ awards more than $30,000 in scholarships and internships to students throughout the country, as well as fellowships for seasoned professionals. Visit its Web site to learn more about the association's programs and services.

National Association of Black Scuba Divers

PO Box 91630
Washington, DC 20090-1630
800-521-6227
http://www.nabsdivers.org
The association promotes an appreciation of diving and an awareness of the aquatic environment. It sponsors an educational program and an annual convention, and provides scholarships for college students studying marine and environmental sciences.

National Association of Blacks in Criminal Justice

North Carolina Central University
PO Box 19788
Durham, NC 27707
919-683-1801
office@nabcj.org
http://www.nabcj.org
This is an association of African-American criminal justice professionals and community leaders dedicated to improving the administration of justice. It offers conferences and training seminars and membership for students.

National Association of Black Social Workers
1220 11th Street, NW
Washington, DC 20001
202 589-1850
http://nabsw-osa.tripod.com
This organization advocates for the productivity and
empowerment of Black families and communities. It
has more than 30 student chapters at schools of social
work throughout the United States. The association
also hosts annual conferences and publishes *The Black
Caucus*, a biannual scholarly journal.

**National Association of Black Telecommunications
Professionals (NABTP)**
2020 Pennsylvania Avenue, NW, Box 735
Washington, DC 20006
800-946-6228
office@nabtp.org
http://www.nabtp.org
This is a membership organization of
telecommunications professionals, small business
owners, and students. The NABTP targets talented
young people for the development of interests
and skills to enter the telecommunications field.
NABTP offers scholarships and sponsors national
competitions, seminars and workshops, and special
community and education projects.

National Association of Health Services Executives
8630 Fenton Street, Suite 126
Silver Spring, MD 20910
202-628-3953
nahsehq@nahse.org
http://www.nahse.org
The association works to promote the advancement and
development of African-American health care leaders.
It is also dedicated to elevating the quality of health
care services rendered to minority and underserved
communities. It maintains a job bank and offers
mentoring, scholarship, and internship opportunities.
It also hosts a Student Forum, where students can
network with tenured health care professionals and
participate in seminars and panels.

National Association of Hispanic Journalists (NAHJ)
1000 National Press Building
529 14th Street, NW
Washington, DC 20045-2001
202-662-7145
nahj@nahj.org

http://www.nahj.org
The NAHJ is dedicated to the recognition and
professional advancement of Hispanics in the news
industry. Programs of the NAHJ include regional
workshops and seminars; a national convention
and career expo, mid-career and professional
development programs, an online job bank,
journalism awards, internship and fellowship listings,
student journalism workshops, a newsletter, and
scholarships.

National Association of Hispanic Nurses (NAHN)
1501 16th Street, NW
Washington, DC 20036
202-387-2477
info@thehispanicnurses.org
http://www.thehispanicnurses.org
As the only national organization representing Hispanic
registered nurses in the United States, the goal of the
NAHN is to increase the leadership development of
Hispanic nurses and to improve the quality of health
care in Latino communities. The NAHN analyzes the
health care needs of the Hispanic community and
works to deliver quality care. It helps Hispanic nurses
receive education and training and assistance from
local, state, and federal agencies. NAHN also works
to increase the number of bilingual and bicultural
nurses. The association has chapters across the
country, hosts an annual conference, and provides
scholarship opportunities.

**National Association of Hispanic Real Estate
Professionals (NAHREP)**
404 Camino del Rio South, Suite 602
San Diego, CA 92108
800-964-5373
membership@nahrep.org
http://www.nahrep.org
The association serves Hispanic real estate professionals
and works to increase home ownership among
Hispanic Americans. It also publishes *Real Voices*
magazine and offers courses and business-based
seminars.

National Association of Mathematicians
Morehouse College
Department of Mathematics
Atlanta, GA 30314
bonvibre@adelphia.net
http://www.math.buffalo.edu/mad/NAM

This organization promotes excellence in the mathematical sciences and encourages underrepresented American minorities to pursue mathematical education and careers. It offers a quarterly newsletter that features job listings, summer opportunities for students, and other information related to the field.

National Association of Minority Contractors (NAMC)

666 11th Street, NW, Suite 520
Washington, DC 20001
866-688-6262
national@namcline.org
http://www.namcline.org
This nonprofit association represents minority contractors across the country, helping contractors to find work opportunities. The NAMC also offers training programs.

National Association of Minority Media Executives (NAMME)

1921 Gallows Road, Suite 600
Vienna, VA 22182
888-968-7658
info@namme.org
http://www.namme.org
The NAMME was formed in 1990 to establish and maintain relationships among minority media executives and to promote the advancement of minorities into management of mainstream media. NAMME membership is open to senior managers and operational directors of newspapers, magazines, radio, and television stations. Visit its Web site for useful resources such as job listings, Mentor's Corner, articles, and training resources.

National Association of Negro Musicians (NANM)

Negro_Musicians@hotmail.com
http://facstaff.morehouse.edu/~cgrimes
The NANM is dedicated to the preservation, encouragement, and advocacy of all genres of the music of African Americans in the world. In its more than 85-year history, the association has awarded more than 170 financial scholarships and awards to talented young musicians throughout the country. Foremost among the activities of the organization are its programs and activities that involve young people. These include national Junior and Youth Divisions and Campus Branches comprising young artists from colleges and universities all over the United States.

National Bankers Association (NBA)

1513 P Street, NW
Washington, DC 20005
202-588-5432
http://www.nationalbankers.org
The NBA represents minority and women-owned banks and monitors legislative issues affecting minority institutions.

National Black Association for Speech-Language and Hearing

Attn: Dr. Elise Davis-McFarland
Trident Technical College
PO Box 118067
Charleston, SC 29423-8067
http://www.nbaslh.org
The association strives to meet the needs and aspirations of African-American speech-language and hearing professionals, African-American students, and the community. It sponsors educational seminars and conferences, as well as a scholarship for graduate students.

National Black Caucus of State Legislators (NBCSL)

444 Capitol Street, NW, Suite 622
Washington, DC 20001
202-624-5457
http://www.nbcsl.com
The NBCSL represents minority legislators across the United States and offers associate membership to corporations and the public at large. Visit its Web site to read its newsletter, *The Legislator*, and other publications.

National Black Chamber of Commerce (NBCC)

1350 Connecticut Avenue, NW, Suite 405
Washington, DC 20036
202-466-6888
info@NationalBCC.org
http://www.nationalbcc.org
The NBCC is the largest minority-oriented trade association in the United States—reaching 100,000 Black-owned businesses. It deals with issues of economics and entrepreneurship in the African-American community. Visit its Web site for useful articles, editorials, webcasts, a business glossary, and other resources.

National Black Law Student Association

Director of Educational Services
1225 11th Street, NW

Washington, DC 20001-4217
202-583-1281
http://www.nblsa.org
This group helps Black students enter legal studies programs by publicizing financial aid opportunities and publishing reports. It also sponsors a training program and hosts an academic retreat. Among its community service programs are voter registration drives, outreach programs for local schools, and a Computer in Schools Program. Visit its Web site for information on scholarships, job fairs, internships, and its College Students Division.

National Black MBA Association (NBMBAA)

180 North Michigan Avenue
Chicago, IL 60601
312-236-2622
http://www.nbmbaa.org
The NBMBAA serves business professionals around the world with 39 chapters across the United States. The organization offers scholarships, hosts a national conference, maintains an employment network, and publishes *Black MBA Magazine*.

National Black Nurses Association (NBNA)

8630 Fenton Street, Suite 330
Silver Spring, MD 20910-3803
800-575-6298
NBNA@erols.com
http://www.nbna.org
This nonprofit organization seeks to advance and retain African-American nurses through improved working and economic conditions, improved patient care skills, and by recruiting students for the nursing profession. The association offers information on scholarships and maintains a job bank at its Web site.

National Black Police Association

3251 Mt. Pleasant Street, NW, 2nd Floor
Washington, DC 20010-2103
202-986-2070
nbpanatofc@worldnet.att.net
http://www.blackpolice.org
The organization of African-American police associations has several chartered organizations throughout the United States, and associate members in Canada, Bermuda, and the United Kingdom. Its Web site offers job listings, information on scholarships for high school seniors, and information regarding its annual conference.

National Business League (NBL)

http://www.thenationalbusinessleague.com
The NBL works to create organizational unity, focusing on the public policy issues affecting African-American business people. It has chapters in 37 states and the District of Columbia.

National Coalition of Black Meeting Planners (NCBMP)

8630 Fenton Street, Suite 126
Silver Spring, MD 20910
202-628-3952
http://www.ncbmp.com
The organization is dedicated to the educational, certification, and professional needs of African-American association executives, meeting planners, and hospitality professionals. It is committed to the improvement of the meetings, conferences, exhibitions, and convocations they manage. Members of the NCBMP include meeting planners from numerous business, civil rights, church, and fraternal organizations.

National Coalition of 100 Black Women

38 West 32nd Street, Suite 1610
New York, NY 10001-3816
212-947-2196
NC100BW@aol.com
http://www.ncbw.org/intro.html
The volunteer organization is dedicated to community service, leadership development, and the enhancement of career opportunities for African Americans through programs and networking. It sponsors conferences, seminars, mentoring, and advocacy.

National Conference of Black Lawyers

PO Box 80043
Lansing, MI 48908-0043
866-266-5091
http://www.ncbl.org/homepage.php
The organization consists of legal workers, including lawyers, legal scholars, judges, law students, and paralegals. It works for social, economic, and political justice for the African-American community. Visit its Web site for job announcements.

National Conference of Black Mayors (NCBM)

1151 Cleveland Avenue, Building D
East Point, GA 30344

404-765-6444
info@ncbm.org
http://www.ncbm.org
The NCBM is a nonprofit, nonpolitical, nonpartisan service organization that provides management and technical assistance to Black mayors and articulates the membership's concerns on national policy issues.

National Conference of Black Political Scientists
President
3695-F Cascade Road, SW, Suite 212
Atlanta, GA 30331
http://www.poli.ncat.edu/ncobps
This organization of African-American political scientists is dedicated to the exchange of scholarly works. The organization sponsors a graduate assistance program for African-American students. It also publishes the *National Political Science Review*.

National Forum for Black Public Administrators
777 North Capitol Street, NE, Suite 807
Washington, DC 20002
202-408-9300
http://www.nfbpa.org
This organization of African-American public administrators links professionals and organizations, offers mentoring programs for youth, and offers programs in executive leadership development. Visit its Web site for job listings and information on its programs.

National Hispana Leadership Institute
1901 North Moore Street, Suite 206
Arlington, VA 22209
703-527-6007
NHLI@aol.com
http://www.nhli.org
This organization is committed to the education and leadership development of Hispanic women. It offers the Latinas Learning to Lead Summer Youth Institute, a one-week program for Latina undergraduate college students that focuses on personal and career planning, health and well-being, and entrepreneurship and leadership skills. Visit its Web site for job listings, links to useful organizations, and a list of recommended books.

National Hispanic Business Association (NHBA)
1712 East Riverside Drive, #208
Austin, TX 78741

512-495-9511
NHBA@ihispano.com
http://www.nhba.org
The NHBA is a "national network of students and alumni whose mission is to promote the development of undergraduate Hispanic business students through educational, professional, and networking opportunities." It addresses many educational and business issues related to Hispanics, and hosts an annual student leadership conference. Members have access to a newsletter, job listings, scholarship opportunities, a resume database, and many networking opportunities.

National Hispanic Corporate Achievers
PO Box 16092
Altamonte Springs, FL 32716
407-228-7267
http://www.hispanicachievers.com
This network of Hispanic professionals across the country works to stimulate job opportunities, introduce new business relationships, and create support for young Hispanics wishing to enter the business arena.

National Hispanic Medical Association
1411 K Street, Suite 1100
Washington, DC 20005
202-628-5895
nhma@nhmamd.org
http://www.nhmamd.org
The mission of the association is to improve the health of Hispanics and other underserved populations; to that end, the NHMA addresses the interests and concerns of licensed physicians and full-time Hispanic medical faculty.

National Institutes of Health (NIH) Black Scientists Association
PO Box 2262
Kensington, MD 20891-2262
http://www.nih.gov/science/blacksci
This association of scientists, physicians, technologists, and science administrators at the NIH works as an advocate for health and scientific issues of importance to underrepresented minority communities. It is concerned with the recruitment and development of Black scientists and clinicians and organizes job fairs, workshops, and conferences.

National Network of Minority Women in Science
1200 New York Avenue, NW
Washington, DC 20005
Minority women in the fields of science and engineering can network with other professionals through this organization.

National Newspaper Publishers Association (NNPA)
3200 13th Street, NW
Washington, DC 20010
202-588-8764
http://www.nnpa.org
The NNPA, also known as the Black Press of America, is a trade organization of publishers of African American-owned newspapers. It provides news, features, and editorial content for the African-American community. It also provides training sessions and conferences, as well as scholarship and internship opportunities for African-American youth.

National Optometric Association (NOA)
3723 Main Street, PO Box F
East Chicago, IN 46312
info@natoptassoc.org
http://www.natoptassoc.org
Optometrists throughout the country participate in the NOA's program, which recruits minority students interested in the field of optometry, counsels and assists them during training, and helps them establish a private practice or find professional employment. Membership in student chapters is also available.

National Organization for the Professional Advancement of Black Chemists and Chemical Engineers (NOBCChE)
PO Box 77040
Washington, DC 20013
800-776-1419
http://www.nobcche.org
The NOBCChE is committed to the professional and educational growth of underrepresented minorities in the sciences. It sponsors an annual meeting and a number of local programs through its network of local chapters. It also provides recognition awards and scholarships to students and professionals annually.

National Organization of Black Law Enforcement Executives
4609 Pinecrest Office Park Drive, Suite F
Alexandria, VA 22312-1442

703-658-1529
noble@noblenatl.org
http://www.noblenatl.org
The membership of this professional organization consists of African-American police chiefs, sheriffs, command-level officers, and others. It conducts research, speaks out on the issues affecting the African-American community, and performs a variety of outreach activities.

National Sales Network
1075 Easton Avenue, Suite 11, #316
Somerset, NJ 08873
732-246-5236
info@salesnetwork.org
http://www.salesnetwork.org
The association is composed of African-American sales professionals from all industries. Local chapters conduct seminars on selling and negotiating skills, job searching, time management, and organization skills. The NSN conducts a national annual conference and circulates a quarterly newsletter.

National Society of Black Engineers (NSBE)
1454 Duke Street
Alexandria, VA 22314
703-549-2207
info@nsbe.org
http://www.nsbe.org
This organization has more than 270 chapters on college and university campuses, 75 Alumni Extension chapters nationwide, and 75 PreCollege chapters. It seeks to increase the number of minority students studying engineering at the undergraduate and graduate levels. Some of the NSBE's activities include tutorial programs, group study sessions, high school/junior high outreach programs, technical seminars and workshops, two national magazines (*NSBE Magazine* and the *NSBE Bridge*), a professional newsletter (*Career Engineer*), career fairs, scholarships, internships, research opportunities, and an annual national convention. Visit its Web site for more information.

National Society of Black Physicists (NSBP)
6704G Lee Highway
Arlington, VA 22205
703-536-4207
http://www.nsbp.org
The NSBP promotes the professions of African-

American physicists within the scientific community and within society at large through a number of activities and programs. It hosts a national conference, and awards undergraduate and graduate scholarships. It also honors outstanding African-American physicists with induction into the NSBP Society of Fellows.

National Society of Hispanic MBAs

1303 Walnut Hill Lane, Suite 300
Irving, TX 75038
877-467-4622
http://www.nshmba.org
The society works to increase the enrollment of Hispanics in graduate management programs. It also assists corporations with the recruitment of Hispanic business professionals and provides many networking opportunities. Members have access to a national conference, newsletter, a MBA prep program, and job listings. The society also offers scholarships.

National Technical Association (NTA)

1761 East 30th Street, 100A
Cleveland, OH 44114
216-298-4425
http://www.ntaonline.org
The National Technical Association is an organization for minority scientists and engineers. It encourages minority youth and women to choose careers in science and technology via science fairs, an annual conference, mentoring, scholarships, and a career fair. NTA consists of regional chapters, publishes *The Journal of the NTA*, and assists members with job searches. Approximately 25 percent of its members are students.

Native American Journalists Association (NAJA)

Al Neuharth Media Center
555 Dakota Street
Vermillion, SD 57069
605-677-5282
info@naja.com
http://www.naja.com
The NAJA, through many programs and activities, promotes journalism, native cultures, and a free press. It monitors and analyzes tribal and national news, maintains educational services, and awards scholarships. Visit its Web site for job listings and additional information about its programs and services.

Northwest Treeplanters and Farmworkers United

300 Young Street
Woodburn, OR 97071
farmworkerunion@pcun.org
http://www.pcun.org
This union represents Oregon's union of farmworkers, nursery, and reforestation workers, and is Oregon's largest Latino organization. It offers information to farmworkers about working conditions, union contracts, pesticides, and other issues of concern.

Oregon Association of Minority Entrepreneurs

4134 North Vancouver Avenue
Portland, OR 97217
503-249-7744
http://www.oame.org
This organization focuses on the special concerns of minority business owners in the Pacific Northwest. It offers a Youth Entrepreneurship Program. Visit its Web site for more information.

Organization of Black Airline Pilots (OBAP)

8630 Fenton Street, Suite 126
Silver Spring, MD 20910
800-538-6227
nationaloffice@obap.org
http://www.obap.org
The OBAP offers educational and mentoring opportunities to African Americans interested in aviation careers. Working in cooperation with several airlines, government agencies, and other private organizations, the OBAP maintains the Aviation Career Enrichment Program, the Pilots in the School Program, the Professional Pilot Development Program (which offers mentorship, scholarships, fellowships, and job placement), and the Summer Ace/Flight Academy Program. Its Web site features a list of aviation educational programs and the Careers in Aviation section.

Organization of Black Designers

300 M Street, SW, Suite N110
Washington, DC 20024-4019
202-659-3918
OBDesign@aol.com
http://www.core77.com/OBD
The Organization of Black Designers is a national professional association for African-American design professionals in the disciplines of graphics design/visual communications, interior design, fashion

design, and industrial design. Its Web site features a member gallery and a job board.

Organization of Black Screenwriters (OBS)

1968 West Adams Boulevard
Los Angeles, CA 90018
323-735-2050
http://www.obswriter.com
The OBS was founded in 1988 to address the lack of Black writers represented within the entertainment industry. Its primary function is to assist screenwriters in the creation of works for film and television and to help them present their work. Visit the OBS Web site to read useful articles and to participate in an online forum.

Professional Hispanics in Energy

20505 Yorba Linda Boulevard, #324
Yorba Linda, CA 92886-7109
714-777-7729
http://www.phie.org
This is an association of Hispanic professionals working in the energy and environmental industries. It provides scholarships, training, and networking opportunities.

Professional Photographers Minority Network (PPMN)

352 Cotton Avenue
Macon, GA 31201
912-741-5151
YCHolmes1@aol.com
http://www.ppmn.org
The purpose of the PPMN is to enhance the professional development of minority professional image-makers, photographers, videographers, and artisans. Membership benefits include a mentor program, scholarship opportunities, a technical support hotline, an annual convention, and educational programs.

Professional Women of Color

PO Box 5196
New York, NY 10185
212-714-7190
TLawr64783@aol.com
http://www.pwcnetwork.org
Professional Women of Color is an organization providing workshops, seminars, group discussions, and networking sessions to assist women of color in the management of their personal and professional lives.

Puerto Rican Studies Association (PRSA)

University of Illinois at Urbana-Champaign
Center on Democracy in a Multiracial Society
1108 West Stoughton Avenue
Urbana, IL 61801
217-244-0188
prsa@uiuc.edu
http://www.puertorican-studies.org
The PRSA is an organization of scholars in the field of Puerto Rican studies. It offers a fellowship to encourage minority students to pursue careers in college teaching.

REFORMA

Attn: Office Manager
PO Box 25963
Scottsdale, AZ 85255-0116
480-471-7452
reformaoffice@riosbalderrama.com
http://www.reforma.org
Reforma is an organization committed to the improvement of library and information services for Spanish-speaking and Hispanic communities. It is dedicated to developing Spanish-language library collections and recruiting bilingual library personnel. It sponsors mentoring programs and workshops, publishes a quarterly newsletter, and awards scholarships. There are 26 Reforma chapters in the United States. Visit its Web site for more information.

Sin Fronteras Organizing Project

201 East Ninth Avenue
El Paso, TX 79901
915-532-0921
sinfront@farmworkers.org
http://www.farmworkers.org
This project is organized to assist farmworkers in West Texas and Southern New Mexico.

Society for Advancement of Chicanos and Native Americans in Science

PO Box 8526
Santa Cruz, CA 95061-8526
877-722-6271
http://www.sacnas.org
SACNAS encourages Chicano/Latino and Native American students "to pursue graduate education and obtain the advanced degrees necessary for research careers and science teaching professions at

all levels." Society membership is composed of science professors, industry scientists, K-12 teachers, and students. The organization offers the SACNAS K-12 Education Program (for elementary, middle, and high school students from traditionally underrepresented minority backgrounds), conferences and workshops, fellowships and scholarships, and a quarterly journal.

Society of Hispanic Professional Engineers (SHPE)
5400 East Olympic Boulevard, Suite 210
Los Angeles, CA 90022
323-725-3970
http://www.shpe.org
SHPE promotes the development of Hispanics in engineering, science, and other technical professions. It has student chapters at many colleges and universities throughout the United States. Visit its Web site for information on scholarships and programs, such as *Advancing Careers in Engineering*.

Society of Mexican American Engineers and Scientists (MAES)
711 West Bay Area Boulevard, Suite 206
Webster, TX 77598-4051
281-557-3677
execdir@maes-natl.org
http://www.maes-natl.org
The society works to increase the number of Mexican Americans and other Hispanics in the technical and scientific fields. It represents the Mexican American community in the technological arena on issues related to education, economics, environment, and research. Visit its Web site to learn more about programs offered for students, undergraduate and graduate scholarships, student chapters, and high school clubs.

United States Hispanic Chamber of Commerce
2175 K Street, NW, Suite 100
Washington, DC 20037
800-874-2286
ushcc@ushcc.com
http://www.ushcc.com
This network of nearly 140 Hispanic Chambers of Commerce and Hispanic business organizations communicates the needs and potential of Hispanic enterprise to the U.S. government and corporate America. Visit its Web site to learn more about available programs.

Urban Financial Services Coalition (UFSC)
1212 New York Avenue, NW, Suite 950
Washington, DC 20005
202-289-8335
http://www.ufscnet.org
The coalition (formerly known as the National Association of Urban Bankers) is an organization of minority professionals in the banking and financial services industries. It supports programs that offer practical benefits for minority financial services professionals, banks, and financial institutions. A variety of scholarships are offered by the UFSC. Visit its Web site for further information.

Walter Kaitz Foundation (WKF)
1724 Massachusetts Avenue, NW
Washington, DC 20036
202-775-3611
info@walterkaitz.org
http://walterkaitz.org
The Walter Kaitz Foundation is dedicated to assisting minority professionals in the cable/broadband industry. Training programs, networking, and mentoring opportunities offered by the WKF allow professionals to develop skills and advance in the industry. The foundation also provides diversity information and resources to industry companies.

OTHER ORGANIZATIONS

A Better Chance
240 West 35th Street, 9th Floor
New York, NY 10001
646-346-1310
http://www.abetterchance.org
The mission of A Better Chance is to substantially increase the number of well-educated minority youth capable of assuming positions of responsibility and leadership in American society. Through a range of programs, A Better Chance works with students of color—from the grades 6 through 11—to help them access expanded educational and career opportunities. Programs include the College Preparatory Schools Program in which academically talented students of color are placed in educational environments that affirm and nurture their academic talent. The Career Services Program provides an exclusive support network to assist students in career exploration and the preparation of individual career paths. The organization also offers study abroad and other summer opportunities.

Abya Yala Fund
PO Box 28386
Oakland, CA 94604
570-763-6553
abyayala@earthlink.net
http://ayf.nativeweb.org
The fund was created by and for indigenous peoples from Central and South America and Mexico. It funds projects that improve life for this population, such as a national rights training program for Mexican women and a community program for environmental entrepreneurs.

African-American Shakespeare Company (AASC)
762 Fulton Street, Suite 306
San Francisco, CA 94102
415-762-2071
general@african-americanshakes.org
http://www.african-americanshakes.org
The AASC is the only company of African-American actors that perform European classical works in the United States. These time-honored works are told within the perspective and cultural dynamic of the African-American culture. The African-American Shakespeare Company's mission is to produce European classical works with an African-American cultural perspective and to provide opportunities and accessibility for minority artists and their community to view these works in a manner that is inclusive of their cultural heritage and identity. The AASC employs actors and designers, and also needs volunteers to assist with productions. The company includes a full production season, an after-school program, a school touring component, and a Summer Youth Troupe. Additionally, its Shake-It-Up Arts Education Program helps low-performing students reach their potential.

African American Speakers Bureau
PO Box 15490
San Francisco, CA 94115-5490
415-346-0199
Aveprsf@amvideos.com
http://www.aasb.net
The bureau provides speakers to address issues of interest to the African-American community. Speaker categories include arts/literature, business, celebrities, entertainment, ethnic health, motivational, politics/legal, relationships, sports, technology, urban culture, and youth.

American Indian Chamber of Commerce of Oklahoma (AICCO)
5103 South Sheridan Road, Suite 695
Tulsa, OK 74145
800-652-4226
Chamber@AICCO.org
http://www.aicco.org
The AICCO works to develop a stronger American Indian business community. It publishes a business directory, provides mentoring and networking opportunities, and advocates for American Indian interests.

American Indian College Fund
PO Box 172449
Denver, CO 80217-9797
800-776-3863
info@collegefund.org
http://www.collegefund.org
The American Indian College Fund provides scholarships and other support for the 34 tribal colleges in the United States. Money from the fund is distributed to these colleges, and the colleges then award scholarships to individual students.

American Indian Higher Education Consortium (AIHEC)

121 Oronoco Street
Alexandria, VA 22314
703-838-9400
aihec@aihec.org
http://www.aihec.org

The AIHEC is a support network for the newly established, tribally controlled colleges—34 in the United States and one in Canada. The organization assists with areas such as faculty development, accreditation, and intergovernmental relations. The AIHEC and the colleges publish a quarterly magazine, *Tribal College Journal*.

Arapaho Business Council

PO Box 396
Ft. Washakie, WY 82514
307-332-6120
http://tlc.wtp.net/arapaho.htm

Residents of the Wind River Reservation have access to a number of services, programs, and grants that are showcased at the council's Web site.

Asian American Arts Alliance

74 Varick Street, Suite 302
New York, NY 10013-1914
212-941-9208
info@aaartsalliance.org
http://www.aaartsalliance.org

Through its programs and services, the Asian American Arts Alliance provides managerial and artistic assistance to Asian American artists and art groups; informs and educates the public about Asian American arts; facilitates connections among Asian American artists; and advocates for increased visibility and opportunities for Asian American artists. Services include: E-Calendar—a biweekly calendar of performances, exhibits, and events happening nationwide; an ongoing series of panel discussions, symposiums, and roundtables featuring artists and arts professionals speaking on issues relevant to Asian American arts and the Asian American community; a resource library consisting of a unique collection of books, periodicals, magazines, and interest binders related to Asian American arts; and a quarterly newsletter, which contains profiles of member organizations and news about the Alliance. Visit its Web site for more information.

Asian American Arts Centre (AAAC)

26 Bowery, 3rd Floor
New York, NY 10013
212-233-2154
aaac@artspiral.org
http://www.artspiral.org/about.html

The AAAC exhibits works by Asian artists and photographers, and maintains an archive of artwork. It also offers gallery talks, panel discussions, art classes, internships, and volunteer opportunities.

Asian American Association

888-411-2742
http://www.aan.net

The Asian American Association is a free membership organization for Asian Americans and other ethnic groups. It helps members save money through special offers and deals from many of its partners, such as DHL, GE Financial Assurance, Liberty Mutual Property and Casualty Insurance, and *Sing Tao Daily Newspaper*.

Asian American Economic Development Enterprises (AAEDE)

216 West Garvey Avenue, Suite E
Monterey Park, CA 91754
626-572-7021
info@aaede.org
http://www.aaede.org

The mission of the AAEDE is to "create business and personal growth for Asian Americans and others through education, employment, and enterprise." For more than 20 years, the AAEDE has provided training and employment services to thousands of Asian Americans throughout Southern California while collaborating with government, not-for-profit organizations, and major corporations in providing programs. It hosts workshops and seminars, which cover topics ranging from international trade and business growth to the commercial use of Internet and other career ideas. It holds an annual job fair that is specifically designed to meet the career transition needs of Asian Americans. Visit its Web site for job listings, useful articles, and information on internships.

Asian American Writers' Workshop

16 West 32nd Street, Suite 10A
New York, NY 10001
212-494-0061
desk@aaww.org
http://www.aaww.org

Asian American Writers' Workshop is an organization dedicated to creative writers. It offers publications, literary awards, and workshops and seminars. Student and other levels of membership are available. Members receive a subscription to *The Asian Pacific American Journal*; discounts off the purchase of books, classes, and seminars; borrowing privileges at its lending library; and a subscription to *Ten*, its literary magazine.

Asian Cultural Council (ACC)

437 Madison Avenue, 37th Floor
New York, NY 10022-7001
212-812-4300
acc@accny.org
http://www.asianculturalcouncil.org
The council supports cultural exchange in the visual and performing arts between the United States and the countries of Asia. The central feature of the ACC is a program that grants fellowships to artists, scholars, and specialists from Asia for the purposes of research, study, and creative work in the United States. Some grants are also made to Americans pursuing similar activities in Asia, and to educational and cultural institutions engaged in projects of special significance to Asian-American exchange.

Asian Media Access

3028 Oregon Avenue South
Minneapolis, MN 55426
612-376-7715
info@amamedia.org
http://amamedia.org
Asian Media Access is a nonprofit media art and education organization inspiring Asian American communities in the Midwest to use media as a means to promote positive social change.

Asian Pacific American Labor Alliance, AFL-CIO

815 16th Street, NW
Washington, DC 20006
202-974-8051
apala@apalanet.org
http://www.apalanet.org
This national organization of nearly 500,000 Asian Pacific American union members seeks better pay, improved benefits, dignity on the job, and a voice in the workplace. It has a national office in Washington, D.C., and chapters across the country.

Asia Society

725 Park Avenue
New York, NY 10021
212-288-6400
info@asiasoc.org
http://www.asiasociety.org
The Asia Society is America's leading institution dedicated to fostering understanding and communication between Americans and the peoples of Asia and the Pacific. A national nonprofit, nonpartisan educational organization, the society provides a forum for building awareness of the more than 30 countries broadly defined as the Asia-Pacific region—the area from Japan to Iran, and from Central Asia to New Zealand, Australia, and the Pacific Islands. Through art exhibitions and performances, films, lectures, seminars, and conferences, publications and assistance to the media, and materials and programs for students and teachers, the Asia Society presents the uniqueness and diversity of Asia to the American people.

ASPIRA Association

1444 Eye Street, NW, Suite 800
Washington, DC 20005
202-835-3600
info@aspira.org
http://www.aspira.org
ASPIRA operates a number of programs across the country to help introduce Hispanic students to opportunities in science and mathematics fields. It offers internship and scholarship opportunities, hosts education conferences, and sponsors a number of math and science initiatives.

Association for Hispanic Theological Education (AETH)

100 East 27th Street
Austin, TX 78705-5711
512-708-0660
office@austinseminary.edu
http://www.aeth.org
The AETH promotes and enhances theological education for Hispanic Americans in Bible institutes, Bible colleges, seminaries, and other programs in the United States, Canada, and Puerto Rico. Membership includes educators and students who are preparing to pursue a career in theological education. The AETH sponsors mentoring programs, a program for Hispanic women in the ministry, and provides technical assistance.

Association of Hispanic Arts Inc.

220 East 106th Street, 3rd Floor, Room 35
New York, NY 10029
212-876-1242
ahanews@latinoarts.org
http://www.latinoarts.org/02docs/home.html
The association serves as a clearinghouse of information about Hispanic arts organizations. It publishes a quarterly newsletter and a directory of organizations, and also maintains a database of information about fellowships and grants. It also offers support grants to eligible Latino arts and cultural organizations throughout the New York tri-state area and offers workshops and seminars for individual artists and arts organizations about topics such as strategic planning, fundraising, grantwriting, marketing, and legal issues.

Association on American Indian Affairs (AAIA)

966 Hungerford Drive, Suite 12-B
Rockville, MD 20850
240-314-7155
general.aaia@verizon.net
http://www.indian-affairs.org
The Association on American Indian Affairs is a citizen-sponsored, national, nonprofit organization assisting American Indian and Alaska Native communities. Its current programs include Repatriation of Sacred Objects and Human Remains, Protection of Sacred Places, Health and Diabetes, Indian Child Welfare, Federal Acknowledgment of Unrecognized Tribes, Tribal Sovereignty, Language Preservation, Youth Summer Camps, and Scholarships. The AAIA is governed by a board of prominent Indian people from such fields as law, education, health, and public service.

Bad River Band of Lake Superior Chippewa

PO Box 39
Odanah, WI 54861
715-682-7111
http://www.glitc.org/tribes/bad_river/default.php
The tribe offers a number of resources and community events to its members. Programs available include housing improvement, family nutrition, economic development administration, student development, health services, and HIV/AIDS prevention.

Ballet Hispanico

167 West 89th Street
New York, NY 10024-1901
212-362-6710
http://www.ballethispanico.org
The Ballet Hispanico Company has been widely recognized as the foremost dance interpreter of Hispanic culture in the United States, with an innovative repertory that blends ballet, modern, and ethnic dance forms into a spirited image of the contemporary Hispanic world. More than 70 new works have been commissioned for Ballet Hispanico's repertory from choreographers of international stature. As part of the company's commitment to new work, Ballet Hispanico also conducts choreographer workshops, which have included a wide range of emerging artists. Additionally, its Ballet Hispanico School offers a balanced curriculum in classical ballet, modern, and Spanish dance.

Bay Area Urban League

2201 Broadway Street
Oakland, CA 94612-3017
510-271-1846
http://www.richmondworks.org/rwmem/urb.htm
The Bay Area Urban League is an interracial, nonprofit community service organization that secures opportunities in American society for African Americans and other minorities. It sponsors advocacy, and education and research programs. Programs include the On The Job Training program, which provides training and employment to San Francisco residents, and the North Cities Coalition (Alameda, Albany, Berkeley, Emeryville, and Piedmont), which helps residents to enroll in certified job training classes or into a guided job search program.

The Black Academy of Arts and Letters

Dallas Convention Center Theater Complex
650 South Griffin Street
Dallas, TX 75202
214-743-2440
info@tbaal.org
http://www.tbaal.org
The academy promotes the work of African Americans in dance, music, theatre, film, literacy, and visual arts. It supports arts education programs, exhibitions, special events, and music, theater, and dance performances.

Black Executive Exchange Program

Attn: National Urban League
120 Wall Street
New York, NY 10005
212-558-5320

http://www.nul.org/programs/education/beep.htm
The Black Executives Exchange Program is dedicated to the need for quality education for African-American students who are interested in high-level industry and government careers. It arranges for professionals to lecture at participating colleges. The program is active at four-year historically Black colleges and universities and on the campus of the University of Nebraska at Omaha.

Blackfeet Nation
PO Box 850
Browning, MT 59417
406-338-7521/7522
http://www.blackfeetnation.com
The Blackfeet Indian Reservation in Northern Montana is home to Blackfeet Community College, and provides information to its members about jobs and economic development.

Black Heritage Museum
PO Box 570327
Miami, FL 33257-0327
305-252-3535
The Museum offers exhibits, talks, and literature about Black history.

Black Leadership Forum Inc. (BLF)
1900 L Street, NW, Suite 405
Washington, DC 20036
  202-659-1881
http://www.blackleadershipforum.org
The BLF empowers African Americans to improve their lives and to fully participate in American social, economic, and political life.

Black Student Fund (BSF)
3636 16th Street, NW, 4th Floor
Washington, DC 20010-1146
202-387-1414
mail@blackstudentfund.org
http://www.blackstudentfund.org
The BSF offers financial assistance to African-American students (grades pre-kindergarten to 12) and their families in the Washington metropolitan area. It works to assure that African-American students have equal access to quality educational opportunities. The BSF's programs include cross-racial communications training to teachers and networking for African-American educators.

Black Women in Sisterhood for Action
PO Box 1592
Washington, DC 20013
202-543-6013
info@bisa-hq.org
http://www.bisa-hq.org
This national nonprofit organization offers hands-on support services for at least 40 students annually during the course of their undergraduate study. Services include financial awards, books, transportation, tutoring, mentoring, counseling (students and parents), networking opportunities, and other resources. Visit its Web site to read its monthly newsletter.

California Indian Basketweavers Association
PO Box 2397
Nevada City, CA 95959
530-272-5500
ciba@ciba.org
http://www.ciba.org
The association works to preserve and promote California Indian basketweaving traditions.

Center for Pan Asian Community Services
3760 Park Avenue
Doraville, GA 30340
770-936-0969
cpacs@cpacs.org
http://www.cpacs.org
This organization provides job training and other social services to the Pan Asian community dealing with problems associated with immigration, refugee, and minority problems.

Center for the History of the American Indian
60 West Walton Street
Chicago, IL 60610-3380
312-255-3564
mcnickle@newberry.org
http://www.newberry.org/mcnickle/L3rdarcy.html
The D'Arcy McNickle Center for American Indian History of the Newberry Library promotes research and teaching about the history of Native Americans. The Center hosts pre- and post-doctoral scholars on long-term fellowships, generally of six to 11 months' duration. Short-term fellows spend between two weeks and two months. Over the years, these long- and short-term fellowships have resulted in nearly 40 books and dozens of scholarly articles. The McNickle

Center has offered short-term fellowships for teachers of Native American history, published bibliographies, offered summer institutes for teachers of American Indian history and American Indian literature, and sponsored conferences, seminars, and workshops for scholars/teachers. The center is currently working with the 13 Committee on Institutional Cooperation universities to create a nationally recognized graduate program in American Indian studies.

Central Council of the Tlingit and Haida Indian Tribes of Alaska

320 West Willoughby Avenue, Suite 300
Juneau, AK 99801
800-344-1432
http://www.ccthita.org
The tribes offer vocational training and other education and job services to its members, which include scholarship opportunities, family and youth services, and health programs. Visit the council's Web site for additional information.

Cheyenne River Sioux Tribe

2001 Main Street, PO Box 590
Eagle Butte, SD 57625
605-964-4155
crstsecretary@lakotanetwork.com
http://www.sioux.org
The tribe offers a variety of resources to its members, including health care and educational opportunities at Si Tanka University.

Chickasaw Nation

530 East Arlington Boulevard, PO Box 1548
Ada, OK 74820
580-436-2603
http://www.chickasaw.net
The tribe offers access to business enterprises, education programs, services, and job information to its members. It also publishes the Chickasaw Times. Visit the nation's Web site to read selected articles.

Chinese-American Planning Council

150 Elizabeth Street
New York, NY 10012
212-941-0920
http://www.cpc-nyc.org
The Chinese-American Planning Council is one of the largest social service programs serving the Chinese American population in the United States. It provides services through more than 50 programs that offer employment and training, education about the culture and arts, and the development of low-income housing. It also sponsors a Summer Youth Employment Program.

Chippewa Cree Tribal Council

Rural Route 1, Box 544
Box Elder, MT 59521
406-395-4282
http://tlc.wtp.net/chippewa.htm
The tribe offers business developmental programs and educational opportunities through Stone Child College (http://www.montana.edu/wwwscc).

Choctaw Nation

PO Drawer 1210
Durant, OK 74702-1210
800-522-6170
http://www.choctawnation.com
The Choctaw Nation sponsors community events, programs, and a Web site that features the Choctaw Artists' Registry—a listing of Choctaw artists around the world. It also offers a variety of employment services to its members.

Citizen Potawatomi Nation

1601 South Gordon Cooper Avenue
Shawnee, OK 74801-8699
800-880-9880
http://www.potawatomi.org
The nation offers employment counseling and business development opportunities to its members.

Columbia River Inter-Tribal Fish Commission

729 NE Oregon Street, Suite 200
Portland, OR 97232
503-238-0667
croj@critfc.org
http://www.critfc.org
The commission represents the fisheries interests of the four Columbia River Treaty Tribes: the Confederated Tribes of the Warm Springs Reservation of Oregon, the Confederated Tribes and Bands of the Yakama Indian Nation, the Confederated Tribes of the Umatilla Indian Reservation, and the Nez Perce Tribe.

Confederated Salish and Kootenai Tribes

PO Box 278
Pablo, MT 59855

888-835-8766
csktcouncil@cskt.org
http://www.cskt.org
The tribe offers educational and career development
  resources to its members.

Confederated Tribes of Siletz Indians
201 Southeast Swan Avenue
Siletz, OR 97380
541-444-2532
hawkeye@ctsi.nsn.us
http://ctsi.nsn.us
A variety of services are available to tribal members,
  including education, career guidance, and alcohol
  and drug counseling.

Confederated Tribes of Warm Springs Oregon
1233 Veterans Street
Warm Springs, OR 97761
541-553-1161
http://www.warmsprings.com
The tribes offer education and employment services to
  their members.

Congressional Black Caucus Foundation (CBCF)
1720 Massachusetts Avenue, NW
Washington, DC 20036
202-263-2800
info@cbcfinc.org
http://www.cbcfinc.org
The CBCF works to increase the influence of African
  Americans in the political, legislative, and public
  policy arenas. It sponsors issue forums and leadership
  seminars, as well as national educational programs.
  These programs include the Congressional Black
  Caucus Spouses (CBC Spouses) Education Scholarship
  Fund, the Fellowship Program, and the Eleanor
  Holmes Norton Congressional Internship Program for
  High School Students.

Congress of National Black Churches (CNBC)
1225 I Street, NW, Suite 750
Washington, DC 20005
202-371-1091
The Congress of National Black Churches is an ecumenical
  coalition of the following major historically African-
  American denominations: African Methodist
  Episcopal, African Methodist Episcopal Zion, Christian
  Methodist Episcopal, Church of God in Christ,
  National Baptist Convention of America, National
  Baptist Convention U.S.A., National Missionary Baptist

Convention of America, and the Progressive National
  Baptist Convention. These denominations represent
  65,000 churches and a membership of more than 20
  million people. CNBC's mission is to foster Christian
  unity, charity, and fellowship.

Cook Inlet Region Inc.
PO Box 93330
Anchorage, AK 99509-3330
907-274-8638
http://www.ciri.com
This Alaska Native regional corporation provides
  shareholder information, job listings, and community
  leadership.

Cow Creek Band of Umpqua Tribe of Indians
2371 Northeast Stephens Street
Roseburg, OR 97470
541-672-9405
http://www.cowcreek.com
The tribe sponsors economic development programs
  for its members. Visit its Web site for information on
  grants.

Dakota Indian Foundation
PO Box 340
Chamberlain, SD 57325
605-234-5472
http://www.dakotaindianfoundation.org
The independent, nonprofit organization provides grants
  to groups and organizations throughout the Sioux
  Nation to support the economic development, social
  enhancement, and cultural preservation of the Dakota
  Sioux Indian people.

Delaware Tribe of Indians
220 NW Virginia Avenue
Bartlesville, OK 74003
918-336-5272
lenape@cowboy.net
http://www.delawaretribeofindians.nsn.us
A number of services are available through the tribal
  council. Visit its Web site for job listings.

East-West Center
1601 East-West Road
Honolulu, HI 96848
808-944-7111
http://www.eastwestcenter.org
The East-West Center is a national and regional source
  of information and analysis about the Asia Pacific

Region, including the United States. The center serves scholars, the government, business professionals, teachers, journalists, and others researching issues of contemporary significance. The center supports the East-West Center Research Program, which researches issues in order to promote understanding and mutually beneficial relations between the United States and the countries of Asia and the Pacific. It offers scholarships, leadership training programs, publications, and student activities.

East West Players (EWP)

120 North Judge John Aiso Street
Los Angeles, CA 90012
213-625-7000
info@eastwestplayers.org
http://www.eastwestplayers.org
East West Players is dedicated to the nurturing and promotion of Asian Pacific American and other culturally diverse talent through the arts. It encourages artists to express themselves by writing stories, creating and producing projects, expanding their performance repertoire, and sharing their work with the community. EWP's Mainstage season consists of productions from musicals, comedies, and dramas to Asian, European, and American classics, and world premieres. EWP sponsors opportunities for new writers and offers grants/scholarships for high school sophomores and juniors, college and graduate school students, and artists. It also hosts the EWP Actors Conservatory and conducts seminars, workshops, and publishes the *East West Players Alliance of Creative Talent Services Directory*.

Eddie Robinson Foundation

575 Pharr Road, #550247
Atlanta, GA 30355
info@eddierobinson.com
http://www.eddierobinson.com
The Eddie Robinson Foundation assists the youth of America with merit and need-based scholarships, grants, and charitable contributions. Eddie Robinson is the winningest coach in college football history. The foundation also develops and supports minority professional golfers through its *Minority Tour Players Association* program.

Equal Rights Advocates (ERA)

1663 Mission Street, Suite 250
San Francisco, CA 94103
415-621-0672
info@equalrights.org
http://www.equalrights.org
The ERA has fought for women's equality for more than 30 years. It offers an advice and counseling hotline (800-839-4372) that helps women understand their rights. It also offers a variety of useful publications at its Web site, including *Sex Discrimination*, *Family and Medical Leave/Pregnancy Discrimination*, *Sexual Harassment at Work*, *Sexual Harassment at School*, *Temporary Workers*, *Tradeswomen's Legal Rights*, *Family and Medical Leave*, *Welfare is a Woman's Issue*, *Women in the Workplace*, *Pay Inequity*, and *Glass Ceiling*.

Falmouth Institute

3702 Pender Drive, Suite 300
Fairfax, VA 22030
800-992-4489
information@falmouthinstitute.com
http://www.falmouthinst.com
The institute offers research, training, and consulting services to Native American communities. Training seminars and courses cover topics such as law, government, education, finance, human resources and management, social services, construction, housing, gaming, natural resources, and law enforcement. In addition, the institute publishes the *American Indian Report* magazine and the *Native American Law Digest*.

First Nations Development Institute

2300 Fall Hill Avenue, Suite 412
Fredericksburg, VA 22401
540-371-5615
info@firstnations.org
http://www.firstnations.org
This Native American nonprofit organization promotes culturally appropriate economic development by and for native peoples. It provides education, advocacy, research, and funding (grants and loans).

Freedom Theatre

1346 North Broad Street
Philadelphia, PA 19121
215-765-2793
http://www.freedomtheatre.org
Freedom Theatre, founded in 1966, is Pennsylvania's oldest African-American theater. Freedom Theatre presents more than 100 performances a year and includes a repertory theater company, a performing arts training program, a lecture series, and a readings series.

Georgia Legislative Black Caucus

18 Capitol Square, SW, Suite 602
Atlanta, GA 30334
404-651-5569
glbc@legis.state.ga.us
http://www.glbcinc.org
The caucus serves the African-American community in Georgia, providing current information on government agencies.

Golden State Minority Foundation (GSMF)

8730 South Vermont Avenue, 2nd Floor
Los Angeles, CA 90044
866-277-4763
education@gsmf.org
http://www.gsmf.org
The GSMF works with local inner-city elementary and middle schools to enrich the educational experience of students in the Los Angeles, Inglewood, Compton, Long Beach, Pasadena, and the Archdiocese of Los Angeles school districts. It provides financial and developmental support to educators and principals from these districts.

Great Lakes Indian Fish and Wildlife Commission

100 Maple Street, PO Box 9
Odanah, WI 54861
715-682-6619
http://www.glifwc.org
Comprised of 11 sovereign tribal governments (Bad River, Lac Courte Oreilles, Lac du Flambeau, Mole Lake/ Sokaogon, Red Cliff, St. Croix, Bay Mills, Keweenaw Bay, Lac Vieux Desert, Fond du Lac, and Mille Lacs) located throughout Minnesota, Wisconsin, and Michigan; the commission's purpose is to protect and enhance treaty-guaranteed rights to hunt, fish, and gather on inland territories, and to provide cooperative management of these resources.

Great Plains Black Museum

2213 Lake Street
Omaha, NE 68110
402-345-2212
The museum serves as an educational resource for students and scholars, and is dedicated to preserving the African-American experience of the Great Plains.

Heard Museum Library and Archives (HMLA)

Billie Jane Baguley Library and Archives
2301 North Central Avenue
Phoenix, AZ 85004-1323
602-252-8840
http://www.heard.org
The HMLA maintains a resource file on 22,000 Native American artists. The file helps researchers, libraries, museums, and other artists learn of people working in all forms of Native American arts.

Hispanas Organized for Political Equality (HOPE)

634 South Spring Street, Suite 920
Los Angeles, CA 90014
213-622-0606
latinas@latinas.org
http://www.latinas.org
HOPE is a nonprofit advocacy organization dedicated to the political education and participation of Latinas and other women in the political process. It sponsors symposiums and hosts workshops including those that educate low-income, high school-aged Latinas about college preparation, financial empowerment, and civic participation.

Hispanic Agenda for Action (HAA)

U.S. Department of Health and Human Services
200 Independence Avenue, SW
Washington, DC 20201
877-696-6775
initiatives@osophs.dhhs.gov
http://www.haa.omhrc.gov
The HAA is a government initiative coordinated by the Office of Minority Health within the Department of Health and Human Services, focusing on such issues as health services and education for Hispanic Americans.

Hispanic Alliance for Career Enhancement (HACE)

Student Development Program
25 East Washington, Suite 1500
Chicago, IL 60602
312-435-0498
abetomas@hace-usa.org
http://www.hace-usa.org
Founded in 1982, the HACE develops initiatives that provide opportunities for Hispanics to participate in professional and managerial positions, as well as in the educational advancement of college students. It offers such programs as the Employer Support Program—a comprehensive candidate referral program designed to assist recruiters with their staffing and recruitment needs. The alliance maintains

a fully computerized database of more than 3,500 professional profiles. It also sponsors annual career development conferences (which includes workshops and a career fair) and offers an internship program for college students, a resume subscription service, high school and college mentoring programs, and job postings at its Web site.

Hispanic Association of Colleges and Universities (HACU)
8415 Datapoint Drive, Suite 400
San Antonio, TX 78229
210-692-3805
hacu@hacu.net
http://www.hacu.net
As a national association representing Hispanic-Serving Institutions, the Hispanic Association of Colleges and Universities works to promote nonprofit, accredited college and universities (more than 400 total institutions) where Hispanics constitute a minimum of 25 percent of the enrollment at either the graduate or undergraduate level. HACU works with its partners in business, government, and industry to accomplish this mission. The association also administers a national internship program for college students, as well as offers scholarships for high school seniors and college students. Publications are produced periodically by the association, including a monthly newsletter, an annual report, and various research-related publications, and other multimedia products. It also maintains an informative Web site with a scholarship database.

Hispanic Association on Corporate Responsibility
1444 I Street, NW, Suite 850
Washington, DC 20005
202-835-9672
hacr@hacr.org
http://www.hacr.org
The association works to ensure that the Hispanic community has active participation in corporate America. It encourages corporations to adopt programs that support diversity and conducts and publishes research about Hispanics in corporate America.

Hispanic Radio Network
1101 Pennsylvania Avenue, NW, 6th Floor
Washington, DC 20004
http://www.hrn.org
The Hispanic Radio Network informs Hispanics about health, environment, education, social justice, and available resources via nine Spanish-language radio programs that are broadcast throughout the United States on more than 100 Spanish-language radio stations. It provides information about local resources via the toll-free National Hispanic Resource Helpline, 800-473-3003.

Hispanic-Serving Health Professions Schools (HSHPS)
1120 Connecticut Avenue, NW, Suite 260
Washington, DC 20036
202-293-2701
hshps@hshps.com
http://www.hshps.com
The mission of HSHPS is to develop educational opportunities in health professions schools to increase the number of Hispanics in health professions careers. Visit its Web site for more information about its programs.

Hispanics in Philanthropy
200 Pine Street, Suite 700
San Francisco, CA 94104
415-837-0427
http://www.hiponline.org/home
Hispanics in Philanthropy is an association of more than 350 grantmakers that advocates for increased philanthropic support of Hispanic communities and greater representation of Hispanics on boards and staff of foundations. HIP commissions and disseminates research findings, convenes conferences and briefings, provides information and referrals, and publishes regular newsletters and other reports. It has regional offices in Colorado, Florida, Minnesota, New York, North Carolina, and Pennsylvania.

Hopi Tribe
PO Box 123
Kykotsmovi, AZ 86039
928-734-3283
info@hopi.nsn.us
http://www.hopi.nsn.us
The Hopi Tribe's Office of Education provides an Adult Vocational Training Program and a Grants and Scholarship Program for tribal members.

International Agency for Minority Artist Affairs (IAMAA)
Adam Clayton Powell Jr. State Office Building
163 West 125th Street, Suite 909
New York, NY 10027

212-749-5298
iamaa@pipeline.com
http://www.aboutharlemarts.org
The IAMAA is committed to the long-range cultural
development of Harlem. It helps make a diverse
variety of high-quality arts experiences available
to the people of Harlem and assists resident art
organizations and artists to reach their full potential.

Inter-Tribal Council of Nevada (ITCN)
680 Greenbrae Drive, Suite 280
Sparks, NV 89431
775-355-0600
request@itcn.org
http://itcn.org/itcn/itcn.html
The ITCN is a tribal organization serving the member
reservations and colonies in Nevada. It plays a
major role in promoting health, educational, social,
economic, and job opportunity programs. The ITCN
also manages federal and state funded programs
aimed at improving the well-being of community
members throughout the state of Nevada. Among
the programs it administers are Head Start and Native
American Workforce.

Intertribal Timber Council (ITC)
1112 NE 21st Avenue
Portland, OR 97232
503-282-4296
itc1@teleport.com
http://www.itcnet.org
The ITC is a "nationwide consortium of Indian Tribes,
Alaska Native corporations, and individuals dedicated
to improving the management of natural resources
of importance to Native American communities."
More than 60 tribes and Alaska Native corporations
currently belong to the ITC. It offers the Truman D.
Picard Scholarship to graduating senior high school
Native American/Alaskan students planning to pursue
education in the field of natural resources. Visit its
Web site for more information.

Jamestown S'Klallam Tribe
1033 Old Blyn Highway
Sequim, WA 98382
360-683-1109
info@jamestowntribe.org
http://www.jamestowntribe.org
The tribe offers economic development opportunities,
family support services, and health and human
services to its members.

Japanese American Citizens League
1765 Sutter Street
San Francisco, CA 94115
415-921-5225
jacl@jacl.org
http://www.jacl.org
The Japanese American Citizens League works to fight
discrimination against people of Japanese ancestry.
It is the largest and one of the oldest Asian American
organizations in the United States. The organization
hosts conferences, publishes books, and supports
scholarship, fellowship, and grant programs.

Japan Foundation North America
152 West 57th Street, 39th Floor
New York, NY 10019
212-489-0299
info@jfny.org
http://www.jfny.org
The Japan Foundation promotes international cultural
exchange and mutual understanding between Japan
and other countries. It conducts a wide range of
programs worldwide, including research and doctoral
fellowships for Japanese studies, institutional grants
above the high school level, Japanese language
instruction, arts and cultural events, intellectual
exchange, and the exchange of persons.

Japanese American Network
231 East 3rd Street, Suite G-104
Los Angeles, CA 90013
213-473-1653
JANet-Info@janet.org
http://www.janet.org
The Japanese American Network is a partnership of
Japanese American organizations encouraging
the use of the Internet to exchange information
about the community. Its Web site offers links to
Japanese American business and professional
associations.

Klamath Tribes
PO Box 436
Chiloquin, OR 97624
541-783-2219
http://www.klamathtribes.org
A number of tribal services and departments assist
members with economic, educational, and career
development. The Klamath Tribes consists of three
tribes: the Klamath, Modoc, and Yahooskin Bands of
Snake Indians.

Latin American Educational Foundation

924 West Colfax Avenue, Suite 103
Denver, CO 80204
303-446-0541
carmen@laef.org
http://www.laef.org
The foundation works to advance the economic and social status of the Hispanic community in Colorado by improving access to higher education through scholarships, community collaboration, and support programs. Its programs include a high school network, mentoring and internship opportunities, and relationships with institutions of higher education focusing on increasing Hispanic enrollment. Its Web site features a useful College Prep section.

Latino Issues Forum (LIF)

160 Pine Street, Suite 700
San Francisco, CA 94111
415-284-7220
http://www.lif.org
Latino Issues Forum is a nonprofit advocacy organization that focuses on public policy issues as they relate to Latinos. It works for better access to higher education, health care, and telecommunications among Latinos. LIF provides community education and training, as well as policy analysis and development.

Latino Medical Student Association

2550 Corporate Place, Suite C202
Monterey Park, CA 91754
lmsaregional@lmsa.net
http://www.lmsa.net
The association is a national organization that represents Hispanic health professions students and professionals. It currently has chapters in California, Arizona, and Utah. It offers a scholarship to assist pre-medical students and a Mentorship Program that provides students with information about curriculum planning, medical applications and interviews, MCAT preparation, and extracurricular activities. Visit its Web site for more information.

League of United Latin American Citizens (LULAC)

2000 L Street, NW, Suite 610
Washington, DC 20036
202-833-6130
http://www.lulac.org
The league operates community-based programs at 700 LULAC councils nationwide. LULAC focuses on education, civil rights, and employment for Hispanics.

LULAC councils provide scholarships to Hispanic students each year and conduct youth leadership training programs. In addition, the LULAC National Educational Service Centers, LULAC's educational arm, provide counseling services to more than 18,000 Hispanic students annually at 16 regional centers. LULAC's employment arm, SER Jobs for Progress, provides job skills and literacy training to the Hispanic community through more than 48 employment training centers located throughout the United States.

Los Angeles Latino International Film Festival

6777 Hollywood Boulevard, Suite 500
Hollywood, CA 90028
323-469-9066
info@latinofilm.org
http://www.latinofilm.org
This annual showcase of Latino films recognizes the makers of feature films, documentaries, and shorts. It offers a number of educational and community outreach programs, including a Latino Screenwriters Lab and a Youth Program. Visit its Web site for more information.

Lumbee Regional Development Association (LRDA)

PO Box 68
Pembroke, NC 28372
910-521-8602
lrda@lumbee.org
http://www.lumbee.org
The association strives to improve services and economic conditions for members of the Lumbee Indian community. Offerings include child services such as Head Start, housing programs, and education and employment resources. Visit the LRDA Web site for additional information.

Magic Johnson Foundation

600 Corporate Pointe, Suite 1080
Culver City, CA 90230
888-624-4205
http://www.magicjohnson.org
The foundation supports community-based organizations serving the health, educational, and social needs of children living in the inner-city. It offers scholarships and mentorships.

MANA, A National Latina Organization

1725 K Street, NW, Suite 501
Washington, DC 20006
202-833-0060

hermana2@aol.com

http://www.hermana.org

This membership organization is dedicated to the empowerment of Latinas of Mexican, Puerto Rican, Dominican, Cuban, Central American, South American, and Spanish decent. It sponsors mentoring and community projects, offers internships, and hosts a leadership development conference.

Marketing Opportunities in Business and Entertainment (MOBE)

47 West Polk Street, Suite 100-261

Chicago, IL 60605

773-651-8008

info@mobe.com

http://www.mobe.com

MOBE sponsors a symposium series and other opportunities for African-American marketers, entertainment executives, promoters, producers, and technologists.

Media Action Network for Asian Americans (MANAA)

PO Box 11105

Burbank, CA 91510

213-486-4433

manaaletters@yahoo.com

http://www.manaa.org

The MANAA monitors all facets of the media for Asian American portrayals and subject matter. It recognizes the achievements of individuals in the entertainment and media industry for their efforts in presenting a balanced image of Asian Americans in the media. The organization also offers scholarship opportunities for college and graduate students interested in pursuing careers in filmmaking and in television production (not broadcast journalism). Visit its Web site to join its discussion group.

Mexican American Legal Defense and Educational Fund (MALDEF)

634 South Spring Street, 11th Floor

Los Angeles, CA 90014

213-629-2512

http://www.maldef.org

The MALDEF works to promote the civil rights of Latinos living in the United States. It works primarily in the areas of employment, education, immigration, political access, and public resource equity and offers scholarship opportunities for law students, legal programs, and programs in education and leadership development. The MALDEF is headquartered in Los

Angeles and has regional offices in Atlanta, Chicago, Los Angeles, San Antonio, and Washington, D.C.; a satellite office in Sacramento, California; and a program office in Houston, Texas.

Minority Business Development Agency (MBDA)

1401 Constitution Avenue, NW

Washington, DC 20230

888-324-1551

http://www.mbda.gov

The MBDA is an agency within the U.S. Department of Commerce, assisting minority-owned businesses. It oversees Minority Business Development Centers and Native American Business Development Centers across the country. Visit its Web site for useful resources.

Mohegan Tribe

PO Box 488

Uncasville, CT 06382

860-862-6100

http://www.mohegan.nsn.us

The tribe sponsors education programs and other community development programs for its members.

Multicultural Marketing Resources (MMR)

286 Spring Street, Suite 201

New York, NY 10013

212-242-3351

http://www.inforesources.com

Multicultural Marketing Resources is a public relations and marketing company with resources for business executives and journalists. MMR publishes the bimonthly *Multicultural Marketing News* newsletter and an annual directory, *The Source Book of Multicultural Experts*. It also offers MMR e-News, a free e-mail-distributed newswire that features profiles of companies that have expertise in reaching multicultural consumers and articles on trends in multicultural marketing.

National African American Student Leadership Conference

145 East Rust Avenue

Holly Springs, MS 38635

662-551-4095

info@naaslc.org

http://www.naaslc.org

This annual conference concerns African-American leadership. It consists of workshops and panel discussions on such topics as education, affirmative action, and international studies.

National Asian American Telecommunications Association

145 Ninth Street, Suite 350
San Francisco, CA 94130
415-863-0814
naata@naatanet.org
http://www.naatanet.org
Through film, video, and new technologies, the association aims to promote better understanding of the Asian Pacific American experience to the broadest audience possible.

National Asian Women's Health Organization

One Embarcadero Center, Suite 500
San Francisco, CA 94111
415-773-2838
info@nawho.org
http://www.nawho.org
This organization works to improve the health status of Asian American women and families through research, education, and public policy advocacy.

National Association for Bilingual Education

1030 15th Street, NW, Suite 470
Washington, DC 20005
202-898-1829
nabe@nabe.org
http://www.nabe.org
This nonprofit national membership organization was founded to address the educational needs of language-minority students in the United States and to advance language competencies and multicultural understanding of all Americans.

National Association for Equal Opportunity in Higher Education

8701 Georgia Avenue, Suite 200
Silver Spring, MD 20910
301-650-2440
http://www.nafeo.org
The association is the national umbrella and public policy advocacy organization for the nation's 120 historically and predominantly Black colleges and universities. It offers an internship program, scholarships, and other resources. Visit its Web site for more information.

National Association for Multicultural Education

733 15th Street, NW, Suite 430
Washington, DC 20005
202-628-6263
name@nameorg.org
http://www.nameorg.org
This organization promotes cultural and ethnic diversity in education, providing information to teachers, administrators, and other educators. It offers an annual conference and publishes a quarterly journal, *Multicultural Perspectives*.

National Association of Latino Elected and Appointed Officials Educational Fund

1122 West Washington Boulevard, 3rd Floor
Los Angeles, CA 90015
213-747-7606
info@naleo.org
http://www.naleo.org
The fund promotes the participation of Latinos in the nation's civic life. It supports programs that promote the integration of Latino immigrants into American society. It also works to develop future leaders among Latino youth, and conducts research on issues of importance.

National Association of Negro Business and Professional Women's Clubs (NANBPWC)

1806 New Hampshire Avenue, NW
Washington, DC 20009
202-483-4206
nanbpwc@aol.com
http://www.nanbpwc.org
The NANBPWC is an organization composed of African-American business and professional women devoted to community service projects. The organization also honors men, women, and youth who have demonstrated outstanding success in their professions and/or an exceptional commitment to the community. It sponsors professional development seminars and workshops, awards scholarships, and hosts a vocal arts competition for emerging artists. It also offers youth clubs for students ages 12 to 18.

National Baptist Convention of America

777 S R Thornton Freeway, Suite 210
Dallas, TX 75203
214-942-3311
http://www.nbcamerica.net
The National Baptist Convention represents several thousand churches and millions of individuals. The convention promotes Christian education and missionary work.

National Baptist Convention USA

1700 Baptist World Center Drive
Nashville, TN 37207
866-531-3054
Dtibbs@NationalBaptist.com
http://www.nationalbaptist.com
Considered the largest African-American organization in the world, this is the larger of the two Baptist conventions, serving more than 30,000 churches. It offers higher education resources at its Web site.

National Black Alcoholism and Addictions Council

5104 North Orange Blossom Trail, Suite 207
Orlando, FL 32810
877-622-2674
mail@nbacinc.org
http://www.nbacinc.org
The council is concerned with the effects of alcoholism among African Americans. It provides information to African-American communities to inform them of the effects of addiction and conducts training on treatment.

National Black Catholic Congress (NBCC)

320 Cathedral Street
Baltimore, MD 21201-4421
nbcc@nbccongress.org
http://www.nbccongress.org
The NBCC represents African-American Roman Catholics. It offers training programs for clergy and for religious and lay leaders, and hosts a high school consortium. Visit its Web site to read articles from its publication, *Black Catholic Monthly*.

National Black United Fund

40 Clinton Street
Newark, NJ 07102
800-223-0866
nbuf@nbuf.org
http://www.nbuf.org
The fund promotes charitable giving among African Americans. It supports educational, cultural, socioeconomic, and social justice programs.

National Bowling Association

377 Park Avenue South, 7th Floor
New York, NY 10016
212-689-8308/8309
TNBACommunications@tnbainc.org
http://www.tnbainc.org

Operated by African Americans, this association is one of the three major governing bodies for amateur bowling. Among its many programs are the Junior Bowling and the Scholarship Award Programs. It also sponsors national tournaments and publishes *Bowler Magazine*.

National Center for American Indian and Alaska Native Mental Health Research

University of Colorado Health Sciences Center
Department of Psychiatry
Nighthorse Campbell Native Health Building
PO Box 6508, Mail Stop F800
Aurora, CO 80045-0508
303-724-1448
http://www.uchsc.edu/ai/ncaianmhr
The center is one of four minority mental health research centers. It pursues research to aid in the mental health care of Native Americans.

National Center for American Indian Enterprise Development (NCAIED)

953 East Juanita Avenue
Mesa, AZ 85204
480-545-1298
http://www.ncaied.org
The NCAIED offers economic development services to American Indians, Native Hawaiians, Alaska Natives, and tribal governments. It seeks to develop and expand the American Indian private sector, increase the number of tribal and individual Indian businesses, and establish business relationships between private industry and Indian enterprises and entrepreneurs

National Congress of American Indians

1301 Connecticut Avenue, NW, Suite 200
Washington, DC 20036
202-466-7767
ncai@ncai.org
http://www.ncai.org
The National Congress of American Indians works to inform the public and Congress on the governmental rights of American Indians and Alaska Natives. The congress consists of 250 member tribes from throughout the United States. Among the group's activities are promotion and support of Indian education, including adult education. Visit its Web site for information about Indian organizations and nations in the United States.

National Council of La Raza (NCLR)

Raul Yzaguirre Building
1126 16th Street, NW
Washington, DC 20036
202-785-1670
http://www.nclr.org
The NCLR is a private, nonprofit, organization that "works to reduce poverty and discrimination, and improve life opportunities for Hispanic Americans." Visit its Web site to learn more about available programs.

National Council of Negro Women (NCNW)

633 Pennsylvania Avenue, NW
Washington, DC 20004
202-737-0120
http://www.ncnw.org
This nonprofit organization works at the national, state, local, and international levels to improve quality of life for women, children, and families. It consists of 38 affiliated national organizations and more than 200 community-based sections. It supports economic development and entrepreneurship and offers career development, community leadership, and mentoring programs for women and youth. For information on these and a variety of other programs, visit the NCNW's Web site.

National Image

PO Box 1368
Bonita, CA 91908
619-934-5277
http://www.nationalimageinc.org
National Image is a national Hispanic organization concerned with employment, education, and civil rights. It hosts a national training conference and convention, and publishes a newsletter, *e-Image*, to keep members updated on organization activities and other items of interest. Visit its Web site to view a database of federal government job openings.

National Indian Council on Aging

10501 Montgomery Boulevard, NE, Suite 210
Albuquerque, NM 87111-3846
505-292-2001
http://www.nicoa.org
The council is a nonprofit advocate for the nation's American Indian and Alaska Native elders. It aids indigenous seniors with employment training and the dissemination of information.

National Indian Education Association (NIEA)

700 North Fairfax Street, Suite 210
Alexandria, VA 22314
703-838-2870
niea@niea.org
http://www.niea.org
The NIEA represents American Indian, Alaska Natives, and Native Hawaiian educators and students. Among its services are conventions and conferences, and the distribution of information about relevant legislation.

National Indian Health Board (NIHB)

101 Constitution Avenue, NW, Suite 8-B02
Washington, DC 20001
202-742-4262
jpetherick@nihb.org
http://www.nihb.org
The NIHB seeks to coordinate and improve Indian health programs and services, and to gather and disseminate relevant information.

National Indian Justice Center

5250 Aero Drive
Santa Rosa, CA 95403
707-579-5507
http://nijc.indian.com
The center is an Indian-owned and -operated nonprofit corporation that works to design and deliver legal education, research, and technical assistance programs in order to improve tribal court systems.

National Indian Telecommunications Institute

110 North Guadalupe, Suite 10
Santa Fe, NM 87501
505-986-3872
karen@niti.org
http://www.niti.org
This organization is dedicated to using the power of electronic technologies to help American Indian, Native Hawaiian, and Alaska Native communities in the areas of economic development, education, language and cultural preservation, tribal policy issues, and self-determination. Visit its Web site for more information.

National Korean American Service and Education Consortium

900 South Crenshaw Boulevard
Los Angeles, CA 90019
323-937-3703

nakasec@nakasec.org
http://www.nakasec.org
This national organization seeks to educate and empower Korean American communities nationwide. It provides bilingual educational materials, cosponsors an annual Summer Youth Program, and organizes seminars, community forums, and conferences.

National Minority AIDS Council
1931 13th Street, NW
Washington, DC 20009
202-483-6622
info@nmac.org
http://www.nmac.org
The council is dedicated to helping communities of color address the challenge of HIV/AIDS. It sponsors advocacy skills training and technical assistance sessions, and advocates for the development of AIDS treatment education programs.

National Minority Business Council (NMBC)
25 West 45th Street, Suite 301
New York, NY 10036
212-997-4753
nmbc@msn.com
http://www.nmbc.org
The NMBC is an umbrella organization that encompasses thousands of small minority businesses located nationally and internationally. It offers short-term loans for working capital in amounts from $1,500 to $25,000, seminars and workshops on topics that include writing a business plan, marketing and sales techniques, and contract procurement, and provides networking opportunities. Visit its Web site for more information.

National Minority Supplier Development Council (NMSDC)
1040 Avenue of the Americas, 2nd Floor
New York, NY 10018
212-944-2430
http://www.nmsdcus.org
The council works to provide a direct link between corporate America and minority-owned businesses. Membership benefits include certification of minority business enterprises, access to a computerized database of minority business suppliers, referrals, and capital loans. The NMSDC has 39 regional councils throughout the United States.

National Native American AIDS Prevention Center
436 14th Street, Suite 1020
Oakland, CA 94612
510-444-2051
information@nnaapc.org
http://www.nnaapc.org
The center is the national headquarters for the campaign to educate Native Americans, Alaska Natives, and Native Hawaiians about AIDS and to improve the quality of life of those infected with or affected by HIV/AIDS.

National Network for Immigrant and Refugee Rights (NNIRR)
310 Eighth Street, Suite 303
Oakland, CA 94607
510-465-1984
nnirr@nnirr.org
http://www.nnirr.org
The NNIRR works for immigrant rights across the country. It is composed of local coalitions and immigrant, refugee, community, religious, civil rights, and labor organizations.

National Organization of Concerned Black Men (NOCBM)
The Thurgood Marshall Center
1816 12th Street, NW, Suite 204
Washington, DC 20009
888-395-7816
info@cbmnational.org
http://www.cbmnational.org
The NOCBM serves as a positive and motivating environment for minority youth by helping them develop skills necessary for their success in the future. It sponsors a number of youth programs and activities. It also offers the Parent Self Improvement Project, which provides low-income working parents with pre-GED instruction, computer training, parenting skills training, and life-skills training. Visit its Web site for more information.

National Congress of Black Women (NCBW)
8484 Georgia Avenue, Suite 420
Silver Spring, MD 20910
877-274-1198
info@npcbw.org
http://www.npcbw.org
The NCBW, formerly the National Political Congress of Black Women, works toward the political

empowerment of African-American women. Activities include mentorship, voter registration, and training in the political process. The organization is dedicated to assisting women in pursuing political office.

National Urban League

120 Wall Street
New York, NY 10005
212-558-5300
info@nul.org
http://www.nul.org

Through advocacy and special programs, the National Urban League assists African Americans in a number of ways. Social and educational development programs help individuals achieve economic self-sufficiency. This community-based organization has more than 100 affiliates across the country, and it offers scholarships, an online career center, assistance to small businesses, education and training programs, and many other resources. It offers a number of publications, including *Achievement Matters: Getting Your Child the Best Education Possible, The State of Black America, Opportunity Journal*, and *National Urban League Institute of Opportunity and Equality Fact Book*.

Native American Public Telecommunications (NAPT)

1800 North 33rd Street
Lincoln, NE 68583
402-472-3522
native@unl.edu
http://www.nativetelecom.org

The mission of the NAPT is supporting the creation, promotion, and distribution of Native American public media through education, training, leadership, and partnerships.

Native American Rights Fund

1506 Broadway
Boulder, CO 80302-6217
303-447-8760
http://www.narf.org

This nonprofit organization provides legal representation and technical assistance to Native American tribes, organizations, and individuals throughout the United States. Among its many activities, the fund offers summer internships for second-year law school students and maintains the National Indian Law Library, a master file of information to help attorneys representing Indians. Visit its Web site to learn more.

Native Americans in Philanthropy

2801 21st Avenue South, Suite 132D
Minneapolis, MN 55407
612-724-8798
http://www.nativephilanthropy.org

Native Americans in Philanthropy was created with a mission to advocate within the philanthropic community with promotion, development, effectiveness, and growth of Native American philanthropy.

Native American Women's Health Education Resource Center

PO Box 572
Lake Andes, SD 57356-0572
605-487-7072
nativewoman@igc.apc.org
http://www.nativeshop.org/nawherc.html

The first resource center to be located on a reservation in the United States, the center is a project of the Native American Community Board of South Dakota. It supports programs that benefit Native Americans locally, nationally, and internationally, including a domestic violence program, adult learning program, a clearinghouse of educational materials, and scholarships for Native American women.

Native Indian American Educational Foundation

PO Box 7465
St. Petersburg, FL 33734-7465
niaef@niaef.org
http://www.niaef.org

The foundation works to raise funds to provide scholarship funding for American Indians in the fields critical to the economic, social, environmental, political, educational, and business development of Indian communities.

Navajo Nation

PO Box 9000
Window Rock, AZ 86515
http://www.navajo.org

The tribe offers employment training, youth opportunities and services, educational resources, and other services to its members.

Northern California Indian Development Council (NCIDC)

241 F Street
Eureka, CA 95501
707-445-8451

http://www.ncidc.org

The NCIDC offers job and career counseling, a computer resource center, and a community mentoring project to Native Americans. It also has offices in Crescent City and Yreka, California.

Office of Minority Health Resource Center (OMHRC)
U.S. Department of Health and Human Services
PO Box 37337
Washington, DC 20013-7337
800-444-6472
http://www.omhrc.gov

The OMHRC is a nationwide service of the Office of Minority Health within the U.S. Department of Health and Human Services. Its mission is to improve the health of racial and ethnic populations through the development of effective health policies and programs that help to eliminate disparities in health. Through the center, minorities have access to an informative Web site and information specialists at the toll-free number.

ONABEN—A Native American Business Network
11825 SW Greenburg Road, Suite B-3
Tigard, OR 97223
800-854-8289
http://www.onaben.org

This nonprofit corporation was created by Northwest Indian tribes to increase the success of private businesses owned by Native Americans. ONABEN offers training and support focused on developing entrepreneurship, and its Web site serves as a resource and directory.

100 Black Men of America
141 Auburn Avenue
Atlanta, GA 30303
800-598-3411
http://www.100blackmen.org

This organization strives to improve life (including educational and economic opportunities) for African Americans. It has chapters throughout the United States and publishes a quarterly magazine, *the onehundred*.

Open Book Program/Open Book Committee
PEN American Center
588 Broadway, Suite 303
New York, NY 10012
212-334-1660

jmartinez@pen.org
http://www.pen.org/page.php/prmID/151

The PEN Open Book Program encourages racial and ethnic diversity within the publishing and literary communities. It works to increase the literature by, for, and about African, Asian, Caribbean, Latin, and Native Americans. Its Open Book Committee serves as a forum for individuals interested in or already a part of the publishing industry. It meets monthly to discuss job concerns and strategies, develop special skills, and to allow members to network among themselves. The committee sponsors the Beyond Margins Awards, which are given to authors of color who submit book length writings that have been published in the United States.

Opera Ebony
2109 Broadway, Suite 1418
New York, NY 10023
212-877-2110
info@operaebony.org
http://www.operaebony.org

Opera Ebony is the oldest African-American opera company in America. Through mainstage productions, tours, and the performance of new and classical works, Opera Ebony introduces performers, conductors, stage directors, choreographers, and other artists to theatrical opera. Its Cross-Cultural Exposure and Development Program introduces opera and musical theatre to young people, ages eight to 18.

Osage Nation
PO Box 779
Pawhuska, OK 74056
800-320-8742
http://www.osagetribe.com

Tribal members are provided with access to employment opportunities, educational programs, and other services. Visit its Web site for complete information and program details.

Pacific Islanders in Communications
1221 Kapi' olani Boulevard, Suite 6A-4
Honolulu, HI 96814
808-591-0059
http://www.piccom.org

Pacific Islanders in Communications is a national nonprofit media organization working to increase national public broadcast programming by and about indigenous Pacific Islanders. It offers internships, workshops, and scholarships to students who are interested in studying media and/or communications.

Pawnee Nation of Oklahoma
PO Box 470
Pawnee, OK 74058
918-762-2541
http://pawneenation.org
The Pawnee Nation offers education and training opportunities, child welfare services, grants, and other support to its members. Visit its Web site for additional information about specific programs and services.

Phelps Stokes Fund
1420 K Street, NW, Suite 800
Washington, DC, 20005
800-874-7797
http://www.psfdc.org
The fund focuses on the education of African Americans, Native Americans, and Africans. It sponsors educational surveys and research studies, administers scholarship and fellowship programs, international exchange programs, and advocates on behalf of its constituents through public education programs.

Piney Woods School
PO Box 100
Piney Woods, MS 39148-9998
601-845-2214
pws@pineywoods.org
http://www.pineywoods.org
One of the few remaining African-American boarding schools in the country, Piney Woods educates children in grades pre-K through 12.

Pinoleville Band of Pomo Indians
367 North State Street, Suite 204
Ukiah, CA 95482
707-463-1454
pgeneral@pinoleville-nsn.gov
http://www.pinoleville.org
The tribe offers employment training, economic resources, social services, and other support to its members.

Port Madison Indian Reservation
PO Box 498
Suquamish, WA 98392
360-598-3311
http://www.suquamish.nsn.us

The reservation hosts a Tribal Center and the Suquamish Community Learning Center, as well as offering other programs and resources.

Prairie Band Potawatomi Nation
16281 Q Road
Mayetta, KS 66509-8970
785-966-2255
http://www.pbpindiantribe.com
The tribe offers education and employment services to its members. Programs include adult education, adult vocational training, higher education scholarships, tribal education and training assistance, graduate student scholarships, and job skills training.

Pueblo of Santa Ana
2 Dove Road
Bernalillo, NM 87004
505-867-3301
info@santaana.org
http://www.santaana.org
The tribe has a development corporation, business enterprises, and sponsors community events.

Quinault Indian Nation
PO Box 189
Taholah, WA 98587-0189
888-616-8211
http://209.206.175.157
This tribe offers educational and training opportunities, employment information, family services, youth programs, and more to its members. Visit the nation's Web site for information about specific services and programs.

Rainbow/PUSH Coalition
930 East 50th Street
Chicago, IL 60615-2702
773-373-3366
http://www.rainbowpush.org
The Rainbow/PUSH Coalition is a multiracial, multi-issue membership organization fighting for social change. Issues include job and economic empowerment, employee rights, and educational access. It has bureaus in Atlanta, Detroit, and New York.

Rankokus Indian Reservation/Powhatan Renape Nation
PO Box 225
Rancocas, NJ 08073

609-261-4747
powhatan@powhatan.org
http://www.powhatan.org
The tribe sponsors social services, training opportunities, and community events for its members.

Rosebud Sioux Tribe
PO Box 517
Rosebud, SD 57570
605-856-5644
resource@gwtc.net
http://www.rosebudsiouxtribe-nsn.gov
Economic development, job services, educational programs, and other community support is sponsored by the tribe. It also offers postsecondary training at Sinte Glesky University.

Saginaw Chippewa Indian Tribe
7070 East Broadway
Mt. Pleasant, MI 48858
989-775-4000
http://www.sagchip.org
The tribe offers educational and job opportunities, and a variety of services to its members. It also offers postsecondary training at Saginaw Chippewa Tribal College.

Saludos Hispanos
800-748-6426
info@saludos.com
http://www.saludos.com
This Hispanic employment service offers free resume postings and a job search database at its Web site. It also publishes Saludos Hispanos magazine.

Sault Tribe of Chippewa Indian
531 Ashmun Street
Sault Ste. Marie, MI 49783
906-635-6050
http://www.sootribe.org
The tribe offers educational opportunities and other services and programs to its youth and adult members. Visit its Web site for additional information.

School of American Research (SAR)
Indian Arts Research Center
PO Box 2188
Santa Fe, NM 87504-2188
505-954-7200
info@sarsf.org
http://www.sarweb.org

The school's Indian Arts Research Center houses one of the world's most significant collections of traditional Southwest Indian arts and artifacts. SAR programs include the Native American Arts Education Program, the Native American Artist Mentor Program, the Resident Scholar Fellowships Program, and the Native American Artist Fellowships. Visit SAR's Web site for more information.

Secretariat for African-American Catholics
United States Conference of Catholic Bishops
3211 Fourth Street, NE
Washington, DC 20017-1194
202-541-3177
saac@usccb.org
http://www.nccbuscc.org/saac
The organization is the official voice of the African-American Catholic community. It provides education and social services to hundreds of Catholic parishes across the United States.

Seminole Nation of Oklahoma
PO Box 1498
Wewoka, OK 74884
405-257-6287
info@seminolenation.com
http://seminolenation.com
The tribe offers educational programs, health and family services, and other support to its members. Visit the nation's Web site for information about specific programs and services.

Seminole Tribe of Florida
6300 Stirling Road
Hollywood, FL 33024
800-683-7800
tribune@semtribe.com
http://www.semtribe.com
The Tribe sponsors a number of educational and community development programs to assist its members with business and career development.

Seneca Nation of Indians
12837 Route 438
Irving, NY 14088
716-532-4900
tlaw@sni.org
http://www.sni.org
The nation consists of three reservations in New York. It provides employment and economic development, education, and health services to its members.

Sitka Tribe of Alaska

456 Katlian Street
Sitka, AK 99835
http://www.sitkatribe.org
A number of tribal services are available to members seeking education and career guidance.

Soul in Motion Players

PO Box 5374
Rockville, MD 20848-5374
800-355-1090
http://www.soulinmotionplayers.org
This touring repertory theater company specializes in African drumming. The group performs for thousands of college students across the country.

Southern Ute Indian Tribe

PO Box 737
Ignacio, CO 81137
970-563-0100
http://www.southern-ute.nsn.us
The tribe offers educational and employment opportunities as well as other support services to its members. Visit its Web site for information.

SPANUSA

1415 Boston Post Road
Larchmont, NY 10538
800-479-8599
info@spanusa.net
http://www.spanusa.net
SPANUSA is an executive search firm specializing in the placement of bilingual Spanish-English speaking professionals and executives.

Spirit Talk Culture Centre

PO Box 477
East Glacier, In the Blackfoot Nation 59434-0477
406-338-2882
blkfoot@3rivers.net
http://www.blackfoot.org
This Web site provides information about the cultural and social practices of the Blackfoot Nation.

Studio Museum in Harlem

144 West 125th Street
New York, NY 10027
212-864-4500
http://www.studiomuseuminharlem.org
The museum offers an educational program, which includes seminars and workshops. It has collections and exhibitions of African American, African-inspired, and Hispanic art. The museum's permanent collection consists of more than 1,500 objects—a collection that exhibits traditional and contemporary African-American art. The museum also offers an Artists-In-Residence Program.

Talento Bilingue de Houston (TBH)

333 South Jensen Drive
Houston, TX 77003-1115
713-222-1213
info@tbhcenter.com
http://www.tbhcenter.com
Talento Bilingue de Houston, formerly the Teatro Bilingue, is Houston's largest Latino cultural arts organization. It is dedicated to presenting and preserving Latin America's rich cultural and artistic heritage, sponsoring varied performances, from ballet to hip-hop. Through mainstage performances, touring exhibitions, and a diverse schedule of cultural and education programs for children and adults, TBH works to instill a sense of cultural pride and affirmation for Latinos in Houston, and foster cross-cultural literacy and understanding for Houston's diverse communities.

Teach for America

315 West 36th, 6th Floor
New York, NY 10018
800-832-1230
admissions@teachforamerica.org
http://www.teachforamerica.org
Teach for America is a national corps of recent college graduates, of all academic majors, who commit two years to teach in underserved and rural public schools.

Thurgood Marshall Scholarship Fund (TMSF)

90 William Street, Suite 1203
New York, NY 10038
212 -573-8888
http://www.thurgoodmarshallfund.org
The Thurgood Marshall Scholarship Fund is the only national organization founded for the sole purpose of providing scholarships to students attending the nation's historically Black public colleges and universities. In addition to scholarships, the TMSF provides unrestricted and restricted support to its 47 member universities. Its Thurgood Marshall Scholarship Fund Career Placement Center provides career services for Thurgood Marshall Students.

Twenty-First Century Foundation
271 West 125th Street, Suite 303
New York, NY 10027-4424
212-662-3700
    info@21cf.org
http://www.21cf.org
The foundation assists with the work of African-American community- and education-based organizations in the form of grants.

United Black Fund
PO Box 7051
Washington, DC 20032
202-783-9300
http://www.ubfinc.org
The United Black Fund is a nonprofit grantmaking institution that provides general, programmatic, and emergency funding to African-American community-based organizations. It presently supports 32 member agencies, and assists yearly additional nonmember agencies on an emergency basis.

United Keetoowah Band of Cherokee Indians in Oklahoma (UKB)
PO Box 746
Tahlequah, OK 74465
918-432-1818
http://www.unitedkeetoowahband.org
The tribe offers educational and employment services, child welfare programs, and a variety of assistance services to its members. Visit the UKB Web site for information.

United National Indian Tribal Youth (UNITY)
PO Box 800
Oklahoma City, OK 73101
405-236-2800
http://www.unityinc.org
UNITY promotes personal development, citizenship, and leadership among Native American youth. It sponsors workshops, a national training conference, and motivational speakers.

United Way of America
701 North Fairfax Street
Alexandria, VA 22314
703-836-7112
http://www.unitedway.org
This national service and training organization assists

minority communities in a variety of ways through its approximately 1,400 local agencies.

Urbanworld Film Festival (UWFF)
Attn: The Tribeca Film Center
375 Greenwich Street, 7th Floor
New York, NY 10013
212-941-3845
info@urbanworld.org
http://www.uwff.com
The mission of the UWFF is to expose independent minority films and entertainment to the widest audience possible. Since its founding in 1997, the UWFF has presented more than 400 features, shorts, and documentaries from around the world. Visit its Web site for more information.

U.S. Indian Arts and Crafts Board
Department of the Interior
1849 C Street, NW, MS 2058-MIB
Washington, DC 20240
888-278-3253
iacb@ios.doi.gov
http://www.doi.gov/iacb
The board is a clearinghouse of information on Indian arts and crafts. It assists federally recognized tribes and their members with economic development through the promotion and marketing of arts and crafts. It also operates the Sioux Indian Museum in Rapid City, South Dakota; the Museum of the Plains Indian in Browning, Montana; and the Southern Plains Indian Museum in Anadarko, Oklahoma.

Vuntut Gwitchin First Nation
PO Box 94
Old Crow, Yukon, Y0B 1N0 Canada
867-966-3261
info@vgfn.net
http://www.oldcrow.ca
The tribe offers adult and youth employment services, social and youth programs, and other support to its members. Visit the nation's Web site for additional information.

Wampanoag Tribe of Gay Head (Aquinnah)
20 Black Brook Road
Aquinnah, MA 02535-1546
508-645-9265
http://www.wampanoagtribe.net

The tribal council serves as a resource to members for information on education, health and human services, and economic development.

Western States Black Research and Educational Center

3617 Montclair Street
Los Angeles, CA 90018-2442
626-794-4677
aclayton@wsbrec.org
http://www.wsbrec.org
Through its collection of films, books, fine art, memorabilia, and music, the center works to preserve the cultural heritage of African Americans. The center's assemblage of African-American resource materials is unique in the Western United States because of its size and scholarly value. It offers research services, workshops, and seminars.

Wichita and Affiliated Tribes

PO Box 729
Anadarko, OK 73005
405-247-2425
info@wichita.nsn.us
http://www.wichita.nsn.us
The Wichita and Affiliated Tribes (Wichita, Keechi, Waco, Tawakonie) help their members pursue higher education and offer job placement and training. Other services and programs the tribes provide include economic development, community and mental health services, housing programs, and more. Visit the Web site for additional information.

Worcester Pipeline Collaborative (WPC)

University of Massachusetts
26 Queen Street
Worcester, MA 01610
508-856-4559
Robert.layne@umassmed.edu
http://www.umassmed.edu/wpc
The WPC encourages, educates, and challenges minority and/or disadvantaged students toward success in health care and science professions, where they are traditionally underrepresented. The WPC partnership includes professionals and K-20 educators from public schools, colleges, universities, biotechnology, health care, and science industries. The WPC offers mentoring, internships, shadowing, after school programs, summer science camp, and professional development. In addition, students may delve into the exploratory nature of science in the Science Laboratory equipped with activities that enhance standards-based school curricula.

Yavapai-Apache Nation

2400 West Datsi Street
Camp Verde, AZ 86322
928-567-1004
http://yavapai-apache-nation.com
The tribe offers educational assistance and job training, among other services and support to its members.

MINORITY COLLEGES AND UNIVERSITIES

MINORITY-SERVING HIGHER EDUCATION ORGANIZATIONS

American Indian College Fund
8333 Greenwood Boulevard
Denver, CO 80221
800-776-3863
info@collegefund.org
http://www.collegefund.org
Colleges or universities controlled by tribal governments typically offer Native American students a unique education based on both traditional academics and native culture. According to the American Indian College Fund, 34 tribal colleges serve more than 30,000 students who represent more than 250 tribes from across the United States, Canada, and Mexico.

Hispanic Association of Colleges and Universities
8415 Datapoint Drive, Suite 400
San Antonio, TX 78229
210-401-1411
http://www.hacu.net/hacu/HACU's_Members_
    EN.asp?SnID=310037736 (list of schools)
The government classifies a Hispanic-Serving Institution (HSI) as a college with at least 25 percent Hispanic undergraduate enrollment. Forty percent of the Hispanic students in postsecondary education are enrolled in Hispanic-Serving Institutions.

White House Initiative on Educational Excellence for Hispanic Americans
400 Maryland Avenue, SW
Washington, DC 20202
202-401-1411
http://www.yesican.gov/wwa
The commission is charged with strengthening the nation's capacity to provide high quality education while increasing opportunities for Hispanic American participation in federal education programs.

All colleges in Puerto Rico are considered Hispanic-Serving Institutions by the U.S. government. These institutions are listed below.

American University of Puerto Rico (Bayamón)
PO Box 2037
Bayamón, PR 00960

787-620-2040
http://www.aupr.edu

Antillean Adventist University
PO Box 118
Mayaguez, PR 00681-0118
787-834-9595
http://www.uaa.edu

Atlantic College
PO Box 3918
Guaynabo, PR 00970
787-720-1022
atlancol@coqui.net
http://www.atlanticcollege-pr.com

Caribbean University (Bayamón)
PO Box 493
Bayamón, PR 00960-0493
787-780-0070
http://www.caribbean.edu

Conservatory of Music of Puerto Rico
350 Rafael Lamar Street
San Juan, PR 00918
787-751-0160
http://www.cmpr.edu

Escuela de Artes Plásticas de Puerto Rico
PO Box 9021112
San Juan, PR 00902-1112
787-725-8120
http://www.eap.edu

Inter-American University of Puerto Rico (Aguadilla)
Recinto de Aguadilla
PO Box 20000
Aguadilla, PR 00605-2000
787-891-0925
http://www.aguadilla.inter.edu

Inter-American University of Puerto Rico (Arecibo)
PO Box 144050
Arecibo, PR 00614-4050
787-878-5475
http://www.arecibo.inter.edu

Inter-American University of Puerto Rico (Barranquitas)
PO Box 517
Barranquitas, PR 00794-0517
787-857-3600
http://www.br.inter.edu

Inter-American University of Puerto Rico (Ponce)
104 Parque Industrial Turpó Road 1
Mercedita, PR 00715-1602
787-284-1912
http://ponce.inter.edu

Inter-American University of Puerto Rico (San Germán)
PO Box 5100
San Germán, PR 00683
800-981-8075
http://www.sg.inter.edu

Polytechnic University of Puerto Rico
PO Box 192017
San Juan, PR 00919-2017
787-622-8000
http://www.pupr.edu

Pontifical Catholic University of Puerto Rico (Ponce)
2250 Avenue Las Americas, Suite 564
Ponce, PR 00731-0777
787-841-2000
http://www.pucpr.edu

Sistema Universitario Ana G. Méndez
PO Box 21345
San Juan, PR 00928-1345
http://www.suagm.edu

Universidad Central del Caribe
PO Box 60327
Bayamon, PR 00960-6032
787-798-3001
http://www.uccaribe.edu

Universidad del Este
PO Box 2010
Carolina, PR 00983
787-257-7373
http://www.suagm.edu/une

Universidad del Turabo
Estacion Universidad, PO Box 3030
Gurabo, PR 00778
787-743-7979
http://www.suagm.edu/ut

Universidad Metropolitana
Apartado 21150
San Juan, PR 00928-1150
787-766-1717
http://www.suagm.edu/umet

University of Puerto Rico (Aguadilla)
PO Box 250160
Aguadilla, PR 00604
787-890-7118
http://www.uprag.edu

University of Puerto Rico (Arecibo)
PO Box 4010
Arecibo, PR 00613
787-815-0000
http://www.upra.edu

University of Puerto Rico (Bayamón)
Industrial Minillas 170 Carr 174
Bayamón, PR 00959-1911
787-786-2885
http://www.uprb.edu

University of Puerto Rico (Carolina)
PO Box 4800
Carolina, PR 00984
787-257-0000
http://www.uprc.edu

University of Puerto Rico (Cayey)
205 Avenida Antonio R. Barceló
Cayey, PR 00736
787-738-2161
http://www.cayey.upr.edu

University of Puerto Rico (Humacao)
Estación Postal CUH 100 Carr
Humacao, PR 00791-4300
787-850-0000
http://www.uprh.edu

University of Puerto Rico (Mayagüez)
PO Box 9000
Mayagüez, PR 00681-9000
787-832-4040
http://www.uprm.edu

University of Puerto Rico (Medical Sciences Campus)
PO Box 365067
San Juan, PR 00936-5067
787-758-2525
http://www.rcm.upr.edu

University of Puerto Rico (Rio Piedras)
PO Box 23302
San Juan, PR 00931-3302
787-764-0000
http://www.uprrp.edu

University of the Sacred Heart
PO Box 12383
San Juan, PR 00914-0383
787-728-1515
http://www.sagrado.edu

White House Initiative on Historically Black Colleges and Universities
1990 K Street, NW, 6th Floor
Washington, DC 20006
202-502-7900
http://www.ed.gov/about/inits/list/whhbcu/edlite-index.html (main site)
http://www.ed.gov/about/inits/list/whhbcu/edlite-list.html (list of colleges)
Historically Black Colleges and Universities (HBCUs) accept applications from all students, but have historically served African American students. These institutions originated to serve the needs of African American communities in a time when Black students could not gain entrance to most colleges. Our nation's 105 HBCUs continue to thrive, enrolling more than 214,000 students annually, according to the U.S. Department of the Interior. They include 40 public four-year, 11 public two-year, 49 private four-year, and five private two-year institutions.

MINORITY-SERVING INSTITUTIONS
Adams State College
208 Edgemont Boulevard
Alamosa, CO 81102
800-824-6494

ascadmit@adams.edu
http://www2.adams.edu
This liberal arts Hispanic-Serving Institution offers bachelor's degrees in 16 majors (including art, biology, English, mathematics, nursing, and Spanish) and graduate degrees in art, counselor education, health and physical education, and teacher education. It also offers associate degrees in chemical analysis, communications technology, general business, geographic information systems, multimedia journalism, and theater.

Alabama Agricultural and Mechanical University
4900 Meridian Street
Huntsville, AL 35811
256-372-5000
http://www.aamu.edu
This Historically Black College and University is a traditional land-grant institution that combines professional, vocational, and liberal arts pursuits. The university provides baccalaureate and graduate studies.

Alabama State University
915 South Jackson Street
PO Box 271
Montgomery, AL 36101-0271
800-253-5037
http://www.alasu.edu
This Historically Black College and University offers undergraduate and graduate instruction in fields such as business, liberal arts, teacher education, the fine arts, the sciences, and other professions.

Alamo Community College District
201 West Sheridan
San Antonio, TX 78204-1429
210-208-8000
http://www.accd.edu
The Alamo Community College District offers associate degree and certificate programs in more than 50 academic and professional fields. Approximately 89,000 students attend its four colleges—Northwest Vista, Palo Alto, St. Philip's, and San Antonio—all of which (listed below) are classified as Hispanic-Serving Institutions.

Northwest Vista College
3535 North Ellison Drive
San Antonio, TX 78251
210-348-2020
nvcinfo@accd.edu
http://www.accd.edu/nvc

Palo Alto College
1400 West Villaret
San Antonio, TX 78224
210-921-5000
http://www.accd.edu/pac/htm

Saint Philip's College
1801 Martin Luther King Drive
San Antonio, TX 78203
210-531-3200
http://www.accd.edu/spc/spcmain/spc.htm
St. Philip's College is also categorized as a Historically
   Black College and University.

San Antonio College
1300 San Pedro Avenue
San Antonio, TX 78212-4299
210-733-2000
http://www.accd.edu/sac/sacmain/sac.htm

Albany State University
504 College Drive
Albany, GA 31705
229-430-4600
Admissions@asurams.edu
http://asuweb.asurams.edu/asu
Albany State University is a Historically Black institution
   in southwest Georgia. It offers bachelor's, master's,
   and education specialist degrees and a variety of
   non-degree educational programs. The university
   emphasizes the liberal arts as the foundation for all
   learning by exposing students to the humanities, fine
   arts, social sciences, and the sciences. Global learning
   is fostered through a broad-based curriculum and
   diverse university activities.

Albuquerque Technical Vocational Institute
525 Buena Vista, SE
Albuquerque, NM 87106
505-224-3000
http://www.tvi.cc.nm.us
Among the educational programs at this community
   college are arts and sciences, adult and
   developmental education, business, health
   occupations, technologies, and distance learning. This
   Hispanic-Serving Institution is New Mexico's largest
   community college.

Alcorn State University
1000 ASU Drive
Alcorn State, MS 39096
601-877-6100
http://www.alcorn.edu
Alcorn State was created in 1871 and has the distinction
   of being the first Historically Black land-grant
   institution and the first state-supported institution for
   the higher education of Blacks in the United States.
   Its student body is predominantly Black; however, it
   includes Caucasian, Asian, African, and West Indian
   students. Alcorn State University is accredited by the
   Commission on Colleges of the Southern Association
   of Colleges and Schools to award the associate,
   baccalaureate, master's, and specialist degrees.
   Currently more than 150 businesses, industries,
   governmental agencies, and school systems
   (including graduate and professional schools) recruit
   on the Alcorn campus.

Allan Hancock College
800 South College Drive
Santa Maria, CA 93454-6399
805-922-6966
http://www.hancock.cc.ca.us
Allan Hancock College is a community college that offers
   degrees and certificates in a variety of study areas. It is
   a Hispanic-Serving Institution.

Allen University
1530 Harden Street
Columbia, SC 29204-1057
803-376-5700
http://www.allenuniversity.edu
Allen University, founded in 1870, is a small,
   coeducational, private institution located in Columbia,
   South Carolina. Its founding institution is the African
   Methodist Episcopal Church. Allen University is an
   academic community whose mission is to provide
   baccalaureate education with a strong, unalterable
   commitment to teaching and community service
   appropriate to the needs of its students. The current
   open admissions policy is designed both for high
   school graduates, as well as those who complete and
   pass the equivalent General Education Development
   tests. Allen University offers baccalaureate degrees in
   nine majors of study.

Alliant International University
10455 Pomerado Road
San Diego, CA 92131-1799
858-635-4772
admissions@alliant.edu
http://www.alliant.edu/sandiego.htm

This Hispanic-Serving Institution offers a variety of
undergraduate and graduate programs through
its School of Organizational Studies, School of
Professional Psychology, College of Business, Arts
and Sciences, and Graduate School of Education.

Amarillo College
PO Box 447
Amarillo, TX 78178-0001
806-371-5000
http://www.actx.edu
This two-year Hispanic-Serving Institution has five
campuses. It offers certificates and associate degrees
in a variety of academic disciplines, including
accounting, art, automotive collision technology,
biotechnology, dental hygiene, engineering,
interior design, mortuary science, nuclear medicine,
nursing, paralegal studies, photography, and surgical
technology.

American Indian College of the Assemblies of God
10020 North 15th Avenue
Phoenix, AZ 85021-2199
602-944-3335
http://www.aicag.edu
The college's stated mission is "Equipping Native
Americans for Christian service, emphasizing Biblical
truths and academic excellence within a Christian
community." Native Americans from approximately 25
tribes attend the school, but it is open to students of
all ethnicities.

Antelope Valley College
3041 West Avenue K
Lancaster, CA 93536
661-722-6300
http://www.avc.edu
This two-year Hispanic-Serving Institution offers a
variety of academic programs through the following
divisions: arts and letters, business, computer and
media arts, health sciences, physical education and
athletics, math and science, social and behavioral
science and family and consumer education, and
technical education.

Arizona Institute of Business and Technology (AIBT)
6049 North 43rd Avenue
Phoenix, AZ 85019-1600
800-793-2428
http://iia-online.com

The AIBT is under the umbrella of the International
Institute of the Americas with campuses is Phoenix,
Mesa, and Tucson. It awards certificates, diplomas,
and associate's and bachelor's degrees in a
variety of academic programs. Hispanics make up
approximately 38 percent of its student body.

Arizona Western College
2020 South Avenue 8 East, PO Box 929
Yuma, AZ 85366-0929
888-293-0392
http://www.awc.cc.az.us
This two-year Hispanic-Serving Institution serves more
than 7,000 students from Yuma and La Paz counties. It
offers associate degrees and certificate in areas such as
agriculture, business, computer information systems,
health, family and consumer sciences, fine arts,
mathematics, nursing, physical education, recreation,
science, and social studies. Day and evening classes
are conducted on campus and at satellite campuses
throughout Yuma and La Paz counties.

Arkansas Baptist College
1600 Bishop Street
Little Rock, AR 72202
501-374-7856
http://www.arbaptcol.edu
Arkansas Baptist College offers six baccalaureate
degrees and five associate degrees. Baccalaureate
degrees include accounting, business administration,
computer science, elementary education, human
services, and theology. Associate degrees include
business administration, child development, Christian
education, computer science, and secretarial science.
The college is predominantly African American.

Bacone College
2299 Bacone Road
Muskogee, OK 74403-1568
888-682-5514
http://www.bacone.edu
Bacone College is a four-year Christian liberal arts
university that was founded in 1880. Majors
include accounting, business administration, child
development, diagnostic medical sonography,
early childhood education, elementary education,
general studies, health and physical education, health
information management, noninvasive cardiology
technology, and nursing. The college also hosts the
Cherokee Nation School of Information Technology.

Bakersfield College

1801 Panaroma Drive
Bakersfield, CA 93305
661-395-4011
http://www.bc.cc.ca.us
Bakersfield College was founded in 1913 and is
one of the nation's oldest continually operating
community colleges. This Hispanic-Serving
Institution serves 15,000 students. Career and
technical programs offered include agriculture
and business management, allied health, animal
science, applied science and technology, business
education, computer science, computer graphics
art, crop science, environmental horticulture, family
and consumer education, forestry, human services,
photography, and public safety. It also offers five
apprenticeship training programs. Bakersfield College
offers students opportunities to earn an associate
degree, transfer to a four-year institution, or to gain
new job skills.

Barber-Scotia College

145 Cabarrus Avenue West
Concord, NC 28025
704-789-2900
http://www.b-sc.edu
Barber-Scotia College offers a liberal arts education
in a community concerned with the interaction of
cultures, Christian heritage, scholarship, citizenship,
and leadership. Barber-Scotia emphasizes a liberal arts
education strengthened by advanced technology.
The college has strong programs dedicated to
teacher education, total student development, other
service-oriented majors, and community services.
Students are expected to demonstrate a true sense
of understanding and value of the local, national, and
international communities.

Barry University

11300 NE Second Avenue
Miami Shores, FL 33161-6695
800-695-2279
admissions@mail.barry.edu
http://www.barry.edu
Barry is an independent, coeducational Catholic
international university. Founded in 1940, this
Hispanic-Serving Institution is sponsored by the
Adrian Dominican Order of Sisters. Barry offers more
than 60 undergraduate programs and 50 graduate
degrees.

Bay Mills Community College

12214 West Lakeshore Drive
Brimley, MI 49715
800-844-BMCC
http://www.bmcc.org
Bay Mills Community College is a tribally controlled
community college located inside the boundaries of
the Bay Mills Indian community on the Eastern Upper
Peninsula of Michigan. Both the on-campus program at
Bay Mills and the Bay Mills Nishnaabek Kinoomaadewin
Virtual College program are based in Native American
culture. Students attending the college, either on
campus or online, receive an education integrated with
American Indian wisdom, culture, and spirituality.

Benedict College

1600 Harden Street
Columbia, SC 29204
803-256-4220
http://www.benedict.edu
Benedict College, founded in 1870, is an independent,
coeducational, private institution located in Columbia,
South Carolina. It has an enrollment of approximately
2,800 students and offers bachelor degree programs
in 29 major areas of study. It is one of 105 Historically
Black College and Universities in the United States.

Bennett College

900 East Washington Street
Greensboro, NC 27401
336-273-4431
http://www.bennett.edu
Bennett College is a small, residential, four-year liberal arts
college affiliated with the United Methodist Church. It
has an enrollment of approximately 600 women, the
majority of whom are of African-American descent.
Bennett offers 24 majors and awards bachelor of arts,
bachelor of science, and bachelor of arts and sciences
degrees in interdisciplinary studies, and bachelor of
social work degrees.

Bethune-Cookman College

640 Dr. Mary McLeod Bethune Boulevard
Daytona Beach, FL 32114-3099
386-481-2000
http://www.bethune.cookman.edu
Founded by Dr. Mary McLeod Bethune in 1904, this
Historically Black College is affiliated with the United
Methodist Church. The coeducational and residential
institution offers degrees in 33 major areas, including

business, education, humanities, nursing, science and mathematics, and social sciences. It also offers preprofessional, nondegree programs in dentistry, engineering, law, medicine, pharmacy, and veterinary medicine.

Bishop State Community College
351 North Broad Street
Mobile, AL 36603-5898
251-690-6801
info@bishop.edu
http://www.bscc.cc.al.us
Bishop State Community College is a state-supported, open-admission, urban community college located in Mobile, Alabama. The college consists of four city campuses dedicated to serving the residents of Mobile and Washington counties in southwest Alabama. Bishop State offers university transfer programs for students wanting to continue their education at a four-year school, or for those who seek to start careers right away, the college's one- and two-year career programs can put students on the fast track to rewarding jobs. It is one of 105 Historically Black College and Universities in the United States.

Blackfeet Community College
PO Box 819
Browning, MT 59417
800-549-7457
http://www.bfcc.org
The Blackfeet Community College is located in Browning, Montana, on the Blackfeet Indian Reservation. The college is a fully accredited, two-year, higher education institution.

Bluefield State College
219 Rock Street
Bluefield, WV 24701
304-327-4000
http://www.bluefield.wvnet.edu
This Historically Black College and University offers undergraduate liberal arts and professional programs in allied health sciences, applied sciences, business, education, engineering technologies, humanities, and social sciences leading to baccalaureate and associate degrees, the nontraditional regents Bachelor of Arts degree, and continuing education opportunities.

Boricua College
3755 Broadway
New York, NY 10032

212-694-1000
acruz@boricuacollege.edu
http://www.boricuacollege.edu
Boricua is a four-year college focusing on the educational needs of Spanish-speaking students with three campuses in the New York area. Majors offered include business administration, childhood education, human services, inter-American studies, and liberal arts and sciences.

Borough of Manhattan Community College
City University of New York
199 Chambers Street
New York, NY 10007
212-220-8000
http://www.bmcc.cuny.edu
This two-year Hispanic-Serving Institution offers a variety of associate degrees, including accounting, allied health sciences, business management, ethnic studies, computer information systems, cooperative education, developmental skills, English, health education, human services, mathematics, modern languages, music and art, nursing, office administration, science, social science, speech, and teacher education.

Bowie State University
14000 Jericho Park Road
Bowie, MD 20715-9465
877-772-6943
http://www.bowiestate.edu
Bowie State University is a Historically Black University. It offers a variety of undergraduate and graduate academic programs through its School of Arts and Sciences, School of Education and Professional Studies, School of Continuing Education and Extended Studies, the Model Institute for Excellence (sponsored by NASA), the University College of Excellence, and the School of Graduate Studies and Research.

Bronx Community College
West 181st Street and University Avenue
Bronx, NY 10453
718-289-5100
admission@bcc.cuny.edu
http://www.bcc.cuny.edu
This Hispanic-Serving Institution offers the Associate in Applied Sciences degree (with career programs including accounting, marketing, nursing, paralegal studies, and pharmaceutical manufacturing technology), the Associate in Arts degree (human

services, liberal arts and sciences), the Associate in Science degree (including business administration, computer science, engineering science, and therapeutic recreation), and certificate programs (including animal care and management, automotive mechanics, and licensed practical nursing).

Broward Community College
111 East Las Olas Boulevard
Fort Lauderdale, FL 33301
954-201-7400
http://www.broward.edu
This Hispanic-Serving Institution offers certificates and associate degrees in more than 100 academic fields. It has eight campuses.

California State Polytechnic University (POMONA)
3801 West Temple Avenue
Pomona, CA 91768
909 869 7659
http://www.csupomona.edu
This Hispanic-Serving Institution offers a variety of undergraduate programs and majors, including accounting, animal science, apparel merchandising and management, computer information systems, education, engineering, hospitality, and music.

California State University
401 Golden Shore
Long Beach, CA 90802-4210
562-951-4000
http://www.calstate.edu
The California State University offers programs in more than 50 academic and professional fields. The university is organized into six schools: Arts and Letters; Business and Economics; Education; Engineering, Computer Science, and Technology; Health and Human Services; and Natural and Social Sciences. Approximately 409,000 students attend its 23 campuses, 10 of which (listed below) are classified as Hispanic-Serving Institutions.

California State University (Bakersfield)
9001 Stockdale Highway
Bakersfield, CA 93311-1022
661-664-2011
http://www.csubak.edu

California State University (Dominguez Hills)
1000 East Victoria Street
Carson, CA 90747
310-243-3696

info@csudh.edu
http://www.csudh.edu

California State University (Fresno)
5241 North Maple Avenue
Fresno, CA 93740-8027
559-278-4240
http://www.csufresno.edu

California State University (Fullerton)
PO Box 34080
Fullerton, CA 92834-9480
714-278-2011
http://www.fullerton.edu

California State University (Long Beach)
1250 Bellflower Boulevard
Long Beach, CA 90840-0106
562-985-4111
http://www.csulb.edu

California State University (Los Angeles)
5151 State University Drive
Los Angeles, CA 90032
323-343-3000
admission@calstatela.edu
http://www.calstatela.edu

California State University (Monterey Bay)
100 Campus Center
Seaside, CA 93955-8001
831-582-3000
http://www.monterey.edu

California State University (Northridge)
18111 Nordhoff Street
Northridge, CA 91330
818-677-1200
http://www.csun.edu

California State University (San Bernardino)
5500 University Parkway
San Bernardino, CA 92407-2397
909-880-5000
http://www.csusb.edu

California State University (Stanislaus)
801 West Monte Vista Avenue
Turlock, CA 95382
209-667-3122
http://www.csustan.edu

Cañada College
4200 Farm Hill Boulevard
Redwood City, CA 94061
650-306-3100
http://canadacollege.net
Cañada College's mission is to ensure that students from diverse backgrounds achieve their educational goals by providing quality instruction in transfer and general education courses, professional/technical programs, basic skills, and activities that foster students' personal development and academic success. The community college has approximately 6,000 students—42 percent of whom are Hispanic.

Cankdeska Cikana Community College
PO Box 269
Fort Totten, ND 58335-0269
701-766-4415
questions@littlehoop.cc
http://www.littlehoop.cc
This college on the Fort Totten Reservation serves Native American students. It is also known as Little Hoop Community College.

Capital Community College
950 Main Street
Hartford, CT 06103
860-906-5000
http://www.ccc.commnet.edu
The college offers 38 associate degree programs and 36 certificate programs in a variety of areas, including accounting, computer and information systems, computer-aided manufacturing, computer technology, early childhood education, fire technology and administration, health science, library technician assistant, local area network operations, medical assisting, microcomputers, nursing, paramedic studies, radiologic technology, and studio art. African Americans and Hispanic Americans make up nearly 60 percent of its student body.

Carlos Albizu University
2173 NW 99th Avenue
Miami, FL 33172
305-593-1223
http://www.ccas.edu
This Hispanic-Serving Institution has campuses in Miami, Florida, and San Juan, Puerto Rico.

Central Arizona College
8470 North Overfield Road
Coolidge, AZ 85228
800-237-9814
http://www.cac.cc.az.us
This Hispanic-Serving Institution offers associate degrees and certificates in more than 55 subject areas, including accounting, chemistry, computers-network administration, computers-Web design, emergency medical services, health occupations, massage therapy, physical education/recreation, sign language (American), theater, and welding. A large percentage of students are Hispanic and Native American.

Central State University (CSU)
PO Box 1004
Wilberforce, OH 45384
973-376-6011
info@csu.ces.edu
http://www.centralstate.edu
Central State University originated as a state-financed department at the African Methodist Episcopal Church's Wilberforce University. Central State is unique as Ohio's only Historically Black public institution of higher education, although the enacting legislation indicated that the Combined Normal and Industrial Department would be "open to all persons of good moral character." Central State University currently grants bachelor of arts, bachelor of science in education, bachelor of manufacturing engineering, and bachelor of music degrees, and master of education degrees through the College of Arts and Sciences, College of Business and Industry, and College of Education. The university typically awards about one-eighth of all bachelor's degrees earned by African Americans at Ohio's public universities.

Central Wyoming College
2660 Peck Avenue
Riverton, WY 82501
307-855-2000
http://www.cwc.cc.wy.us
This is a public, two-year college near the Wind River Reservation. About one-fifth of the enrolled students are Native American. The college offers two educational tracks: a Transfer Program and a Career/Technical Program. Majors include art, automotive parts, business administration, computer networking technologies, electronic media, equine studies,

human services, Native American studies, nursing, theatre, and welding.

Cerritos College
11110 Alonda Boulevard
Norwalk, CA 90650
562-860-2451
http://www.cerritos.edu
Founded in 1955, Cerritos College is a public community college that offers degrees and certificates in more than 80 areas of study. Hispanics, Asians, African Americans, Pacific Islanders, and Native Americans together account for more than 60 percent of the students.

Chaffey College
5885 Haven Avenue
Rancho Cucamonga, CA 91737-3002
909-987-1737
http://www.chaffey.edu
This community college offers more than 100 degree and certificate programs. It is a Hispanic-Serving Institution.

Charles Drew University of Medicine and Science
1731 East 120th Street
Los Angeles, CA 90059
323-563-4800
http://www.cdrewu.edu
Born out of the ashes of the Watts rebellion, Charles R. Drew Postgraduate School was founded in 1966 in response to the lack of adequate medical facilities in the area, which featured a large population of African Americans. The institution later became a university and changed its name in 1987 to reflect its expanded academic role and identity. Today the university offers training in the following medical specialties: anesthesiology, emergency medicine, family medicine, internal medicine, neurosurgery, obstetrics and gynecology, opthalmology, oral maxillofacial, otolaryngology, pathology, pediatrics, psychiatry, radiology, and surgery.

Cheyney University of Pennsylvania
1837 University Circle, PO Box 200
Cheyney, PA 19319-0200
610-399-2000
http://www.cheyney.edu
Founded in 1837 as the Institute for Colored Youth, Cheyney University of Pennsylvania is the oldest Historically Black Institution of higher education in the nation. Cheyney is a coeducational public institution that admits all qualified students regardless of race, creed, or ethnicity. It offers baccalaureate degrees in more than 30 disciplines and the master's degree in education.

Chicago State University
9501 South King Drive
Chicago, IL 60628
773-995-2000
http://www.csu.edu
Chicago State University is a public institution of higher learning located on the south side of Chicago. It offers 36 degree and certificate programs at the undergraduate level and 29 degree and certificate programs at the graduate level. The university's academic programs include accounting, education, finance, health information administration, information systems, management, marketing, nursing, and occupational therapy. A large percentage of its students are African American.

Chief Dull Knife College
PO Box 98
Lame Deer, MT 59043
406-477-6215
http://www.cdkc.edu
Chief Dull Knife College is located on the Northern Cheyenne Indian Reservation in southeastern Montana, and serves the reservation and surrounding communities. The college offers associate degrees and certificate programs.

Citrus College
1000 West Foothill Boulevard
Glendora, CA 91741-1899
626-914-8511
admissions@citruscollege.edu
http://www.citrus.cc.ca.us
This public community college offers associate degrees and career/technical programs in a variety of subject areas, including administration of justice, architecture, art, automotive technology, business education, child development, computer science, dance, digital and Web design, forestry, heating and air conditioning, information technology, licensed vocation nursing, music-instrumental, music-vocal, teaching (K-12), theatre arts, and truck technology. Its student body is 39 percent Hispanic.

City College of New York, University of New York
138th Street and Convent Avenue
New York, NY 10031
212-650-7000
admissions@ccny.cuny.edu
http://www.ccny.cuny.edu
This Hispanic-Serving Institution includes the College
of Liberal Arts and Science, along with Schools of
Architecture, Education, Engineering, and the Sophie
Davis School of Biomedical Education/CUNY Medical
School. Long renowned as a great teaching institution,
CCNY has also become internationally known for the
research activities of its faculty in a host of fields such
as molecular modeling, laser optics, and AIDS. Students
from more than 85 countries attend the university.

City College of San Francisco (Phelan)
50 Phelan Avenue
San Francisco, CA 94112
415-239-3000
http://www.ccsf.edu
This Hispanic-Serving Institution offers undergraduate
and graduate degrees in many areas, including
aeronautics, Asian American studies, automotive
technology, broadcast electronic media arts,
computer and information science, computer
networking and information technology, culinary
arts/hospitality studies, environmental horticulture
and floristry, fashion, labor studies, Latin American
and Latino studies, licensed vocational nursing,
registered nursing, paralegal-legal studies, Philippine
studies, skilled trades, and theatre arts.

City Colleges of Chicago
District Office
226 West Jackson Boulevard
Chicago, IL 60606
312-553-2500
http://www.ccc.edu
The seven City Colleges of Chicago (listed below) are
some of the most ethnically diverse colleges in the
nation. Students attending the colleges can pursue
associate degrees in Career/Technical Programs,
General Studies Programs, and Transfer Programs.

City Colleges of Chicago, Harold Washington College
30 East Lake Street
Chicago, IL 60601
312-553-5600
http://hwashington.ccc.edu

City Colleges of Chicago, Kennedy-King College
6800 South Wentworth Avenue
Chicago, IL 60621
773-602-5000
http://kennedyking.ccc.edu
The college's students are predominantly African
American.

City Colleges of Chicago, Malcolm X College
1900 West Van Buren Street
Chicago, IL 60612
312-850-7000
http://malcolmx.ccc.edu
More than 25 percent of the students at Malcolm X
College are Hispanic.

City Colleges of Chicago, Olive-Harvey College
10001 South Woodlawn
Chicago, IL 60628
773-291-6100
http://oliveharvey.ccc.edu

City Colleges of Chicago, Richard J. Daley College
7500 South Pulaski Road
Chicago, IL 60652
773-838-7500
http://daley.ccc.edu
More than 25 percent of the students at Richard J. Daley
College are Hispanic.

City Colleges of Chicago, Truman College
1145 West Wilson Avenue
Chicago, IL 60640
773-907-4000
tradmissions@ccc.edu
http://www.trumancollege.cc

City Colleges of Chicago, Wilbur Wright College
4300 North Narragansett Avenue
Chicago, IL 60634
773-777-7900
http://wright.ccc.edu
More than 25 percent of students at Wilbur Wright
College are Hispanic.

Claflin College
400 Magnolia Street
Orangeburg, SC 29115-9970
800-922-1276
http://www.claflin.edu

Claflin College is a private, coeducational, Historically Black, United Methodist Church-related four-year institution. Claflin offers 34 majors leading to the bachelor's degree. These majors help students pursue careers in fields such as teaching, the ministry, the service professions, government, business, scientific research, mass communications, and the arts. The college also offers preprofessional programs in medicine, dentistry, law, Christian ministry, and engineering. It offers a Master of Business Administration degree and a Master of Science in Biotechnology.

Clark-Atlanta University
223 James P. Brawley Drive, SW
Atlanta, GA 30314
404-880-8000
http://www.cau.edu
Clark-Atlanta University, one of 105 Historically Black Colleges and Universities in the United States, offers undergraduate and graduate degrees in more than 50 fields.

Clinton Junior College
1029 Crawford Road
Rock Hill, SC 29730
877-837-9645
http://www.clintonjuniorcollege.edu
One of 105 Historically Black Colleges and Universities in the United States, this two-year institution offers programs in Christian ministries, liberal arts, small business, and religious studies.

Clovis Community College
417 Schepps Boulevard
Clovis, NM 88101
505-769-2811
info@clovis.edu
http://www.clovis.edu
This two-year Hispanic-Serving Institution offers certificates and associate degrees in more than 25 academic disciplines.

Coahoma Community College
3240 Friars Point Road
Clarksdale, MS 38614
662-627-2571
http://www.ccc.cc.ms.us
Coahoma Community College is a two-year coeducational community college offering degrees or certificates in more than 50 majors. Academic division

majors include accounting, art, athletic administration and coaching, biology, chemistry, child development, computer science, criminal justice, education, English, mathematics, radio and television broadcasting, and social work. Vocational-technical division majors include business and office systems technology, child development technology, collision repair technology, cosmetology, hotel and restaurant management technology, industrial maintenance mechanic technology, practical nursing, residential carpentry technology, and welder/welding technology. African Americans make up a large percentage of the student body at the college.

Coastal Bend College
3800 Charco Road
Beeville, TX 78102
361-358-2838
http://vct.coastalbend.edu
Coastal Bend College is a two-year Hispanic-Serving Institution that offers associate degrees and certificates. Study areas include business technology, dental hygiene, kinesiology and health, mathematics and physics, protective services, visual arts, and vocational nursing. In addition to its main campus in Beeville, the college also has campuses in Alice, Kingsville, and Pleasanton, Texas. According to the college, more than three-quarters of its graduates are either working or earning university degrees.

Cochise College
4190 West State Highway 80
Douglas, AZ 85607-6190
520-364-7943
http://www.cochise.edu
This two-year Hispanic-Serving Institution offers academic programs in airport/aviation, athletics, motor transportation, nursing, and other disciplines. In addition to its Douglas campus, Cochise College has campuses in Sierra Vista, Wilcox, Benson, and Fort Huachuca, Arizona.

College of Menominee Nation
PO Box 1179
N 172 Highway 47/55
Keshena, WI 54135
800-567-2344
http://www.menominee.edu
The College of Menominee Nation is a two-year tribal college offering many programs of study, including

business administration, computer science, early childhood education, human services/social work, natural resources, nursing, nutrition and food science, and sustainable development. It also offers a pre-apprenticeship carpentry certificate.

College of Mount Saint Vincent
6301 Riverdale Avenue
Riverdale, NY 10471-1093
800-665-2678
admissns@mountsaintvincent.edu
http://www.mountsaintvincent.edu
This Hispanic-Serving Institution offers a variety of undergraduate and graduate majors, including allied health studies, international studies, religious studies, and Spanish. It also offers certificate programs in allied health, education, and nursing.

College of Santa Fe
1600 Saint Michael's Drive
Santa Fe, NM 87505
800-456-2673
http://www.csf.edu
This Hispanic-Serving Institution is an independent college in the Lasallian Catholic tradition with academic emphases on the arts, business, and education.

College of the Desert
43-500 Monterey Avenue
Palm Desert, CA 92260
760-346-8041
http://www.desert.cc.ca.us
This community college offers degrees and certificates in more than 70 disciplines, including agriculture, air conditioning /HVAC, art, automotive technology, advanced transportation technologies, business and hospitality industries, culinary arts, early childhood education, health sciences, and social sciences. Approximately 52 percent of its students are Hispanic.

College of the Sequoias
915 South Mooney Boulevard
Visalia, CA 93277
559-730-3700
http://www.cos.edu
This Hispanic-Serving Institution offers associate degrees and certificates in many areas, including architecture, math and engineering, nursing/health sciences, and vocational education.

College of the Southwest
6610 Lovington Highway
Hobbs, NM 88240
800- 530-4400
http://www.csw.edu
This Christian Hispanic-Serving Institution offers undergraduate in 17 majors, including education, environmental management, sport management, and theatre. Graduate degrees are offered in counseling, curriculum and instruction, educational administration, and educational diagnostics.

Colorado State University (Pueblo)
2200 Bonforte Boulevard
Pueblo, CO 81001-4901
719-549-2461
info@colostate-pueblo.edu
http://www.colostate-pueblo.edu
This Hispanic-Serving Institution offers undergraduate study in more than 25 majors (including automotive industry management, Chicano studies, and foreign languages/Spanish) and graduate study in six majors (including applied natural science, industrial and systems engineering, and nursing).

Columbia Basin College
2600 North 20th Avenue
Pasco, WA 99301
509-547-0511
http://www.cbc2.org
This two-year Hispanic-Serving Institution offers a variety of associate degrees and certificates.

Community College of Denver
PO Box 173363
Denver, CO 80217-3363
303-556-2600
http://ccd.rightchoice.org
The college offers 125 degree and certificate programs through its Center for Arts and Sciences, Center for Business and Technology, Center for Educational Advancement, and Center for Health Sciences. Minorities make up 58 percent of its student body.

Compton Community College
1111 East Artesia Boulevard
Compton, CA 90221
310-900-1600
info@compton.edu
http://www.compton.cc.ca.us

Compton Community College offerings range from vocational programs to fine arts. The student body is almost evenly divided among African American and Hispanic American students.

Concordia College

1804 Green Street
Selma, AL 36701
334-874-5700
http://www.concordiaselma.edu
One of 105 Historically Black Colleges and Universities in the United States, this institution offers study options in elementary education, general education, and teacher certification. It also offers a Lutheran teacher diploma. Concordia is affiliated with the Lutheran Church-Missouri Synod.

Coppin State College

2500 West North Avenue
Baltimore, MD 21216-3698
800-635-3674
http://www.coppin.edu
Coppin, a Historically Black College, provides undergraduate and graduate education opportunities through its Division of Arts and Sciences, Division of Education, Division of Nursing, Division of Graduate Studies, and Division of Honors.

Crownpoint Institute of Technology

Lower Point Road, State Road 371
PO Box 849
Crownpoint, NM 87313
505-786-4100
http://www.cit.cc.nm.us
Crownpoint Institute of Technology's two campuses are situated on the eastern edge of the Navajo Nation in Crownpoint, New Mexico. It offers the following certification programs: accounting, administrative assistant, alternative energy, applied computer technology, automotive technology, carpentry, commercial driver license, computer-aided drafting, construction technology, culinary arts, early childhood multicultural development, electrical trades, environmental science and natural resources, nursing assistant, and small business development. It also offers associate degree programs in accounting, administrative assistant, applied computer technology, computer-aided drafting, environmental science and natural resources, law advocate, legal assistant, public administration, and veterinary technician.

Delaware State University

1200 North Dupont Highway
Dover, DE 19901
302-857-6060
http://www.dsc.edu
This public institution is one of 105 Historically Black Colleges and Universities in the United States. Degrees are offered in art, business administration, science, social work, and technology, among other fields.

Del Mar College

101 Baldwin Boulevard
Corpus Christi, TX 78404-3897
800-652-3357
colrel@delmar.edu
http://www.delmar.edu
This comprehensive, two-year Hispanic-Serving Institution is located in Corpus Christi, Texas. It offers academic, occupational, technical, and noncredit programs.

Denmark Technical College

500 Solomon Blatt Boulevard
PO Box 327
Denmark, SC 29042
803-793-5176
http://www.denmarktech.edu
This two-year institution offers technical certificates, one-year diplomas, and two-year degrees in a variety of areas, including advanced welding, automotive heating/air conditioning, automotive technology, automotive transmission/transaxle, barbering, brick masonry, carpentry, computer technology, cosmetology, criminal justice, culinary arts, early childhood development, electronics technology, general business, general technology, human services, industrial electricity/electronics, industrial electricity/electronics, office systems technology, plumbing, and welding. It is one of 105 Historically Black Colleges and Universities in the United States.

Dillard University

2601 Gentilly Boulevard
New Orleans, LA 70122
504-283-8822
http://www.dillard.edu
Dillard University is a private, undergraduate liberal arts university founded in 1869. It has been cited in *U.S. News and World Report* as a top southern liberal arts

college. This Historically Black College and University offers more than 30 undergraduate majors.

Diné College
PO Box 67
Tsaile, AZ 86556-0067
928-724-6630
http://www.dinecollege.edu
Diné College was established to meet the educational needs of the Navajo people. It offers two-year programs according to the needs of the Navajo Nation. Diné College has eight campuses in Arizona and New Mexico. All campuses offer educational programs that prepare students for transfer to four-year colleges/ universities and for entry into the workforce.

Donnelly College
608 North 18th Street
Kansas City, KS 66102
913-621-6070
http://www.donnelly.edu
This Hispanic-Serving Institution offers a variety of associate degrees and certificates and also offers an intensive English program.

Eastern New Mexico University (Roswell)
PO Box 6000
Roswell, NM 88202-6000
800-243-6687
http://www.roswell.enmu.edu
This Hispanic-Serving Institution awards certificates, associate degrees, and certificates of occupational training in contemporary career/technical programs and general transfer academic programs.

East Los Angeles College
1301 Avenida Cesar Chavez
Monterey Park, CA 91754
323-265-8650
http://www.elac.cc.ca.us
This Hispanic-Serving Institution offers both academic transfer courses, which prepare students for admission to four-year colleges and universities, and occupational programs that prepare students for careers in two years or less.

Edward Waters College
1658 Kings Road
Jacksonville, FL 32209
888-898-3191

http://www.ewc.edu
Edward Waters College is a private residential institution. This four-year, liberal arts college was established in 1866 to educate recently emancipated African Americans. Today, it continues to educate this group while at the same time welcoming other racial and ethnic groups.

El Camino College
16007 Crenshaw Boulevard
Torrance, CA 90506
866-352-2646
http://www.elcamino.cc.ca.us
This Hispanic-Serving Institution offers certificates and associate degrees in a wide array of academic areas.

El Centro College
801 Main Street
Dallas, TX 75202-3604
214-860-2037
http://www.elcentrocollege.edu
This two-year Hispanic-Serving Institution offers certificates and associate degrees in more than 25 fields, including biotechnology, diagnostic medical sonography, fashion design, interior design, Internet development technologies, invasive cardiovascular technology, medical transcription, and respiratory care.

Elizabeth City State University
1704 Weeksville Road
Elizabeth City, NC 27909
800-347-3278
admissions@mail.ecsu.edu
http://www.ecsu.edu
Elizabeth City State University is a public baccalaureate university offering more than 20 majors in the arts and sciences and in some professional and preprofessional areas; it also offers a master's degree in elementary education. It is one of 105 Historically Black Colleges and Universities in the United States.

El Paso Community College
PO Box 20500
El Paso, TX 79998
915-831-2000
http://www.epcc.edu
This Hispanic-Serving Institution offers associate degrees, certificates, and transfer courses. It also offers programs for career guidance and job placement.

According to its Web site, it is the nation's fastest growing community college.

Estrella Mountain Community College

3000 North Dysart Road
Avondale, AZ 85323
623-935-8000
http://www.emc.maricopa.edu
The college offers numerous associate degrees, university transfer partnerships, and 17 specialized certificate programs. Minority students make up more than 42 percent of the 11,000 students enrolled at the school.

Faulkner University

5345 Atlanta Highway
Montgomery, AL 36109
800-879-9816
http://www.faulkner.edu
Faulkner University is a Christian College that has African-American enrollment of about 25 percent.

Fayetteville State University

1200 Murchison Road
Fayetteville, NC 28301
910-672-1111
http://www.uncfsu.edu
Fayetteville State University is one of 105 Historically Black Colleges and Universities in the United States. Its offers a variety of undergraduate and graduate degrees through its College of Humanities and Social Sciences, College of Basic and Applied Sciences, School of Business and Economics, School of Education, and Extended Learning Center.

Fisk University

1000 17th Avenue, North
Nashville, TN 37208-3051
615-329-8500
http://www.fisk.edu
Fisk offers 20 undergraduate degrees and four graduate degrees. Black Enterprise recently ranked the university as one of the top 50 colleges and universities for African-American students in the United States.

Florida Agricultural and Mechanical University

Tallahassee, FL 32307
850-599-3560
http://www.famu.edu
Florida A&M University is a coeducational, residential, multilevel land-grant university offering a broad range of instruction, research, and service programs at the undergraduate, professional, and graduate levels. It is one of 105 Historically Black Colleges and Universities in the United States.

Florida International University (University Park)

11200 Southwest Eighth Street
Miami, FL 33199
305-348-2000
http://www.fiu.edu
A member of the State University System of Florida, this Hispanic-Serving Institution is a research university offering a diverse selection of undergraduate, graduate, and professional programs. It offers more than 190 baccalaureate, master's, and doctoral degree programs in 19 colleges and schools.

Florida Memorial University

15800 Northwest 42nd Avenue
Miami Gardens, FL 33054
305-626-3600
http://www.fmuniv.edu
Florida Memorial University is a private, four-year, coeducational liberal arts college. FMC offers 38 degree programs through its seven academic divisions, including programs in aviation, business, computer science, education, engineering, liberal arts, and sciences. It is one of 105 Historically Black Colleges and Universities in the United States.

Fond du Lac Tribal and Community College

2101 14th Street
Cloquet, MN 55720
800-657-3712
http://www.fdl.cc.mn.us
Fond du Lac Tribal and Community College is unique in the United States because it is jointly a tribal college and a member of the Arrowhead Community College Region in Minnesota. It offers liberal arts and sciences transfer programs, career and technical education programs, and certificate programs.

Fort Belknap College

PO Box 159
Harlem, MT 59526
406-353-2607
http://www.fbcc.edu
Fort Belknap College provides postsecondary educational opportunities for Native American residents of the Fort Belknap communities. Fort Belknap College offers

one degree, an associate of arts in general studies with an emphasis in business, human services, data processing, liberal arts, Native American studies, preprofessional, or natural resources. Certificates of completion in early childhood education and computer applications are also available.

Fort Berthold Community College (FBCC)
220 8th Avenue, PO Box 490
New Town, ND 58763
701-627-4738
http://www.fbcc.bia.edu
One of 34 tribal colleges in the United States, FBCC offers a variety of associate degree programs, including accounting/business administration, addiction studies, agriculture transfer, agriculture division-management option, agriculture division-agribusiness sales and service option, computer information systems, computer science, early childhood development, environmental science, human services, information management specialist, liberal arts, liberal arts-emphasis elementary education, mathematics, medical secretarial services, public/tribal administration, science, and water treatment technology. It also offers vocational certificates in administrative assisting, child development, construction technology, emergency medical services, farm/ranch management, graphic arts technology, home health care technology, horticulture science, and marketing/entrepreneurship.

Fort Peck Community College
PO Box 398, 605 Indian
Poplar, MT 59255
406-768-6300
http://www.fpcc.edu
Fort Peck, one of 34 tribal colleges in the United States, offers a variety of associate degrees and certificates.

Fort Valley State University
1005 State College Drive
Fort Valley, GA 31030-4313
478-825-6211
http://www.fvsu.edu
This Historically Black College and University is accredited by the Commission on Colleges of the Southern Association of Colleges and Schools to award associate, baccalaureate, master's, and specialist's degrees. The university has three academic colleges: The College of Agriculture, Home Economics and Allied Programs; The College of Arts, Sciences and

Education; and The College of Graduate Studies and Extended Education.

Fresno City College
1101 East University Avenue
Fresno, CA 93741
866-245-3276
http://www.fresnocitycollege.com
This two-year Hispanic-Serving Institution offers more than 100 areas of study.

Fullerton College
321 East Chapman Avenue
Fullerton, CA 92832-2095
714-992-7568
admissions@fullcoll.edu
http://www.fullcoll.edu
This community college offers 90 associate degree programs and 111 vocational certificate programs. Its student body is approximately 31 percent Hispanic and 15 percent Asian.

Gadsden State Community College
PO Box 227
Gadsden, AL 35902-0227
256-549-8200
http://www.gadsdenstate.edu
The institution offers a variety of academic programs, including applied technology, engineering technology, business, health sciences, information technology, science and aquatic science, and social science. It is one of 105 Historically Black Colleges and Universities in the United States.

Gavilan College
5055 Santa Teresa Boulevard
Gilroy, CA 95020
408-848-4801
http://www.gavilan.cc.ca.us
This public, two-year Hispanic-Serving Institution offers associate degrees and certificates in a variety of subject areas, including administration of justice, allied health, business, computer graphics and design, computer science and information systems, digital media, media arts, and Spanish.

Glendale Community College
1500 North Verdugo Road
Glendale, CA 91208
818-240-1000

info@glendale.edu
http://www.glendale.edu
This two-year Hispanic-Serving Institution offers a
variety of majors, including animation, aviation,
computer science/information systems, culinary arts,
ethnic studies, fashion design merchandising, mass
communications, nursing, and sign language.

Grambling State University
100 Main Street
Grambling, LA 71245
800-569-4714
http://www.gram.edu
Grambling State University was founded in 1901 as a
private industrial school to educate African Americans.
It offers undergraduate, graduate, professional, and
continuing education programs.

Hampton University
Hampton, VA 23668
757-727-5000
admissions@hamptonu.edu
http://www.hamptonu.edu
This Historically Black College and University provides
a liberal arts foundation for its professional and
scientific disciplines. Some of the major areas of
study are aviation science, architecture, business,
computer sciences, education, emergency medical
systems management, English, entrepreneurship,
environmental and marine science, chemistry,
electrical and chemical engineering, mass media,
music engineering technology, nursing, and systems
management. Students may earn the bachelor's
and/or master's degree in many areas. Hampton offers
38 undergraduate programs, 14 master's degree
programs, and four doctoral degree programs.

Hampton University School of Nursing
Hampton, VA 23668
757-727-5251
http://www.hamptonu.edu/nursing
The Hampton University School of Nursing is the oldest
baccalaureate nursing program in Virginia as well as
the oldest graduate nursing program in a Historically
Black College or University. The school offers
traditional LPN-to-BS and RN-to-BS programs.

Harris-Stowe State College
3026 Laclede Avenue
St. Louis, MO 63103

314-340-3366
http://www.hssc.edu
This Historically Black College and University's degree
programs cover five main areas: arts and sciences,
business administration, continuing education,
teacher education, and urban education.

Hartnell College
156 Homestead Avenue
Salinas, CA 93901
831-755-6700
http://www.hartnell.cc.ca.us
Hartnell College awards associate degrees and
certificates. Hispanics make up approximately 52
percent of its student body.

Haskell Indian Nations University
155 Indian Avenue
Lawrence, KS 66046
785-749-8404
http://www.haskell.edu/haskell
Students at this four-year tribal university can pursue
an academic program that prepares them to enter
baccalaureate programs in elementary teacher
education, American Indian studies, business
administration, and environmental science; to transfer
to another baccalaureate degree-granting institution;
or to directly enter the workforce.

H. Councill Trenholm State Technical College
1225 Air Base Boulevard
Montgomery, AL 36108
334-420-4200
http://www.trenholmtech.cc.al.us
This Historically Black two-year technical college offers
technical certificate and degree programs.

Heald College
670 Howard Street
San Francisco, CA 94105
415-808-1400
http://www.heald.edu
This Hispanic-Serving Institution with 11 campuses
offers associate degrees, short-term diplomas,
and certification training programs in business,
technology, and health care.

Heritage College
3240 Fort Road
Toppenish, WA 98948

888-272-6190
http://www.heritage.edu
Heritage College is a nonprofit, independent, nondenominational accredited institution of higher education
offering undergraduate and graduate education. Its
most popular programs include business, computer
science, environmental science, natural resources
science, psychology, social work, teacher education,
and school counseling. Approximately 37 percent of
the students attending Heritage are Hispanic and 10
percent are Native American.

Hostos Community College
City University of New York
500 Grand Concourse
Bronx, NY 10451
718-518-4444
http://www.hostos.cuny.edu
The college offers bilingual degree and certificate
programs for Spanish-speaking students.

Houston Community College System
3100 Main Street
Houston, TX 77266-7517
713-718-2000
http://www.hccs.edu
The Houston Community College System confers more
than 30 certificates and associate degrees to students
at five campuses in the Houston metropolitan area.
Approximately 39 percent of its students are Hispanic.

Howard University
2400 Sixth Street, NW
Washington, DC 20059-0001
202-806-6100
http://www.howard.edu
This private Historically Black College and University
offers academic programs encompassing some 180
areas of study leading to undergraduate, graduate,
and professional degrees.

Hudson County Community College
70 Sip Avenue
Jersey City, NJ 07306
201-714-7100
http://www.hccc.edu
This Hispanic-Serving Institution offers associate-degree
and certificate programs in allied health, business,
computer science, culinary arts, education, engineer-
ing/technology, liberal arts, and the social sciences.

Huston-Tillotson University
900 Chicon Street
Austin, TX 78702
512-505-3000
http://www.htc.edu
Huston-Tillotson University is an independent Historically
Black Institution. It is affiliated with the United
Methodist Church, the United Church of Christ,
and the United Negro College Fund. It awards
undergraduate degrees in business, education, the
humanities, natural sciences, and social sciences.

Imperial Valley College
380 East Aten Road, PO Box 158
Imperial, CA 92251
760-352-8320
http://www.imperial.cc.ca.us
This two-year Hispanic-Serving Institution provides
vocational training and transfer preparation for
four-year-college and university-bound students.

Institute of American Indian Arts
83 Avan Nu Po Road
Santa Fe, NM 87508
505-424-2300
http://www.iaiancad.org
The Institute of American Indian Arts is a four-year
academic institution that offers degrees in creative
writing, media studies, studio arts, and visual
communications.

Interdenominational Theological Center
700 Martin Luther King Jr. Drive
Atlanta, GA 30314-4143
404-527-7700
info@itc.edu
http://www.itc.edu
The center supports research into the integration of
African-American perspectives on the ministry. With
its resources and facilities, the center supports study
into theological curriculum and religion.

International Institute of the Americas
6049 North 43rd Avenue
Phoenix, AZ 85019-1600
877-702-7900
http://iia-online.com
This Hispanic-Serving Institution offers diploma programs
in automated accounting, business technology,
clinical technology, computer technology, detention

and security, medical assisting, and patient care. It offers associate programs in accounting, business technology, clinical technology, justice administration, legal assisting, medical transcription, medical assisting, microcomputer networking, nursing, and patient care. It also offers a bachelor degree program in management. The institute has five campuses.

Iowa Central Community College
330 Avenue M
Fort Dodge, IA 50501
800-362-2793
http://www.iccc.cc.ia.us
The College offers certificates and associate degrees in more than 30 academic areas, including automotive technology, aviation science/professional pilot, broadcasting, commercial construction, computer networking technology, fire service administration, nursing, and radiologic technology. At least 25 percent of the students attending its Storm Lake campus are Hispanic.

Jackson State University
1400 Lynch Street
Jackson, MS 39217
800-848-6817
http://www.jsums.edu
Jackson State is one of America's leading Historically Black Colleges and Universities. The university is organized into the following academic units: College of Business; College of Education and Human Development; College of Liberal Arts; Division of Graduate Studies; College of Science, Engineering and Technology; College of Public Service; and College of Lifelong Learning.

Jarvis Christian College
PO Box 1470
Hawkins, TX 75765
903-769-5700
http://www.jarvis.edu
This is a private, four-year, accredited, coeducational liberal arts college that is affiliated with the Christian Church (Disciples of Christ). It is one of 105 Historically Black Colleges and Universities in the United States.

J. F. Drake State Technical College
3421 Meridian Street North, PO Box 17439
Huntsville, AL 35810-7439
888-413-7253
http://dstc.cc.al.us
Students at J.F. Drake, one of 105 Historically Black Colleges and Universities in the United States, receive training in specialized areas of specific job placement/advancement. The college offers associate's degrees in applied technology in such areas as accounting, computer information, and drafting and design.

John Jay College of Criminal Justice
899 Tenth Avenue
New York, NY 10019
212-237-8000
http://www.jjay.cuny.edu
The John Jay College of Criminal Justice, which is affiliated with City University of New York, is not only a college of criminal justice but also a liberal arts college. It offers associate, bachelor's, and master's degrees. At least 25 percent of its students are Hispanic.

Johnson C. Smith University
100 Beatties Ford Road
Charlotte, NC 28216
800-782-7303
admissions@jcsu.edu
http://www.jcsu.edu
This Historically Black College and University offers a wide variety of majors through the following departments: Business Administration and Economics; Communication Arts, Music and Fine Arts; Computer Science and Engineering, Education; English and Foreign Languages-Liberal Arts Program; Health and Human Performance; Natural Sciences and Mathematics; Psychology; Social Sciences; and Social Work.

Kentucky State University
400 East Main Street
Frankfort, KY 40601
502-597-6000
http://www.kysu.edu
This Historically Black College and University offers a comprehensive, liberal studies curriculum.

Knoxville College
901 Knoxville College Drive
Knoxville, TN 37921
800-743-5669
http://www.knoxvillecollege.edu
Knoxville College, one of 105 Historically Black Colleges

and Universities in the United States, offers a variety of associate and bachelor's degrees. It also offers preprofessional programs in dentistry, law, medicine, nursing, and theology.

Lac Courte Oreilles Ojibwa Community College

13466 West Trepania Road
Hayward, WI 54843-2181
888-526-6221
http://www.lco-college.edu
The Lac Courte Oreilles Ojibwa Community College provides, within the Indian community, a system of postsecondary and continuing education with an associate degree and certificate granting capabilities.

La Guardia Community College

City University of New York
31-10 Thomson Avenue
Long Island City, NY 11101
718-482-5000
http://www.lagcc.cuny.edu
This branch of the City University of New York serves western Queens and the larger New York metro area. The Hispanic-Serving Institution offers more than 35 academic majors.

Lane College

545 Lane Avenue
Jackson, TN 38301
731-426-7500
http://www.lanecollege.edu
Founded in 1882 by a former slave, Lane College is one of the nation's oldest Historically Black Colleges. It offers 17 majors and 18 minors.

Langston University

PO Box 728
Langston, OK 73050
405-466-3428
admissions@lunet.edu
http://www.lunet.edu
This Historically Black College and University offers a variety of undergraduate programs through its School of Agriculture and Applied Sciences, School of Arts and Sciences, School of Business, School of Education and Behavioral Science, School of Nursing and Health Professions, and School of Physical Therapy. It also offers graduate degrees in education, rehabilitation counseling, and physical therapy.

Laredo Community College

Memorial Hall, Room 125
West End Washington Street
Laredo, TX 78040-4395
956-721-5117
admissions@laredo.edu
http://www.laredo.cc.tx.us
This community college offers 24 one-year certificates, 28 associate degrees, and two two-year certificates. Hispanics make up a significant percentage of students at the college.

Lawson State Community College

3060 Wilson Road
Birmingham, AL 35221
205-925-2515
http://www.ls.cc.al.us
One of 105 Historically Black Colleges and Universities in the United States, Lawson State offers educational programs in business and information technologies; career, technical, and occupational programs; general education; health and physical education; health professions; humanities; math and science; and social science.

Leech Lake Tribal College

PO Box 180, 113 Balsam Avenue
Cass Lake, MN 56633
888-829-4240
http://www.lltc.org
This tribal college offers a wide variety of study areas, including art, business management, carpentry, child development, education, electrical, English, information technology, law enforcement, math, music, nutrition, and science.

Lehman College

250 Bedford Park Boulevard West
Bronx, NY 10468-1589
877-534-6261
http://www.lehman.cuny.edu
This branch of the City University of New York offers more than 20 undergraduate and graduate degrees in a wide variety of disciplines, including anthropology; art; biological sciences; Black studies; chemistry; early childhood and childhood education; economics, accounting, and business administration; English; environmental, geographic, and geological sciences; health sciences; history;

languages and literature; Latin American and Puerto Rican studies; mathematics and computer science; middle and high school education; music; nursing; philosophy; physics and astronomy; political science; psychology; sociology and social work; and speech-language-hearing sciences. It is a Hispanic-Serving Institution.

LeMoyne-Owen College

807 Walker Avenue
Memphis, TN 38126
901-942-7302
http://www.loc.edu
One of 105 Historically Black Colleges and Universities in the United States, LeMoyne-Owen College offers the Bachelor's of Arts, Bachelor's of Science, and Bachelor's of Business Administration degrees. It also offers the Master's of Science in Education through its Division of Graduate Studies.

Lewis College of Business

17370 Meyers Road
Detroit, MI 48235
313-862-6300
http://www.lewiscollege.edu
This Historically Black College and University offers degree programs in business administration, computer information systems, and office information systems.

Lexington College

310 South Peoria Street
Chicago, IL 60607
312-226-6294
adm@lexingtoncollege.edu
http://www.lexingtoncollege.edu
This "Roman Catholic-inspired" college touts itself as "*the* women's hospitality management college in the United States." It offers associate and bachelor's degrees in hospitality management, and has a diverse student body.

Lincoln University of Missouri

820 Chestnut Street
Jefferson City, MO 65102
800-521-5052
http://www.lincolnu.edu
This Historically Black College and University offers a wide variety of undergraduate and graduate degrees.

Lincoln University of the Commonwealth of Pennsylvania

PO Box 179
Lincoln University, PA 19352
610-932-8300
admiss@lu.lincoln.edu
http://www.lincoln.edu
Lincoln University is a four-year liberal arts institution located in southern Chester County, Pennsylvania. Chartered in 1854, Lincoln is the oldest Historically Black College and University in the United States.

Little Big Horn College

1 Forest Lane
Crow Agency, MT 59022
406-638-3104
http://main.lbhc.cc.mt.us
Little Big Horn College is a public two-year community college chartered by the Crow Tribe of Indians.

Little Priest Tribal College

601 East College Drive
Winnebago, NE 68071
402-878-2380
dbales@lptc.bia.edu
http://www.lptc.bia.edu
Little Priest Tribal College offers two-year associate degree programs, certificate programs, and community education programs.

Livingstone College

701 West Monroe Street
Salisbury, NC 28144
800-835-3435
http://www.livingstone.edu
Livingstone College is a Historically Black Institution. This private, church-supported, liberal arts college was founded in 1879 by ministers of the African Methodist Episcopal Zion Church. It consists of two schools: an undergraduate college of arts and sciences, and a graduate school of theology.

Long Beach City College

4901 East Carson Street
Long Beach, CA 90808
562-938-4353
http://www.lbcc.cc.ca.us
This community college offers a variety of academic and vocational programs through the following

schools: Business and Social Science, Creative Arts and Applied Science, Health and Science, Language Arts and Physical Education, and Trade and Industrial Technologies. Minorities make up approximately 46 percent of Long Beach's student body.

Los Angeles City College
855 North Vermont Avenue
Los Angeles, CA 90029
323-953-4000
http://www.lacitycollege.edu
More than 25 academic programs are available at this community college. Approximately 41 percent of its students are Hispanic.

Los Angeles County College of Nursing and Allied Health
1237 North Mission Road
Los Angeles, CA 90033
323-226-4911
http://www.ladhs.org/lacusc/lacnah
Hispanic students make up more than 25 percent of the student body at this institution.

Los Angeles Harbor College
1111 Figueroa Place
Wilmington, CA 90744
310-233-4000
http://www.lahc.cc.ca.us
This two-year institution offers more than 25 areas of study. Approximately 42 percent of the students at this community college are Hispanic.

Los Angeles Mission College
13356 Eldridge Avenue
Sylmar, CA 91342
818-364-7600
http://www.lamission.cc.ca.us
This two-year Hispanic-Serving Institution offers more than 60 academic programs, including accounting, engineering, food service management, microbiology, and photography.

Los Angeles Trade Technical College
400 West Washington Boulevard
Los Angeles, CA 90015
213-763-7000
http://www.lattc.cc.ca.us
More than 52 percent of students at this two-year institution are Hispanic. The areas of study most in demand (in descending order) at the college are electrical construction and maintenance, nursing-RN, liberal arts and science, child development, and fashion design.

Los Angeles Valley College
5800 Fulton Avenue
Valley Glen, CA 91401-4096
818 947-2600
http://www.lavc.edu
The college offers a variety of associate degrees and certificates. Approximately 37 percent of its students are Hispanic.

Luna Community College
366 Luna Drive
Las Vegas, NM 87701 800-588-7232
http://www.lvti.cc.nm.us
This Hispanic-Serving Institution is the only vocational technical community college in northeastern New Mexico. It offers more than 30 areas of study.

MacCormac College
29 East Madison Street
Chicago, IL 60602
312-922-1884
http://www.maccormac.edu
This Hispanic-Serving Institution offers the following associate degree and certificate programs: accounting, business administration, business office technology, computer information systems, court reporting, international business, legal office technology, medical office technology, paralegal studies, and travel and hospitality.

Martin University
2171 Avondale Place
Indianapolis, IN 46218-0567
317-543-3235
admissions@martin.edu
http://www.martin.edu
Martin University is a private, not-for-profit, nondenominational institution dedicated to the higher education of adult learners, low-income persons, minorities, the elderly, and prison inmates.

Marygrove College
8425 West McNichols Road
Detroit, MI 48221
313-927-1200

info@marygrove.edu
http://www.marygrove.edu
This is a four-year and master's degree college with
a predominantly Black enrollment.

Mary Holmes College
PO Drawer 1257
West Point, MS 39773-1257
662-494-6625
mhcinfo@maryholmes.edu
http://www.maryholmes.edu
Mary Holmes College is an open admission, two-year,
Historically Black, coeducational, primarily residential
institution related to the Presbyterian Church
(USA). Majors at the college include education, law,
medicine, and religion.

Medgar Evers College
City University of New York
1665 Bedford Avenue
Brooklyn, NY 11225
718-270-6024
http://www.mec.cuny.edu
This branch of the City University of New York offers certificate, associate, and baccalaureate degrees in business,
computer applications, elementary education, liberal
arts, marketing, nursing, public administration, science,
and other areas. Medgar Evers College's students are
predominantly African American.

Meharry Medical College
1005 Dr. D.B. Todd Jr. Boulevard
Nashville, TN 37208
615-327-6000
http://www.mmc.edu
Meharry Medical College is the largest private Historically
Black Institution exclusively dedicated to educating
health care professionals and biomedical scientists in
the United States.

Merced College
3600 M Street
Merced, CA 95348-2898
209-384-6000
http://www.merced.cc.ca.us
This diverse institution awards associate degrees in more
than 70 areas of study, including environmental
technologies, horse management, HVAC technology,
lab technology, nursing-RN, nursing-vocational,
and radiologic technology. It offers certificates in

more than 50 areas, including agriculture business,
automotives, biotechnology, commercial art,
corrections, diagnostic medical sonography, electrical
technology, and paralegal studies.

Metropolitan College of New York
75 Varick Street
New York, NY 10013
800-338-4465
http://www.metropolitan.edu
This Hispanic-Serving Institution offers certificates, and
associate, bachelor's, and master's degrees in a variety
of academic disciplines, including arts, business,
business administration, childhood education,
emergency and disaster management, and media
management.

Midland College
3600 North Garfield
Midland, TX 79705-6399
432-685-4500
http://www.midland.edu
This two-year Hispanic-Serving Institution offers associate
degrees and certificates in more than 50 fields.

Miami-Dade Community College
300 NE Second Street
Miami, FL 33132
305-237-3000
http://www.mdc.edu/college_wideMiami-Dade
Community College offers more than 150 associate's
degrees. Approximately 160,000 students attend its
six campuses, five of which (listed below) are classified
as Hispanic-Serving Institutions.

Miami-Dade Community College (Homestead)
500 College Terrace
Homestead, FL 33030-6009
305-237-5555
http://www.mdc.edu/homestead

Miami-Dade Community College (Kendall)
11011 Southwest 104th Street
Miami, FL 33176-3393
305-237-2222
http://www.mdc.edu/kendall

Miami-Dade Community College (Medical Center)
950 Northwest 20th Street
Miami, FL 33127-4622

305-237-4160
http://www.mdc.edu/medical

Miami-Dade Community College (North Campus)
11380 Northwest 27th Avenue
Miami, FL 33167-3418
305-237-1111
http://www.mdc.edu/north

Miami-Dade Community College (Wolfson)
300 Northeast Second Street
Miami, FL 33132-2204
305-237-3000
contact@mdc.edu
http://www.mdc.edu/wolfson

Miles College
PO Box 3800
Birmingham, AL 35208
205-929-1000
info@mail.miles.edu
http://www.miles.edu
This Historically Black College is a four-year liberal arts
    institution for African-American students and other
    ethnic groups. It offers bachelor degree programs
    with majors in accounting, biology, biology education,
    business administration, chemistry, chemistry
    education, communications, elementary education,
    English, environmental science, language arts
    education, mathematics, mathematics education,
    political science, social science education, and social
    work.

Mississippi Valley State University
14000 Highway 82 West
Itta Bena, MS 38941
800-844-6885
http://www.mvsu.edu
This Historically Black College and University offer
    opportunities for concentrated study in the arts,
    humanities, sciences, technology, and professional
    fields of business, education, special services, and
    preprofessional health services.

Modesto Junior College
435 College Avenue
Modesto, CA 95354
209-575-6498
mjcadmissions@mail.yosemite.cc.ca.us
http://www.mjc.yosemite.cc.ca.us
This Hispanic-Serving Institution offers associate

degrees and certificates through the following
academic divisions: Agriculture and Environmental
Sciences; Allied Health, Family and Consumer
Sciences; Arts, Humanities, and Communications;
Business; Behavioral and Social Sciences; Literature
and Language Arts; Physical, Recreation, and
Health Education; Public Safety; Science, Math and
Engineering; and Technical Education.

Morehouse College
830 Westview Drive, SW
Atlanta, GA 30314
404-681-2800
http://www.morehouse.edu
Morehouse College was founded in 1867 and is the
    nation's only private, four-year liberal arts institution
    for African-American men. Degrees can be obtained
    through the bachelor's level.

Morehouse School of Medicine
720 Westview Drive, SW
Atlanta, GA 30310-1495
404-752-1500
http://www.msm.edu
The Morehouse School of Medicine is a Historically Black
    Institution established to recruit and train minority
    and other students as physicians and biomedical
    scientists committed to the primary health care needs
    of the underserved.

Morgan State University
1700 East Cold Spring Lane
Baltimore, MD 21251
443-885-3333
info@morgan.edu
http://www.morgan.edu
This Historically Black College and University awards
    more bachelor's degrees to African-American
    students than any other school in Maryland.
    Historically, the university has ranked among the top
    public campuses nationally in the number of Black
    graduates subsequently receiving doctorates from
    U.S. universities.

Morris Brown College
643 Martin Luther King Jr. Boulevard
Atlanta, GA 30314
404-739-1000
http://www.morrisbrown.edu
Morris Brown College is fully accredited by the Southern
    Association of Colleges and Schools with majors

offered in more than 40 areas of study, including business sciences, computer science, chemistry, biology, and hospitality administration. It is one of 105 Historically Black Colleges and Universities in the United States.

Morris College
100 West College Street
Sumter, SC 29150-3599
803-934-3200
http://www2.morris.edu
Morris College is a Historically Black, coeducational, liberal arts college, operated by the Baptist Educational and Missionary Convention of South Carolina. It offers degrees in biology, business administration, broadcast media, Christian education, criminal justice, early childhood education, elementary education, English, health science, history, journalism, liberal studies, mathematics, organizational management, pastoral ministry, political science, recreation administration, and sociology. It also offers teacher preparatory certification in biology, English, history, mathematics, and social studies.

Morton College
3801 South Central Avenue
Cicero, IL 60804
708-656-8000
http://www.morton.edu
Besides its highly rated university transfer program, this two year Hispanic-Serving Institution provides programs in vo-tech education, liberal studies, continuing education, and community service.

Mountain View College
4849 West Illinois Avenue
Dallas, TX 75211
214-860-8600
http://www.mountainviewcollege.edu
This community college offers a wide range of associate degree and certificate programs, including computer information technology, criminal justice, electronics technology, geographic information systems, teacher education, and welding technology. Hispanics make up a significant percentage of its student body.

Mount Saint Mary's College
12001 Chalon Road
Los Angeles, CA 90049
310-954-4000

http://www.msmc.la.edu
Mount St. Mary's College is an independent, Catholic, liberal arts college. Hispanic students earn 74 percent of associate degrees and 44 percent of bachelor's degrees at the college.

Mt. San Antonio College
1100 North Grand
Walnut, CA 91789
909-594-5611
info@mtsac.edu
http://www.mtsac.edu
This community college offers more than 200 associate degree and certificate programs. Hispanics make up nearly 42 percent of its student population.

Mt. San Jacinto College
1499 North State Street
San Jacinto, CA 92583
951-487-6752
http://www.msjc.edu
This Hispanic-Serving Institution offers certificate and associate degree programs in more than 50 areas. In addition to San Jacinto, the college has campuses in Menifee and Temecula.

Myers University
112 Prospect Avenue East
Cleveland, OH 44115
877-366-9377
http://www.dnmyers.edu
This is a four-year university with a predominantly Black enrollment. Myers University offers master's degrees in business administration, bachelor's of science degrees, associate's in science degrees, and associate's in arts degrees, in addition to a number of certificate programs.

National Hispanic University
14271 Story Road
San Jose, CA 95127
408-254-6900
http://www.nhu.edu
The university offers degree, credential, and certificate programs in business administration, computer information systems, liberal studies, mathematics and science, and teacher education.

Native American Educational Services College
2838 West Peterson
Chicago, IL 60659

773-761-5000

http://www.naes.edu

This college is the only independent, Native American-owned and -controlled college in the United States. It offers a single degree, a bachelor of arts degree in public policy. In addition to its Chicago campus, NAES has campuses in Minneapolis, Minnesota, and on the Menominee Reservation in Keshena, Wisconsin.

Nebraska Indian Community College

PO Box 428

Macy, NE 68039

888-843-6422

admissions@thenicc.edu

http://www.thenicc.edu

This is a two-year college established to meet the unique education needs of the state's Native American community. The college is located on the Omaha and Santee Sioux reservations and also includes the Yankton Sioux Tribe of Marty.

New Jersey City University

2039 Kennedy Boulevard

Jersey City, NJ 07305-1597

888-441-6528

http://www.njcu.edu

This public Hispanic-Serving Institution offers more than 25 undergraduate degree programs, as well as graduate programs and teacher certification programs.

New Mexico Highlands University

PO Box 9000

Las Vegas, NM 87701

877-850-9064

http://www.nmhu.edu

This Hispanic-Serving Institution offers graduate and undergraduate programs in arts and sciences, business, education, and social work.

New Mexico Junior College

5317 Lovington Highway

Hobbs, NM 88240

800-657-6260

http://www.nmjc.cc.nm.us

This Hispanic-Serving Institution offers certificates and associate degrees in many academic areas, including accounting, athletic training, business information systems, chemistry, computer animation, computer assisted drafting, computer Web page design, early childhood education, elementary education, law enforcement, mathematics, nursing, paralegal, physics, radiological control and waste handling, secondary education, sociology, and theatre.

New Mexico State University

PO Box 30001

Las Cruces, NM 88003-8001

505-646-0111

http://www.nmsu.edu

New Mexico State University offers 76 baccalaureate degree programs, 51 master's degree programs, and 22 doctoral programs. In addition, it has four branch campuses, three of which (listed below) are classified as Hispanic-Serving Institutions.

New Mexico State University (Alamogordo)

2400 North Scenic Drive

Alamogordo, NM 88310

505-439-3600

http://alamo.nmsu.edu

New Mexico State University (Carlsbad)

1500 University Drive

Carlsbad, NM 88220

505-234-9200

http://www.cavern.nmsu.edu

New Mexico State University (Dona Ana)

MSC 3DA, PO Box 30001

Las Cruces, NM 88003-8001

505-527-7500

http://dabcc-www.nmsu.edu

New York City Technical College

City University of New York

300 Jay Street

Brooklyn, NY 11201

718-260-5500

http://www.citytech.cuny.edu

This Hispanic-Serving Institution offers more than 30 career-specific baccalaureate, associate, and specialized certificate programs. Interesting baccalaureate degree programs include electromechanical engineering technology, graphic arts and advertising production management, hospitality management, human services, legal assistant studies, occupational/technology teacher education, stage technology, and telecommunications technology.

Norfolk State University

700 Park Avenue
Norfolk, VA 23504
757-823-8600
http://www.nsu.edu

NSU is a four-year, coeducational, state-assisted public institution. It is one of 105 Historically Black Colleges and Universities in the United States.

North Carolina Agricultural and Technical State University

1601 East Market Street
Greensboro, NC 27411
336-334-7500
http://www.ncat.edu

North Carolina A&T State University is comprised of six schools and two colleges. Among them: the School of Agriculture and Environmental Science, the School of Business and Economics, the College of Engineering, and the School of Technology.

North Carolina Central University

1801 Fayetteville Street
Durham, NC 27707
919-530-6100
http://www.nccu.edu

North Carolina Central University is a comprehensive university offering programs at the undergraduate and graduate levels. It is the nation's first public liberal arts institution founded for African Americans.

Northeastern Illinois University

5500 North Saint Louis Avenue
Chicago, IL 60625-4699
773-442-4050
http://www.neiu.edu

The university offers more than 80 undergraduate and graduate majors. Approximately 45 percent of its students are minorities.

Northern New Mexico Community College

921 Paseo de Onate
Española, NM 87532
505-747-2100
http://www.nnmcc.edu

More than 50 certificate and degree programs are offered by this Hispanic-Serving Institution, including accounting, business administration, computer science, design foundation, computer-aided drafting, early childhood education, fine arts, human services, library technology, micro electronics, management information systems, nursing, radiography, science, substance abuse counselor, and welding technology.

Northwest Indian College

2522 Kwina Road
Bellingham, WA 98226
360-676-2772
http://www.nwic.edu

Northwest Indian College provides postsecondary educational opportunities for Native Americans. The curriculum includes academic, vocational, continuing, cultural, community service, and adult basic education.

Nova Southeastern University

3301 College Avenue
Fort Lauderdale-Davie, FL 33314-7796
800-541-6682
http://www.nova.edu

This Hispanic-Serving Institution offers more than 100 undergraduate and graduate degrees in areas such as athletic training, information security, marine biology, pharmacy, and sport and wellness studies.

Oakwood College

7000 Adventist Boulevard
Huntsville, AL 35896
256-726-7000
http://www.oakwood.edu

Founded in 1896, this Historically Black four-year college focuses primarily on liberal arts and is a Seventh-Day Adventist institution. It is one of America's premier colleges in the preparation of African Americans for medical school and health science careers.

Oglala Lakota College

PO Box 490
Kyle, SD 57752
605-455-6000
http://www.olc.edu

Oglala Lakota College was one of the first tribally-controlled colleges in the United States. From its initial status as a community college, Oglala Lakota has grown to offer baccalaureate degrees and a master's degree in Lakota leadership. Besides its Kyle campus, the college has 11 other campuses in various locations across South Dakota, including a nursing program in Pine Ridge.

Otero Junior College

1802 Colorado Avenue
La Junta, CO 81050
719-384-6831
http://www.ojc.cccoes.edu
This Hispanic-Serving Institution offers associate degree programs in administrative assisting, behavioral science, business, business administration, business management, early childhood, elementary education, nursing, premedicine, psychology, secondary education, sports medicine, and other areas. Certificate programs include accounting clerk, administrative assistant, auto CAD, automotive technology, children's group leader, Cisco CCNA and CCNP, drafting, farm/ranch business management, law enforcement training, and microcomputer operations.

Our Lady of the Lake University

411 Southwest 24th Street
San Antonio, TX 78207
210-434-6711
http://www.ollusa.edu
This Hispanic-Serving Institution offers 58 undergraduate degree programs, 48 graduate degree programs and two doctoral degree programs in the arts and sciences, business, education, clinical studies, and social work.

Oxnard College

4000 South Rose Avenue
Oxnard, CA 93033
805-986-5800
http://www.oxnard.cc.ca.us
This Hispanic-Serving Institution provides studies leading to associate degrees and certificates of achievement in transfer programs and occupational/professional fields.

Paine College

1235 15th Street
Augusta, GA 30901
706-821-8200
http://www.paine.edu
One of 105 Historically Black Colleges and Universities in the United States, Paine College offers bachelor of arts and bachelor of science degrees in a variety of subjects. Minors and concentrations are also available.

Palomar College

1140 West Mission Road
San Marcos, CA 92069-1487
760-744-1150
http://www.palomar.edu
This Hispanic-Serving Institution offers more than 250 associate degree and certificate programs.

Palo Verde College

One College Drive
Blythe, CA 92225
760-921-6168
http://www.paloverde.cc.ca.us
This Hispanic-Serving Institution offers a variety of associate degrees and certificate through the following academic divisions: Allied Health; History, Social and Behavior Sciences; Language Arts and Communication Studies; Mathematics and Sciences; and Professional Technologies.

Pasadena City College

1570 East Colorado Boulevard
Pasadena, CA 91106
626-585-7123
http://www.pasadena.edu
This community college offers more than 100 academic and vocational programs. Approximately 36 percent of its students are Hispanic, and more than 27 percent are Asian or Pacific Islander.

Passaic County Community College

One College Boulevard
Paterson, NJ 07505
973-684-6868
http://www.pccc.cc.nj.us
This two-year Hispanic-Serving Institution offers associate degrees and certificate in many areas, including applied computer science, business administration, computer and information sciences, criminal justice, health science, liberal arts, medical transcription, and nursing.

Paul Quinn College

3837 Simpson Stuart Road
Dallas, TX 75241
800-237-2648
http://www.pqc.edu
Founded in 1872, Paul Quinn College is the oldest liberal arts college for African Americans in

Texas and west of the Mississippi River. Areas of academic study include accounting, biology, business administration, communications, computer science, engineering technology, English, criminal justice, elementary education, history, mathematics, organizational management, physical education, religion, secondary education, and sociology.

Philander Smith College
One Trudie Kibbe Reed Drive
Little Rock, AR 72202800-446-6772
http://www.philander.edu
This four-year Historically Black College and University offers bachelor degrees in more than 25 fields.

Phoenix College
1202 West Thomas Road
Phoenix, AZ 85013
602-285-7500
http://www.pc.maricopa.edu
This Hispanic-Serving Institution offers associate degrees and certificates in more than 30 academic areas.

Pima Community College
4905 East Broadway
Tucson, AZ 85709-1010
800-860-7462
infocenter@pima.edu
http://www.pima.edu
This Hispanic-Serving Institution offers more than 100 associate degrees and certificates.

Ponce School of Medicine
PO Box 7004
Ponce, PR 00732-7004
787-840-2575
info@psm.edu
http://www.psm.edu
This Hispanic-Serving Institution offers programs in a variety of science-related areas, including anatomy, biochemistry, medicine, pharmacology, psychiatry, and surgery.

Porterville College
100 East College Avenue
Porterville, CA 93257
559-791-2200
http://www.pc.cc.ca.us

The college offers a variety of associate degree and certificate programs. Hispanics make up a large percentage of its student body.

Prairie View A&M University
PO Box 519
Prairie View, TX 77446-0519
936-857-3311
http://www.pvamu.edu
This Historically Black College and University offers a broad range of undergraduate and graduate academic programs through seven colleges and one school: College of Agriculture and Human Sciences; College of Arts and Sciences; College of Business; College of Education; College of Engineering; College of Juvenile Justice and Psychology; College of Nursing; and the School of Architecture.

Pueblo Community College
900 West Oman Avenue
Pueblo, CO 81004-1499
888-642-6017
http://www.pueblocc.edu
This Hispanic-Serving Institution offers more than 40 associate degree and certificate programs. In addition to it Pueblo campus, the college has campuses in Canon City, Cortez, and Pagosa Springs.

Reedley College
995 North Reed Avenue
Reedley, CA 93564
559-638-3641
http://www.reedleycollege.edu
This two-year Hispanic-Serving Institution offers a variety of associate degrees and certificates through the following academic divisions: agriculture and natural resources; business; composition and literature; counseling and guidance; fine arts, social and behavioral science; industrial technology; math, science and engineering; physical education and health (including criminal justice, child development and dental assisting); and reading, speech, English as a second language, and foreign language.

Rio Hondo College
3600 Workman Mill Road
Whittier, CA 90601
562-692-0921
http://www.rh.cc.ca.us

This community college awards degrees in more than 40 disciplines and certificates in nearly 30 subjects. Approximately 68 percent of its students are Hispanic.

Riverside Community College-Riverside Campus
4800 Magnolia Avenue
Riverside, CA 92506-1299
951-222-8000
http://www.rcc.edu
This two-year Hispanic-Serving Institution offers more than 100 programs that lead to an associate degree, career certificate, or transfer to a four-year college or university. In addition to its Riverside campus, the college has campuses in Moreno Valley and Norco, California.

Robert Morris College
401 South State Street
Chicago, IL 60605
800-762-5960
enroll@robertmorris.edu
http://www.robertmorris.edu
This private Hispanic-Serving Institution offers associate and bachelor's degrees in business, culinary arts, graphic arts, health care, and other fields.

Rust College
150 Rust Avenue
Holly Springs, MS 38635
662-252-8000
http://www.rustcollege.edu
This private, Historically Black College offers associate and bachelor's degrees in business, education, humanities, science and mathematics, and social sciences. Preprofessional programs are also available in nursing, engineering, law, medical technology, and medicine.

Saginaw Chippewa Tribal College
7070 East Broadway
Mount Pleasant, MI 48858
989-775-4000
http://www.sagchip.org/tribalcollege
This tribal college offers associate degrees in business, general studies, and Native American studies.

Saint Augustine College
1333-1345 West Argyle
Chicago, IL 60640-3594
773-878-8756
http://www.staugustinecollege.edu

A member of the Association of Episcopal Colleges, St. Augustine College is the only bilingual (English/Spanish) institution of higher education in the Midwest that has North Central Association of Colleges and Schools accreditation.

Saint Augustine's College
1315 Oakwood Avenue
Raleigh, NC 27610
919-516-4000
http://www.st-aug.edu
This private, Historically Black, coeducational institution awards degrees in 32 different majors or areas of concentration, including biology education, community economic development, elementary education, industrial mathematics, music business, premedical sciences, and visual arts.

Saint Edward's University
3001 South Congress Avenue
Austin, Texas 78704
512-448-8400
http://www.stedwards.edu
This private, Catholic liberal arts institution offers undergraduate and graduate degrees in a wide array of academic disciplines. Nearly 27 percent of its students are Hispanic.

Saint Mary's University
One Camino Santa Maria
San Antonio, TX 78228-8503
800-367-7868
http://www.stmarytx.edu
This independent, Roman Catholic institution offers a variety of degrees from the bachelor's to the doctoral level. More than 50 percent of its students are Hispanic.

Saint Paul's College
115 College Drive
Lawrenceville, VA 23868
434-848-3111
http://www.saintpauls.edu
One of 105 Historically Black Colleges and Universities in the United States, St. Paul's offers a variety of majors, including business administration, computer science, English, and political science.

Saint Peter's College
2641 Kennedy Boulevard
Jersey City, NJ 07306

888-772-9933
http://www.spc.edu
The college offers four master's programs, 38 bachelor's programs, and 10 associate degree programs. Hispanics make up approximately 29 percent of its student body, and African Americans make up about 20 percent of its students.

Saint Thomas University
16401 Northwest 37th Avenue
Miami, FL 33054
305-628-6546
http://www.stu.edu
This Hispanic-Serving Institution offers undergraduate, graduate, and professional studies programs. Saint Thomas is the only Catholic Archdiocesan-sponsored university in Florida, but welcomes students of all faiths.

Salish Kootenai College
52000 Highway 93, PO Box 70
Pablo, MT 59855
406-275-4800
http://www.skc.edu
Salish Kootenai College is one of 34 tribal colleges in the United States. It is a fully accredited institution providing opportunities for one-, two-, and four-year degrees. Key degree areas include building trades, business, computer science, dental assisting, education, environmental science, heavy equipment operation, human services, medical records, Native American studies, nursing, and office professions.

San Bernardino Valley College
701 South Mount Vernon Avenue
San Bernardino, CA 92401
909-384-4400
http://www.valleycollege.edu
This two-year Hispanic-Serving Institution offers a variety of associate degrees and certificates in business and information technology, criminal justice, health science, humanities, physical education and athletics, science and math, social sciences, technical, and transportation.

San Diego State University (Imperial Valley)
720 Herber Avenue
Calexico, CA 92231
760-768-5500
http://www.ivcampus.sdsu.edu

This Hispanic-Serving Institution offers certificates, bachelor's degrees, and master's degrees in many academic areas, including applied arts and sciences, business administration, court interpreting, and Latin American studies.

Santa Fe Community College
6401 Richards Avenue
Santa Fe, NM 87508-4887
505-428-1000
info@sfccnm.edu
http://www.sfccnm.edu
The college offers a wide variety of associate degree and certificate programs. Approximately 37 percent of its students are Hispanic.

Santa Monica College
1900 Pico Boulevard
Santa Monica, CA 90405
310-434-4000
http://www.smc.edu
This two-year Hispanic-Serving Institution offers certificates and associate degrees in more than 25 academic disciplines.

Savannah State University
3219 College Street
Savannah, GA 31404
912-356-2181
http://www.savstate.edu
Savannah State University, established in 1890, is the oldest public Historically Black University in the state of Georgia.

Scottsdale Community College
American Indian Programs
9000 East Chaparral Road
Scottsdale, AZ 85256-2626
480-423-6000
http://www.sc.maricopa.edu/aip
Scottsdale Community College is located on the Salt River Pima-Maricopa Community and offers a tribal development and American Indian studies program, which awards certificates and associate degrees. The college also offers a Gaming Institute.

Selma University
1501 Lapsley Street
Selma, AL 36701
334-872-2533
http://www.selmauniversity.com

This four-year, private institution affiliated with the Alabama State Missionary Baptist Convention offers certificates, associate degrees, and bachelor degrees. It is one of 105 Historically Black Colleges and Universities in the United States.

Shaw University

118 East South Street
Raleigh, NC 27601
919-546-8200
http://www.shawuniversity.edu
Shaw is one of 105 Historically Black Colleges and Universities in the United States.

Shelton State Community College

9500 Old Greensboro Road
Tuscaloosa, AL 35405
205-391-2211
http://www.sheltonstate.edu/sscc
This Historically Black College and University offers certificates and associate degrees in many academic disciplines, including air conditioning and refrigeration, automotive technology, business, carpentry, commercial art, computer science, cosmetology, culinary arts, electrical technology, engineering, fine arts, industrial electronics technology, industrial maintenance technology, mathematics, natural sciences, nursing, office administration, and truck driving.

Sinte Gleska University

150 East Second Street, PO Box 105
Mission, SD 57555
605-856-8100
http://sinte.indian.com
Sinte Gleska University is located on the Rosebud Sioux Indian Reservation. Its academic programs include computer science, and a master's degree in education program. The university is also the home of the Native American Mathematics and Science Educational Leadership Program.

Sisseton Wahpeton College

PO Box 689
Sisseton, SD 57262
605-698-3966
http://www.swc.tc
SWC was chartered by the Sisseton Wahpeton Sioux Tribe in 1979 and provides associate degrees in selected fields of study.

Si Tanka University

333 Ninth Street, SW
Huron, SD 57350
800-710-7159
http://www.sitanka.edu
This tribal college offers baccalaureate and graduate degrees in athletic training, business management, criminal justice, education, information technology, and nursing.

Sitting Bull College

1341 92nd Street
Fort Yates, ND 58538
701-854-3861
info@sbci.edu
http://www.sittingbull.edu
Sitting Bull College, one of 34 tribal colleges in the United States, offers certificates and associate degrees in many academic fields, including agribusiness, bison management, business administration, early childhood education, Native American studies, and nursing. In cooperation with other universities, the college also offers bachelor's degrees in business administration, elementary/secondary education, and environmental science.

South Carolina State University

300 College Street, NE
Orangeburg, SC 29117
800-260-5956
http://www.scsu.edu
South Carolina State is one of 105 Historically Black Colleges and Universities in the United States. It offers a variety of majors through its College of Business and Applied Professional Sciences; College of Education, Humanities, and Social Sciences; College of Science, Mathematics, and Engineering Technology; and School of Graduate Studies.

Southern University and A& M College (Baton Rouge-Main Campus)

Southern University System
PO Box 9901
Baton Rouge, LA 70813
225-771-4500
http://www.subr.edu
This Historically Black College and University offers programs of study ranging from associate degrees to doctoral and professional degrees.

Southern University at New Orleans

6400 Press Drive
New Orleans, LA 70126
504-286-5000
http://www.suno.edu
Southern University at New Orleans is an open-enrollment university, serving Louisiana, southern Mississippi, and the greater New Orleans area. It is also a Historically Black College and University, and so was created to serve the needs of the African-American community.

Southern University at Shreveport

3050 Martin Luther King Jr. Drive
Shreveport, LA 71107
800-458-1472
http://www.susla.edu
One of 105 Historically Black Colleges and Universities in the United States, Southern University offers a variety of associate degrees and certificates through the following academic divisions: allied health, behavioral sciences and education, business studies, humanities, science and technology, and nursing.

South Mountain Community College

7050 South 24th Street
Phoenix, AZ 85042
602-243-8000
http://www.smc.maricopa.edu
This Hispanic-Serving Institution offers degree and certificate programs in many areas, including art, business administration, chemistry, political science, pre-engineering, and teleservices technology.

South Plains College

1401 South College Avenue
Levelland, TX 79336
806-894-9611
http://www.spc.cc.tx.us
This Hispanic-Serving Institution offers two-year academic programs that allow for transfer to a major university; it also offers technical programs and associate degrees.

South Texas College

PO Box 9701
McAllen, TX 78502-9701
800-742-7822
http://www.southtexascollege.edu

This two-year Hispanic-Serving Institution offers associate degrees and certificates in more than 95 academic disciplines through the following divisions: business, math, science, and technology; liberal arts and social sciences; and nursing and allied health.

Southwestern Christian College

PO Box 10
Terrell, TX 75160
972-524-3341
http://www.swcc.edu
This Historically Black College and University awards associate and bachelor's degrees, including a bachelor's degree in Bible and religious education.

Southwestern College

900 Otay Lakes Road
Chula Vista, CA 91910
619-421-6700
http://www.swc.cc.ca.us
This Hispanic-Serving Institution offers more than 285 associate degree and certificate options. Minorities make up a large percentage of its student population.

Southwestern Indian Polytechnic Institute

9169 Coors Road, NW
PO Box 10146
Albuquerque, NM 87196
800-586-7474
http://www.sipi.bia.edu
The Southwest Indian Polytechnic Institute offers programs of study in environmental science and industrial hygiene, graphic arts technology, liberal arts, natural resources technology, and optical technologies.

Southwest Texas Junior College

2401 Garner Field Road
Uvalde, TX 78801-6297
830-278-4401
http://www.swtjc.net
This Hispanic-Serving Institution offers a wide range of associate degree and certificate programs, including agriculture business, air conditioning and refrigeration, automotive technology, business, business management, child development, computer information systems, cosmetology, criminal justice, diesel technology, education, engineering, homeland security, law enforcement, office systems technology, and vocational nursing.

Spelman College

350 Spelman Lane, SW
Atlanta, GA 30314-4399
404-681-3643
http://www.spelman.edu
This well-known Historically Black College and University offers 26 majors and 25 minors.

Stillman College

PO Box 1430
Tuscaloosa, AL 35403
800-841-5722
http://www.stillman.edu
Stillman College is a four-year liberal arts college offering bachelor of arts and bachelor of science degrees. Stillman offers majors in a variety of areas, including business, computer science, health and physical education, international studies, and music. Stillman also has preprofessional programs in engineering, law, medicine, ministry, and social work. It is one of 105 Historically Black Colleges and Universities in the United States.

Stone Child College

Rural Route 1, Box 1082
Box Elder, MT 59521
406-395-4313
http://www.montana.edu/wwwscc
Stone Child College is one of 34 tribal colleges in the United States. It offers certificate and associate's degree programs in mathematics and science, business, computer, human services, and Native American studies.

Sul Ross State University

PO Box C-114
Alpine, TX 79832
432-837-8011
http://www.sulross.edu
This Hispanic-Serving Institution offers 27 undergraduate degree programs and 23 graduate degree programs.

Talladega College

627 West Battle Street
Talladega, AL 35160
256-761-6128
http://www.talladega.edu
This Historically Black College and University offers majors in the following areas: business and administration,

humanities and fine arts, natural sciences and mathematics, and social sciences and education.

Tennessee State University

John A. Merritt Boulevard, PO Box 9609
Nashville, TN 37209-1561
888-463-6878
http://www.tnstate.edu
This Historically Black College and University offers a variety of academic study areas, including allied health, arts and sciences, business, education, engineering and technology, home economics, human services, nursing, and public administration.

Texas A&M International University

5201 University Boulevard
Laredo, TX 78041
956-326-2001
http://www.tamiu.edu
This Hispanic-Serving Institution offers baccalaureate and master's programs in the arts; humanities; business; education; physical, biological, and social sciences.

Texas A&M University (Corpus Christi)

6300 Ocean Drive
Corpus Christi, TX 78412
361-825-5700
pioweb@falcon.tamucc.edu
http://www.tamucc.edu
This Hispanic-Serving Institution confers more than 60 undergraduate and graduate degrees through its College of Arts and Humanities, College of Business, College of Education, and College of Science and Technology.

Texas A&M University (Kingsville)

700 University Boulevard
Kingsville, TX 78363-8202
361-593-2111
http://www.tamuk.edu
The university offers more than 60 undergraduate and graduate programs, including accounting, agribusiness, animal science, art, bilingual education, business administration, chemical engineering, chemistry, civil engineering, computer information systems, computer science, counseling and guidance, criminology, fashion and interiors merchandising, finance, food and nutrition science, geography, horticulture, international business management,

kinesiology, mathematics, mechanical engineering, music, natural gas engineering, physics, plant and soil science, political science, range and wildlife science, range and wildlife management, school health, social work, theatre arts, and wildlife science. Approximately 62 percent of its students are Hispanic.

Texas College

2404 North Grand Avenue
Tyler, TX 75702-1962
800-306-6299
http://www.texascollege.edu
Texas College, a Historically Black College and University, offers baccalaureate degree programs in art, biology, business administration, computer science, English, education, history, mathematics, music, physical education, political science, liberal studies, social work, and sociology. It also offers associate degrees in early childhood education and general studies.

Texas Southern University

3100 Cleburne
Houston, TX 77004
713-313-7011
http://www.tsu.edu
This Historically Black College and University's academic programs include arts and sciences, business, education, pharmacy, and technology. It also has a graduate school and a school of law.

Texas State Technical College

1902 North Loop 499
Harlingen, TX 78550
800-852-8784
http://www.harlingen.tstc.edu
This Hispanic-Serving Institution offers associate degrees and certificates in more than 30 disciplines, including agriculture; business, commerce, and service; engineering and manufacturing; health and sciences; information technology and telecommunications; and transportation and aviation.

Tohono O'odham Community College

PO Box 3129
Sells, AZ 85634
520-383-8401
http://www.tocc.cc.az.us
This two-year tribal college serves the residents of the Tohono O'odham Nation and others who seek to pursue higher education. As a requirement for graduation, students must take two classes in Tohono O'odham culture.

Tougaloo College

500 County Line Road
Tougaloo, MS 39174
601-799-7700
http://www.tougaloo.edu
Tougaloo College is a Historically Black, private, coeducational, church-related, four-year, liberal arts institution.

Trinidad State Junior College

600 Prospect Street
Trinidad, CO 81082
800-621-8752
http://www.trinidadstate.edu
This two-year Hispanic-Serving Institution offers a wide variety of associate degrees and certificates.

Turtle Mountain Community College

PO Box 340
Belcourt, ND 58316
701-477-7862
http://www.turtle-mountain.cc.nd.us
One of 34 tribal colleges in the United States, Turtle Mountain offers associate degrees and certificates in more than 50 disciplines. It also offers a bachelor's of science degree in elementary education.

Tuskegee University

Tuskegee, AL 36088
800-622-6531
admissions@tuskegee.edu
http://www.tuskegee.edu
Tuskegee University is the number one producer of AfricanAmerican aerospace science engineers in the nation, and the number two producer of African-American engineering graduates in three other engineering fields in the country. It is the only Historically Black College and University approved to offer the doctor of philosophy (Ph.D.) in materials science and engineering.

Union County College

1033 Springfield Avenue
Cranford, NJ 07016
908-709-7000
http://www.ucc.edu
This two-year Hispanic-Serving Institution with four

campuses offers certificate and associate degrees in more than 75 academic areas, including American sign language and deaf studies, biotechnology, bioterrorism, deaf-blind interpreting, dental hygiene, English for speakers of other languages, game design development, gerontology, multimedia development, restaurant management, and visual arts/fine arts.

United Tribes Technical College

3315 University Drive
Bismarck, ND 58504
701-255-3285
http://www.uttc.edu
The college was founded to provide opportunities through which Native Americans can obtain a technical education and become self-sufficient. It provides not only occupational education and training, but also a comprehensive set of support services to adults and their children.

University of Arizona South

1140 North Colombo Avenue
Sierra Vista, AZ 85635
520-458-8278
http://www.uas.arizona.edu
This Hispanic-Serving Institution offers certificates and undergraduate and graduate degrees in academic areas such as commerce, computer science, elementary education, elementary education-bilingual option, family studies, history, Latin American studies, mathematics, political science, psychology, and secondary education.

University of Arkansas (Pine Bluff)

1200 North University Drive
Pine Bluff, AR 71601
870-575-8000
http://www.uapb.edu
The University of Arkansas at Pine Bluff is a multicultural institution and one of 105 Historically Black Colleges and Universities in the United States. Undergraduate and graduate degrees are offered through four academic programs: arts and sciences; agriculture, fisheries, and human sciences; business and management; and education.

University of Houston (Downtown)

One Main Street
Houston, TX 77002
713-221-8522

uhdadmit@dt.uh.edu
http://www.dt.uh.edu
Minorities make up nearly 63 percent of the student body at this four-year institution.

University of La Verne

1950 Third Street
La Verne, CA 91750
909-593-3511
http://www.ulv.edu
The university offers 88 bachelor's and master's degrees programs and four doctorates. Approximately 53 percent of its students are African American, Asian American, Native American and/or Latino. Majors most in demand at the school are business administration, liberal studies, psychology, and criminology.

University of Maryland Eastern Shore (UMES)

11868 Academic Oval
Princess Anne, MD 21853
410-651-2200
http://www.umes.edu
A Historically Black University on the rural Eastern Shore, UMES grants degrees in the arts and sciences, agriculture, and business.

University of Miami

Coral Gables, FL 33124
305-284-2211
http://www.miami.edu
The university offers 150 undergraduate, 130 master's, 60 doctoral, and two professional areas of study. Minorities make up approximately 44 percent of its student body.

University of New Mexico (Main Campus)

PO Box 4895
Albuquerque, NM 87196-4895
505-277-0111
http://www.unm.edu
This Hispanic-Serving Institution's main and branch campuses offer 88 certificates, 97 associate degrees, 145 bachelor's degrees, 83 master's degrees, 42 doctorate degrees, three professional degrees, and 11 post-master's certificates. Approximately 30 percent of the students attending its main campus are Hispanic.

University of New Mexico (Valencia)

280 La Entrada
Los Lunas, NM 87051

505-925-8500
http://www.unm.edu/~unmvc
The university offers study options in business
     administration, business and technology, computer-
     aided drafting, fine arts, language and literature, and
     mathematics and statistics. Nearly 55 percent
     of students at the university are Hispanic.

University of St. Thomas
3800 Montrose
Houston, TX 77006
713-522-7911
http://www.stthom.edu
This Roman Catholic Hispanic-Serving Institution offers
     undergraduate and graduate degrees in more
     than 40 areas, including bioinformatics, business
     administration, Catholic studies, environmental
     studies, international studies, liberal arts, pastoral
     theology, and Spanish.

University of Texas
601 Colorado Street
Austin, TX 78701-2982
512-499-4200
http://www.utsystem.edu
The University of Texas system has nine academic
     universities that serve approximately 182,000
     undergraduate, graduate, and professional school
     students. Of its universities, six (listed below) are
     classified as Hispanic-Serving Institutions.

University of Texas (Brownsville)
80 Fort Brown
Brownsville, TX 78520
956-544-8200
http://www.utb.edu

University of Texas (El Paso)
500 West University Avenue
El Paso, TX 79968
915-747-5000
http://www.utep.edu

**University of Texas (Health Science Center
     at San Antonio)**
7703 Floyd Curl Drive
San Antonio, TX 78229-3900
210-567-7000
http://www.uthscsa.edu

University of Texas (Pan American)
1201 West University Drive
Edinburg, TX 78541
956-381-8872
http://www.panam.edu

University of Texas (the Permian Basin)
4901 East University
Odessa, TX 79762-0001
432-554-2605
http://www.utpb.edu

University of Texas (San Antonio)
6900 North Loop 1604 West
San Antonio, TX 78249
210-485-4011
http://www.utsa.edu

University of the District of Columbia
4200 Connecticut Avenue, NW
Washington, DC 20008
202-274-5000
http://www.udc.edu
The University of the District of Columbia is the only
     public institution of higher education in the District of
     Columbia—and one of 105 Historically Black Colleges
     and Universities. It offers undergraduate and graduate
     programs.

University of the Incarnate Word
4301 Broadway
San Antonio, TX 78209
800-749-9673
admis@universe.uiwtx.edu
http://www.uiw.edu
This Hispanic-Serving Institution offers 45 undergraduate
     majors, four minors, 24 graduate degree programs,
     and a Ph.D. program with four specializations.

University of the Virgin Islands
Two John Brewers Bay
St. Thomas, VI 00802-9990
340-693-1150
pr@uvi.edu
http://www.uvi.edu/pub-relations/uvi.htm
The University of the Virgin Islands is the only Historically
     Black College and University outside of the continental
     United States. It enrolls approximately 3,200 full-time
     and part-time students at its two campuses. It offers
     courses in five areas of study: business, education,

humanities, nursing, and science and math. The university has campuses on St. Thomas and St. Croix, and an ecological research station on St. John.

Vaughn College of Aeronautics and Technology
86-01 23rd Avenue
Flushing, NY 11369
800-682-8446
http://www.aero.edu
This Hispanic-Serving Institution (formerly known as the College of Aeronautics) is one of the country's premier aviation institutions, and is located at LaGuardia Airport in Queens, New York. The college offers associate's and bachelor's degrees.

Ventura College
4667 Telegraph Road
Ventura, CA 93003
805-654-6400
http://www.venturacollege.edu
Ventura College offers more than 100 associate degrees and certificates. Of the students attending the college, approximately 36 percent are Hispanic.

The Victoria College
2200 East Red River
Victoria, TX 77901
361-573-3291
http://www.victoriacollege.edu
This community college offers a wide array of associate degree and certificate programs. Approximately 32 percent of its student body is Hispanic.

Victor Valley Community College
18422 Bear Valley Road
Victorville, CA 92392-5849
760-245-4271
http://www.vvc.edu
This Hispanic-Serving Institution offers certificates and associate degrees in more than 25 academic fields.

Virginia State University
Petersburg, VA 23806
804-524-5000
http://www.vsu.edu
Virginia State University was America's first fully state-supported, four-year institution of higher learning for Blacks. It is a comprehensive university and one of two land-grant institutions in Virginia. The university

is accredited by the Commission on Colleges of the Southern Association of Colleges and Schools to award bachelor's and master's degrees, and a certificate of advanced graduate study.

Virginia Union University
1500 North Lombardy Street
Richmond, VA 23220
804-257-5600
http://www.vuu.edu
VUU is a charter member of The College Fund/UNCF, a consortium of select Historically Black Colleges and Universities across the nation. It requires that all students complete a core curriculum of courses from the humanities, natural sciences, mathematics, and social sciences.

Vorhees College
PO Box 678
Denmark, SC 29042
803-793-1290
http://www.voorhees.edu
Vorhees College, a Historically Black College and University, is a four-year, private liberal arts college with 10 degree programs. Financial aid is available, as well as a special program for single mothers to earn a college degree.

Western Carolina University
College of Arts and Science
Cherokee Studies
McKee Building 105A-C
Cullowhee, NC 28723
828-227-3841
jeastman@email.wcu.edu
http://www.wcu.edu/cherokeestudies
In addition to its undergraduate and graduate programs, the university offers a program in Cherokee studies.

Western New Mexico University
PO Box 680
Silver City, NM 88062
800-872-9668
http://www.wnmu.edu
This Hispanic-Serving Institution offers certificate, associate, baccalaureate, and graduate programs through the following academic divisions: applied technology, business administration and criminal justice, education, expressive arts, humanities, mathematics and computer science, natural sciences,

nursing, occupational therapy and rehabilitation services, social sciences, social work, and wellness and movement science.

Western Texas College
6200 South College Avenue
Snyder, TX 79549
325-573-8511
http://www.wtc.edu
This two-year Hispanic-Serving Institution offers more than 25 academic majors, including agriculture, computer science, government, mass communications, physical education, Spanish, and speech.

West Hills Community College
990 Cody Street
Coalinga, CA 93210
800-266-1114
http://www.westhillscollege.com
This two-year Hispanic-Serving Institution offers certificates and associate degrees in a variety of subjects, including chemistry, computer information systems, and health science. It also offers a bachelor's degree program in partnership with California State University-Fresno. West Hills has two campuses.

West Los Angeles College
9000 Overland Avenue
Culver City, CA 90230
310-287-4200
http://www.wlac.edu
This Hispanic-Serving Institution offers more than 50 associate degree and certificate programs.

West Virginia State College
PO Box 1000
Institute, WV 25112-1000
800-987-2112
http://www.wvsc.edu
West Virginia State College is a Historically Black College and University that provides a broad range of undergraduate and graduate programs for residential and commuting students. It has 21 academic departments, including art, biology, business, chemistry, communications, criminal justice, economics, education, English, foreign languages, health, history, mathematics, music, physics, political science, psychology, social work, and sociology.

White Earth Tribal and Community College
202 South Main Street
Mahnomen, MN 56557
218-935-0417
http://www.wetcc.org
This liberal arts institution of higher education is one of 34 tribal colleges in the United States.

Whittier College
13406 Philadelphia, PO Box 634
Whittier, CA 90608-0634
562-907-4200
http://www.whittier.edu
Whittier College is an Anishinabe-controlled liberal arts institution of higher education. It is one of 34 tribal colleges in the United States.

Wilberforce University
1055 North Bickett Road, PO Box 1001
Wilberforce, OH 45384-1001
937-376-2911
http://www.wilberforce.edu
Wilberforce University is the oldest, private, Historically Black, liberal arts school in the nation. Since 1856, its mission has been to educate students of all colors, creeds, and religious denominations. Wilberforce is affiliated with the African Methodist Episcopal Church.

Wiley College
711 Wiley Avenue
Marshall, TX 75670
903-927-3300
http://www.wileyc.edu
Wiley College is a four-year, coeducational, liberal arts, private institution. It is affiliated with the United Methodist Church and was the first accredited Historically Black College west of the Mississippi. Wiley has an average enrollment of 650 students, with many attending from Texas, southeastern Oklahoma, western Arkansas, and western Louisiana. It offers 17 fields of study, including accounting, biology, business administration, chemistry, computer information systems, computer science, criminal justice, elementary education (K-4), English, history, hospitality and tourism administration, mathematics, music, organizational management, physical education, secondary education, and sociology.

Winston-Salem State University

601 Martin Luther King Jr. Drive
Winston-Salem, NC 27110
800-257-4052
http://www.wssu.edu
Winston-Salem State University is a public university that offers educational programs at the baccalaureate level for diverse and motivated students. Master's and intermediate level programs for professional study are also available. It is one of 105 Historically Black Colleges and Universities in the United States.

Woodbury University

7500 Glenoaks Boulevard
Burbank, CA 91510-7846
800-784-9663
info@woodbury.edu
http://www.woodbury.edu
This Hispanic-Serving Institution offers more than 15 undergraduate and graduate programs, including accounting, business and management, animation arts, architecture, fashion design, graphic design, interior architecture, communication, computer information systems, fashion marketing, marketing, organizational leadership, politics and history, and psychology.

Xavier University of Louisiana

One Drexel Drive
New Orleans, LA 70125
504-486-7411
http://www.xula.edu

Xavier University is the nation's only institution of higher learning that is both Historically Black and Catholic. Xavier offers preparation in 36 majors on the undergraduate, graduate, and professional degree levels. According to the U.S. Department of Education, Xavier continues to rank first nationally in the number of African-American students earning undergraduate degrees in biology and the life sciences. It is also ranks first in the number of doctor of pharmacy degrees awarded to African Americans and first in placing African-American students into medical schools.

York College

City University of New York
94-20 Guy R. Brewer Boulevard
Jamaica, NY 11451
718-262-2000
http://www.york.cuny.edu
York College, a senior college of The City University of New York, was founded in 1967. It offers professional degree programs and more than 40 baccalaureate options. Multicultural and international education have long been important themes at the college.

FRATERNITIES AND SORORITIES

The majority of these service organizations were founded by members of specific minority groups, but offer membership and services to people from all ethnic backgrounds.

Alpha Kappa Delta Phi Sorority
http://www.akdphi.org
An Asian American–interest sorority founded in 1990.

Alpha Kappa Educational Advancement Foundation
5656 Stony Island Avenue
Chicago, IL 60637
773-947-0026
http://www.akaeaf.org
An African-American co-ed service organization.

Alpha Phi Alpha Fraternity
2313 St. Paul Street
Baltimore, MD 21218-5234
410-554-0040
http://www.alphaphialpha.net
An African-American–interest fraternity.

Alpha Phi Gamma Sorority
PO Box 971
Northbrook, IL 60065-0971
http://www.alphaphigamma.org
An Asian American–interest sorority.

Alpha Rho Lambda Sorority
61-17 63rd Street
Middle Village, NY 11379
http://www.alpharholambda.org
A Hispanic-interest sorority.

Alpha Sigma Lambda Fraternity
600 Lincoln Avenue
Charleston, IL 61920
217-581-7106
alsiglam@www.eiu.edu
http://www.alphasigmalambda.org
A fraternity for adult students in higher education.

Chi Alpha Delta Sorority
uclachis@ucla.edu
http://www.chialphadelta.com
An Asian American–interest sorority.

Delta Psi Epsilon Christian Sorority
cu_poet@hotmail.com
http://www.angelfire.com/ca2/deltapsiepsilon
A Christian African-American–interest sorority.

Delta Sigma Theta Sorority
1707 New Hampshire Avenue, NW
Washington, DC 20009
202-986-2400
http://www.deltasigmatheta.org
An African-American–interest sorority.

Delta Xi Phi Sorority
PO Box 5218
Chicago, IL 60680
http://www.geocities.com/~deltaxiphi
A multicultural sorority.

Gamma Phi Eta Fraternity
PO Box 17793
Statesboro, GA 30460
912-681-9252
http://www.angelfire.com/ga/GAMMAPHIETA/page.
    html
A multicultural sorority.

Gamma Phi Omega Sorority
PO Box 4680
Chicago, IL 60608
877-899-3286
http://www.gammaphiomega.org
A Hispanic American-interest sorority.

Gamma Phi Sigma Fraternity
http://www.gammaphisigma.org
A Hispanic-interest fraternity.

Gamma Zeta Alpha Fraternity
http://www.gammas.org
A Hispanic-interest fraternity.

Iota Phi Lambda Sorority
http://www.iota1929.org
An African-American–interest sorority.

Iota Phi Theta Fraternity
8417 Locust Grove Drive
Laurel, MD 20707
888-835-5109
http://www.iotaphitheta.org
An African-American–interest fraternity.

Kappa Alpha Psi Fraternity
2322-24 North Broad Street
Philadelphia, PA 19132-4590
215-228-7184
http://www.kappaalphapsi1911.com
An African-American–interest fraternity.

Kappa Phi Iota Sorority
kappa_phi_iota@hotmail.com
http://www.angelfire.com/nj/kappaphiiota
An African-American–interest sorority.

Kappa Phi Lambda Sorority
university@kappaphilambda.org
http://www.kappaphilambda.org
An Asian American–interest sorority.

Lambda Alpha Upsilon Fraternity
29 John Street, PMB 181
New York, NY 10038
http://www.lambdas.com
A Hispanic-interest fraternity.

Lambda Phi Epsilon Fraternity
http://www.lambdaphiepsilon.com
An Asian American–interest fraternity.

Lambda Psi Delta Sorority
PO Box 260128
Hartford, CT 06106-0128
nationals@lambdapsidelta.org
http://www.lambdapsidelta.org
This is a multicultural sorority.

Lambda Theta Nu Sorority
1220 Rosecrans, #543
San Diego, CA 92106
http://www.lambdathetanu.org
A Hispanic-interest sorority.

Lambda Upsilon Lambda Fraternity
PMB 39, 511 Sixth Avenue
New York, NY 10011
http://www.launidadlatina.org
A Hispanic-interest fraternity.

National Pan-Hellenic Council
http://www.nphchq.org
This is a co-ed service organization for African
    Americans.

Nu Alpha Kappa Fraternity
PO Box 12102
San Luis Obispo, CA 93406
http://www.naknet.org
A Hispanic-interest fraternity.

Omega Delta Phi Fraternity
PO Box 2235
Phoenix, AZ 85002-2235
http://www.omegadeltaphi.com
A Hispanic-interest fraternity.

Omega Phi Beta Sorority
Director@OmegaPhiBeta.org
http://www.omegaphibeta.org
A Hispanic-interest sorority.

Omega Psi Phi Fraternity
3951 Snapfinger Parkway
Decatur, GA 30035
404-284-5533
http://www.omegapsiphifraternity.org
An African-American–interest fraternity.

Omega Xi Delta Fraternity
California Polytechnic State University
PO Box 65
San Luis Obispo, CA 93403
http://www.omegaxidelta.com
An Asian American–interest fraternity.

Phi Beta Sigma Fraternity
145 Kennedy Street, NW
Washington, DC 20011-5434
202-726-5434
http://pbs1914.org
An African-American–interest fraternity.

Phi Delta Psi Fraternity
8200 East Jefferson, Suite 907
Detroit, MI 48214
pdpsi@phideltapsifraternity.org
http://www.phideltapsifraternity.org
An African-American–interest fraternity.

Phi Iota Alpha Fraternity
49 East 41st Street, Suite 449
New York, NY 10165
212-642-1087
council@phiota.org

http://www.phiota.org
A Hispanic-interest fraternity.

Phi Rho Eta Fraternity
contactus@phirhoeta.org
http://www.phirhoeta.org
An African-American–interest fraternity.

Pi Delta Psi Fraternity
Church Street Station, PO Box 2920
New York, NY 10008-2920
http://www.pideltapsi.com
An Asian American–interest fraternity.

Pi Psi Fraternity
PO Box 2784
Farmington Hills, MI 48333
info@pipsi.org
http://www.pipsi.org
An African-American–interest fraternity.

Sigma Gamma Rho Sorority
1000 Southhill Drive, Suite 200
Cary, NC 27513
888-747-1922
http://sgrho1922.org
An Asian American–interest sorority.

Sigma Iota Alpha Sorority
Prince Street Station, PO Box 237
New York, NY 10012
neb@hermandad-sia.org
http://www.hermandad-sia.org
A Hispanic-interest sorority.

Sigma Lambda Gamma Sorority
Iowa Memorial Union
Iowa City, IA 52242-1317
888-486-2382
http://www.sigmalambdagamma.com
A Hispanic-interest sorority.

Sigma Lambda Upsilon Sorority
Grand Central Station, PO Box 4170
New York, NY 10163
http://www.sigmalambdaupsilon.org
A Hispanic-interest sorority.

Sigma Psi Zeta Sorority
http://www.sigmapsizeta.org
An Asian American–interest sorority.

Sigma Theta Psi Sorority
sigmathetapsi@yahoo.com
http://www.geocities.com/CollegePark/5012
This is a multicultural sorority.

Tau Beta Sigma Sorority
PO Box 849
Stillwater, OK 74076-0849
800-543-6505
kkytbs@kkytbs.org
http://www.kkytbs.org
This is an honorary band sorority.

Zeta Phi Beta Sorority
1734 New Hampshire Avenue, NW
Washington, DC 20009
202-387-3103
IHQ@zPhiB1920.org
http://www.zphib1920.org
An African-American–interest sorority.

ADDITIONAL RESOURCES

A variety of career aids can be found in this section, including boys' and girls' programs, internships, minorities studies and minorities research programs, publications, online resources, and information on other career and education directories for minorities.

BOYS' AND GIRLS' PROGRAMS

American Indian Science and Engineering Society
PO Box 9828
Albuquerque, NM 87119-9828
505-765-1052
http://www.aises.org
The society encourages young American Indians to pursue careers in science, technology, and engineering. It offers membership to students from kindergarten to 12th grade (whom they refer to as "pre-college students"), a National American Indian Science and Engineering Fair, and a High School Day and Career Fair as part of its annual conference.

American Indian Workshop at Michigan Technological University
Michigan Technological University
Youth Programs Office, Alumni House
1400 Townsend Drive
Houghton, MI 49931-1295
906-487-2219
http://youthprograms.mtu.edu
Michigan Technological University's American Indian Workshop introduces Native Americans ages 12 to 15 to college coursework through the study of computers and mathematics. Contact the Youth Programs Office for more information.

Association of American Indian Physicians
1225 Sovereign Row, Suite 103
Oklahoma City, OK 73108
405-946-7072
aaip@aaip.com
http://www.aaip.com
This association seeks to increase the recruitment and retention of Native American high school and college students into the medical and health professions (including the allied health professions, such as dentistry, veterinary, medicine, optometry, and pharmacy). Many opportunities are available via its Health Careers Opportunity Program, including a mentoring program that allows students to correspond with Native American health professionals via mail, phone, e-mail, or by personal contact; a live-in shadowing program in which students spend four to seven days observing health care professionals; Pre-Admission Workshops; and a Student Enrichment Academy for Reaching Careers in Health, a six-week

summer academy for Native American students ages 14 to 17 at the University of Oklahoma Health Sciences Center in Oklahoma City.

Bay Area Multicultural Media Academy
San Francisco State University
Center for Integration and Improvement of Journalism
1600 Holloway Avenue, Humanities 307
San Francisco, CA 94132
415-338-2083
ciij@sfsu.edu
http://www.ciij.org/workshops or http://xpress.sfsu.edu/bamma
The Bay Area Multicultural Media Academy is a two-week summer program for Asian American, African American, Latino American, Native American, and low-income youth who are interested in learning more about careers in journalism. Applicants must be attending Bay Area high schools. Graduates of the program work in radio, television, print, and online journalism. Contact the center for more information.

Center for Education Integrating Science, Mathematics, and Computing at Georgia Institute of Technology
Georgia Institute of Technology
Summer Camps
760 Spring Street
Atlanta, GA 30332-0282
404-894-0777
http://www.ceismc.gatech.edu
The center offers summer camps that help to expand elementary, middle, and high school students' interest in mathematics, science, and engineering. The program is open to both males and females, but females and underrepresented minorities are strongly encouraged to take advantage of the center's programs. The camps last five days and feature demonstrations, laboratory exercises, discussion groups, presentations, and some recreational activities. Contact the center for information on application requirements, costs, and program dates.

Explorations in Engineering Program at Michigan Technological University
Michigan Technological University
Youth Programs Office, Alumni House
1400 Townsend Drive

Houghton, MI 49931-1295
906-487-2219
http://youthprograms.mtu.edu
Michigan Technological University (MTU) offers the
Explorations in Engineering Program, which
helps high school students explore computers
and engineering in a college setting. This
residential program is for minority or economically
disadvantaged students; freshmen, sophomores,
and juniors are eligible. While living on campus for
one week, participants engage in informational
discussions and technical projects with MTU faculty
and other professional engineers and computer
scientists. The program is usually held in June or July.

Girls Incorporated

120 Wall Street
New York, NY 10005-3902
800-374-4475
http://www.girlsinc.org
Girls Incorporated is a national network of programs
that serves nearly 700,000 girls (including those in
high-risk, underserved areas) between the ages of
six to 18 through a network of 1,000 affiliates in the
United States and Canada. Its Web site lists contact
information by state for Girls Incorporated sites.
Its Operation SMART program encourages girls to
explore their natural curiosity in math, science, and
technology and consider nontraditional careers such
as auto mechanic, astronaut, and microsurgeon.

HERMANITAS Program

MANA, A National Latina Organization
1725 K Street, NW, Suite 201
Washington, DC 20006
202-833-0060
hermana2@aol.com
http://www.hermana.org/orgfrm.htm
MANA's HERMANITAS Program was created to encourage
Hispanic girls to stay in school and reach academic
goals. Students work with mentors to stay on track in
their personal and academic lives. Additionally, MANA
offers the National HERMANITAS Summer Institute.
Contact MANA for more information on the Program.

Hispanic Alliance for Career Enhancement (HACE)

Student Development Program
25 East Washington, Suite 1500
Chicago, IL 60602
312-435-0498

abetomas@hace-usa.org
http://www.hace-usa.org
The alliance offers an internship program for high
school students, as well as high school and college
mentoring programs. Contact the HACE for more
information.

Idaho JEMS Summer Workshop at the University of Idaho

University of Idaho
College of Engineering
Attn: Program Director
Idaho JEMS Summer Workshop
PO Box 441011, JEB B40
Moscow, ID 83844-1011
208-885-4934
isgc@uidaho.edu
http://www.uidaho.edu/engr/jems
The University of Idaho's College of Engineering sponsors
Idaho JEMS (Junior Engineering Math & Science
program) each summer for rising high school seniors.
Students live on the university campus for two
weeks and take classes with College of Engineering
professors. Such classes may include computer
programming, engineering design, human factors,
and engineering problem-solving. Successful
completion of the classes leads to college engineering
credits from the University of Idaho. In addition
to course work, participants explore engineering
through lab exercises, field trips, and guest speakers.
Female and minority students are especially
encouraged to apply, but the program is open to all
qualified applicants. For more information and an
application, contact the program director.

Magic Johnson Foundation

9100 Wilshire Boulevard, Suite 700 East
Beverly Hills, CA 90212
310-246-4400
http://www.magicjohnson.org/tm_index.php
The foundation offers a scholarship program for minority
high school students that features mentorship and
internship components. Applicants must be residents
of Atlanta, Cleveland, Houston, Los Angeles, or New
York. Contact the foundation for more information.

MentorNet

1275 South Winchester Boulevard, Suite E
San Jose, CA 95128-3910
408-296-4405

http://www.mentornet.net
MentorNet is a program that "addresses the retention and success of those in engineering, science, and mathematics, particularly, but not exclusively, women and other underrepresented groups." Its mentors work with college students one-on-one, via e-mail.

Minority Introduction to Engineering at Tuskegee University

Tuskegee University
College of Engineering, Architecture and Physical Sciences
Attn: Assistant to the Dean for Student Development and Special Programs
Tuskegee, AL 36088
334-727-8946
http://tuskegee.edu/global/Story.asp?s=1172515
The College of Engineering, Architecture and Physical Sciences at Tuskegee University invites minority students who are rising high school juniors or seniors to apply to the Minority Introduction to Engineering (MITE). MITE is a two-week summer program that allows students to fully experience campus life, from living in the dormitories to studying with current staff and students. Participants spend time exploring engineering and other math and science careers and attending laboratory demonstrations by engineering faculty. For further details and application information, contact the Assistant to the Dean for Student Development and Special Programs.

Minority Introduction to Engineering, Entrepreneurship and Science at Massachusetts Institute of Technology

Massachusetts Institute of Technology (MIT)
Attn: Karl Reid, Program, MITE2s Program
77 Massachusetts Avenue, Room 1-123
Cambridge, MA 02139
617-253-3298
mites@mit.edu
http://web.mit.edu/mites/www
Minority Introduction to Engineering, Entrepreneurship and Science, or MITE2s, is a six-week residential, summer program for high school juniors who are interested in engineering, science, and entrepreneurship. Students spend 30 to 35 hours in classes and lab each week and participate in seminars, competitions, and field trips. Contact the program director for more information.

Multicultural Journalism Workshop at the University of Alabama

University of Alabama
Journalism Department
Box 870172
Tuscaloosa, AL 35487-0172
205-348-8607
http://www.ccom.ua.edu/mjw
The University of Alabama's Multicultural Journalism Program helps educate minority students about journalism. Students in the program participate in mentoring with journalism professionals, work with other students to create a newspaper, and receive job placement. A Multicultural Journalism Workshop is also offered to high school students. Participants learn reporting, writing, editing, graphics, photography, production, and basic communication skills. Contact the journalism department for more information.

Multiethnic Introduction to Engineering at Purdue University

Purdue University
Attn: Marion Blalock, Director of Pre-Engineering and Alumni Relations
400 Centennial Mall Drive, Engineering Administration Building, Room 222
West Lafayette, IN 47907-2016
765-494-3974
mep@ecn.purdue.edu
https://engineering.purdue.edu/MEP/pre_college/mite
Purdue University's Multiethnic Introduction to Engineering runs for two weeks in mid-July. Rising high school seniors with a strong academic background take part in computer sessions, laboratory experiences, engineering design projects, and lectures by faculty members and engineering professionals. Participants live on campus and have access to a wide range of recreational events and facilities. For more information about the program and details about application procedures, contact the Director of Pre-Engineering and Alumni Relations.

National Society of Black Engineers (NSBE)

1454 Duke Street
Alexandria, VA 22314
703-549-2207
http://www.nsbe.org/membership/mempci.php
The Society offers the Pre-College Initiative (PCI) program. The PCI program links professional NSBE members with students to encourage their interests

in math and science. PCI students in grades six through 12 are eligible to become NSBE Jr. members. These young members can participate in activities such as "camping conferences" and college admissions and financial aid workshops. The society also offers extensive programs for minority college students, including an Academic Tech Bowl.

Organization of Black Airline Pilots (OBAP)
8630 Fenton Street, Suite 126
Silver Spring, MD 20910
800-538-6227
nationaloffice@obap.org
http://www.obap.org
Working in cooperation with several airlines, government agencies, and other private organizations, the OBAP maintains the Pilots in the School Program (which features educational visits by pilots to high schools) and the Professional Pilot Development Program (which offers mentorship, scholarships, fellowships, and job placement). It also offers the Summer Ace/ Flight Academy Program, which introduces children ages 13 to 18 to the field of aviation. Activities include model aircraft building, field trips to military and commercial facilities, aircraft orientation flights, aviation seminars, and other opportunities.

Planning for the Future Program at the University of Wisconsin-Milwaukee
University of Wisconsin-Milwaukee
PO Box 413
Milwaukee, WI 53201
414-229-5940
http://www.uwm.edu/Dept/DSAD/PRECOLL
The Planning for the Future Program helps minority fourth through eighth graders learn the value of academic achievement and the benefits of attending college. The program is conducted during the regular academic year. Workshops cover study habits, personal values, career options, decision-making, and the importance of planning for their future. Contact the university for more information.

Promotion and Awareness of Careers in Engineering and Science Program
MAES: The Society of Mexican American Engineers and Scientists Inc.
711 West Bay Area Boulevard, Suite 206
Webster, TX 77598-4051
281-557-3677

execdir@maes-natl.org
http://www.maes-natl.org
Promotion and Awareness of Careers in Engineering and Science is a national program that introduces Hispanic students at the junior high school and high school levels to the fields of engineering and science. At the junior high level, the program consists mainly of seminars that educate students and parents about college options and careers in science and engineering. High school-level activities include assistance with research on financial aid and colleges, tutoring, and field trips to universities and technology-related settings. Contact the society for more information.

Student Introduction to Engineering (SITE) at North Carolina State University
North Carolina State University
College of Engineering
Attn: SITE Coordinator
Campus Box 7904
Raleigh, NC 27695-7904
919-515-9669
http://www.engr.ncsu.edu/summerprograms
The Student Introduction to Engineering (SITE) is a summer program sponsored by the College of Engineering at North Carolina State University (NCSU). Open to rising high school juniors and seniors from all backgrounds, SITE offers students a realistic look at the professional lives of engineers and the preparation needed to pursue such a career via 11 programs, including computer science, aerospace engineering, autonomous robotics, civil engineering/construction management, materials science and engineering, mechatronics, biological engineering, chemical engineering, textiles (including textile engineering), Wolfpack Motorsports, and a Young Investigators Program in Nuclear Technology. Underrepresented minorities (Hispanic Americans, African Americans, and Native Americans, and women) are strongly encouraged to apply to the program. A program for middle school students is also available. For more information and a copy of the application form, contact the SITE coordinator.

Student Success Program at the University of Wisconsin-Milwaukee
University of Wisconsin-Milwaukee
PO Box 413
Milwaukee, WI 53201

414-229-5940

http://www.uwm.edu/Dept/DSAD/PRECOLL

The Student Success Program helps minority rising 10th, 11th, and 12th graders succeed academically and prepare for college. The program has a six-week summer component, which helps students prepare for their core classes the next school year, and an academic year component, which helps students to reinforce the skills they learned in the summer by offering specialized workshops, career development, life skills, academic skill building, tutoring, community service, academic advising, and field trips. Contact the university for more information.

Uninitiates' Introduction to Engineering Program

Junior Engineering Technical Society (JETS)

1420 King Street, Suite 405

Alexandria, VA 22314-2794

703-548-5387

info@jets.org

http://www.jets.org

JETS, in conjunction with the U.S. Army Research Office, offers The Uninitiates' Introduction to Engineering Program, which helps minority high school students prepare for college through summer classes. The classes introduce students to an educational experience that parallels that of a freshmen student in a university engineering program. Learning methods include academic classes, hands-on activities, and team-based learning. Participating schools include Colorado State University, Florida International University, New Mexico MESA, the University of Delaware, and the University of Detroit-Mercy.

University Familiarization Program for Minorities in Engineering at Mississippi State University

Mississippi State University (MSU)

Bagley College of Engineering

Attn: Emma Seiler, Coordinator for Educational Outreach and Student Programs

Box 9544

Mississippi State, MS 39762

662-325-1360

eseiler@engr.msstate.edu

http://www.engr.msstate.edu/outreach

The University Familiarization Program for Minorities in Engineering introduces minority students to the various engineering disciplines taught at MSU via a one-week residential summer program. Applicants may be rising 10th, 11th, and 12th graders. Contact the Coordinator for Educational Outreach and Student Programs for more information.

Visit in Engineering Week (VIEW) Summer Program at Pennsylvania State University

Pennsylvania State University

Visit in Engineering Week (VIEW) Summer Program

Attn: Program Director

208 Hammond Building

University Park, PA 16802

800-848-9223

http://www.engr.psu.edu/mep/VIEW.htm

The Pennsylvania State University invites rising high school freshman, sophomores, and juniors to apply to its Visit in Engineering Week (VIEW) residential summer program. Participants must be academically talented, motivated, and genuinely interested in computer engineering or other engineering disciplines. Members of underrepresented minority groups are especially encouraged to apply. There are three-week long VIEW sessions each summer for current juniors; freshmen and sophomores are invited to participate in a three-day program. Each session provides experiences in design, modeling and implementation, communications, group dynamics, and project management. Participants explore many different areas within the field of engineering and also sample college life as an engineering student.

Women in the Sciences and Engineering (WISE) Week at Pennsylvania State University

Pennsylvania State University

319 Boucke Building

University Park, PA 16802

814-865-3342

WISE@psu.edu

http://www.equity.psu.edu/wise/wisecamp.asp

The Pennsylvania State University (Penn State) offers a residential Women in the Sciences and Engineering (WISE) Week program each June for female rising juniors and seniors. Participants are academically talented with strong math and science skills, headed for college, and considering career paths in health, science, and engineering. Members of minority groups and students with physical disabilities are strongly encouraged to apply. For further information about WISE Week and the application process, contact the program.

Worcester Pipeline Collaborative (WPC)
University of Massachusetts
26 Queen Street
Worcester, MA 01610
508-856-4559
http://www.umassmed.edu/wpc
The WPC helps minority and/or disadvantaged students
   in Central Massachusetts learn more about health
   care and science professions. The WPC partnership
   includes professionals and K-20 educators from
   public schools, colleges, universities, biotechnology,
   health care, and science industries. The WPC offers
   a mentoring program for elementary, middle, high
   school, and college students; internships for high
   school students at select high schools; a shadowing
   program for seventh and eighth grade students, a
   summer science camp for sixth, seventh, and eighth
   graders; and other programs. Contact the WPC for
   more information.

**Young Engineering and Science Scholars Program
   at California Institute of Technology**
California Institute of Technology
Office of Minority Student Affairs
Mail Code 255-86
Pasadena, CA 91125
626-395-6207
yess@caltech.edu
http://www.yess.caltech.edu
The Young Engineering and Science Scholars Program
   introduces minority high school sophomores and
   juniors to careers in science and engineering via a
   three-week summer program. This residential program
   offers lectures, research and laboratory work, field
   trips, faculty speakers, and an interactive workshop on
   the complete college admissions process. Applicants
   are typically from ethnic groups (such as Native
   American, Hispanic American, and African American)
   that are traditionally underrepresented in science
   and engineering—although students from all ethnic
   groups are considered.

INTERNSHIPS

ACT Inc.

500 ACT Drive, PO Box 168
Iowa City, IA 52243-0168
http://www.act.org/humanresources/jobs/intern.html
ACT Inc., a nonprofit educational testing and assessment organization, offers a Summer Internship Program for doctoral students interested in careers related to assessment and educational studies. The eight-week program has a special goal of increasing the number of women and minorities in measurement and related fields. Internships are available in four categories: Educational and Social Research, Industrial-Organizational Psychology, Psychometrics and Statistics, and Career and Vocational Psychology. Interns receive a stipend of $5,000 and round-trip transportation between their graduate institution and Iowa City (the headquarters of ACT Inc.).

American Association of Advertising Agencies

405 Lexington Avenue, 18th Floor
New York, NY 10174-1801
212-682-2500
ameadows@aaaa.org
http://www.aaaa.org/diversity/maip/about.htm
The MultiCultural Advertising Intern Program (MAIP) program encourages African American, Asian American, Hispanic American, and Native American college students to consider careers in advertising. In recent years, the program has been expanding with more students and more agencies becoming involved. Each year, approximately 50 to 70 qualified undergraduate and graduate students are selected from colleges and universities nationwide to spend 10 summer weeks interning at member agencies in various U.S. cities. The top MAIP intern receives a scholarship of $5,000.

American College of Healthcare Executives

One North Franklin, Suite 1700
Chicago, IL 60606-3424
312-424-2800
hr-intern-fellow@ache.org
http://www.ache.org/carsvcs/internship.cfm
The American College of Healthcare Executives offers three-month summer internships to students who are interested in careers in health care management. Interns rotate through the college's major divisions, including administration, communications and marketing, education, executive office, finance, health administration press, management information systems, membership, regional services, and research and development. Minorities who have completed at least one year of graduate study in health care or association management are eligible to apply. Interns receive a salary of approximately $16.60 per hour.

American Indian Science and Engineering Society (AISES)

Attn: Program Officer
2305 Renard, SE, Suite 200, PO Box 9828
Albuquerque, NM 87119-9828
505-765-1052
shirley@aises.org
http://www.aises.org/highered/internships/index.html
The AISES offers a 10-week summer internship program that provides its student members with opportunities to explore work at the following federal agencies: Bonneville Power Administration: Environment, Fish and Wildlife; Centers for Disease Control and Prevention; Central Intelligence Agency; NASA Goddard Space Flight Center; National Science Foundation; U.S. Department of Commerce; U.S. Department of State; and U.S. Department of Veterans Affairs. Applicants must be pursuing a degree at a college or university on a full-time basis; have a GPA of at least 3.0 (2.5 for the Bonneville Power internship); be college or university sophomores, juniors, seniors, or graduate students at the time their internship begins; and be U.S. citizens or permanent residents. Applicants who are pursuing education in the following fields will receive special consideration: accounting/finance, business, computer science/technology, economics, engineering, graphic design, health policy, health support, human resources/personnel, international relations, logistics, medical/premed, nursing, political science, psychology, public administration, and science (all fields). Interns receive a weekly stipend, a local transportation allowance, round-trip airfare or mileage to their internship site, and dormitory lodging.

Asian American Journalists Association (AAJA)

AP Internship
1182 Market Street, Suite 320
San Francisco, CA 94102

415-346-2051
national@aaja.org
http://www.aaja.org/programs/for_students/internships
The AAJA, in cooperation with the Associated Press (AP), offers the Associated Press Internship Program, a 12-week summer internship for college juniors and seniors and graduate students interested in careers in print journalism. Applicants who are nominated by the AAJA will receive strong consideration. Interns receive a paid internship at an AP bureau and have the opportunity to cover breaking news.

Asian American Journalists Association (AAJA)
Cox Reporting Internship
1182 Market Street, Suite 320
San Francisco, CA 94102
415-346-2051
national@aaja.org
http://www.aaja.org/programs/for_students/internships
The AAJA, in cooperation with Cox Newspapers, offers the Cox Reporting Internship. This summer internship offers one intern the opportunity to work as a general assignment reporter in the Cox Washington Bureau in Washington, D.C. Applicants must be college juniors or seniors, graduate students, or recent graduates with an interest in journalism. College newspaper experience or internship experience is preferred. A $300 weekly stipend, free airfare, and a furnished apartment are provided to interns.

Asian American Journalists Association (AAJA)
AAJA/Sports Journalism Institute Program
1182 Market Street, Suite 320
San Francisco, CA 94102
415-346-2051
national@aaja.org
http://www.aaja.org/programs/for_students/internships
The AAJA, in cooperation with Associated Press Sports Editors (APSE), offers the Sports Journalism Institute Program, a nine-week summer internship for Asian American college sophomores or juniors interested in sports journalism careers. Interns receive a paid internship in the sports department of a daily newspaper, the opportunity to attend and work at the APSE's annual convention, and a $500 scholarship on completion of the program.

Asian American Journalists Association (AAJA)
AAJA/NPR Internship
1182 Market Street, Suite 320

San Francisco, CA 94102
415-346-2051
national@aaja.org
http://www.aaja.org/programs/for_students/internships
The AAJA, in cooperation with National Public Radio, offers 10-week internships to AAJA student members in Washington, D.C., each summer. Students receive a stipend for the 10 weeks, but are responsible for paying for their travel to and from Washington, DC.

Asian American Journalists Association (AAJA)
Siani Lee Broadcast Internship
1182 Market Street, Suite 320
San Francisco, CA 94102
415-346-2051
national@aaja.org
http://www.aaja.org/programs/for_students/internships
The AAJA offers the Siani Lee Broadcast Internship for Television, which is hosted each summer by CBS affiliate KYW-TV in Philadelphia, Pennsylvania. Applicants must be at least 18 years of age, have an interest in broadcast journalism, have a GPA of at least 2.7 (3.0 in major courses), and be currently enrolled in a postsecondary institution that offers credit for the internship. Interns receive a stipend of $2,500 to help cover travel and lodging costs.

Asian Immigrant Women Advocates
310 Eighth Street, Suite 301
Oakland, CA 94607
510-268-0192
info@aiwa.org
http://www.aiwa.org
This organization seeks to empower low-income Asian immigrant women. It offers unpaid internships throughout the year. Hours and length of internship are flexible.

AT&T Undergraduate Research Program
Attn: AT&T Labs Fellowship Administrator
Room C103
180 Park Avenue
Florham Park, NJ 07932-0971
http://public.research.att.com/index.cfm?portal=20
The AT&T Labs Fellowship Program seeks to assist women and minority U.S. citizens in computer science, math, statistics, electrical engineering, operations research, systems engineering, industrial engineering, or related fields. The Fellowship covers all school-related expenses during the academic year. Candidates

should be available to participate in a research internship during the first summer of their fellowship. Interns work on individual projects that are part of ongoing research in the lab.

Aunt Lute Books

PO Box 410687
San Francisco, CA 94141
415-826-1300
books@auntlute.com
http://www.auntlute.com

Aunt Lute Books is a nonprofit, multicultural women's press. Aunt Lute Books seeks part-time, unpaid interns to assist in all phases of book production, including order fulfillment, marketing, Web research, grants, and book production. Interns work a minimum of 10 hours a week for six months or one semester. Academic credit may be arranged; a number of informal classes on publishing are given.

Chips Quinn Scholars

Attn: Karen Catone, Director
Freedom Forum
1101 Wilson Boulevard
Arlington, VA 22209
703-284-3934
kcatone@freedomforum.org
http://www.chipsquinn.org

College juniors, seniors, and graduates with journalism majors or career goals in newspapers may apply for the Chips Quinn Scholars program, a paid training and internship opportunities for minority students. Programs are offered in the spring and summer. Interns participate in a four-day orientation in Arlington, Virginia, which is followed by a 10- to 12-week internship at a newspaper. Applicants must be U.S. citizens or permanent residents and have a car.

Congressional Black Caucus Foundation

1720 Massachusetts Avenue, NW
Washington, DC 20036
202-263-2800
info@cbcfinc.org
http://www.cbcfinc.org/Leadership%20Education/Internships/summer.html

The foundation's Congressional Internship Program offers undergraduate students the opportunity to learn about government in the office of a Congressional Black Caucus Member. Interns in this nine-week summer program receive a $2,500 stipend to cover personal expenses and free housing in the District of Columbia. Applicants must be interested in the legislative and public policy processes, demonstrate academic achievement and leadership, and contribute to their communities. The foundation also offers a fall and spring internship program.

Congressional Hispanic Caucus Institute

911 Second Street, NE
Washington, DC 20002
202-543-1771
http://www.chci.org/chciyouth/internship/internships.htm

The caucus offers an eight-week summer internship program to Hispanic American students. Interns work in the offices of U.S. representatives and receive firsthand knowledge of how government works. They also participate in a community service project in Washington, D.C., and attend weekly policy discussion sessions with political and business leaders. Applicants must be currently enrolled undergraduate students, have a GPA of at least 3.0, be U.S. citizens or permanent legal residents, have strong writing and analytical skills, and show evidence of participation in public service-oriented activities. The caucus provides participants with a $2,000 stipend, domestic round-trip transportation to Washington, D.C., and housing.

Dow Jones Newspaper Fund

4300 Route One North, PO Box 300
South Brunswick, NJ 08852
609-452-2820
newsfund@wsj.dowjones.com
http://djnewspaperfund.dowjones.com/fund/cs_internships.asp

The Dow Jones Newspaper Fund offers a summer Business Reporting Internship for minority sophomores and juniors interested in careers in business journalism. Interns begin the program by attending a one-week training seminar at New York University's Department of Journalism and Mass Communication and then spend nine weeks covering business and consumer news at a daily newspaper or news service. Weekly salaries for interns start at $350. Scholarships of $1,000 are awarded to students who return to college full time at the completion of their internship.

Dow Jones Newspaper Fund, Newspaper Copy Editing Internship

4300 Route One North, PO Box 300
South Brunswick, NJ 08852
609-452-2820
newsfund@wsj.dowjones.com
http://djnewspaperfund.dowjones.com/fund/cs_internships.asp

The Dow Jones Newspaper Fund offers a summer Newspaper Copy Editing Internship for minority sophomores and juniors and graduate students. Interns work as copy editors at daily newspapers. Weekly salaries for interns start at $350. Scholarships of $1,000 are awarded to students who return to college full-time at the completion of their internship.

Dow Jones Newspaper Fund, Sports Copy Editing Internship

4300 Route One North, PO Box 300
South Brunswick, NJ 08852
609-452-2820
newsfund@wsj.dowjones.com
http://djnewspaperfund.dowjones.com/fund/cs_internships.asp

The Dow Jones Newspaper Fund offers a summer Sports Copy Editing Internship for minority students. Interns work at sports copy desks at daily newspapers and attend two-week seminars at the University of Nebraska-Lincoln. Weekly salaries for interns start at $350. Scholarships of $1,000 are awarded to students who return to college full-time at the completion of their internship.

Fermilab National Accelerator Laboratory

Fermilab Summer Internships in Science and Technology for Minority Students
PO Box 500, MS 117
Batavia, IL 60510-0500
630-840-3415
sist@fnal.gov
http://sist.fnal.gov

The laboratory offers paid summer internships to minorities who have been historically underrepresented in science and technology. Applicants must have completed at least one year of education at a four-year institution in the United States, be U.S. citizens or foreign nationals with proper work visas, and have a GPA of at least 3.0. Preference will be given to qualifying students of Native American, Hispanic American, and African American ethnicities.

Harvard School of Public Health

Attn: Ms. Janice Stenger
Division of Biological Sciences
665 Huntington Avenue, Building 1-1312
Boston, MA 02115-6021
617-432-4470
dbs@hsph.harvard.edu
http://www.hsph.harvard.edu/sip

The Undergraduate Internship Program for Minority Students is designed to expose minority college science students to the rewards of research directed toward solving important public health problems such as cancer, cardiovascular disease, infections, etc. To qualify for this program, applicants must be U.S. citizens or permanent residents and a member of an ethnic group currently underrepresented in science: African American, Mexican American, Chicano, Native American (American Indian, Aleut, Eskimo), Pacific Islander (Polynesian or Micronesian), or Puerto Rican. The nine-week summer internship includes a stipend of $3,200, a travel allowance of up to $475, and free dormitory housing.

Hispanic Association of Colleges and Universities

One Dupont Circle, NW, Suite 605
Washington, DC 20036
202-467-0893
HNIP@HACU.net
http://www.hnip.net

The Hispanic Association of Colleges and Universities' National Internship Program places Hispanic students in internships in a wide array of federal government and private organizations, including laboratories, hospitals, airports, national forests and parks, and departments of public affairs, accounting, human resources and information technology. Internships are offered in the spring, summer, and fall. Applicants should have a GPA of at least 3.0 on a 4.0 scale, be enrolled in an undergraduate or graduate degree program (and have completed their freshmen year before the their internship begins), and be able to work by law in the United States. Federal interns receive stipends that range from $420 to $520 by level of education and round-trip airfare. Compensation for corporate interns is set by the corporation.

Hispanic-Serving Health Professions Schools (HSHPS)

HSHPS/CDC Student Internship
1120 Connecticut Avenue, NW, Suite 260
Washington, DC 20036

202-293-2701
mconde@hshps.com
http://www.studentinternshipprogram.com
Hispanic-Serving Health Professions Schools, in
cooperation with the Centers for Disease Control
(CDC) and Prevention, offers the HSHPS/CDC Student
Internship Program. The program was created to
"foster the development of public health and research
skills of Hispanic medical and public health students
in order to increase the number of students who
pursue careers in epidemiology, preventive medicine,
and public health research." Applicants must be
currently enrolled in a master's or doctoral program
at an HSHPS-member institution, be U.S. citizens or a
permanent residents, and have an interest in Hispanic
health issues. The program is targeted toward
Hispanic students, but students from all backgrounds
may apply. Program participants receive stipends that
range from $2,000 to $2,500; free transportation to
Atlanta, Georgia (where the program is held); partial
coverage of local travel expenses; and free housing.

INROADS Inc.

10 South Broadway, Suite 300
St. Louis, MO 63102
314-241-7488
info@inroads.org
http://www.inroads.org/interns/internPublic.jsp
INROADS is an organization that seeks to develop and
place minority youth in business and industry via paid
internships with Fortune 1000 companies. Applicants
for internships must have an interest in allied health
care, business, computers and information sciences,
engineering, health care management, marketing,
or sales; be graduating high school seniors, college
freshmen, or college sophomores; have a B average or
above; have a combined SAT score of at least 1000 or
an ACT score of 20 or better; demonstrate leadership
ability; and plan to or currently pursuing a bachelor's
degree in one of the aforementioned fields.

Institute for Tribal Environmental Professionals

Northern Arizona University
PO Box 86011
Flagstaff, AZ 86011
928-523-9555
ITEP@nau.edu
http://www4.nau.edu/eeop/eeop_internships.html
This organization offers the Environmental Education
Outreach Program, which coordinates summer

programs and internships in environmental science
for Native American students with the Environmental
Protection Agency and with tribal environmental
offices.

InternJobs.com

http://www.internjobs.com
InternJobs.com is a searchable database of internships
located throughout the world. You can search by
geographic location, type of job, or keyword (such as
"minorities").

Internships.com

Internships LLC
2020 Pennsylvania Avenue, NW, PMB 336
Washington, DC 20006
http://internships.com
This useful Web site provides a database of internships.
The database is searchable by major (such as African
American Studies, Asian Studies, etc.) and country.

Kaiser Family Foundation

Attn: Penny Duckham, Executive Director
Kaiser Media Fellowships Program
2400 Sand Hill Road
Menlo Park, CA 94025
650-234-9220
pduckham@kff.org
http://www.kff.org/about/mediainternships.cfm
Kaiser Media Internship in Health Reporting provides
work experience to minority college or graduate
students who want to specialize in health reporting.
Minority college or graduate students studying
journalism or a related field may apply for this 12-
week, summer program if their career goals are to be
reporters on health matters. This program provides a
stipend of $500 per week and all travel expenses.

The Leadership Alliance

015 Sayles Hall, Box 1963
Providence, RI 02912
401-863-1474
http://www.theleadershipalliance.org/html/under.html
The Leadership Alliance is an alliance of 31 top research
and teaching academic institutions "dedicated to
improving the participation of underserved and
underrepresented students in graduate studies and
Ph.D. programs." Its Leadership Alliance Summer
Research Early Identification Program offers
underrepresented minorities the chance to participate

in an eight- to 10-week internship with a mentor at an Alliance institution. Interns must present a written report and/or abstract and complete a program evaluation at the end of the program. Applicants must have a GPA of at least 3.0; have completed at least two semesters, but have at least one semester of undergraduate study remaining, at the beginning of their internship; plan to pursue graduate study; and be U.S. citizens or permanent residents.

MANA, A National Latina Organization

Internships
1725 K Street, NW, Suite 201
Washington, DC 20006
202-833-0060
hermana2@aol.com
http://www.hermana.org
MANA seeks to empower Hispanic women through leadership development and community action. In addition to scholarships, MANA offers the opportunity to gain valuable educational and work experience through internships at its national headquarters in Washington, D.C., as well as at the local chapter level.

mun2 Television

Telemundo
2470 West Eighth Avenue
Hialeah, FL 33010
305-882-8700
mcampirano@latcominc.com
http://www.mun2television.com
Hispanic students studying communications, broadcasting, and marketing can participate in the mun2 internship program sponsored by mun2 Television, Telemundo's cable channel for young Hispanics. The four-month unpaid internship is offered throughout the year in Los Angeles, California; Miami, Florida; New York, New York; San Antonio, Texas; and San Jose, California. Applicants must be enrolled in an accredited college or university, able to earn academic credit for the internship, and willing to work a minimum of three nights a week.

National Action Council for Minorities in Engineering

440 Hamilton Avenue, Suite 302
White Plains, NY 10601-1813
914-539-4010
http://www.nacme.org/university
The council offers an online resume directory that lists internship opportunities at partner companies

that share its goal of increasing the number of underrepresented minorities in engineering.

National Association of Black Journalists (NABJ)

University of Maryland
8701-A Adelphi Road
Adelphi, MD 20783-1716
301-445-7100
nabj@nabj.org
http://www.nabj.org/programs/internships/index.html
The NABJ provides summer internships to African American students who are interested in pursuing careers in journalism. Students participate in 10-week paid internships with newspapers, television and radio stations, and online news services throughout the United States. Internships are available in print journalism (reporting, business reporting, health reporting, copy editing, and graphic design), broadcast journalism (radio and television), online journalism, sports journalism, and photojournalism. Applicants must have prior journalism experience (collegiate or professional), be members of the NABJ, and meet other specific requirements based on the type of internship in which they wish to participate. Interns receive $400 to $600 a week. They must pay for transportation, housing, and other living expenses.

National Association of Latino Elected and Appointed Officials (NALEO)

Attn: Lourdes Ferrer
1122 West Washington Boulevard, 3rd Floor
Los Angeles, CA 90015
213-747-7606, ext. 127
http://www.naleo.org
The NALEO Educational Fund, in cooperation with Ford Motor Company, offers the NALEO Ford Motor Company Fellows Program to help Hispanic students learn about government and public policy. Fellows participate in workshops, attend NALEO's annual conference, and complete a five-week internship with a member of Congress or at a federal agency in Washington, D.C. Applicants must be Hispanic; be U.S. citizens or legal residents; live in California, Florida, Illinois, Michigan, Texas, or Puerto Rico (note: additional interns will be selected from a pool of national applicants); and be rising seniors, graduate students, or recent graduates. Fellows receive a $1,500 stipend; free airfare to and from San Juan, Puerto Rico, and Washington, D.C.; and housing accommodations while participating in NALEO-sponsored activities.

National Association of Latino Elected and Appointed Officials (NALEO)
Attn: Lourdes Ferrer
1122 West Washington Boulevard, 3rd Floor
Los Angeles, CA 90015
213-747-7606, ext. 127
http://www.naleo.org
The NALEO Educational Fund, in cooperation with Shell Oil Company, offers the Shell Legislative Internship Program to help Hispanic students learn about government at all levels.

National Heart, Lung, and Blood Institute
PO Box 30105
Bethesda, MD 20824-0105
301-592-8573
http://www.nhlbi.nih.gov
The Minority Institutional Research Training Program is a National Research Service Award Program intended to support training of graduate and health professional students and individuals in postdoctoral training at minority schools. Training is intended to increase students' awareness of cardiovascular, pulmonary, hematologic, and sleep disorders. Applicants must have a strong career interest in cardiovascular, pulmonary, hematologic, or sleep disorders research. They must also be U.S. citizens, noncitizen nationals, or legal permanent residents of the United States.

100 Hispanic Women Inc.
358 Fifth Avenue, Suite 504
New York, NY 10001
212-239-1430
http://www.100hispanicwomen.org/scholarships/index.html
100 Hispanic Women Inc., a nonprofit, nonpartisan women's organization, provides internship and other training opportunities to female Hispanic students via its Young Latinas Leadership Institute. Contact the organization for details.

Smithsonian Institution
Office of Fellowships
750 Ninth Street, NW, Suite 9300
MRC 902, PO Box 37012
Washington, DC 20013-7012
202-275-0655
siofg@si.edu
http://www.si.edu/ofg/intern.htm
The Smithsonian Institution's Office of Fellowships offers the James E. Webb Internship for Minority Undergraduate Seniors and Graduate Students in Business and Public Administration. Interns work in offices, museums, and research institutes throughout the Smithsonian Institution. Undergraduate seniors and graduate students majoring in areas of business or public administration may apply. Internships last 10 weeks and are available each summer. Interns receive a stipend of $450 per week.

Smithsonian Institution
Office of Fellowships
750 Ninth Street, NW, Suite 9300
MRC 902, PO Box 37012
Washington, DC 20013-7012
202-275-0655
siofg@si.edu
http://www.si.edu/ofg/intern.htm
The Smithsonian Institution's Office of Fellowships offers 10-week internships to minority undergraduate and beginning graduate students "who are underrepresented in Smithsonian scholarly programs, in the disciplines of research conducted at the Institution, and in the museum field." Internships are available in the spring, summer, and fall. Interns receive a stipend of $400 per week.

Smithsonian Institution
Office of Fellowships
750 Ninth Street, NW, Suite 9300
MRC 902, PO Box 37012
Washington, DC 20013-7012
202-275-0655
siofg@si.edu
http://www.si.edu/ofg/intern.htm
The Smithsonian Institution's Office of Fellowships provides 10-week internships to Native American undergraduate and graduate students to participate in "internship projects related to Native American topics and using Native American resources at the Smithsonian." Internships are available in the spring, summer, and fall. Interns receive a stipend of $400 per week and a travel allowance.

Student Action With Farmworkers
Attn: Lupe Huitron, Apprentice/Internship Coordinator
1317 West Pettigrew Street
Durham, NC 27705
919-660-3652
itfcampo@duke.edu

http://www-cds.aas.duke.edu/saf/internship.htm
Student Action With Farmworkers is a non-profit organization that brings students and farmworkers together to work for fairness in agriculture. Participants in its Into the Fields Internship Program work in migrant education programs, rural health clinics, legal services, immigrant assistance organizations, policy and research groups, and with community and labor organizing projects in North and South Carolina. Interns receive a $1,200 stipend, free housing, a post-service scholarship of $1,500, and potential academic credit.

StudentJobs.gov

http://www.studentjobs.gov
StudentJobs.gov provides a searchable database of jobs and internships with the federal government. The database is searchable by keyword, geographic location, occupation, and other criteria.

United Negro College Fund (UNCF)

UNCF Corporate Scholars Program
8260 Willow Oaks Corporate Drive
Fairfax, VA 22031
866-671-7237
internship@uncf.org
http://www.uncf.org/internships/index.asp
The UNCF's Corporate Scholars Program helps African American students obtain valuable experience in corporate settings via paid internships. Eligibility requirements vary by internship. Contact the UNCF for more information.

United States Hispanic Leadership Institute

431 South Dearborn Street, Suite 1203
Chicago, IL 60605
312-427-8683
ushli@aol.com
http://www.ushli.com/leadershipprg.htm
The 21st Century Leaders Internship Program is a paid 10-week summer internship program that helps Hispanic college students learn how to be strong community organizers and leaders. Interns work closely with elected officials or directors of community organizations with the overall goal of registering 500 new voters.

Utah Department of Health

Office of Ethnic Health
288 North 1460 West
Salt Lake City, UT 84116
hledo.chazots@state.ut.us
http://health.utah.gov
The Utah Department of Health offers a part-time paid internship to minority students through the UDOH Ethnic Health Workforce Program. The intern works within the Office of Ethnic Health on various projects aimed to ensure that Utah's ethnic populations are adequately served and represented in respect to health services. The student will have a background in sociology, ethnic studies, anthropology, family and consumer studies, or related subject with a demonstrated interest in ethnic minority issues.

Washington Center for Internships and Academic Seminars

2301 M Street, NW, 5th Floor
Washington, DC 20037
202-336-7600
info@twc.edu
http://www.twc.edu
The Washington Center for Internships and Academic Seminars is a nonprofit organization that provides internships to students (including minorities) in the Washington, D.C., metropolitan area. Program components include a week-long academic seminar to develop students' leadership skills; an internship experience affording them the chance to compare theory with daily experience within a given academic field; and an academic course that challenges fellows to connect their academic background with their respective field experiences. Applicants must be at least college sophomores and have a GPA of at least 2.75. The center charges a fee for its internship programs; 80 percent of program participants receive some form of financial assistance.

WetFeet Inc.

The Folger Building
101 Howard Street, Suite 300
San Francisco, CA 94105
415-284-7900
http://wetfeet.internshipprograms.com
WetFeet is a recruiting organization that helps large companies locate the most-qualified workers. Visit its Web site to access its Internship Search Engine, which allows you to search thousands of internship opportunities by geographic location and career. WetFeet also offers The Ideal Internship, a print and online resource that provides advice and resources on landing an internship.

Women's Sports Foundation
Attn: Intern Program Manager
Eisenhower Park
East Meadow, NY 11554
800-227-3988
wosport@aol.com
http://www.womenssportsfoundation.org/cgi-bin/iowa/
funding
Women of color who are interested in learning more
about sports-related careers are eligible to apply for
Jackie Joyner-Kersee/Minority Internships. Applicants
may be undergraduate students, graduate students,
or adults. Interns must be willing to participate
in an internship (typically 40 hours a week) at the
foundation's headquarters in East Meadow, New York.
Stipends range from $450 to $1,000 a month. College
credit for the internship is also possible.

Women's Sports Foundation
Attn: Intern Program Manager
Eisenhower Park
East Meadow, NY 11554
800-227-3988
wosport@aol.com
http://www.womenssportsfoundation.org/cgi-bin/iowa/
funding
Women of color who are interested in learning more
about sports-related careers are eligible to apply for
Zina Garrison/Minority Internships. Undergraduate
students, graduate students, and adults may apply.
Interns must be willing to participate in an internship
(typically 40 hours a week) at the foundation's
headquarters in East Meadow, New York. Stipends
range from $600 to $1,000 a month. College credit
for the internship is also possible.

Worcester Art Museum
55 Salisbury Street
Worcester, MA 01609
508-799-4406, ext. 3014
katrinastacy@worcesterart.org
http://www.worcesterart.org/Education/mip.html
The museum offers summer internships to minority
students from the central Massachusetts area. Interns
work with museum professionals in the five major
divisions of the Museum: education, curatorial,
administration, marketing, and development. The
internships last eight weeks and interns receive $9
an hour.

Y.E.S. TO JOBS
PO Box 3390
Los Angeles, CA 90078-3390
http://www.yestojobs.org
Y.E.S. TO JOBS provides internship opportunities to
minority high school and college students to help
introduce them to behind-the-scenes careers in the
entertainment industry. High school internships
are full time and last eight to 10 weeks. They are
available in Atlanta, Georgia; Los Angeles, California;
Nashville, Tennessee; Miami, Florida; New York, New
York; Washington, D.C.; and other cities. Applicants
must be 16 to 18 years of age, have a GPA of at least
2.8, and have an attendance record of at least 90
percent. College internships are offered year round
in Los Angeles and New York. Applicants must be
between the ages of 18 and 24, enrolled in a college
or university, and have a GPA of at least 2.5. Interns are
typically paid minimum wage and must provide their
own housing and transportation.

MINORITY STUDIES AND MINORITY RESEARCH PROGRAMS

Minority studies/research programs typically conduct interdisciplinary scholarship and research relating to a particular ethnic group. This section offers a listing of professional organizations that provide support to minority studies scholars and researchers and a listing of colleges and universities that have minority studies programs (majors, minors, and concentrations) and research centers on campus. Minority groups covered in this section include African Americans, Asian Americans, Hispanic Americans, and Native Americans.

PROFESSIONAL ORGANIZATIONS

Association for Asian American Studies
Asian American Studies Program
Cornell University
420 Rockefeller Hall
Ithaca, NY 14853-2502
607-255-3320
ssh13@cornell.edu
http://www.aaastudies.org/index.tpl

Association for the Study of American Indian Literatures
Attn: Siobhan Senier
University of New Hampshire
Department of English
Hamilton Smith Hall, 95 Main Street
Durham, NH 03824
http://oncampus.richmond.edu/faculty/ASAIL

Consortium of Latin American Studies Programs
Attn: Stone Center for Latin American Studies
Tulane University
100 Jones Hall
New Orleans, LA 70118-5698
504-865-5164
http://www.claspprograms.org

National Association of African American Studies
PO Box 325
Biddeford, ME 04005-0325
207-839-8004
naaasconference@earthlink.net
http://www.naaas.org

COLLEGES AND UNIVERSITIES
African American
Amherst College
Department of Black Studies
PO Box 5000
Amherst, MA 01002-5000
413-542-5800
blackstudies@amherst.edu
http://www.amherst.edu/~blackstudies

California State University-Los Angeles
Department of Pan-African Studies
5151 State University Drive
Los Angeles, CA 90032
323-343-2290
pas@calstatela.edu
http://www.calstatela.edu/academic/pas

Clark Atlanta University
African and African American Studies Program
223 James P. Brawley Drive, SW
Atlanta, GA 30314
404-880-6810
jbradley@cau.edu
http://www.cau.edu/acad_prog/default.html

Colby College
African American Studies Department
4705 Mayflower Hill Drive
Waterville, ME 04901
207-872-3133
ctgilkes@colby.edu
http://www.colby.edu/afr.amer

Columbia University
School of International and Public Affairs
Institute of African-American Studies
1103 International Affairs Building
420 West 118th Street, Mail Code 3331
New York, NY 10027
212-854-4633
http://www.columbia.edu/cu/sipa/regional/ias

Cornell University
Africana Studies and Research Center
310 Triphammer Road

Ithaca, NY 14853-2599
607-255-4625
spt1@cornell.edu
http://www.asrc.cornell.edu

Duke University
African and African American Studies
John Hope Franklin Center
2204 Erwin Road, Box 90252
Durham, NC 27708
919-684-2830
blackmor@duke.edu
http://www.duke.edu/web/africanameric/grad.html

Florida International University
African New World Studies
University Park
11200 SW Eighth Street DM298A
Miami, FL 33199
305-348-6860
africaup@fiu.edu
http://www.fiu.edu/~africana

Georgetown University
African American Studies
37th and O Streets, NW
Washington, DC 20057
202-687-6376
alm22@georgetown
http://www.georgetown.edu/departments/
    africanamericanstudies

Harvard University
Department of African and African American Studies
12 Quincy Street, Barker Center, 2nd Floor
Cambridge, MA 02138
617-495-4113
http://www.fas.harvard.edu/~afroam

Indiana University
Department of African American and African Diaspora
    Studies
Memorial Hall M18, 1021 East Third Street
Bloomington, IN 47405
812-855-3875
aaads@indiana.edu
http://www.indiana.edu/~afroamer

Morehouse College
Department of African-American Studies
Brawley Hall, 830 Westview Drive, SW, Room 212

Atlanta, GA 30314
404-681-2800
http://www.morehouse.edu/academics/humsocsci/
    africanamericanstudies/index.html

Morgan State University
Department of History and Geography
Holmes Hall, 1700 East Cold Spring Lane, Room 326-I
Baltimore, MD 21251
443-885-3190
apalmer@moac.morgan.edu
http://www.morgan.edu/academics/Grad-Studies/
    programs/aframer.asp

Ohio State University
Department of African American and African Studies
486 University Hall, 230 North Oval Mall
Columbus, OH 43210
614-292-3700
Boykin.1@osu.edu
http://aaas.osu.edu

Princeton University
Program in African American Studies
112 Dickinson Hall
Princeton, NJ 08544
609-258-4270
jeanw@princeton.edu
http://www.princeton.edu/%7Eaasprog/homepage.html

Temple University
Department of African American Studies
810 Gladfelter Hall, 1115 West Berks Street
Philadelphia, PA 19122
215-204-8491
afam@temple.edu
http://www.temple.edu/AAS

University of California-Berkeley
Department of African American Studies
688 Barrows Hall, #2572
Berkeley, CA 94720
510-642-7972
lherbert@berkeley.edu
http://violet.berkeley.edu/~africam

University of California-Los Angeles
Interdepartmental Program in Afro-American Studies
160 Haines Hall, Box 951545
Los Angeles, CA 90095

310-825-7403
http://www.afro-am.ucla.edu

University of California-Santa Barbara
Department of Black Studies
South Hall, Room 3631
Santa Barbara, CA 93106-3150
805-893-3800
http://www.blackstudies.ucsb.edu/index.html

University of Georgia
Institute for African American Studies
312 Holmes/Hunter Academic Building
Athens, GA 30602
706-542-5197
afam@arches.uga.edu
http://www.uga.edu/iaas

University of Iowa
African-American World Studies Program
436 English-Philosophy Building
Iowa City, IA 52242-1408
319-335-0317
afam-world-studies@uiowa.edu
http://english.uiowa.edu/africanamerican

University of Maryland-College Park
African American Studies Department
2169 LeFrak Hall
College Park, MD 20742
http://www.bsos.umd.edu/aasp

University of Massachusetts-Amherst
Department of Black Studies
PO Box 5000
Amherst, MA 01002-5000
413-542-5800
http://www.amherst.edu/~blackstudies

University of Nebraska-Omaha
Department of Black Studies
6001 Dodge Street, 184 Arts and Sciences Hall
Omaha, NE 68182
402-554-2412
http://www.unomaha.edu/wwwblst

University of North Carolina-Chapel Hill
Department of African and Afro-American Studies
Battle Hall, CB#3395
Chapel Hill, NC 27599-3395

919-966-5496
http://www.unc.edu/depts/afriafam

University of Pennsylvania
Center for Africana Studies
3401 Walnut Street, Suite 331A
Philadelphia, PA 19104-6228
215-898-4965
africana@sas.upenn.edu
http://www.sas.upenn.edu/africana

University of Texas-Austin
Center for African and African American Studies
One University Station, Jester Center A232A
Austin, TX 78705
512-471-1784
caaas@uts.cc.utexas.edu
http://www.utexas.edu/cola/depts/caaas

University of Virginia
Carter G. Woodson Institute for Afro-American
    and African Studies
108 Minor Hall, PO Box 400162
Charlottesville, VA 22904-4162
434-924-3109
woodson@gwis.virginia.edu
http://www.virginia.edu/woodson/courses/courses.
    html

University of Wisconsin-Madison
Department of Afro-American Studies
600 North Park, 4141 HC White
Madison, WI 53706
608-263-1642
jscomsto@wisc.edu
http://polyglot.lss.wisc.edu/aas

Xavier University
Institute for Black Catholic Studies
One Drexel Drive, Box 49
New Orleans, LA 70125
504-520-7691
IBCS@xula.edu
http://www.xula.edu/IBCS

Yale University
African American Studies Program
493 College Street, Yale Station, PO Box 203388
New Haven, CT 06520-3388
203-432-1170

robert.stepto@yale.edu
http://www.yale.edu/afamstudies

Asian American
Arizona State University
Asian Pacific American Studies Program
Social Sciences Building, Room 100, PO Box 874401
Tempe, AZ 85287-4401
480-965-9711
apastudies@asu.edu
http://www.asu.edu/clas/apas

California State University-Fullerton
Asian American Studies Program
800 North State College Boulevard, Humanities 314
Fullerton, CA 92834-6868
714-278-4099
bgreen@fullerton.edu
http://hss.fullerton.edu/asian-american

California State University-Long Beach
Department of Asian and Asian American Studies
1250 Bellflower Boulevard
Long Beach, CA 90840-1002
562-985-4645
akamin@csulb.edu
http://www.csulb.edu/depts/as

California State University-Northridge
Asian American Studies Department
18111 Nordhoff Street
Northridge, CA 91330-8251
818-677-4966
teresa.k.williams@csun.edu
http://www.csun.edu/aas

City University of New York-Hunter College
Asian American Studies Program
695 Park Avenue, Room 503, Thomas Hunter
New York, NY 10021
212-772-5559
goh@hunter.cuny.edu
http://www.hunter.cuny.edu/aasp

City University of New York-Queens College
Asian/American Center
Kissena Hall, Room 315
65-30 Kissena Boulevard
Flushing, NY 11367
718-997-3050

HWu@Qc1.Qc.edu
http://qcpages.qc.cuny.edu/cmal

Claremont McKenna College
Intercollegiate Department of Asian American Studies
Seaman Hall, #222
Claremont, CA 91711
909-607-2828
david.yoo@claremontmckenna.edu
http://programs.academic.claremontmckenna.edu/
    asian-american-studies

Columbia University
Center for the Study of Ethnicity and Race
Asian American Studies Program
424 Hamilton Hall, 1130 Amsterdam Avenue, MC 2880
New York, NY 10027
212-854-0507
gyo3@columbia.edu
http://www.columbia.edu/cu/cser

Cornell University
Department of Asian Studies
350 Rockefeller Hall
Ithaca, NY 14853
607-255-5095
http://lrc.cornell.edu/asian

Loyola Marymount University
Asian Pacific American Studies Program
One Loyola Marymount Drive
Los Angeles, CA 90045-8319
310-338-4491
epark@lmu.edu
http://bellarmine.lmu.edu/apam

New York University
Asian/Pacific/American Studies Program & Institute
41 East 11th Street, 7th Floor
New York, NY 10003
212-998-3700
apa.studies@nyu.edu
http://www.apa.nyu.edu

Northwestern University
Asian American Studies Program
Crowe Hall 1-117, 1860 Campus Drive,
Evanston, IL 60208-2166
847-467-7114
asianamerican@northwestern.edu
http://www.wcas.northwestern.edu/asianamerican

Pitzer College
Intercollegiate Department of Asian American Studies
Mead Hall 131, 1050 North Mills Avenue, Box A76
Claremont, CA 91711
909-607-9508
idaas@pomona.edu
http://www.idaas.pomona.edu/majorminor_pitzer.htm

San Francisco State University
Asian American Studies Department
1600 Holloway Avenue, PSY 103
San Francisco, CA 94132-4252
415-338-2698
aas@sfsu.edu
http://www.sfsu.edu/~aas

San Jose State University
Asian Studies Program
One Washington Square, FO 127
San Jose, CA 95192-0092
408-924-4465
http://www.sjsu.edu/asianstudies

Stanford University
Asian American Studies Program
Building 240, Room 110
Stanford, CA 94305-2152
650-723-8449
mibarra@stanford.edu
http://www.stanford.edu/dept/AAS/index.shtml

University of California-Berkeley
Department of Ethnic Studies
Asian American Studies
506 Barrows Hall, #2570
Berkeley, CA 94720-2570
510-642-6644
btung@uclink.berkeley.edu
http://socrates.berkeley.edu/~ethnicst

University of California-Davis
Asian American Studies Program
3102 Hart Hall
Davis, CA 95616
530-752-3625
ifujimoto@ucdavis.edu
http://asa.ucdavis.edu

University of California-Irvine
Department of Asian American Studies
300 Murray Krieger Hall

Irvine, CA 92697-6900
949-824-2746
mcclelld@uci.edu
http://www.hnet.uci.edu/aas

University of California-Los Angeles
Department of Asian American Studies
3230 Campbell Hall, Box 951546
Los Angeles, CA 90095-1546
310-825-2974
isoriano@ucla.edu
http://www.sscnet.ucla.edu/asianam

University of California-Santa Barbara
Department of Asian American Studies
5044 Humanities and Social Science Building
Santa Barbara, CA 93106
805-893-8039
phillips@asamst.ucsb.edu
http://www.asamst.ucsb.edu

University of Connecticut-Storrs
Asian American Studies Institute
354 Mansfield Road, U-2091
Storrs, CT 06269-2091
860-486-4751
fe.delos-santos@uconn.edu
http://asianamerican.uconn.edu

University of Illinois-Urbana-Champaign
Asian American Studies Program
1208 Nevada Street, MC 142
Urbana, IL 61801
217-244-9530
aasp@uiuc.edu
http://www.aasp.uiuc.edu

University of Massachusetts-Boston
Asian American Studies Program
100 Morrissey Boulevard
Boston, MA 02125-3393
617-287-5000
http://www.umb.edu/academics/undergraduate/asian_
    american_studies/index.html

University of Pennsylvania
Asian American Studies Program
166 McNeil Building
Philadelphia, PA 19104-6299
215-898-1782

asam@ccat.sas.upenn.edu
http://paachweb.vpul.upenn.edu/asamnew

University of Texas-Austin
Center for Asian American Studies
Geography Building, 210 West 24th Street, Suite 220
Austin, TX 78712-0135
512-471-1393
aas@austin.utexas.edu
http://www.utexas.edu/cola/depts/aas

University of Wisconsin-Madison
Asian American Studies Program
303 Ingraham Hall, 1155 Observatory Drive
Madison, WI 53705
608-263-2976
lbow@wisc.edu
http://polyglot.lss.wisc.edu/aasp

Hispanic American
Adelphi University
Center for Latin American Studies Program
Harvey Hall, Room 224, PO Box 701
Garden City, NY 11530-0701
516-877-4054
amador@adelphi.edu
http://academics.adelphi.edu/artsci/latam

Albright College
Johnson Center for Latin American Studies
13th and Bern Streets, PO Box 15234
Reading, PA 19612-5234
610-921-2381
betsyk@alb.edu
http://www.albright.edu/academics/depts/latin-
   american-studies.html

Allegheny College
Latin American Studies Center
Quigley Hall, 520 North Main
Meadville, PA 16335
814-332-3349
smattiac@allegheny.edu
http://webpub.allegheny.edu/group/LAS

American University
Department of Language and Foreign Studies
Latin American Studies
Asbury Building, 4400 Massachusetts Avenue, NW,
   Room 324

Washington, DC 20016
202-885-2381
lfs@american.edu
http://www.american.edu/cas/department_language.
   shtml

Arizona State University
Center for Latin American Studies
PO Box 874502
Tempe, AZ 85287-4502
480-965-5127
LatAm.Studies@asu.edu
http://www.asu.edu/clas/latin

Austin Community College
Latino/Latin American Studies Center
Building 2000, 3401 Webberville Road, Eastview Campus,
   Room 2127
Austin, TX 78702
512-223-5224
marianod@austincc.edu
http://www.austincc.edu/rss/centro/index.htm

Baylor University
Latin American Studies Program
One Bear Place 97206
Waco, TX 76798-7206
254-710-4531
Lilly_Fuertes@baylor.edu
http://www.baylor.edu/Latin_American/index.
   php?id=8637

Boston University
Department of International Relations
Interdisciplinary Program in Latin American Studies
152 Bay State Road
Boston, MA 02215
617-353-9279
ir@bu.edu
http://www.bu.edu/ir/las

Brandeis University
Latin American Studies Program
415 South Street, Mailstop 036
Waltham, MA 02454
781-736-2293
mbrooks@brandeis.edu
http://www.brandeis.edu/departments/latinam

Brigham Young University
David Kennedy Center for International Studies
211 HRCB
Provo, UT 84602
801-422-7151
kennedy@byu.edu
http://kennedy.byu.edu/academic/LAS/index.php

Brown University
Center for Latin American Studies
111 Thayer Street, Box 1970
Providence, RI 02912
401-863-2106
http://www.watsoninstitute.org/CLAS

Bucknell University
Latin American Studies Program
Moore Avenue
Lewisburg, PA 17837
570-577-2000
http://www.bucknell.edu/Academics/Academic_
    Programs/Latin_American_Studies/index.html

California State University-Chico
Office of International Programs
Latin American Studies Program
211 Tehama Hall, 400 West First Street
Chico, CA 95929
530-898-6880
grin@csuchico@edu
http://www.csuchico.edu/catalog/cat03/programs/inst/
    min_last.html

California State University-Fullerton
Latin American Studies Program
PO Box 6846
Fullerton, CA 92834-6846
714-278-3161
splinggi@fullerton.edu
http://hss.fullerton.edu/latinamerican

California State University-Los Angeles
Department of Latin American Studies
5151 State University Drive, KHB 3006
Los Angeles, CA 90032
323-343-2180
las@calstatela.edu
http://www.calstatela.edu/academic/las

Carleton College
Latin American Studies Program
One North College Street

Northfield, MN 55057
507-663-4204
jlevi@carleton.edu
http://www.acad.carleton.edu/curricular/ltam/index.
    html

Catholic University of America
Latin American Center for Graduate Studies in Music
620 Michigan Avenue, NE
Washington, DC 20064
202-319-5000
http://lamc.cua.edu

City University of New York-Brooklyn College
Caribbean Studies Program
3107 James Hall, 2900 Bedford Avenue
Brooklyn, NY 11210
718-951-4596
bthomas@brooklyn.cuny.edu
http://websql.brooklyn.cuny.edu/course_search/acad/
    dept_info.jsp?div=U&dept_code=11&dept_id=181

City University of New York-City College
Latin American and Latino Studies
160 Convent Avenue, NA 6/108B
New York, NY 10031
212-650-7527
ilopez@ccny.cuny.edu
http://www1.ccny.cuny.edu

City University of New York-Queens College
Latin American Studies
65-30 Kissena Boulevard
Flushing, NY 1136
718-997-2800
http://www.soc.qc.edu/laas

College of William and Mary
Hispanic Studies Program
PO Box 8795
Williamsburg, VA 23187-8795
757-221-3590
gxgree@wm.edu
http://www.wm.edu/modlang/hispanic_studies/index.
    php

Columbia University
Institute of Latin American Studies
420 West 118th Street, 8th Floor, IAB
New York, NY 10027
212-854-4643

majordomo@columbia.edu
http://www.columbia.edu/cu/ilas

Cornell University
Latin American Studies Program
190 Uris Hall
Ithaca, NY 14853-7801
607-255-3345
lasp@is.cornell.edu
http://www.einaudi.cornell.edu/LatinAmerica

Dartmouth College
Latin American, Latino, and Caribbean Studies
304B Silsby Hall
Hanover, NH 03755-18042
603-646-1640
israel.reyes@dartmouth.edu
http://www.dartmouth.edu/~lalacs

DePaul University
Latin American and Latino Studies Program
2320 North Kenmore Avenue, Schmitt Academic Center,
    #5 A-H
Chicago, IL 60614
773-325-4818
lalsp@depaul.edu
http://lals.velkat.com

Drake University
Latin American Studies
2507 University Avenue
Des Moines, IA 50311-4505
515-271-3181
http://www.choose.drake.edu/admissions/academic/
    programs/artsci/latinamerican.asp

Duke University
Duke Center for Latin American and Caribbean Studies
2114 Campus Drive, Box 90254
Durham, NC 27708-0255
919-681-3980
http://www.duke.edu/web/las

Emory University
Latin American and Caribbean Studies Program
1385 Oxford Road, NE, Suite 110
Atlanta, GA 30322
404-727-6562
lacs@emory.edu
http://www.lacsp.emory.edu

Flagler College
Department of Liberal Arts
Latin American Studies
PO Box 1027
St. Augustine, FL 32085-1027
904-829-6481
liberalstudies@flagler.edu
http://www.flagler.edu/academics/la.html

Florida International University
Latin American and Caribbean Center
University Park, DM 353
Miami, FL 33199
305-348-2894
lacc@fiu.edu
http://lacc.fiu.edu

George Mason University
Latin American Studies Program
Robinson, #B-371A
Fairfax, VA 22030
703-993-1010
mkarush@gmu.edu
http://chnm.gmu.edu/las

Georgetown University
Center for Latin American Studies
ICC484
Washington, DC 20057
202-687-0140
clas@georgetown.edu
http://www.georgetown.edu/sfs/programs/clas

Grand Valley State University
Latin American Studies
115 Lake Ontario Hall
Allendale, MI 49401
616-331-3898
ashmoret@gvsu.edu
http://www4.gvsu.edu/las

Grinnell College
Latin American Studies
PO Box 805
Grinnell, IA 50112-0806
641-269-4000
aparicio@grinnel.edu
http://web.grinnell.edu/latinamericanstudies

Harvard University
David Rockefeller Center for Latin American Studies
1730 Cambridge Street

Cambridge, MA 02138
617-495-3366
drclas@fas.harvard.edu
http://drclas.fas.harvard.edu

Hood College
Latin American Studies Center
401 Rosemont Avenue
Frederick, MD 21701
301-663-3131
http://www.hood.edu/academic/forlang/index.
    cfm?pid=_prog_latin_amer_study.htm

Indiana University
Center for Latin American and Caribbean Studies
1125 East Atwater Avenue
Bloomington, IN 47401
812-855-9097
clacs@indiana.edu
http://www.indiana.edu/~clacs

Johns Hopkins University
Program in Latin American Studies
3400 North Charles Street, Greenhouse 003
Baltimore, MD 21218
410-516-5488
plas@jhu.edu
http://web.jhu.edu/plas

Kansas State University
Latin American Studies Program
215 Eisenhower Hall
Manhattan, KS 66506-1004
785-532-1988
ias@ksu.edu
http://www.k-state.edu/ias/lassec.htm

Michigan State University
Center for Latin American and Caribbean Studies
300 Delia Koo International Academic Center
East Lansing, MI 48824
517-353-1690
clacs@msu.edu
http://www.isp.msu.edu/clacs

Mount Holyoke College
Latin American Studies Program
50 College Street
South Hadley, MA 01075
413-538-2000
http://www.mtholyoke.edu/acad/latam

New Mexico State University
Center For Latin American and Border Studies
Department 3LAS, Box 30001
Las Cruces, NM 88003-0001
505-646-6814
krebecca@nmsu.edu
http://www.nmsu.edu/~clas

The New School, A University
Janey Program in Latin American Studies
65 Fifth Avenue, Room 425
New York, NY 10003
212-229-5905
Jung@newschool.edu
http://www.newschool.edu/gf/centers/programs.htm

New York University
Center for Latin American and Caribbean Studies
53 Washington Square South, Floor 4W
New York, NY, 10012
212-998-8686
clacs.info@nyu.edu
http://www.nyu.edu/gsas/program/latin

Northern Illinois University
Center for Latinos and Latin American Studies
515 Garden Road
Dekalb, IL 60115
815-753-1531
latinostudies@niu.edu
http://www.clas.niu.edu/latino

Oberlin College
Latin American Studies
52 West Lorain Street
Oberlin, OH 44074
440-775-8450
registrar@oberlin.edu
http://www.oberlin.edu/catalog/college/latinam.html

Ohio State University
Center for Latin American Studies
306 Oxley Hall, 1712 Neil Avenue
Columbus, OH 43210
614-688-4881
unzueta.1@osu.edu
http://oia.osu.edu/clas

Ohio University
Latin American Studies
Yamada International House, 56 East Union Street

Athens, OH 45701-2979
740-593-1840
LatStudy@ohio.edu
http://www.ohio.edu/latinamerican

Princeton University
Program in Latin American Studies
58 Prospect Avenue
Princeton, NJ 08544-2006
609-258-4177
plas@princeton.edu
http://www.princeton.edu/plasweb

Providence College
Latin American Studies
302 Howley Hall, 549 River Avenue
Providence, RI 02918-0001
401-865-2752
http://www.providence.edu/Academics/Undergraduate
    +Studies/Areas+of+Study/Latin+American.htm

Rhode Island College
Latin American Studies Program
600 Mount Pleasant Avenue,146 Craig-Lee
Providence, RI 02908-1991
401-456-8029
despinosa@ric.edu
http://www.ric.edu/academics/dept_latin.html

Richard Stockton College of New Jersey
Latin American and Caribbean Studies Program
PO Box 195
Pomona, NJ 08240
609-652-1776
http://loki.stockton.edu/~greenel/LACS/lacs_homepage.
    htm

Rollins College
Latin American and Caribbean Affairs Program
Cornell Social Science Building, 1000 Holt Avenue,
    Box 2761
Winter Park, FL 32789
407-646-2370
http://www.rollins.edu/laca

Rose-Hulman Institute of Technology
Department of Humanities and Social Science
Latin American Studies
5500 Wabash Avenue
Terre Haute, IN 47803

812-877-8276
Merry.Chambers@rose-hulman.edu
http://www.rose-hulman.edu/hss/courses/latin.htm

Rutgers University
Latin American Studies Program
105 George Street, Cook/Douglas Campus
New Brunswick, NJ 08901-1414
732-932-9323
cbpinto@spanport.rutgers.edu
http://www.rci.rutgers.edu/~rulas

Rutgers University-Camden
Latin American Studies Program
Armitage Hall, 311 North Fifth Street
Camden, NJ 08102
856-225-6136
cgiaudro@camden.rutgers.edu
http://www.camden.rutgers.edu/dept-pages/forlangs

Saint Joseph's University
Latin American Studies Program
5600 City Avenue
Philadelphia, PA 19131
610-660-3088
cfaccini@sju.edu
http://www.sju.edu/cas/latin_studies

Saint Olaf College
Hispanic Studies Program
1520 St. Olaf Avenue, Old Main 22D
Northfield, MN 55057
507-646-3470
carullo@stolaf.edu
http://www.stolaf.edu/depts/hispanic-studies

San Diego State University
Center for Latin American Studies
146 Storm Hall
San Diego, CA 92182-4446
619-594-1103
http://www-rohan.sdsu.edu/%7Elatamweb

Smith College
Latin American & Latino/A Studies
Seelye Hall
Northampton, MA 01063
413-585-3591
kgauger@email.smith.edu
http://www.smith.edu/las

South Dakota State University

Latin American Area Studies
Department of Military Science, Box 2236
Brooking, SD 57007-0494
605-688-4277
maria_ramos@sdstate.edu
http://www3.sdstate.edu/Academics/CollegeOfArts
    AndScience/redirect/LatinAmericanAreaStudies

Southern Methodist University

Latin American Studies
320 Clements Hall
Dallas, TX 75275
214-768-4366
lmanzett@mail.smu.edu
http://www.smu.edu/dedman/majors/latinstudies

Stanford University

Stanford University Center for Latin American Studies
Bolívar House, 582 Alvarado Row
Stanford, CA 94305
650-723-4444
boho-calendar@lists.stanford.edu
http://www.stanford.edu/group/las

Syracuse University

Latino-Latin American Studies Program
435 Hall of Languages
Syracuse, NY 13244
315-443-9475
tpaniagu@syr.edu
http://www-hl.syr.edu/depts/llas/index.html

Texas Tech University

Latin American and Iberian Studies Program
Box 42071
Lubbock, TX 79409
806-742-1562
julian.perez@ttu.edu
http://www3.tltc.ttu.edu/Perez/default.htm

Trinity University

International Programs and Studies
One Trinity Place, Box 100
San Antonio, TX 78212-7200
210-999-7011
web@trinity.edu
http://www.trinity.edu/departments/int_studies/
    index.asp

University of Alabama

Latin American Studies Program
Box 870246
Tuscaloosa, AL 35487-0246
205-348-8472
thomas.jennings@ua.edu
http://www.as.ua.edu/las/links.htm

University of Arizona

Center for Latin American Studies
Marshall Building, Suite 280, PO Box 210158B
Tucson, AZ 85721-0158
520-626-7242
laac@u.arizona.edu
http://las.arizona.edu

University of Arkansas

Latin American Studies Program
425 Kimpel Hall
Fayetteville, AR 72701
479-575-2951
sbell@uark.edu
http://www.uark.edu/depts/lastinfo

University of California-Berkeley

Center for Latin American Studies
2334 Bowditch Street, #2312
Berkeley, CA 94720
510-642-2088
clas@uclink4.berkeley.edu
http://socrates.berkeley.edu:7001/About/index.html

University of California-Los Angeles

Latin American Studies Program
10373 Bunche Hall, Mail Code 148703, Box 951487
Los Angeles, CA 90095-1487
310-206-6571
cramirez@isop.ucla.edu
http://www.isop.ucla.edu/idps/las

University of California-Riverside

Latin American Studies Program
2416 HMNSS Building
Riverside, CA 92521
951-827-2742
ami.flori@ucr.edu
http://www.latinamericanstudies.ucr.edu

University of California-San Diego
Center for Iberian and Latin American Studies
10111 North Torrey Pines Road
Gildred Latin American Studies Building, Institute
    of the Americas Complex
La Jolla, CA
858-534-6050
latamst@ucsd.edu
http://cilas.ucsd.edu

University of California-Santa Barbara
Latin American and Iberian Studies
Phelps Hall 4206
Santa Barbara, CA 93106-4150
805-893-3161
LAISDirector@lais.ucsb.edu
http://www.lais.ucsb.edu

University of California-Santa Cruz
Latin American and Latino Studies
Casa Latina, Lower Level
Santa Cruz, CA 95064
831-459-4284
lals@ucsc.edu
http://lals.ucsc.edu

University of Central Florida
Latin American, Caribbean, and Latino Studies
PO Box 161998
Orlando, FL 32816-1998
407-823-1174
martfern@mail.ucf.edu
http://www.cas.ucf.edu/CAS2/2004-departments-lacls.php

University of Chicago
Center for Latin American Studies
Kelly Hall 310, 5848 South University Avenue
Chicago, IL 60637
773-702-8420
clas@uchicago.edu
http://clas.uchicago.edu

University of Connecticut
Center for Latin American and Caribbean Studies
843 Bolton Road, Unit 1161
Storrs, CT 06269-1161
860-486-4964
LatinAmerica@uconn.edu
http://clacs.uconn.edu

University of Delaware
Latin American Studies Program
325 Smith Hall
Newark, DE 19716
302-831-0439
csc@udel.edu
http://www.udel.edu/AreaStudies/latam.html

University of Florida
Center for Latin American Studies
319 Grinter Hall, PO Box 115530
Gainesville, FL 32611-5530
352-392-0375
http://www.latam.ufl.edu

University of Idaho
Latin American Studies Program
305-A Administration Building, 875 Perimeter Drive
Moscow, ID 83844
208-885-8956
http://www.uidaho.edu/LS/LASt

University of Illinois-Chicago
Latin American and Latino Studies Program
1527 University Hall, 601 South Morgan Street
Chicago, IL 60607-7115
312-996-2445
martae@uic.edu
http://www.uic.edu/las/latamst

University of Illinois-Urbana-Champaign
Center for Latin America and Caribbean Studies
201 International Studies Building, 910 South Fifth
    Street, MC-481
Champaign, IL 61820
217-333-3182
clacs@uiuc.edu
http://www.clacs.uiuc.edu

University of Iowa
Latin American Studies Program
252 International Center
Iowa City, IA, 52242-1802
319-335-0096
william-reisinger@uiowa.edu
http://intl-programs.uiowa.edu/academic/lasp

University of Kansas
Center of Latin American Studies
1440 Jayhawk Boulevard, Suite 320

Lawrence, KS 66045-7574
785-864-4213
latamst@ku.edu
http://www.ku.edu/~latamst

University of Kentucky
Program in Latin American Studies
1115 Patterson Office Tower
Lexington, KY 40506-0027
859-257-9576
kristie.bulleit@uky.edu
http://www.as.uky.edu/interprog/las

University of Maryland
Latin American Studies Center
0128-B Holzapfel Hall
College Park, MD 20742
301-405-6459
lasc@umd.edu
http://www.lasc.umd.edu

University of Massachusetts
924 Thompson Hall, 200 Hicks Way
Amherst, MA 01003-9277
413-545-4648
las@econs.umass.edu
http://www.umass.edu/clacls/index.html

University of Miami
Center for Latin American Studies
125-A Memorial Building
Coral Gables, FL 33124-2302
305-284-3117
lasgrad@miami.edu
http://www.as.miami.edu/lasp/master.htm

University of Miami
Latin American Studies
Ashe Building, Room 505, PO Box 248093
Coral Gables, FL 33124-4650
305-284-4858
las@miami.edu
http://www.as.miami.edu/lasp/default.htm

University of Michigan
Latin American and Caribbean Studies
International Institute Building
1080 South University Street, 2607 Social Work
Ann Arbor, MI 48109-1106
734-763-0553

lacs.office@umich.edu
http://www.umich.edu/~iinet/lacs

University of Minnesota
Institute for Global Studies
Latin American Studies
214 Social Sciences Building
267 19th Avenue South
Minneapolis, MN 55455
612-625-9353
http://www.catalogs.umn.edu/ug/cla/cla46.html

University of Minnesota-Morris
Latin American Area Studies Program
600 East Fourth Street
Morris, MN 56267
888-866-3382
alvarez@morris.umn.edu
http://www.mrs.umn.edu/academic/laas

University of Nebraska-Lincoln
Latino and Latin American Studies Program
309 Seaton Hall
Lincoln, NE 68588-0686
402-472-9983
http://www.unl.edu/unlies/latino/latino.htm

University of Nebraska-Omaha
Office of Latino/Latin American Studies
    of the Great Plains
Arts and Sciences Hall, Room 106
Omaha, NE 68182
402-554-3358
lgouveia@mail.unomaha.edu
http://www.unomaha.edu/ollas

University of New Mexico
Latin American and Iberian Institute
801 Yale, NE, MSC02 1690
Albuquerque, NM 87131-0001
505-277-2961
info@laii.unm.edu
http://laii.unm.edu

University of North Carolina-Chapel Hill
Institute of Latin American Studies
223 East Franklin Street, Campus Box 3205
Chapel Hill, NC 27599-3205
919-966-1484
http://www.unc.edu/depts/ilas

University of Oklahoma
Latin American Area Studies
729 Elm, Hester Hall, Room 207
Norman, OK 73129-0535
405-325-1584
rhcox@ou.edu
http://www.ou.edu/cas/ias/Latam/LATINAM.htm

University of Pennsylvania
Latin American and Latino Studies Program
3624 Market Street, Suite 1E, Room 164
Philadelphia, PA 19104-2615
215-898-9919
lals@sas.upenn.edu
http://www.sas.upenn.edu/lals

University of Pittsburgh
Center for Latin American Studies
4E04 Wesley W. Posvar Hall
Pittsburgh, PA 15260
412-648-7392
clas@pitt.edu
http://www.ucis.pitt.edu/clas

University of South Carolina
Latin American Studies Program
408 Gambrell Hall
Columbia, SC 29208
803-777-0437
AEkingso@gwm.sc.edu
http://www.cas.sc.edu/lasp

University of Tennessee
Latin American Studies Program
617 McClung Tower
Knoxville, TN 37996
865-974-5421
handelsman@utk.edu
http://web.utk.edu/~LatAmer

University of Texas-Austin
Teresa Lozano Long Institute of Latin American Studies
One University Station D0800
Austin, TX 78712
512-471-5551
adibble@mail.utexas.edu
http://www.utexas.edu/cola/llilas

University of Texas-El Paso
Center for InterAmerican and Border Studies
500 West University Avenue

Liberal Arts Building, 200 de Wetter Center, Room 343
El Paso, TX 79968
915-747-5196
cibs@utep.edu
http://www.utep.edu/catalogs/undergrad/libart/latin.htm

University of Washington
Latin American Studies Program
122 Thomson Hall, Box 353650
Seattle WA 98195
206-685-3435
lasuw@u.washington.edu
http://jsis.artsci.washington.edu/programs/latinam

University of Wisconsin-Madison
Latin American, Caribbean, and Iberian Studies Program
209 Ingraham Hall, 1155 Observatory Drive
Madison, WI 53706
608-262-2811
gpodesta@wisc.edu
http://polyglot.lss.wisc.edu/laisp

University of Wisconsin-Milwaukee
Center for Latin American and Caribbean Studies
Pearse Hall, 2513 East Hartford Avenue, #168
Milwaukee, WI 53201-0413
414-229-4401
clacs@uwm.edu
http://www.uwm.edu/Dept/CLACS

Vanderbilt University
Center for Latin American and Iberian Studies
2301 Vanderbilt Place, VU Station B, #351806
Nashville, TN 37235-1806
615-322-2527
norma.g.antillon@vanderbilt.edu
http://www.sitemason.vanderbilt.edu/clais

Washington University
Latin American Studies
One Brookings Drive
St. Louis, MO 63130
314-935-5145
mmorana@artsci.wustl.edu
http://www.artsci.wustl.edu/~ias/latinamstudies.shtml

Wesleyan University
Latin American Studies Program
Center for the Americas, Room 201

Middleton, CT 06459
860-685 2396
awightman@wesleyan.edu
http://www.wesleyan.edu/last

West Chester University
Latin American Studies
111 Main Hall
West Chester, PA 19383
610-436-2372
ebraidotti@wcupa.edu
http://www.wcupa.edu/_ACADEMICS/sch_cas/lat_stu

Western Kentucky University
Department of Modern Languages
Latin American Studies
1906 College Heights Boulevard, #11066
Bowling Green, KY 42101-1066
270-745-5334
oip@wku.edu
http://www.wku.edu/modernlanguages/programs/
    latinamerica.html

Woodrow Wilson International Center for Scholars
Latin American Program
1300 Pennsylvania Avenue, NW, One Woodrow
    Wilson Plaza
Washington, DC 20004-3027
202-691-4030
lap@wwic.si.edu
http://www.wilsoncenter.org/index.cfm?fuseaction=
    topics.home&topic_id=1425

Native American
Arizona State University
American Indian Studies
PO Box 874603
Tempe, AZ 85287-4603
480-965-3634
ais@asu.edu
http://www.asu.edu/clas/americanindian

Bemidji State University
American Indian Resource Center
1500 Birchmont Drive, NW
Bemidji, MN 55601
218-755-2590
lcook@bemidjistate.edu
http://www.bemidjistate.edu/airc

Black Hills State University
American Indian Studies
1200 University Street, Unit 9502
Spearfish, SD 57799-9502
605-642-6578
LowellAmiotte@bhsu.edu
http://www.bhsu.edu/prospective/summary/
    Majors-Menu/H&SS_ais.htm

Colgate University
Native American Studies Program
12 Hascall Hall, 13 Oak Drive
Hamilton, NY 13346
cvecsey@mail.colgate.edu
http://www.colgate.edu/frameset.aspx?nwURL=http://
    departments.colgate.edu/nast

Creighton University
Native American Studies Program
2500 California Plaza
Omaha, NE 68178
402-280-3587
bucko@creighton.edu
http://puffin.creighton.edu/nas/index.htm

Dartmouth College
Native American Studies Center
Sherman House, 37 North Main Street, HB 6152
Hanover, NH 03755
603-646-3530
colin.calloway@dartmouth.edu
http://www.dartmouth.edu/~nas

Evergreen State College
Northwest Indian Applied Research Institute
2700 Evergreen Parkway, NW, SEM 3122
Olympia, WA 98505
360-867-6614
nwindian@evergreen.edu
http://www.evergreen.edu/nwindian

Humboldt State University
Native American Studies Department
One Harpst Street
Arcata, CA 95521-8299
707-826-4329
ferris@laurel.humboldt.edu
http://www.humboldt.edu/~nasp

Northeastern State University
Native American Studies Program
Department of Social Sciences
Tahlequah OK 74464
918-456-5511
http://arapaho.nsuok.edu/%7Esocsci/NAS/NAS-
    Frameset-1.htm

Northern Arizona University
Department of Applied Indigenous Studies
PO Box 15018
Flagstaff, AZ 86011
928-523-6624
d-ais@jan.ucc.nau.edu
http://www.ais.nau.edu

Northland College
Native American Studies
1411 Ellis Avenue
Ashland, WI 54806-3999
715-682-1699
http://www.northland.edu/Northland/Academics2/
    ProgramsOfStudy/NativeAmericanStudies

University of Alaska-Fairbanks
Alaska Native Studies Department
319 Brooks Building, PO Box 756300
Fairbanks, AK 99775-6300
904-474-7181
http://www.uaf.edu/ans/index.html

University of California-Berkeley,
Department of Ethnic Studies
506 Barrows Hall, #2570
Berkeley, CA 94720-2570
510-643-0796
http://socrates.berkeley.edu/~ethnicst

University of California-Davis
Department of Native American Studies
One Shields Avenue
Davis CA 95616
530-752-3237
mjmacri@ucdavis.edu
http://cougar.ucdavis.edu/nas

University of California-Riverside
Native American Student Programs
224 Costo Hall
Riverside, CA 92521

951-827-4143
sisto@ucr.edu
http://www.nasp.ucr.edu

University of Minnesota-Twin Cities
Department of American Indian Studies
Two Scott Hall, 72 Pleasant Street, SE
Minneapolis, MN 55455
612-624-1338
aminstud@tc.umn.edu
http://cla.umn.edu/amerind/amin.html

University of Montana
Native American Studies
600 University Avenue
Missoula MT 59812
406-243-5831
http://www.umt.edu/nas

University of Nebraska-Lincoln
Institute for Ethnic Studies
303 Seaton Hall
Lincoln, NE 68588-068
402-472-1663
http://www.unl.edu/unlies

University of New Mexico
Native American Studies
Mesa Vista, Room 3080, MSC 06 3740
Albuquerque, NM 87131-0001
505-277-3917
nasinfo@unm.edu
http://www.unm.edu/~nasinfo

University of North Carolina-Pembroke
Department of American Indian Studies
PO Box 1510
Pembroke, NC 28372-1510
910-521-6266
ais@uncp.edu
http://www.uncp.edu/ais

University of North Dakota
Indian Studies Department
PO Box 7103
Grand Forks, ND 582
701-777-4314
merry_ketterling@und.nodak.edu
http://www.und.edu/dept/indian

University of Oklahoma
Native American Studies
Ellison Hall, 633 Elm Avenue, Room 216
Norman, OK 73019-3113
405-325-2312
nas@ou.edu
http://www.ou.edu/cas/nas

University of South Dakota
Institute of American Indian Studies
414 East Clark Street
Vermillion, SD 57069
605-677-5209
iais@usd.edu
http://www.usd.edu/iais

University of the Incarnate Word
Native American Studies
4301 Broadway
San Antonio, TX 78209
210-829-6005
http://www.uiw.edu/ugcat0305/01.html

University of Wisconsin-Eau Claire
American Indian Studies Program
Hibbard Hall 150
Eau Claire, WI 54702-4004
715-836-6045
martinlt@uwec.edu
http://www.uwec.edu/AIS

ONLINE RESOURCES

Affiliated Tribes of Northwest Indians

http://www.atnitribes.org

ATNI is a nonprofit organization representing 54
   Northwest tribal governments from Oregon, Idaho,
   Washington, southeast Alaska, Northern California,
   and western Montana. Its Web site includes a calendar
   of events, lists of powwows and cultural gatherings,
   and information from committees on economic
   development, education, health, and other issues.

African American Business Directory

http://africanamericanbusinessdirectory.com

This fee-based site features career resources (job and
   resume posting), a directory of businesses, free e-mail
   accounts, and a business center with information for
   the entrepreneur.

African American Business Link

http://www.aabl.com

Offers a business directory and information about
   promoting your business online.

African American Shopping Mall

http://www.aasm.com

The Shopping Mall is a directory of links to products
   and services of interest to the African-American
   community. It allows African-American merchants to
   showcase their wares.

African American Web Connection

http://www.aawc.com

An African-American Web directory of organizations,
   business sites, and publications online.

Afronet

http://www.afronet.com

An Internet service offering free Internet access, message
   boards, chat, and departments focusing on such
   subjects as business and technology.

Asian Women in Business

http://www.awib.org

Asian Women in Business seeks to assist Asian women
   in realizing their entrepreneurial potential. Its
   Web site contains a business reference library for
   those starting a small business, with topics such as
   legal considerations, how to write a business plan,

designing your own Web site, and evaluating your
   employees.

BlackApolis

http://www.blackapolis.com

This Web site provides an overview of U.S. cities from
   the perspective of multi-cultural professionals. It lists
   minority organizations and resources in each city, as
   well as grades each city on its appeal to minorities.

Black Athlete Sports Network

http://blackathlete.com

This Web site covers the sports industry and the concerns
   of African-American athletes.

Black Atlanta.com

http://www.blackatlanta.com

This is Web directory provides information and links
   to business, cultural, and other topics of interest to
   African Americans in Atlanta, Georgia.

Black Career Women

http://www.bcw.org

Black Career Women is an advocacy organization for
   African-American women in the workforce. Visit its
   Web site for statistics, career resources, an assessment
   test, and job listings.

BlackNLA

http://www.blacknla.com

This online directory lists African-American businesses,
   organizations, and events in the Los Angeles,
   California, area.

BlackTexas.com

http://www.blacktexas.com/news.php

This Web site lists organizations and resources available
   to African Americans in Texas.

Black Voices

http://www.blackvoices.com

This online community for African Americans features a
   career center with job and resume postings.

Blackworld

http://www.blackworld.com

This Internet directory of resources for African Americans

provides links to arts and culture, business, education, finance, and government sites.

The Black World Today
http://www.tbwt.org
The Black World Today is an online collective of African-American journalists, writers, artists, communicators, and entrepreneurs.

BPNetwork: The Black Professional Network
http://www.bpnetwork.com
BPNetwork provides business services and resources for African-American professionals. Visitors can browse company Web pages, job listings, and lists of mutual funds.

Collegeboard.com
http://apps.collegeboard.com/cbsearch_ss/welcome.jsp
This testing service (PSAT, SAT, etc.) also offers a scholarship search engine. It features scholarships worth nearly $3 billion. Users can search by minority group, gender, specific major, and a variety of other criteria.

CollegeNET
http://mach25.collegenet.com/cgi-bin/M25
CollegeNET features 600,000 scholarships worth more than $1.6 billion. Users can search by keyword (such as "minority") or by creating a personality profile of their interests.

CVLatino.com
http://www.cvlatino.com
This site allows Hispanic professionals to share their curriculum vitae with other professionals and global companies. The site features many job listings for individuals who speak Spanish, Portuguese, and English.

Denver Black Pages
http://www.denverblackpages.com
This Web site provides business, entertainment, and news to African Americans in Denver, Colorado.

District of Columbia Internet Black Pages
http://www.dcblackpages.com
This directory provides links to African-American businesses, organizations, and other resources in Washington, D.C.

Diversity/Careers in Engineering and Information Technology
http://www.diversitycareers.com
This online magazine covers the rapidly growing IT industry, and focuses on companies with diversity initiatives. The magazine publishes feature articles, provides access to back issues, and features an annual college issue. A resume database is also available.

DiversityInc.com
http://www.diversityinc.com
This fee-based Web site features articles on diversity in the workplace and in business relations.

Ethnic Majority
http://www.ethnicmajority.com
This organization seeks to advance African Americans, Hispanic Americans, and Asian Americans in business, politics, in the workplace, and society in general.

FastWeb
http://fastweb.monster.com
FastWeb is one of the largest scholarship search engines around. It features 600,000 scholarships worth more than $1 billion. Free registration is required to use this resource.

GuaranteedScholarships.com
http://www.guaranteed-scholarships.com
This Web site offers lists (by college) of scholarships, grants, and financial aid that "require no interview, essay, portfolio, audition, competition, or other secondary requirement."

ihispano.com
http://www.ihispano.com
This Web site serves as a career recruiting/job search resource for Hispanics; it allows users to create a profile and to search for jobs.

IMDiversity.com
http://www.imdiversity.com
This Web site provides career and self-development information to all minorities.

Job Latino
http://www.joblatino.com
This employment database for Hispanic job seekers and employers also features links to Hispanic organizations, job training programs, and scholarships and fellowships.

LatPro Professional Network
http://www.LatPro.com
The network assists Hispanic and bilingual professionals in meeting industry recruiters. The site also features news and forums for commentary.

MBNet.com
http://www.mbnet.com
MBNet.com is a business information and resource service. It provides opportunities for minorities to market and expand their businesses.

Milwaukee Black Online
http://www.thembo.com/home.htm
This Web site provides resources of interest to African Americans in Milwaukee, Wisconsin.

Minority Career Network
http://www.minoritycareernet.com/aboutus.shtml
This is an online employment service for job seekers and employers.

National Diversity Newspaper Job Bank
http://www.newsjobs.com
This job bank promotes diversity in the newspaper industry and allows users to view or post jobs, submit a resume, and link to job Web sites.

Native American Public Telecommunications
http://www.nativetelecom.org
This Indian-owned and -operated network is dedicated to establishing and developing affordable public access, computerized information, and telecommunication services for American Indians and Alaskan Natives.

NativeTech
http://www.nativetech.org
This educational Web site covers Native American art—specifically the arts of Eastern Woodland Indian Peoples.

Native Web
http://www.nativeweb.org
Contains listings of resources for indigenous cultures around the world. Features news features, message boards, job listings, and links to Web sites.

Pew Hispanic Center
http://pewhispanic.org
This Web site provides comprehensive research on the Hispanic experience in the United States, including demographic patterns, economics, education, identity, immigration, employment, and politics.

Princeton Review
http://www.princetonreview.com
Princeton Review is a great site to find comprehensive college reviews and information. Check out the site's annual rankings to read how schools stack up in academics, social scene, diversity, and other areas.

Red Ibis
http://www.redibis.com
Red Ibis connects Internet industry professionals of color. The site contains message boards, mailing lists, and an educational center.

RedWire: The Diversity E-Business Network
http://www.minoritybusiness.com
RedWire is an online directory of minority businesses and professionals sponsored by Hispanic Business.

San Diego BLAACK Pages
http://www.sdbp.com
A Web directory with links to pages on black history, education, organizations, classifieds, and discussion forums.

Scholarships.com
http://www.scholarships.com
Scholarships.com offers a free college scholarship search engine (although registration is required) and financial aid information.

South Asian Women's Network
http://www.umiacs.umd.edu/users/sawweb/sawnet
This Web site for and about women from Bangladesh, Bhutan, India, Maldives, Nepal, Pakistan, and Sri Lanka lists resources, including contact information and links, for South Asian women's organizations, books and articles by and for South Asian women, careers, grants, funding, and electronic resources. The site also hosts a forum discussing various issues of interest to South Asian women.

Universal Black Pages
http://www.ubp.com
A directory of African-American educational opportunities, professional and student organizations, and other resources.

OTHER DIRECTORIES

Directory of Selected Scholarship, Fellowship, and Other Financial Aid Opportunities for Women and Ethnic Minorities in Psychology and Related Fields
American Psychological Association
750 First Street, NE
Washington, DC 20002-4242
http://forms.apa.org/pi/financialaid
This is a free, online database of financial aid resources for minorities and women who are planning to or currently pursuing study in psychology or related fields. The directory is searchable by institution name, education level, and type of financial aid.

East West Players Alliance of Creative Talent Services Directory
East West Players
120 North Judge John Aiso Street
Los Angeles, CA 90012
213-625-7000
info@eastwestplayers.org
http://www.eastwestplayers.org/acts.htm
This annual publication lists Asian Pacific American actors, writers, directors, and other theatre artists.

Financial Aid for African Americans
Reference Service Press
5000 Windplay Drive, Suite 4
El Dorado Hills, CA 95762-9600
916-939-9620
info@rspfunding.com
http://www.rspfunding.com
This directory provides detailed descriptions of scholarships, fellowships, loans, grants, awards, and internships available to African Americans at any level (from high school through professional and postdoctoral). Entries are arranged by program type and indexed by sponsor, title, geographic coverage, subject, and deadline.

Financial Aid for Asian Americans
Reference Service Press
5000 Windplay Drive, Suite 4
El Dorado Hills, CA 95762-9600
916-939-9620
info@rspfunding.com
http://www.rspfunding.com
This publication contains detailed descriptions of funding opportunities open to Chinese Americans, Japanese Americans, Korean Americans, Vietnamese Americans, Filipinos, and other Americans of Asian ancestry. Entries are arranged by program type and indexed by sponsor, title, geographic coverage, and subject.

Financial Aid for Hispanic Americans
Reference Service Press
5000 Windplay Drive, Suite 4
El Dorado Hills, CA 95762-9600
916-939-9620
info@rspfunding.com
http://www.rspfunding.com
This publication contains detailed descriptions of scholarships, fellowships, loans, grants, awards, and internships available to Hispanic Americans, including Mexican Americans, Puerto Ricans, Cuban Americans, and others of Latin American origin. Entries are arranged by program type and indexed by sponsor, title, geographic coverage, subject, and deadline.

Financial Aid for Native Americans
Reference Service Press
5000 Windplay Drive, Suite 4
El Dorado Hills, CA 95762-9600
916-939-9620
info@rspfunding.com
http://www.rspfunding.com
This publication lists funding opportunities open to American Indians, Native Alaskans, and Native Pacific Islanders (including Native Hawaiians and Samoans). Entries are arranged by program type and indexed by sponsor, title, geographic coverage, subject, and deadline.

Grants for Minorities
The Foundation Center
79 Fifth Avenue/16th Street
New York, NY 10003-3076
800-424-9836
http://fdncenter.org
This publication lists grants of $10,000 or more recently awarded to programs for minority populations, such as African Americans, Hispanic Americans, Asian Americans, Native Americans, gay men, lesbians,

immigrants, and refugees. Information is indexed by the type of organization receiving the grant, and the geographic area in which the program is located.

Hispanic Scholarship Directory
National Hispanic Press Foundation
941 National Press Building
    Washington, DC 20045
202-662-7250
hispanicscholars@aol.com
http://www.scholarshipsforhispanics.org
This directory lists more than 1,000 financial aid entries for Hispanic students. A free online version is also available.

National Directory of Hispanic Organizations
Congressional Hispanic Caucus Institute
911 Second Street, NE
Washington, DC 20002
205-543-1771
http://www.chci.org/publications/nd.html
This directory provides information on Hispanic organizations at the state, regional, and national level. It also includes demographic information on the Hispanic population including income, workforce participation, purchasing power, population, home ownership, educational attainment, and voting statistics.

Scholarships for African-American Students
Peterson's
2000 Lenox Drive, PO Box 67005
Lawrenceville, NJ 08648
800-338-3282, ext. 5660
custsvc@petersons.com
http://www.petersons.com

This directory provides an overview of financial aid opportunities that are available to Hispanic students. Information is indexed by award name; sponsor; academic field/career goal; civic, professional, social, or union affiliation; corporate affiliation; employment experience; military service; religious affiliation; state of residence; and talent.

Scholarships for Asian-American Students
Peterson's
2000 Lenox Drive, PO Box 67005
Lawrenceville, NJ 08648
800-338-3282, ext. 5660
custsvc@petersons.com
http://www.petersons.com
This directory provides an overview of financial aid opportunities that are available to Asian American students. Information is indexed by award name; sponsor; academic field/career goal; civic, professional, social, or union affiliation; corporate affiliation; employment experience; military service; religious affiliation; state of residence; and talent.

Sources of Financial Aid Available to American Indian Students
Indian Resource Development
New Mexico State University
Box 30001, Department 3IRD
Las Cruces, NM 88003-8001
gina@nmsu.edu
http://www.nmsu.edu/~ird
This directory lists financial aid resources for undergraduate and graduate students of Native American heritage.

PUBLICATIONS

This section lists publications (magazines, journals, newspapers), directories, and Web sites of relevance to minorities looking to develop their careers.

African-American Career World Magazine
Equal Opportunity Publications
445 Broad Hollow Road, Suite 425
Melville, NY 11747
631-421-9421
info@eop.com
http://www.eop.com
This publication links African-American students with job opportunities at major corporations. It features career-guidance columns, profiles of African Americans in all fields, and news and trends.

American Indian Report
Falmouth Institute
3702 Pender Drive, Suite 300
Fairfax, VA 22030
800-992-4489
http://www.falmouthinst.com
The leading news source for the nation's tribal leaders and legislators, educators, business leaders, and environmentalists.

The Asian American Psychologist
Asian American Psychological Association
PMB #527
5025 North Central Avenue
Phoenix, AZ 85012
602-230-4257
http://www.aapaonline.org
This newsletter keeps association members up to date on developments in the field and association initiatives.

Asian Enterprise (AE)
23824 Twin Pines Lane
    Diamond Bar, CA 91765
909-860-3316
http://www.asianenterprise.com
Asian Enterprise focuses on small business enterprises of Asian Pacific Americans nationwide. On a monthly basis, AE provides important information to a growing number of Asian Pacific American entrepreneurs, addressing issues that impact the Asian Pacific American business community.

Asian Pacific American Journal
Asian American Writers' Workshop
16 West 32nd Street, Suite 10A
New York, NY 10001
212-494-0061
http://www.aaww.org
The *Asian Pacific American Journal* publishes fiction, poetry, essays, reviews, and interviews from Asians and Pacific Islanders.

Black Collegian
140 Carondelet Street
New Orleans, LA 70130
832-615-8871
http://www.blackcollegian.com
This national career opportunities magazine offers general feature articles and career planning/job search information. It is available free online and in college career offices.

Black Congressional Monitor
Len Mor Publications
PO Box 75035
Washington, DC 20013
202-488-8879
http://www.bcmonitor.com
The *Black Congressional Monitor* is a twice-monthly report of federal government news by and about, and of interest and benefit to African Americans. It presents information on available grant awards, contract and subcontract opportunities, public meetings, public notices, publications, and other public policy documents. In addition, it reports on the legislative initiatives of African Americans in the U.S. Congress (e.g., public laws enacted, bills and resolutions introduced, hearings held, reports to and by Congress, statements made on the House and Senate floors, and thoughts about Congressional intent).

Black Enterprise
130 Fifth Avenue, 10th Floor
New York, NY 10011-4399
212-242-8000
http://www.blackenterprise.com
This is one of the leading publications covering the world of African-American businesses and corporations.

Black MBA Magazine
National Black MBA Association
180 North Michigan Avenue

Chicago, IL 60601
312-236-2622
http://www.nbmbaa.org
The official publication of the National Black MBA
   Association, *Black MBA Magazine* provides useful
   articles on business-related issues for African-
   American students and professionals.

The Black Scholar

PO Box 22869
Oakland, CA 94618
510-547-6633
BlkSchlr@aol.com
http://www.theblackscholar.org
This journal of African-American studies and research
   publishes criticism and interviews by scholars and
   other writers.

Black Talent News

PO Box 34899
Los Angeles, CA 90034-0899
310-203-1336
info@blacktalentnews.com
http://www.blacktalentnews.com
The *Black Talent News* is a national trade publication for
   African Americans in the entertainment industry.

Callaloo

Attn: Project MUSE
2715 North Charles Street
Baltimore, MD 21218-4319
410-516-6989
muse@muse.jhu.edu
http://muse.jhu.edu/journals/callaloo
This African and African-American literary journal features
   original works by and critical studies of Black writers
   worldwide.

Career Engineer

National Society of Black Engineers
1454 Duke Street
Alexandria, VA 22314
703-549-2207
info@nsbe.org
http://www.nsbe.org
This magazine for African-American engineers provides
   information on careers, leadership and training
   opportunities, and other topics.

Cultural Diversity at Work

13751 Lake City Way, NE, Suite 210
Seattle, WA 98125-8612
206-362-0336
orders@diversitycentral.com
http://www.diversityhotwire.com
This journal addresses cultural diversity in the workplace
   and the business world.

DateLine AAJA

Asian American Journalists Association (AAJA)
1182 Market Street, Suite 320
San Francisco, CA 94102
415-346-2051
national@aaja.org
http://www.aaja.org
This is the official quarterly newsletter of the association.

Diverse: Issues In Higher Education

10520 Warwick Avenue, Suite B-8
Fairfax, VA 22030-3136
800-783-3199
http://www.diverseeducation.com
Formerly known as *Black Issues in Higher Education*, this
   magazine is dedicated to addressing issues that affect
   minorities in higher education.

DiversityInc

http://www.diversityinc.com
**This magazine provides articles about diversity in the
   workplace and in business relations.**

The Ebony Cactus

PO Box 24982
Tempe, AZ 85285-4982
602-821-8191
http://www.theebonycactus.com
This publication provides support and informational
   resources to African-American businesspeople in
   the American Southwest.

Equal Opportunity

Equal Opportunity Publications
445 Broad Hollow Road, Suite 425
Melville, NY 11747
631-421-9421
info@eop.com
http://www.eop.com
Equal Opportunity is a career guidance and recruitment
   magazine distributed free of charge to minority
   college students and professionals in all fields.

Hispanic Business
425 Pine Avenue
Santa Barbara, CA 93117-3709
805-964-4554
http://www.hispanicbusiness.com
This magazine for Hispanic professionals features the latest business news and its effect on the Hispanic community.

Hispanic Career World
Equal Opportunity Publications
445 Broad Hollow Road, Suite 425
Melville, NY 11747
631-421-9421
info@eop.com
http://www.eop.com
This publication links Hispanic students with job opportunities at major corporations. It features career-guidance columns, profiles of Hispanics in all fields, and news and trends.

Hispanic Journal
PO Box 810650
Dallas, TX 75381
214-350-4774
sales@hispanicjournal.com
http://www.hispanicjournal.com
Hispanic Journal features articles about Hispanic Americans in business, politics, and culture.

Hispanic Magazine
6355 NW 36th Street
Miami, FL 33166
305-744-3550
http://www.hisp.com
A magazine and online service for the general interests of the Hispanic community.

Hispanic Outlook in Higher Education
210 Route Four East, Suite 310
Paramus, NJ 07652
201-587-8800
http://www.hispanicoutlook.com
This magazine covers issues of interest to Hispanic students and educators.

How to Run A Minority High School Journalism Workshop
Dow Jones Newspaper Fund
PO Box 300
Princeton, NJ 08543-0300
609-452-2820
newsfund@wsj.dowjones.com
http://www.dj.com/newsfund
This online publication offers advice to educators on how to set up and run a minority high school journalism workshop.

Indian Country
3059 Seneca Turnpike
Canastota, NY 13032
888-327-1013
http://www.indiancountry.com
A nationwide newspaper covering stories and issues relevant to Native Americans; serves as a major source of information for Native American schools and colleges.

The Journal of Negro Education
Howard University
School of Education
PO Box 311
Washington DC 20059
202-806-8120
jne@howard.edu
http://www.journalnegroed.org
This publication features scholarly articles on African American-related educational issues.

The Legislator
National Black Caucus of State Legislators
444 North Capitol Street, NW, Suite 622
Washington, DC 20001
202-624-5457
http://www.nbcsl.com/legislator.html
This newsletter provides updates on caucus activities.

Minority Business Entrepreneur Magazine
3528 Torrance Boulevard, Suite 101
Torrance, CA 90503
310-540-9398
http://www.mbemag.com
A bimonthly publication for and about minority and women business owners.

Minority Engineer
Equal Opportunity Publications
445 Broad Hollow Road, Suite 425
Melville, NY 11747
631-421-9421
info@eop.com

http://www.eop.com
A free publication for minority engineering, computer science, and information technology professionals.

Mosaic Literary Magazine

314 West 231st Street, #470
Bronx, NY 10463
718-530-9132
magazine@mosaicbooks.com
http://www.mosaicbooks.com/maginfo.htm
A literary magazine featuring original fiction, poetry, and reviews by African American writers.

National Black Law Journal

435 West 116th St.
New York, NY 10027-7297
212-854-3318
nblj@law.columbia.edu
http://www.law.columbia.edu/current_student/student_service/Law_Journals/black_law
The journal publishes scholarly studies of law and the African-American community.

National Minority Business Council Business Report

National Minority Business Council
25 West 45th Street, Suite 301
New York, NY 10036
212-997-4753
nmbc@msn.com
http://www.nmbc.org
The report provides updates on business opportunities and developments for minorities.

Native American Law Digest

Falmouth Institute
3702 Pender Drive, Suite 300
Fairfax, VA 22030
800-992-4489
http://www.falmouthinst.com
A monthly summary of all legal decisions significant to the American Indian community.

Native Peoples Magazine

5333 North Seventh Street, Suite 224
Phoenix, AZ 85014
602-265-4855
http://www.nativepeoples.com
This magazine covers the art and lifestyle of Native Americans, and features the work of Native American writers and photographers.

Network Journal: Black Professionals and Small Professional News

39 Broadway, Suite 2120
New York, NY 10006
212-962-3791
http://www.tnj.com
Features business and trade news of interest to the African American and Caribbean American community.

NSBE Bridge

National Society of Black Engineers (NSBE)
1454 Duke Street
Alexandria, VA 22314
703-549-2207
info@nsbe.org
http://www.nsbe.org
NSBE Bridge seeks to introduce African-American youth to opportunities in the math and sciences.

NSBE Magazine

National Society of Black Engineers (NSBE)
1454 Duke Street
Alexandria, VA 22314
703-549-2207
info@nsbe.org
http://www.nsbe.org
This publication for students, technical experts, and engineering educators offers articles on a variety of engineering and technology disciplines.

the onehundred

100 Black Men of America
141 Auburn Avenue
Atlanta, GA 30303
800-598-3411
http://www.100blackmen.org/theonehundredmagazine/index.html
This magazine details the organization's programs to improve life (including educational and economic opportunities) for African Americans.

Onyx Woman

PO Box 91362
Pittsburgh, PA 15221
412-731-5159
onyxwomanmag@aol.com
http://www.onyxwoman.com
A career and entrepreneur development magazine for women of color

Opportunity Journal
National Urban League
120 Wall Street, 8th Floor
New York, NY 10005
212-558-5300
info@nul.org
http://www.nul.org
This scholarly journal provides in-depth coverage of issues related to the Civil Rights Movement.

Packaging Horizons
Women in Packaging, Inc.
4290 Bells Ferry Road, Suite 106-17
Kennesaw, GA 30144-1300
678-594-6872
  wpstaff@womeninpackaging.org
http://www.womeninpackaging.org
Packaging Horizons is the official publication of Women in Packaging and is also available by subscription to nonmembers. It seeks to change stereotypes and raise awareness and visibility of women and minorities in the packaging industry and industry in general.

Psychology Education and Careers: Guidebook for College Students of Color
American Psychological Association
750 First Street, NE
Washington, DC 20002-4242
800-374-2721
http://www.apa.org/pi/online.html
This free, online publication provides advice to minority college students who are interested in pursuing careers in psychology.

Psychology Education and Careers: Guidebook for College Students of Color Applying to Graduate and Professional Programs
American Psychological Association
750 First Street, NE
Washington, DC 20002-4242
800-374-2721
http://www.apa.org/pi/online.html
This free, online publication provides tips and advice to minority students who are applying to graduate psychology programs.

Psychology Education and Careers: Guidebook for High School Students of Color
American Psychological Association
750 First Street, NE
Washington, DC 20002-4242

800-374-22721
http://www.apa.org/pi/online.html
This free, online publication provides advice to minority high school students who are interested in pursuing careers in psychology.

Saludos Hispanos
800-748-6426
info@saludos.com
http://www.saludos.com/saludosmagazine/saludosmagazine.html
This is a bilingual career and education publication for Hispanic students.

Spectrum Magazine
National Association of Black Accountants (NABA)
7429-A Hanover Parkway
Greenbelt, MD 20770
301-474-6222
http://www.nabainc.org
Spectrum Magazine is the annual publication of the NABA. It features news on the accounting, finance, and business professions.

The State of Black America
National Urban League
120 Wall Street, 8th Floor
New York, NY 10005
212-558-5300
info@nul.org
http://www.nul.org
The State of Black America is an annual report produced by the league that examines the progress of African Americans in education, home ownership, entrepreneurship, health, and other important areas.

Surviving and Thriving in Academia: A Guide for Women and Ethnic Minorities
American Psychological Association
750 First Street, NE
Washington, DC 20002-4242
800-374-2721
http://www.apa.org/pi/online.html
This free, online publication addresses issues faced by minority and women postsecondary educators.

Tribal College Journal of American Indian Higher Education
PO Box 720
Mancos, CO 81328
970-533-9170

info@tribalcollegejournal.org
http://tribalcollegejournal.org
The journal provides information about American Indian higher education.

Upscale Magazine
2141 Powers Ferry Road
Marietta, GA 30067
770-988-0015
http://www.upscalemagazine.com
This publication for African-American professionals features articles on business, technology, entertainment, and travel.

Urban Influence Magazine
National Urban League
120 Wall Street, 8th Floor
New York, NY 10005
212-558-5300
info@nul.org
http://www.nul.org
This magazine profiles minority professionals in fast-growing industries and provides advice to would-be and current entrepreneurs and business people.

VISTA Magazine
305-416-4644
croiz@hisp.com
http://www.vistamagazine.com
This publication provides comprehensive coverage of social, cultural, and economic issues of interest to Hispanic Americans.

The Voice
Hispanic Association of Colleges and Universities (HACU)
8415 Datapoint Drive, Suite 400
San Antonio, TX 78229
210-692-3805
hacu@hacu.net
http://www.hacu.net
The Voice provides timely articles on HACU activities and developments in higher education that affect Hispanics. Sample copies are available online.

Winds of Change
American Indian Science and Engineering Society Publishing, Inc.
4450 Arapahoe Avenue, Suite 100
Boulder, CO 80303
http://www.wocmag.org
This magazine provides career and educational resources to Native American students. An annual college guide is included with each subscription.

Workforce Diversity for Engineering and IT Professionals
Equal Opportunity Publications
445 Broad Hollow Road, Suite 425
Melville, NY 11747
631-421-9421
info@eop.com
http://www.eop.com
This magazine is distributed free to minority engineering and Information Technology professionals.

PART IV
INDEXES

INSTITUTION AND
FINANCIAL AID INDEX

INSTITUTION AND FINANCIAL AID INDEX

STATE INDEX

STATE INDEX

ACADEMIC INDEX

ACADEMIC INDEX

MINORITY INDEX

MINORITY INDEX